ANALYZING AND SOLVING
INTERMEDIATE ACCOUNTING PROBLEMS
USING LOTUS 1-2-3®

by

David R. Koeppen, Ph.D., C.P.A.
University of Wisconsin-La Crosse

Sharon M. O'Reilly, M.B.A., C.P.A.
MicroAge of La Crosse

Donald E. Kieso, Ph.D., C.P.A.
Northern Illinois University

Jerry J. Weygandt, Ph.D., C.P.A.
University of Wisconsin-Madison

JOHN WILEY & SONS

New York   Chichester   Brisbane   Toronto   Singapore

ISBN 0-471-84288-5

Printed in the United States of America

10 9 8 7 6 5 4 3

CONTENTS

Note to Students:

The primary purpose of this manual is not to teach you how to use computers; rather, it is intended to help you learn more about accounting by using the computer. Our approach is to take the computer for what it is--a tool which can be used to help you gain a better understanding of accounting and its role in business. We have designed the manual to challenge your accounting knowledge and to increase your awareness of how the computer and electronic spreadsheets can be used to enhance your accounting skills.

To help achieve these purposes, we have designed most of the manual to be interactive--we believe that you should be *doing* and not just reading about doing! The manual is based on the premise that the best way to learn how to *use* the computer and electronic spreadsheets is to do just that--*use* them!

Part I of the manual provides an *introduction* to computers and electronic spreadsheets for those who are not already familiar with these tools. We encourage everyone to read or review this part.

In **Part II**, we have provided you with sixteen spreadsheet *templates*. These are preprogrammed spreadsheets for which you must *identify* and enter the relevant input data *and* evaluate and interpret the output data generated by the template.

Part III provides a set of tutorials designed to help you learn how to prepare your own spreadsheets. You will then be able to begin building spreadsheets to solve other accounting problems that you may encounter!

In **Part IV**, you are provided with a selection of partially completed problems. These problems are intended to remove some of the tedium of preparing the spreadsheet from scratch, while at the same time testing your accounting knowledge and your developing computer skills.

Finally, if you're ready for a challenge, try **Part V**. This part contains ten comprehensive problems designed to challenge both your accounting skills and your computer skills. You are responsible for all aspects of the construction of these spreadsheets--from conceptual development to design to programming to interpretation of results!

If your accounting skills are enhanced through the use of this manual, our primary purpose will have been served. If you also learn something about computers along the way, we (and you) will have been doubly successful!

Acknowledgments

We would like to express our appreciation to the many people who contributed to the development of this manual through their comments, ideas, and constructive criticism. We extend special thanks to: Claudia Bierman, Whitworth College; David R. Finley, University of Houston; Louis Geller, CUNY--Queens College; Loomis H. Toler, Mississippi State University; and Ron Turner, SOPH-WARE Supplements.

Our sincere thanks go to the following persons who painstakingly reviewed both the manuscript and the computer applications and suggested numerous improvements: Jean Ann Beskar; Tina Bournoville; Ann Freeman; Lea Lawrence; Mark Nelson; Marcia Sarnowski; and especially Kevin Hinsdill.

We also appreciate the support given us by the people at John Wiley & Sons, Inc. Publishers, particularly Susan Saltrick and Lew Hollerbach, and especially Lucille Sutton.

ABOUT USING THIS MANUAL

Several conventions which are used throughout this manual are described below. Familiarizing yourself with these conventions will make the manual easier for you to understand and use.

Actions: Whenever you are required to perform a task, whether it be placing a disk in the computer, typing an entry, pressing a special key, or otherwise, the action is emphasized in **bold** text and offset from the other text. The remaining text, while important, is used in most cases to explain or clarify the action you have taken or are about to take.

>S Actions to be taken when using SuperCalc3[1] are preceded by a *greater than* (>) symbol and "S".

>L Actions to be taken when using Lotus 1-2-3[2] are preceded by a *greater than* (>) symbol and "L".

>SL Actions which are the same for both SuperCalc3 and Lotus 1-2-3 are preceded by the *greater than* (>) symbol and "SL".

Characters to be typed: When you are asked to type one or more characters, quotation marks are used to offset the characters to be typed from the regular text. These quotation marks should *not* be typed unless you are explicitly told to do so.

Letters to be typed are shown in upper case (capital) in order to emphasize the characters to be typed. No differentiation is made by the programs between upper case and lower case, so it may be more convenient to enter letters in lower case and avoid using the [shift] or [Cap lock] keys.

When special keys are to be used, they are offset using brackets. For example, the escape key is shown as [Esc], the return or enter key as [enter], and the special function key F1 as [F1].

---

[1]SuperCalc3 is a registered trademark of Sorcim Corporation.
[2]Lotus and 1-2-3 are registered trademarks of Lotus Development Corporation.

PART I

INTRODUCTION

CHAPTER 1 - COMPUTERS AND ACCOUNTING

Using computers to perform accounting tasks is a logical outgrowth of the need for more timely and cost effective financial information. The high-speed processing capabilities of computers help accountants to prepare financial information in a fraction of the time it would have taken to prepare by other means. This provides users of financial data with more timely information with which to make decisions. Time savings also provide the accountant with an opportunity to spend more time on activities which were previously not cost-effective. That is, the accountant can spend time to gather and prepare information which was previously not available.

The Development of Computer Hardware and Software

The first commercially available computers were introduced in the early 1950's. The hardware, or physical components of these computers, were massive pieces of equipment, often occupying entire rooms and even buildings. Enormous amounts of electrical power were required by these computers and they were very sensitive to temperature and humidity. Because of their size and sensitivity to their environment, they required continual maintenance in order to be kept running. Computer "downtime" was a common problem.

The software programs, or instructions telling the computer how to run, were also very primitive in comparison with today's standards. Programs were designed to perform specific tasks and frequently were tailored specifically to the hardware of the computer being used. It was necessary to know and understand the computer language, the task which was being programmed *and* the computer hardware in order to develop a program. Needless to say, most computer facilities were centralized in order to take maximum advantage of the people who had the expertise to run the computer.

Accounting tasks which were frequently computerized in this early stage included the general ledger, accounts receivable and accounts payable subsidiary ledgers, payroll and inventory control. Successfully computerizing these tasks involved the use of highly specific software programs which were difficult to modify or change.

In the mid-60's, the first minicomputers were introduced in business. Technological changes allowed the computer hardware to shrink in size and price. People using these computers frequently did not need to interact through a central computer. These types of changes permitted a much broader distribution of computers and computer users throughout an organization.

A distinction was also developing between the software used to run the computer hardware (called the operating system) and the software used to develop and run a specific task. Standardized programming languages such as Fortran and Cobal were developed and prewritten packages known as "applications software" began to appear. Knowledge of the computer's hardware was becoming less important, but computer languages were still not very user-friendly.

By the mid-to-late 70's, the first desk-top and portable computers became available. These microcomputers have proven to be extremely popular in the workplace. They are commonly used in all of the functional areas of business and at all levels of management.

The hardware and software innovations which accompanied the advent of the microcomputer have resulted in greatly reduced costs. A system which might have cost over $100,000 in the mid-70's can now be purchased for around $10,000--a ten-fold decrease--and the price keeps dropping.

The Changing Nature of Software

Programming languages are increasingly easier to learn and use--becoming what are referred to as high-level languages. High-level languages have a much greater end-user orientation and oftentimes utilize easy-to-interpret words along with mathematical operations and formulas. These languages are meant to be used by people who may not understand how the computer works internally--and who don't really need to!

The instructions which allow you to create and manage disk files, to run your programs and to run the computer hardware, can be kept separate from the applications you create to perform accounting tasks. These instructions, comprising the Disk Operating System (commonly referred to as "DOS"), must be loaded into the computer before you can begin using an application. This is a very simple process, and it is described in CHAPTER 4.

The ability to separate DOS (the control of the computer's hardware) from specific tasks has resulted in the development of many general purpose application programs. These general purpose application programs allow you to spend more of your time concentrating on identifying the relevant inputs to a problem, how those inputs should be processed, and what the output should look like--all without having to worry about how the computer works internally.

Electronic Spreadsheets

Electronic spreadsheets are just one example of general purpose application software. Electronic spreadsheets are so flexible that you can customize the spreadsheet to meet *your* specific needs. But just what is an electronic spreadsheet? Basically, an electronic spreadsheet is a software program which can be used to automate many of the tasks we might otherwise do using a pencil and paper.

Much of an accountant's work is prepared on spreadsheets, which are simply large pieces of paper which are ruled into a grid of rows and columns. The accountant uses this grid to organize his/her work in an orderly and logical manner so that it is easier to understand and interpret. Unfortunately, each time that the accountant begins another task, a new spreadsheet must be created because of the uniqueness of each set of numbers. This is true even if the task is similar to an earlier one.

The electronic spreadsheet is also a grid of rows and columns. Thus, what the accountant could do with pencil and paper can be done on the computer. This adds the computer's processing speed to the accomplishment of the task--a *major* benefit.

However, the electronic spreadsheet has an additional benefit of great importance to the accountant. This is the ability to "remember" the logical relationships between the entries made on the spreadsheet. For example, once you have calculated a total at the bottom of a column of numbers, this calculation can be "remembered" by the spreadsheet. Thus, if you were to change one of the numbers in the column to be totaled, the spreadsheet would automatically retotal the column, incorporating the new number into the total. This means that the accountant can now create a basic spreadsheet--called a *template*--which can be used over and over again to perform tasks of a similar nature. Thus, once a template has been prepared, it can be used for similar tasks simply by changing the numbers. In addition, even if a template doesn't do exactly what you would like, you can modify it to better meet your specific needs.

Most electronic spreadsheets also utilize functions (such as minimums and maximums, if/then statements, dates, etc.) which further increase the efficiency of the spreadsheet and ease the accountant's tasks.

Future Software Directions

Another major change in application programs is already underway and you will see it evidenced in your electronic spreadsheet programs. This change is the integration of several general purpose application programs into a single package. For example, your spreadsheet program is no longer just an electronic spreadsheet. It is also a database management program and a graphics program--all three programs combined in one. Other packages have also integrated word-processing programs and advanced telecommunications capabilities with spreadsheets, database management, and graphics. The computing power available to you, as a student or as an accountant, is increasing every day.

CHAPTER 2 - WHAT YOU DO NEED TO KNOW ABOUT HARDWARE

General purpose application programs, such as the electronic spreadsheet, enable you to be a successful end user without requiring extensive knowledge about your microcomputer. What follows is a brief description of what you should know before starting to use your microcomputer.

First, your microcomputer consists of three basic hardware components. These components are:

1. The system unit.
2. The monitor.
3. The keyboard.

In addition, your microcomputer may have one or more extras--non-essential components called peripherals. Peripherals might include a printer, a mouse or joystick and other hardware; however, since they are non-essential, they will not be discussed.

The System Unit

The primary workings of your microcomputer are contained within the system unit. If you were to take the cover off your computer, you might be surprised to see that the computer boards and chips--the heart of the computer's memory and processing capabilities--take up very little space. In fact, technological innovations have made these parts so small that many system units appear to be empty!

A large part of the space within the system unit is taken up by the disk drives. These drives electronically read and write to and from your floppy disks and correspondingly must be at least as large as a disk. The disk drives are also the primary moving parts in your computer--almost everything else is electronic.

In some systems, the disk drives are separate from the system unit and are connected to the system unit by "cables." Still other system units may contain a "hard-disk" drive in place of one of the floppy disk drives. Since hard-disk drives are fixed in place in the system unit, they operate much faster than floppy disk drives and they can contain a great deal more information than a floppy disk.

System units are *delicate* instruments and they should always be handled with great care.

The Monitor

The monitor is your "window to the world". Just as you cannot see all of the world around you when you look out a window, you cannot see all of what is in the computer by looking at the monitor. For example, when you view an electronic spreadsheet on the monitor, you will only be able to see a small fraction of the entire worksheet which is available to you!

Monitors are generally of two types--those with the ability to do on-screen graphics and those without that ability. A few of the templates in this manual use graphics to help illustrate certain points (these graphics are not essential to completing the assignments). However, if you wish to use graphics, you should check with your instructor or computer lab assistant to find out if your monitor has graphics capability (since it may not be obvious from the type of monitor).

The Keyboard

Your primary means of entering instructions or information to the microcomputer is through the keyboard. What you enter on the keyboard, you will usually see displayed on the monitor. While the keyboard resembles a typewriter keyboard, it has some special keys that you should be familiar with before beginning to use the computer. These keys are listed below along with the abbreviations or descriptions of the symbols *usually* used to denote each key. Make sure that you can locate them on the keyboard illustrated in Exhibit 2-1 and on your microcomputer's keyboard before you begin using your spreadsheet!

Key	Common Abbreviation or Description
Escape key	Esc
Control key	Ctrl
Alternate key	Alt
Insert key	Ins
Delete key	Del
Backspace key	Key with a single arrow pointing to the left.
Enter (return) key	Key with a bent arrow pointing to the left, or labeled enter or return.
Shift key(s)	Key(s) with non-solid arrows pointing towards the top of the keyboard
Tab key	Key with both left and right pointing arrows.
Directional (cursor movement) keys	Keys (usually four), each with an arrow pointing either up, down, left or right.
Special function keys	Keys labeled [F1] through [F10], located at the left side of the keyboard.
Home key	Home
Page up (1-2-3 only)	PgUp
Page down (1-2-3 only)	PgDn
End key (1-2-3 only)	End
Slash key	/ (on same key with the question mark)
Print Screen key	PrtSc
Number pad lock	Num Lock

Note: You can use the number pad in conjunction with the directional keys by using the [shift] key. If you press the [shift] key and simultaneously press one of the number pad keys, a number will be entered. If you release the [shift] key, then the directional keys can be used. Alternatively, if you press the [Num Lock] key, then pressing a key on the number pad will enter a number--pressing the [shift] key and simultaneously pressing a key on the number pad will allow you to use the directional keys. (Press the [Num Lock] key a second time to return to the normal keyboard setting.)

Exhibit 2-1

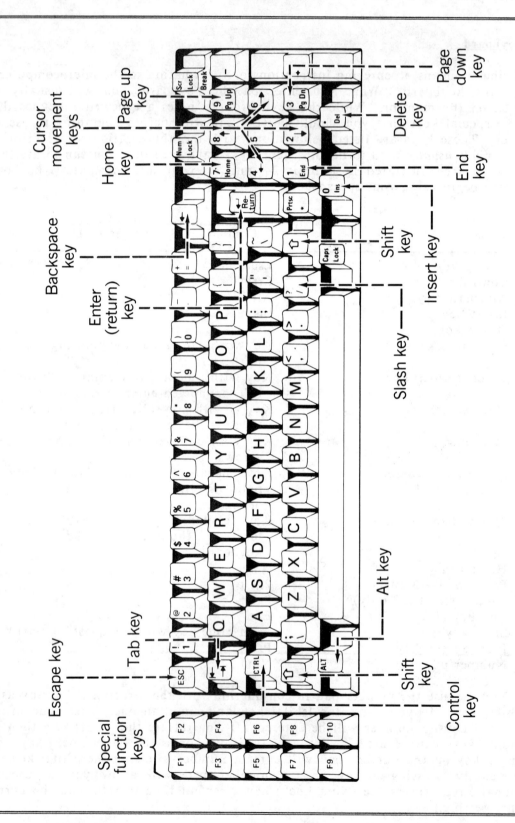

CHAPTER 3 - CARE AND FEEDING OF FLOPPY DISKS

The final components needed to run your microcomputer are the floppy disks containing the software; that is, the instructions to run the computer and your applications programs. While floppy disks are technically hardware, many people equate them with software, which is probably a good idea since floppy disks are just that--soft and floppy! This means that you should take special care to protect your disks since they can be accidentally damaged or destroyed in many ways. Remember that your disk is a *sensitive* electronic medium. Following are some things that you should and shouldn't do with your disk:

DISK HANDLING--*Do's and Don'ts*

Insert disks carefully in the disk drives. Jamming them in can result in bends, creases, or folds which can make it impossible for the computer to read from and/or write to the disk. Use similar care when removing disks from the drives.

Keep your disk in its protective sleeve whenever it is not in the computer so that dust and other foreign objects cannot reach it.

Make it a practice not to eat or drink around your disks--sooner or later (probably sooner) an accident will happen and your disk may be destroyed.

Handle a disk only by its protected surfaces--Never touch the exposed surfaces of the disk with your fingers. Even the natural oils on *clean* fingers can destroy the disk surface.

Use a felt-tip pen if you need to write on the disk label. Never use a ball-point pen or pencil as they can crease the disk surface. For similar reasons, never put a paper clip on the edge of the disk.

Don't carry your disk *between* heavy books since a book edge (or even the weight) may crease or damage the disk surface.

Avoid magnetic fields. Remember, your disk is magnetically written to by the computer. Don't take it through x-ray equipment in airports, electronic book checks in libraries, or similar checkpoints. If in doubt, don't take a chance--take the disks around the electronic checker.

Your disk is also sensitive to extremes of heat and cold. Don't leave it in your car on a hot summer day or through a cold winter night. If you do forget, give your disk a chance to return to a normal temperature before you try to use it.

Keep a backup copy of your disk if possible. Procedures for saving files to a disk are discussed in Chapter 5. Check with your instructor or computer lab assistant about making a backup of your entire disk.

Remember, all it takes is *one* careless mistake and your disk is *useless*!

CHAPTER 4 - PREPARING TO USE YOUR ELECTRONIC SPREADSHEET

Loading the Disk Operating System: Before loading the electronic spreadsheet program, the disk operating system (DOS)[1] must be loaded in your computer.[2]

If the computer is turned off:

>SL **Insert a copy of DOS version 2.0 (or a version with a higher numerical rating than 2.0) in drive A of your computer, close the drive door, and turn on the computer.**

Drive A is the default disk drive--the one which automatically engages a few moments after the computer is turned on. This would be the left-hand drive on an IBM-PC.[3]

If the computer is already turned on:

>SL **Insert a copy of DOS 2.0 or higher in drive A of your computer, close the drive door, and then press the [Ctrl], [Alt], and [Del] keys simultaneously.**

This will restart (reboot) the computer.

After a few moments the red indicator light for drive A should come on--*Never open the drive door when the light is on!* Before the computer finishes loading DOS, it will prompt you to enter a date.

>SL **It is best to enter a date (in the format mm/dd/yy), but it is not essential and you may skip this step.**

Entering a date, however, will result in the date being associated with any files you create. This can be very helpful if you later try to determine when your files were last updated.

>SL **Continue by pressing the [enter] key.**

The computer will then prompt you for the time--

>SL **Press the [enter] key to continue.**

After you have responded to the requests for a date and a time, the A> should appear. If it does not, repeat the procedures above or seek assistance.

>SL **Remove the DOS disk from drive A and replace it with the electronic spreadsheet program disk.**

---

[1]It may be possible to make your electronic spreadsheet auto-loading by using an autoexec file. Check with your instructor or computer assistant to see if this can be (or has been) done with the program disk.

[2]If your computer is equipped with a hard-disk drive, check with your instructor or computer lab assistant for the proper start-up procedures.

[3]IBM PC is a trademark of International Business Machines Corporation.

Next, go to the appropriate section for **Using SuperCalc3** (see below) or **Using Lotus 1-2-3** (page 19) and follow that set of instructions.

USING SUPERCALC^3

The educational version: Your educational version of SuperCalc3 is only slightly different from the commercially available version of SuperCalc3. There are three significant differences between the two versions:

1.   The educational version has only 26 columns and 40 rows. The commercial version has 63 columns and 254 rows. While this may seem to be a significant limitation, you will probably find that you can do a tremendous amount of work within this relatively "small" area. You may find, however, that you need to plan your applications more carefully to make them fit within the confines of the spreadsheet.

2.   The maximum size of an entry in a cell is 80 characters in the educational version. In the commercial version, 115 characters per cell are permitted. Unless you are writing very sophisticated formulas, you shouldn't encounter any problems with this limit.

3.   Files created using the educational version cannot be used with the commercial version and vice-versa.

To begin using SuperCalc3:

>S   **Type "SC3" and press the [enter] key.**

The quotation marks are used merely to highlight the characters to be typed and should not be entered--it also does not matter whether you type in upper case (capital) or lower case letters--they will be interpreted in the same manner by DOS and by SuperCalc3.

After a few moments, the SuperCalc3 screen should appear as shown in Exhibit 4-1.

To begin using the spreadsheet:

>S   **Press the [enter] key.**

The initial SuperCalc3 screen should be replaced by a spreadsheet showing a series of columns and rows designated by letters A-H (columns) and numbers 1-20 (rows) as is illustrated in Exhibit 4-2. These columns and rows represent the upper left-hand corner of your spreadsheet. Remember, your spreadsheet has A through Z (26) columns and 40 rows.

The intersection of any column and any row is referred to as a cell. For example, the intersection of column B and row 10 is referred to as cell B10.

Exhibit 4-1

SuperCalc3(tm)
Educational Version
Version 1.00
I B M   P C
S/N-000000, IBM DOS

Copyright 1984
SORCIM/IUS.
San Jose, CA.

Enter "?" for HELP or "return" to start.
F1 = Help; F2 = Erase Line/Return to Spreadsheet; F9 = Plot; F10 = View

The spreadsheet status lines: At the bottom of the screen are the status lines.

The <u>first status line</u> tells you what cell the cursor is in. The cell reference on the first status line should indicate cell A1 (>A1). The character (>) immediately in front of the cell reference shows the direction the cursor will move in if the [enter] key is pressed. (SuperCalc3 has an automatic cursor advance which is activated by pressing the [enter] key. Note that this feature has been *turned off* in most of the templates in this manual.) The first status line will also show the contents of the cell in which the cursor is located; however, since we have not yet entered anything in cell A1, the remainder of the line is blank.

The <u>second status line</u> shows:

1.   The width of the column. Nine characters is the standard (or default) setting; it may be increased or decreased in size. (Changing column widths is described in Chapter 22.)

2.   The amount of memory remaining in your computer; for example, 130k in Exhibit 4-2. This amount is dependent on your computer's hardware. Part of the memory is taken by DOS and by SuperCalc3. The amount shown tells you how much memory is available for your spreadsheet. Most of the less complicated templates used with Part II of the manual require only 2-5k of memory. The more sophisticated templates (such as pensions), however, require up to 25k of memory.

3.   The lower right hand corner (last column/row) in which an entry has been made. This should be cell A1 since nothing has been entered yet.

4.   How to gain access to a help screen (type a question mark).

The third status line, which is blank at this time except for the character counter (1>), will show what you are currently entering into a cell. The character counter, 1>, tells you that the next character which is typed will be in the first space in the cell where the cursor is located. As you type, this counter will always tell you at what space the next character will appear.

Below the third status line, at the bottom of the screen, are some helpful reminders. By pressing the special function key [F1], you can obtain a help screen. This key can be used instead of typing a question mark (?) for help. Pressing the special function key [F2] enables you to erase what you have typed on the third status line. For example, you start typing a formula and get hopelessly confused--pressing [F2] will eliminate what you have typed and allows you to start your entry over. (We'll try this in a moment.) If your computer is connected to a printer which will plot graphs, pressing the special function key [F9] will allow you to print the graphs which you have created. Finally, pressing the special function key [F10] allows you to view graphs which you create from your spreadsheet.

Moving about the spreadsheet:

Cell A1 should now be highlighted with the cursor block. The cursor (technically referred to as a reverse-video bar) can be moved to any cell using the four directional arrow keys on the number pad at the right hand side of your keyboard. Moving the cursor across the screen is similar to moving the tip of your pencil across a piece of paper (spreadsheet).

>S   **Try moving the cursor around using the four directional arrow keys.**

On most keyboards, if you hold an arrow key down, the cursor will automatically continue moving in that direction until it reaches an edge of the spreadsheet. Note how the column headings and row numbers change when your cursor moves outside of the initial screen (that is, if you move the cursor below row 20 or to the right beyond column H). Note that the cursor's location at any time is shown on the first status line.

You can move directly to any cell by using the GOTO command, which is designated by the equals (=) sign.

>S   **Type "=C14" (the quotation marks again are used merely to highlight the entry and should not be typed) and press the [enter] key.**

Exhibit 4-2

	A	B	C	D	E	F	G	H
1								
2								
3								
4								
5								
6								
7								
8								
9								
10								
11								
12								
13								
14								
15								
16								
17								
18								
19								
20								

```
> A1
Width:  9  Memory:130 Last Col/Row:A1     ? for HELP
 1>
F1 = Help; F2 = Erase Line/Return to Spreadsheet; F9 = Plot; F10 = View
```

See how the cursor has jumped to cell C14! You can also return to cell A1 from anywhere on the spreadsheet by pressing the [Home] key on the number pad.

>S   **Press the [Home] key to return to cell A1.**

If you enter a letter designating a column, but without a number, the cursor will jump to row 1 of the column you specified.

>S   **Type "=Z" and press the [enter] key. Where did your cursor end up?**

If you enter a number designating a row, but without a letter, the cursor will jump to column A of the row you specified.

>S   **Type "=32" and press the [enter] key. Where has the cursor moved to?**

>S   **Return to cell A1 by pressing the [Home] key.**

Entering text and correcting typing errors:

Let's try making a couple of entries.

>S   **Type your name.**

See how what you are typing appears on the third status line to let you know what you have typed.

If you make an error when typing an entry, you can use the backspace key to go back and correct your error by typing over the incorrect characters.

>S   **Press the [enter] key to insert your name in the spreadsheet.**

If the cursor has automatically advanced to another cell (B1 or A2), move the cursor back to cell A1. See how your name now appears on the first status line to let you know what has been entered in cell A1. (Note that if your name is longer than 9 spaces, the program allows it to "spill over" to cell B1.)

>S   **Begin typing some gibberish; for example "jkljkljkl".**

Note that what you are typing appears on the third status line.

>S   **Before pressing the [enter] key, you realize that you do not wish to enter this text--press the special function key [F2].**

This eliminates what you have typed from the third status line and returns you to the spreadsheet.

If you have already entered an incorrect entry into a cell, simply type and reenter the correct entry in the same cell.

>S   **With the cursor in any cell but A1 (where your name is), enter a number. For example, type "66" in cell B1 and press the [enter] key.**

This illustrates a difference between text such as your name and numbers. The text is left-hand justified in each cell while numbers are right-hand justified in each cell. That is, text begins at the left-hand side of a cell; numbers are "pushed" over to the right-hand side of a cell. SuperCalc3 distinguishes between text and numbers--a very important feature when we start performing mathematical operations such as adding a column of numbers.

Slash commands

In addition to using text, numbers, and formulas, you can also use SuperCalc3's commands. These commands, referred to as *slash commands* since they begin by typing a slash (/), represent the programming steps which you can use in developing, saving and retrieving, and manipulating spreadsheets.

>S   **Type a slash (/).**

The slash is located on the same key with the question mark. Don't confuse it with the backslash key (\).

On the second status line, you will see a series of letters and other characters. Each of these characters stands for a specific command. In later chapters, we will make use of many of these commands.

>S   **For now, press the special function key [F2] to cancel the slash commands.**

Starting over:

Finally, if you wish to start over on your spreadsheet, or start a new template or spreadsheet, you must first erase or clear your current spreadsheet from the computer's temporary memory.

If you don't erase the current spreadsheet before you load a new file from the disk, SuperCalc3 will load the new file over the existing one. This can produce some very strange results!

>S   **Type "/Z", which calls up the slash command for "Zap the spreadsheet."**

Using this command will clear the screen and the computer's temporary memory.

>S   **Type "Y" for Yes to indicate that you do wish to zap the spreadsheet.**

The current spreadsheet will then be cleared from the computer's temporary memory and you are ready to begin anew.

WARNING: Since the spreadsheet which you see on the screen is not automatically saved when you finish working on it, you must decide whether or not you wish to save it before clearing the screen . . . see Chapter 5 on saving and retrieving files (spreadsheets).

>S   **If you wish to quit at this time, type "/QY" for Quit,Yes.**

Recalculation:

SuperCalc3 recalculates all of the entries in a spreadsheet when you press the [enter] key. When you are working with complex spreadsheets, the cursor will disappear temporarily while the calculation is taking place. Make sure that you wait for the cursor to reappear before attempting to make any further entries.

Waiting for the cursor to reappear can be time-consuming when you have a large spreadsheet. To speed the entry of data, you can instruct the program to recalculate only when you want it to. This procedure is described in detail in several of the templates in Part II, but will also be introduced here for people who wish to work ahead.

To recalculate manually, instead of automatically, you would use a slash command. Once the spreadsheet is displayed on the screen, simply type "/GM". This stands for "/Global,Manual" (which will be displayed on the third status line when you type "/GM") and means that the entire (or global) worksheet will recalculate only when you instruct it to (manually). You can then instruct the spreadsheet to recalculate by typing an exclamation point (!). If you wish, you can change back to automatic recalculation at any time by typing "/GA", which stands for "/Global,Automatic".

Automatic Cursor Movement:

Another feature which you may wish to use to speed the entry of data is the automatic cursor advance. As was mentioned previously, this feature has been turned off in most of the templates and tutorials. It can be turned back on by using a slash command. Once the template is displayed on the screen, simply type "/GN". This stands for "/Global,Next" (which will be displayed on the third status line when you type "/GN") and means that the cursor will advance to the next cell whenever you press the [enter] key. If you wish, you can turn the automatic cursor advance off again by typing "/GN" a second time.

USING LOTUS 1-2-3

To begin using Lotus 1-2-3:

>L   **Type "123" and press the [enter] key.**[4]

The quotation marks are used merely to highlight the characters to be typed and should not be entered. Remember that it also does not matter whether you type in upper case (capital) or lower case *letters*--they will be interpreted in the same manner by DOS and Lotus 1-2-3.

After a few moments, the Lotus 1-2-3 screen should appear as in Exhibit 4-3 (or similar to this exhibit).

To begin using the spreadsheet:

>L   **Press the [enter] key.**

The Lotus 1-2-3 copyright screen should be replaced by a spreadsheet showing a series of columns and rows designated by letters A through H (columns) and numbers 1 to 20 (rows) as is illustrated in Exhibit 4-4. These columns and

---

[4] You may also begin by entering "LOTUS" instead of "123". The initial Lotus 1-2-3 screen which will be displayed is referred to as the Lotus Access System. When this screen appears, simply press the [enter] key to select 1-2-3 and continue following the instructions. If DOS 2.0 or higher has been installed on your Lotus 1-2-3 program disk, it is not necessary to load DOS into the computer separately. Place the Lotus 1-2-3 program disk in drive A of the computer instead of the DOS disk and follow the instructions for responding to the time and date prompts. The Lotus Access System will appear as the first screen. Continue as suggested above.

rows represent the upper left-hand corner of your spreadsheet. The entire spreadsheet has A through IV (256) columns and 2,048 rows.

Exhibit 4-3

---

1 - 2 - 3

Copyright (C) 1982,1983
Lotus Development Corporation
All Rights Reserved
Release 1A
*

(Press Any Key To Continue)

Exhibit 4-4

A1:   READY

```
        |  A  |  B  |  C  |  D  |  E  |  F  |  G  |  H  |
   1  |
   2  |
   3  |
   4  |
   5  |
   6  |
   7  |
   8  |
   9  |
  10  |
  11  |
  12  |
  13  |
  14  |
  15  |
  16  |
  17  |
  18  |
  19  |
  20  |
```

The intersection of any column and any row is referred to as a cell. For example, the intersection of column B and row 10 is referred to as cell B10.

The control panel: At the top of the screen is the control panel.

The first line of the control panel tells you what cell the cursor is in. The cell reference on the first line should indicate cell A1. This line will also indicate what we have entered in the cell where the cursor is located. (Nothing is displayed yet since we have not entered anything.) The first line also indicates the "mode" that the spreadsheet is in-- which should currently be READY.

The second and third lines (which are currently blank) will be used to indicate what you type in a cell or various command options you may select from. We'll discuss these lines later when they come into use.

Moving about the spreadsheet:

Cell A1 should now be highlighted with the cursor block. The cursor (technically referred to as a reverse-video bar) can be moved to any cell using the four directional arrow keys on the number pad at the right hand side of your keyboard, as well as by using several special keys. Moving the cursor across the screen is similar to moving the tip of your pencil across a piece of paper (spreadsheet).

>L   **Try moving the cursor around using the four directional arrow keys.**

On most keyboards, if you hold an arrow key down, the cursor will automatically continue moving in that direction until it reaches an edge of the spreadsheet. Note how the column headings and row numbers change when your cursor moves outside of the initial screen (that is, if you move the cursor below row 20 or to the right beyond column H). Note that the cursor's location at any time is shown on the first line of the control panel.

You can move directly to any cell by using the GOTO command, which is designated by the special function key [F5].

>L   **Press [F5]. Type "C14" (the quotation marks again are used merely to highlight the entry and should not be typed) and press the [enter] key.**

See how the cursor has jumped to cell C14! You can also return to cell A1 from anywhere on the spreadsheet by pressing the [Home] key on the number pad.

>L   **Press the [Home] key to return to cell A1.**

You can also use the pageup [PgUp], pagedown [PgDn], [tab] and [backtab] keys to move the cursor.

>L   **Press [PgDn].**

The cursor has jumped down one screen to cell A21. Each time you press this key, the cursor will jump down one additional screen.

The [PgUp] key works in the same manner except that the cursor will jump up one additional screen each time this key is pressed.

>L   **Press the [tab] key.**

The cursor will jump one screen to the right when this key is pressed. You should now see columns I through P.

The [backtab] key works the same way except that it moves the cursor to the left. Note that the backtab is selected by pressing the [shift] key and the [tab] key simultaneously.

Finally, you can also move the cursor by pressing the [End] key followed by pressing a directional arrow key.

>L   **Press [End], followed by the "down" arrow key.**

Since the cursor was in a "blank" cell, the program searched in the direction indicated for the next cell which contained an entry. Since we have not made any entries, the cursor has jumped all the way to row 2,048 at the bottom of the spreadsheet. Had the cursor been located in a cell with an entry, the program would have searched for the first cell which did not have an entry.

>L   **Press the [Home] key to return to cell A1.**

Entering text and correcting typing errors:

Let's try making a couple of entries.

>L   **Type your name.**

See how what you are typing appears on the second line of the control panel to let you know what you have typed.

If you make an error when typing an entry, you can use the backspace key to go back and correct your error by retyping the correct characters.

>L   **Press the [enter] key.**

See how your name appears on the first line of the control panel to let you know what has been entered. (Note that if your name is longer than nine characters, the program will allow it to "spill over" into cell B1.)

An alternative to pressing the [enter] key is to simply move the cursor to a different cell. Whatever you have typed in a cell will automatically be entered when you move the cursor to another cell.

>L   **With the cursor in cell A1, begin typing some gibberish; for example "jkljkljkl".**

Note how this appears on the second line of the control panel.

>L   **Before pressing the [enter] key or moving to another cell, you realize that you do not wish to enter this text in the cell which contains your name. Press the [Esc] key.**

This eliminates what you have typed from the second line of the control panel.

If you have already entered an incorrect entry into a cell, simply type and reenter the correct entry in the same cell.

>L   **Move the cursor to any cell except A1 (where your name is). Enter a number. For example, type "66" and press the [enter] key.**

This illustrates a difference between text such as your name and numbers. The text is left-hand justified in each cell while numbers are right-hand justified in each cell. That is, text begins at the left-hand side of a cell; numbers are "pushed" over to the right-hand side of a cell. Lotus 1-2-3 distinguishes between text and numbers--a very important feature when we start performing mathematical operations such as adding a column of numbers.

Slash commands

In addition to using text, numbers, and formulas, you can also use Lotus 1-2-3's commands. These commands, referred to as *slash commands* since they begin by typing a slash (/), represent the programming steps which you can use in developing, saving and retrieving, and manipulating spreadsheets.

>L   **Type a slash (/).**

The slash is located on the same key as the question mark. Don't confuse it with the backslash (\) key.

On the second line of the control panel, you will see a series of words. Each of these words stands for a specific command. In later chapters, we will use many of these commands. On the third line of the control panel is another series of words. These words represent options under the command which is highlighted on the second line of the control panel.

You can select a command by typing the first letter of the command. Another way to select the command is to use the left and right cursor movement keys to move the highlight on the second line to the command you wish to select and pressing the [enter] key.

>L   **For now, press the [Esc] key to cancel the slash commands.**

Starting over:

Finally, if you wish to start over on your spreadsheet, or start a new template or spreadsheet, you should first erase or clear your current spreadsheet from the computer's temporary memory.

This is a good habit to get into because many spreadsheets will load one spreadsheet over the top of another, leading to some very strange results!

>L   Type "/W" which calls up the slash command for Worksheet, followed by "E" which calls up the slash command for Erase.

Using these commands will clear the screen and the computer's temporary memory.

>L   Type "Y" for Yes to indicate that you do wish to erase the spreadsheet.

The current spreadsheet will then be cleared from the computer's temporary memory and you are ready to begin anew.

WARNING: Since the spreadsheet which you see on the screen is not automatically saved when you finish working on it, you must decide whether or not you wish to save it before clearing the screen . . . see Chapter 5 on saving and retrieving files (spreadsheets).

>L   If you wish to quit at this time, type "/QY" for Quit,Yes.

Recalculation:

Lotus 1-2-3 recalculates all of the entries in a spreadsheet when you press the [enter] key. When you are working with complex spreadsheets, you will need to wait for a brief time before making any further entries. While this recalculation is occurring, the mode indicator will display WAIT as a reminder to you.

Waiting for the cursor to reappear can be time-consuming when you have a large spreadsheet. To speed the entry of data, you can instruct the program to recalculate only when you want it to. This procedure is described in detail in several of the templates in Part II, but will also be introduced here for people who wish to work ahead.

To recalculate manually, instead of automatically, you would use a slash command. Once the spreadsheet is displayed on the screen, simply type "/WGRM". This stands for "/Worksheet,Global,Recalculation,Manual" and means that the entire (or global) worksheet will recalculate only when you instruct it to (manually). You can then instruct the spreadsheet to recalculate by pressing the special function key [F9]. If you wish, you can change back to automatic recalculation at any time by typing "/WGRA", which stands for "/Worksheet,Global,Recalculation,Automatic".

CHAPTER 5 - SAVING, RETRIEVING, AND PRINTING SPREADSHEETS

Being able to save and retrieve your spreadsheets adds to the power of the computer to assist you in your work. There are, however, several hazards to watch out for when saving and retrieving files.

Cautions about saving and retrieving files:

First, make sure that you type the correct commands to serve your purpose. That is, if you wish to save a spreadsheet, make sure that you type the proper save command--or if you wish to retrieve a spreadsheet, make sure that you type the proper command to load the spreadsheet into the computer. It is easy to type the wrong command, particularly since these commands usually require only one letter to be typed, with potentially disastrous consequences.

For example, let's assume that you have just finished loading the spreadsheet program in the computer and now wish to load a spreadsheet called DOLLAR from a file. If you accidentally type the save command, the blank spreadsheet shown on your screen may be saved to the disk under the name of DOLLAR and your original file will be gone! You can help prevent this from happening by keeping a write protect tab on your disk at all times and removing it only when you are actually planning to save a spreadsheet. (The write protect tab should cover the small notch in the side of your disk.) A piece of tape can be substituted for a write-protect tab.

The opposite situation may also arise. Let's assume that you have just finished a spreadsheet which you have been working on over the last few days. At the end of each day, you have saved the partially completed spreadsheet under the file name of BUSINESS. Now you wish to save the completed spreadsheet. By accident, you type the command to retrieve the file called BUSINESS and the spreadsheet program loads the file you saved yesterday over today's completed spreadsheet and everything you did today is lost! To avoid this situation, you should always use a different file name when you save a spreadsheet. Had you used a new name for the file, such as BUSDONE and accidentally typed the retrieve command, the spreadsheet program would have been unable to find a file by this name and would not have overwritten your current day's work.

Second, beware of power outages and other power fluctuations. Since your spreadsheet is in RAM, or temporary memory, accidentally kicking the plug from the wall will result in a complete loss of your work. While it is impossible to prevent this loss should you lose all power, the damage can be minimized by making frequent backups (saving your spreadsheet to disk) while you work, rather than waiting until you are completely done. Then, you only lose the work you've done since you last saved the spreadsheet.

Finally, if you are working on a particularly valuable spreadsheet, you should consider using at least one backup disk. That is, save your work on several different disks. That way, if one disk goes bad, which is not an uncommon occurrence, you won't lose your work.

Incidentally, it doesn't take long for a spreadsheet to be worth more than the small cost of a backup disk. Any spreadsheet which takes you longer than an hour to prepare is certainly worth the added cost of a backup.

Retrieving a SuperCalc3 Spreadsheet from a Disk File

>S   Load SuperCalc3 in the computer using the procedures described in Chapter 4 so that you are viewing a blank spreadsheet.

>S   Place the disk containing the file you wish to retrieve in either drive A or drive B.

>S   Type a slash (/) followed by "L" for Load.

On the third status line, you will see "/Load," displayed. On the second status line, you will be prompted for the file name used for the spreadsheet.

>S   If your file disk is in drive A, type the name of the file (for example, "TIMEVAL") followed by a comma (,). The comma lets the program know that you have finished entering the file name. (If you wish, you can press the [enter] key instead of typing the comma, and the program will automatically enter the comma for you.)

On the third status line, you will see "/Load,TIMEVAL," displayed. On the second status line, you will be prompted to specify how much of the file (among other options) that you wish to load.

>S   Type "A" for All and the file will be loaded from drive A.

In summary, you should have typed "/LTIMEVAL,A".

Remember that it will not make any difference whether you type upper case or lower case letters--all letters used for commands are interpreted in the same manner.

>S   If your file disk is in drive B, the procedures are the same except that you must tell the computer what drive the file disk is in by typing "B:" before the file name, the comma, and the "A" for all.

In summary, if your disk is in drive B, you should type "/LB:TIMEVAL,A" and you will see "/Load,B:TIMEVAL,All" displayed on the third status line prior to the file being loaded.

The SuperCalc3 File Directory: If you would like to review the SuperCalc3 files on a disk, load SuperCalc3 in the computer and:

>S   Type "/L".

>S   Press the [enter] key to view the directory. You should see the directory options menu displayed.

If your files are on the disk in drive A:

>S   Type "S" for See to display the SuperCalc3 files on the disk in drive A.

If your files are on the disk in drive B:

>S   Type "C" for Change followed by "B" to change the logged data disk drive to drive B.

Note that if you use this procedure, you can enter a file name to be loaded or saved without the "B:" drive designation. The program will assume that the file is in drive B.

>S   Type "S" for See to display the SuperCalc3 files on the disk in drive B.

To continue:

>S   Press the [space bar] to see any additional files on the disk and/or to return to the directory options menu.

>S   Either type "E" for Enter and continue loading a file as described earlier or press the special function key [F2] to abort the load command and return to the spreadsheet.

Saving a SuperCalc3 Spreadsheet to a Disk File

>S   Place a formatted disk on which you wish to save the spreadsheet in either drive A (left-hand drive) or drive B (right-hand drive).

(Check with your computer lab assistant or your instructor about procedures for formatting a disk.)

>S   Decide on a file name for your spreadsheet.

Remember, it is best not to use the same name as an existing file. File names may be up to eight characters long and you should use a name which is easy to remember. For example, you might use "WORKSHTA" to indicate that you have completed part A of a worksheet problem. Later you might use "WORKSHTB" to indicate that you have completed part B. By using such a sequence (A,B,C, . . .), you will also be able to tell which file is your most recent spreadsheet.

>S   Type a slash (/) followed by "S" for Save.

On the third status line, "/Save," will be displayed. On the second status line, you will be prompted for the file name to be used for the spreadsheet.

>S   If your file disk is in drive A, type the name of the file (for example, "WORKSHTA") followed by a comma (,). The comma lets the program know that you have finished entering the file name. (If you wish, you can press the [enter] key instead of typing the comma, and the program will automatically enter the comma for you.)

On the third status line, you will see "/Save,WORKSHTA," displayed. On the second status line, you will be prompted to specify how much of the file that you wish to save. (If another file with the same file name already exists on the disk, you will be asked whether you wish to change the file's name, make the existing file into a backup, or overwrite the existing file before continuing.)

>S   **Type "A" for All to save the entire spreadsheet, including any formulas.**

Once you have typed "A" for All, the computer will save the file to the disk.

In summary, you should have typed "/SWORKSHTA,A".

Remember that it will not make any difference whether you type upper case or lower case letters--all letters used for commands are interpreted in the same manner.

>S   **If your file disk is in drive B, the procedures are the same except that you must tell the computer what drive the file disk is in by typing "B:" before the file name, the comma, and the "A" for All.**

In summary, if your disk is in drive B, you should type "/SB:WORKSHTA,A" and you will see "/Save,B:WORKSHTA,All" displayed on the third status line prior to the file being saved.

After the red "in-use" light goes out, exit the program by typing "/Q" for Quit and "Y" for Yes.

>S   **Type "/QY" to exit SuperCalc3.**

When the SuperCalc3 screen has cleared, you may remove your disk(s) and turn off the computer.

Printing a SuperCalc3 Spreadsheet

Your spreadsheet can be printed in several different ways. The two most important ways are described below:

Printing values: Most often, you will probably want to print the values in a spreadsheet as they appear on the screen. This can be done as follows:

>S   **Type "/GB". This stands for "/Global,Borders" and removes the row and column headings (borders) so that they will not be printed.**

(Before removing the borders, you should note the range of cells which you wish to print as discussed below.)

>S   **Type "/OD". This represents "/Output,Display," and will be shown on the third status line.**

On the second status line, you are prompted to enter the range to be printed. This range can be one cell or a range of cells. Typically, it will be a range of cells. A print range is specified by the locations of the cells in the upper left-hand and lower right-hand corners of the range you wish to print. Enter the cell in the upper left-hand corner, followed by a colon (:), then the location of the cell in the lower right-hand corner, and type a comma (or press the [enter] key) to let the program know that you have finished specifying the print range.

>S   For example, if you wish to print a spreadsheet which is located in columns A and B, rows 5 through 20, you would type "A5:B20," to specify the entire spreadsheet as the print range. If you wanted to print only the lower two-thirds of the spreadsheet, you would type "A11:B20,". Or, if you wanted to print only the part of the spreadsheet in column A, you would type "A5:A20,".

The range which you enter will also be displayed on the third status line. Once you enter a print range, you must tell the program that you wish to have the range printed on a printer.

>S   Type "P" for Printer and the range you have specified will be printed.
>S   Press any key to continue after printing.

If you have problems, make sure that your computer is connected to a printer and that it is on-line! If you wish to continue using the spreadsheet after printing, you may want to replace the row and column headings.

>S   Type "/GB" to replace the borders on the spreadsheet.

Printing formulas: Sometimes you will want to print the formulas in a spreadsheet instead of the values which are normally displayed on the screen. This process is *identical* to printing values *except* that we must first specify that we would like formulas to be output *and* you need not remove the spreadsheet borders. This can be done as follows:

>S   Type "/OC". This command represents "/Output,Content".

Contents is the command which tells SuperCalc3 to print the formulas and cell references (contents) instead of the values displayed in each cell. Each cell in which an entry has been made will be printed along with the related entry. Each cell's contents will be printed on a separate line. The remaining commands are the same:

>S   Enter a cell range to be printed.
>S   Type "P" for Printer to print the specified range.
>S   Press any key to continue after printing.

Retrieving a Lotus 1-2-3 Spreadsheet from a Disk File

>L   Use the procedures given in Chapter 4 for loading the Lotus 1-2-3 program with one modification. Place the disk containing the file you wish to retrieve in drive B at the same time you place the program disk in drive A.

(If your computer has only one drive, load the Lotus 1-2-3 program using the procedures in Chapter 4. When the program has loaded, you will be prompted to insert the file disk in the drive. Remove the program disk, insert the file disk in the drive, and press any key to continue.)

If you are using the disk containing the files accompanying this manual, a menu of templates and options will appear on the screen.[1]

>L   **Press the [Alt] key and simultaneously type the letter corresponding to the template or option you wish to select. To return to the menu from a template, press the [Alt] key and simultaneously type the letter "M" for Main menu.**

If you are using a different file disk than the one accompanying this manual:

>L   **Type a slash (/) followed by "F" for File.**

Note that you can use the *pointer* in the menu of commands that appear at the top of the screen after typing the slash. For example, use the left and right directional arrow keys to move the cursor to File and then press the [enter] key.

>L   **Type "R" or select Retrieve by using the pointer and the [enter] key.**

If your file disk is in the drive configured for the data disk, 1-2-3 will display the file names in the control panel.

You will then be prompted for the file name of the spreadsheet you wish to retrieve.

>L   **You may select the file by either using the left and right directional arrow keys to point to the appropriate file, or by typing the file name.**

>L   **Press the [enter] key and the file will be loaded by the program.**

In summary, you should have typed "/FR", selected or typed the file name, and pressed the [enter] key.

Remember that it will not make any difference whether you type upper case (capital) or lower case letters--all letters used for commands are interpreted in the same manner.

---

[1]If your Lotus 1-2-3 system disk is formatted for use with a hard disk drive (drive c:), then the menu will not automatically appear unless the data files have been saved on the hard disk (drive c:). Follow the procedures for using a different file disk than the one accompanying this manual.

The Lotus 1-2-3 file listing:

If you would like to review the Lotus 1-2-3 files on a file disk, load Lotus 1-2-3 in the computer, place the file disk in the appropriate drive, and:

>L   **Type "/F" followed by "L" for List.**
>L   **Type "W" to display all Worksheet files on the disk.**

>L   **Press the [enter] key to return to the spreadsheet.**

Saving a Lotus 1-2-3 Spreadsheet to a Disk File

>L   **Place a formatted disk on which you wish to save the spreadsheet in the drive configured for the data disk (normally drive B, the right-hand drive). (Check with your computer lab assistant or your instructor about procedures for formatting a disk.)**

>L   **Decide on a file name for your spreadsheet.**

Remember, it is best not to use the same name as an existing file. File names may be up to eight characters long and you should use a name which is easy to remember. For example, you might use "STATEMTA" to indicate that you have completed part A of a financial statement problem. Later you might use "STATEMTB" to indicate that you have completed part B. By using such a sequence (A,B,C, . . .), you will also be able to tell which file is your most recent spreadsheet.

>L   **Type a slash (/) followed by "F" for File.**

Note that you can also use the pointer in the menu of commands that appear after typing the slash. For example, use the left and right directional arrow keys to move the cursor to File and then press the [enter] key.

>L   **Type "S" or select Save by using the pointer and the [enter] key.**

You will then be prompted for the file name to be used for the spreadsheet.

>L   **Type the name of the file (for example, "STATEMTA") and press the [enter] key.**

In summary, you should have typed "/FS", typed the file name, and pressed the [enter] key.

Once you have pressed the [enter] key, the computer will save the file to the disk. (If another file on the disk already has the same name which you entered, a prompt will appear to ask you whether to replace the existing file with the new spreadsheet or if the save command should be cancelled.)

Remember that it will not make any difference whether you type upper case or lower case letters--all letters used for commands are interpreted in the same manner.

>L   After the red "in-use" light goes out, exit from Lotus 1-2-3 by typing "/Q" for Quit and "Y" for Yes.

>L   If the Lotus Access System screen appears, exit this system by typing "E" for Exit and "Y" for Yes.

When the Lotus Access System screen has cleared, you may remove your disk(s) and turn off the computer.

Printing a Lotus 1-2-3 Spreadsheet

Your spreadsheet can be printed in several different ways. Three of these ways are described below:

Printing values: Most often, you will probably want to print the values in a spreadsheet as they appear on the screen. This can be done in several ways:

The *templates in Part II* include what are called print macros.   These macros automate the print procedures so that printing is much simpler. For each of these templates, you can print the results as follows:

>L   Press the [Alt] key and simultaneously type a "P" for print. (Make sure that the paper in your printer is properly aligned first.)

If you have problems, make sure that your computer is connected to a printer and that it is on-line!

The other Parts in the manual do not have print macros. Thus, you must manually enter the print commands required by Lotus 1-2-3.

>L   Type "/PPR", which represents "/Print,Printer,Range."

On the second line of the control panel, you will be prompted to enter the range to print. This range can be one cell or a range of cells. Typically, it will be a range of cells. A print range is specified by the locations of the cells in the upper left-hand and lower right-hand corners of the range you wish to print. Move the cursor to the cell in the upper left-hand corner of the range, type a period (.), then move the cursor to the lower right-hand corner and press the [enter] key to let the program know that you have finished specifying the print range.

>L   For example, if you wish to print a spreadsheet which is located in columns A and B, rows 5 through 20, you would place the cursor in cell A5, type a period (.), move the cursor to cell B20 and press the [enter] key. If you wanted to print only the lower two-thirds of the spreadsheet, then you would place the cursor in cell A11, type a period, move the cursor to cell B20 and press the [enter] key. Or, if you wanted to print only the part of the spreadsheet in column A, you would move the cursor to cell A5, type a period, move the cursor to cell A20 and press the [enter] key.

The range which you enter will be displayed on the second line of the control panel. Once you enter a print range, you must specify several other important factors.

>L   Check to make sure that the paper in your printer is properly aligned with the printhead and type "A" for Align. This command tells the program where the top of the page is.
>L   Type "G" for Go to print the spreadsheet.
>L   Finally, type "Q" to Quit the print function and continue.

Printing formulas: Sometimes you may want to print the formulas in a spreadsheet instead of the values which are normally displayed on the screen. This process is identical to printing values as just described (without print macros) except that we must specify that we would like formulas to be printed.

>L   Anytime after typing "/PP" and before typing "G" for Go, type "O" for Options.
>L   Type "O" a second time to select Other.
>L   Type "C" to select Cell-Formulas.
>L   Type "Q" to Quit the Options menu and continue with the usual print procedures.

Cell-Formulas is the command which tells Lotus 1-2-3 to print the formulas and cell references instead of the values displayed for each cell. The location of each cell in which an entry has been made will be printed along with that entry. Each cell is printed on a separate line.

If you wish to print the values instead of the formulas in the spreadsheet at a later time, you will need to reenter the Options menu and specify that you wish to print the values.

>L   While in the print command menu, type "OO" for Options,Other, followed by "A" for As-Displayed and then "Q" to Quit the Options menu.

PART II

TEMPLATES

CHAPTER 6 - TIME VALUE OF MONEY

Objective: This spreadsheet will enable you to determine future amounts and present values under three different cash flow assumptions:

1. A lump sum.
2. An ordinary annuity.
3. An annuity due at the beginning of each period.

The spreadsheet provides a fast and efficient means of evaluating the effects of changes in the cash flows, the number of years, the number of times interest is compounded annually, and the annual interest rate.

Compatible Textbook Problems: E6-2bc, E6-3, E6-4ac, E6-5ab, E6-6ab, E6-7, E6-8, E6-9, E6-10, E6-13ab, E6-14, E6-15, E6-16, E6-18, E6-19, E6-20, P6-1, P6-2, P6-5, P6-6, P6-7, P6-8, P6-11, P6-16.

Chapter 6

Spreadsheet Name: TIMEVAL

Print Range: A1:F27

Required Input Information: Before beginning, you should identify:

1. The dollar amount of each periodic cash flow.
2. The number of years after which a lump sum payment or receipt will occur, or the number of years in which each periodic cash flow will occur.
3. The number of times interest is compounded each year.
4. The annual interest rate.

Using the Spreadsheet:

>S   **Load the spreadsheet from the file disk in drive B by typing "/L" followed by "B:TIMEVAL,A".**

>L   **Load the spreadsheet from the file disk by pressing the [Alt] key and simultaneously typing the letter "A" from the menu.**

When the spreadsheet has finished loading, the screen display should appear similar to that shown in Exhibit 6-1.

Example problem: Mary Covington has $10,000 which she wishes to invest. The Bolivar State Bank has told her that she can earn 12% compounded semiannually if she will deposit the money with the bank for a period of five years. How much will Mary's investment amount to at the end of five years?

Entering the problem data: You must now enter the required input information in cells F4, F6, F8, and F10.

>SL   **Move the cursor to cell F4 and enter $10,000 as the dollar amount of the investment.**

This amount should be entered without commas or dollar signs, which will be added automatically.

>SL   **In cell F6, enter the number of years the investment will be outstanding (five (5) in this example).**

>SL   **In cell F8, enter the number of times interest is compounded annually (for example, semiannually = 2).**

>SL   **In cell F10, enter the annual interest rate as a decimal (for example, 12% equals .12).**

Note that the total number of interest periods and the effective interest rate per period are automatically calculated by the spreadsheet. This is the *only* template which has been designed to do this. In all other templates, you will be required to calculate these amounts!

>SL   **By using the cursor to scroll down to row 27, you can see that the spreadsheet has calculated the future amounts and the present values of a lump sum, an ordinary annuity, and an annuity due.**

The answer to our example problem is the future amount of a lump sum, displayed in cell F19. This amount equals $17,908.48!

Printing: If your computer is connected to a printer, you may want to print out the results. Make sure that your printer is turned on and that it is on-line!

>S   Type "/GB" to remove the spreadsheet borders (row and column headings).
>S   Type "/ODA1:F27,P".
>S   Press any key to continue.
>S   Type "/GB" to replace the spreadsheet borders if you wish to continue.

>L   Press the [Alt] key and "P" simultaneously. (Alt + P)

You may now manipulate the spreadsheet to examine the effect of changes in the input variables. In fact, the spreadsheet may be used on a trial and error, or iterative, basis to determine an unknown interest rate or other unknown variable.

Example problem: George Brown has $15,000 to invest. If he wishes to have $21,000 at the end of four years, then what annual interest rate must he earn?

>SL   **In cell F4, enter $15,000; in cell F6, enter four (4) years; in cell F8, enter one (1); and in cell F10, enter zero (0).**

Note at this point that the future amount of a lump sum as shown in cell F19 is $15,000 since no interest rate has been specified.

>SL   **Enter an interest rate in cell F10.**

Note the effect on the future amount of a lump sum as shown in cell F19.

>SL **If the amount in cell F19 is greater than $21,000, enter a lower interest rate; if the amount in cell F19 is less than $21,000, enter a higher interest rate.**

By repeating this process, you can find an accurate approximation of the effective interest rate without having to interpolate. (In this example, you should find an interest rate of approximately 8.77573% after a few iterations.)

If you wish to quit at this time:

>S **Type "/QY" to quit using SuperCalc3.**

>L **Type "/QY" to quit using Lotus 1-2-3. (Type "EY" if needed to exit from the Lotus access system menu.)**

After the screen clears and the red in-use light has gone off, you may remove your disks and turn off the computer.

Exhibit 6-1

	A	B	C	D	E	F
1|	TIME VALUE OF MONEY		Future Amounts and Present Values			
2							
3|	Amount of lump sum payment or receipt, or					
4|	Amount of each periodic annuity ....$					.00
5							
6|	Number of years					0
7|	Number of interest payments per year					
8|	(for example, quarterly = 4)					1
9							
10|	Annual interest rate (.00)					0
11|	===					
12|	Number of interest periods		=	0 years times		
13|				1 payment(s) =		0
14|				--		
15|	The interest rate per period		= .0000	divided by		
16|				1 payment(s) =		0
17|				--		
18							
19|	Amount of a lump sum equals ....$					.00
20|	Amount of an ordinary annuity equals ....$					.00

Problems:

1.   Jasper Laurel, age 25, wants to invest a total of $2,000 each year in his Individual Retirement Account until he retires at age 65.   He is having trouble deciding where to open his account, but wants to select the institution which will provide him with the largest dollar amount at the time of his retirement.   He has contacted several financial institutions and has narrowed his choices to the following three: Second State Bank, which offers an IRA yielding 10.25% compounded annually; Creative Credit Union, which offers only 6.0% and requires equal quarterly payments, but which also offers interest compounded quarterly; and Valley Bank, which offers 8.8% and requires equal semiannual payments with interest compounded semiannually. Under each of these plans, calculate the amount which would be available for Jasper at the time of retirement. Which institution should Jasper select?

$\underline{\hspace{5cm}}$ Second State Bank's IRA

$\underline{\hspace{5cm}}$ Creative Credit Union's IRA

$\underline{\hspace{5cm}}$ Valley Bank's IRA

Decision:

2.   Wanda Smith is considering purchasing a home. Wanda's loan payments would be $551.95 at the end of each month for 25 years. The annual interest rate stated in the loan agreement is 11.5%. What is the amount of the loan?

$\underline{\hspace{4cm}}$

Assuming instead that Wanda could invest these monthly payments and earn 11.5%, how much would she have at the end of 25 years? (Ignore income taxes.)

$\underline{\hspace{4cm}}$

3.   Randy Barr has just bought a new car for a purchase price of $11,000. Randy paid $3,000 down and financed the remainder.   When Randy negotiated his deal, he based the amount of the loan on how much he could afford to pay each month. As a result, he agreed to pay $236.15 at the end of each month for 3 1/2 years. To the nearest tenth of one percent, what annual interest rate is Randy being charged?

$\underline{\hspace{5cm}}$%

CHAPTER 7 - NOTES RECEIVABLE

Objective: The notes receivable spreadsheet will enable you to determine the present value of a long-term note receivable and, correspondingly, whether or not the note will involve a premium or a discount. The spreadsheet can be used to rapidly evaluate the effects of differences between the rates of interest which a note pays and the imputed interest rate required by the holder of the note. The spreadsheet also prepares an amortization schedule of up to eighteen periods using the effective interest method. Data from this schedule may be used to prepare journal entries.

Compatible Textbook Problems: E7-21, E7-22, P7-13, P7-14, P7-18, E10-7, E10-8.

Chapter 7

Spreadsheet Name: NOTES

Print Range: A1:F40

Required Input Information: Before beginning, you should identify:

1. The face amount of the note receivable.
2. The stated interest rate *per period.*
3. The imputed interest rate *per period.*
4. The number of *interest periods.*

Using the Spreadsheet:

>S   **Load the spreadsheet from the file disk in drive B by typing "/L" followed by "B:NOTES,A".**

>L   **Load the spreadsheet from the file disk by pressing the [Alt] key and simultaneously typing the letter "B" from the menu.**

When the spreadsheet has finished loading, the screen display should appear similar to that shown in Exhibit 7-1.

Example problem: The Lakemont Company has accepted a three-year, 6%, $100,000 note from the Tallulah Corporation, a major customer of Lakemont's. Lakemont agreed to the 6% rate, which is payable semiannually, even though similar notes are carrying a market interest rate of 17%. Determine the effects of this note receivable on the balance sheet and the income statement of Lakemont.

Entering the problem data: You must now enter the required input information in cells F3, F4, F5, and F6.

>SL   **Move the cursor to cell F3 and enter the face amount of the note receivable ($100,000).**

This amount should be entered without commas or dollar signs, which will be added automatically.

>SL   **In cell F4, enter the stated interest rate of 3% (6% divided by two semi-annual periods). This is the rate of interest actually paid in cash.**

>SL   **In cell F5, enter the imputed interest rate of 8.5% (17% divided by two semiannual periods) for the holder of the note (the effective rate for similar notes).**

Each of these rates must be input as a decimal (for example, 6% equals .06) and must be *the rate per period* (for example, 6% compounded semiannually is 3% (.03) per semiannual interest period).

>SL   **In cell F6, enter 6 (3 years times 2 semiannual periods per year) as the number of interest periods.**

Your entry in this cell must also consider how often interest will be compounded. *For example, a 3-year note paying interest semiannually results in 6 semiannual interest periods.*

Note that the spreadsheet has calculated the present values of the note's interest payments (row 8), the face amount of the note (row 9), and the note receivable as a whole (row 11).

>SL   **By using the cursor to scroll down to row 40, you can see that the spreadsheet has also prepared an amortization schedule for up to eighteen periods using the effective interest method in rows 13 through 40.**

From these calculations, you can determine the amount at which the note will be recorded, and the annual interest income to be recognized.

(Note that while the spreadsheet will accept a larger number of interest periods, the amortization schedule will only display the first eighteen interest periods and the subsequent totals in row 39 will be incorrect.)

Printing: If your computer is connected to a printer, you may want to print the results. Make sure that your printer is turned on and that it is on-line!

>S   **Type "/GB" to remove the spreadsheet borders (row and column headings).**

>S   **Type "/ODA1:F40,P".**

>S   **Press any key to continue.**

>S   **Type "/GB" to replace the spreadsheet borders if you wish to continue.**

>L   **Press the [Alt] key and "P" simultaneously. (Alt + P)**

You may now manipulate the spreadsheet to examine the effect of changes in the input variables. The spreadsheet may be used to evaluate the effects of imputed interest rates both above and below the note's stated rate of interest on the note's market value. This information may be used to evaluate the effect of accepting a note on a company's net income. Thus, changing market interest rates might lead a company to be more (or less) willing to accept a note because of the related interest income.

If you wish to quit at this time:

>S   Type "/QY" to quit using SuperCalc3.

>L   Type "/QY" to quit using Lotus 1-2-3. (Type "EY" if needed to exit from the Lotus access system menu.)

After the screen clears and the red in-use light has gone off, you may remove your disks and turn off the computer.

Exhibit 7-1

	A	B	C	D	E	F
1	LONG-TERM NOTES RECEIVABLE					
2						
3	Face value of the note					$0
4	Stated interest rate (per period)					0
5	Imputed interest rate (per period)					0
6	Number of interest periods (max=18)					0
7	===					
8	Present value of interest payments equals					$0
9	Present value of the face amount equals					0
10						-----------------
11	Present value of long-term note receivable equals					$0
12						============
13	Schedule of Note Discount (Premium) Amortization					
14	Effective Interest Method					
15						
16		Cash	Effective	Disc(Prem)	Unamort.	Present Value
17	Period	Interest	Interest	Amortized	(Disc)Prem	of Note
18	---					
19	0	0	0	0	0	0
20	1	0	0	0	0	0

Problems:

1. On January 1, 1986, Talladega Forest Products Company recorded a $50,000 sale on account to J. B. Crenshaw, Inc., a small construction company. In exchange, J. B. Crenshaw, Inc. signed a five-year, $50,000, non-interest bearing note. Jane Sipsey, your newly hired assistant, has tried to convince you that the sale was appropriately recorded at $50,000. You are unsure because similar notes currently bear interest at the rate of 15%.

    A. Assuming that the note will be fully collectible five years from now, determine the present value of the note:

    Present value of long-term note receivable equals: $_____

    B. Prepare any necessary journal entry to adjust the amount of the note receivable recorded and the amount of sales recorded to the correct balances.

    C. Prepare the necessary journal entry at December 31, 1986.

    D. Prepare any necessary entry to adjust the note receivable recorded and the sales recorded if the note pays a stated rate of interest of 5%. Explain why this entry is the same/different from the entry in Part B.

2.   Bankhead Products, Inc. is negotiating a sale of goods to the Bynum Compressor Company. Bynum has offered to give Bankhead a $120,000 non-interest bearing note due in three years in exchange for the goods. Similar notes currently bear interest at the rate of 17%.

A. If Bankhead accepts the note in exchange for the goods, calculate the discount on the note which must be recognized. Explain what the effect of this discount is on Bankhead's income statement (sales) at the time they accept the note.

B. Assume, instead, that Bankhead is unwilling to record sales of less than $100,000. What amount of principal (to the nearest dollar) must the note be written for in order to ensure that the amount of sales to be recorded will be at least $100,000?

C. Assume, instead, that the note principal will be fixed at $120,000 and that the note will be interest bearing, but that Bankhead is still unwilling to record less than $100,000 in sales. What rate of interest must the note bear in order to ensure that Bankhead's sales will be $100,000?

Objective: This spreadsheet will enable you to determine the dollar amount of ending inventory under the Dollar-Value Lifo method for up to eleven periods. The spreadsheet enables you to rapidly assess and evaluate the effects of changes in price levels, as well as changes in levels of inventories, on the dollar balance of ending inventory.

Compatible Textbook Problems: E8-17, E8-18, P8-11, P8-12.

Spreadsheet Name: LIFO

Print Range:

Inputs and Schedule of Changes in Inventory Layers A1:F19
G1:L19
M1:R19
Computation of Inventory at End-of-Year Prices A21:F40
G21:L40
M21:R40
S21:X40

Required Input Information: Before beginning, you should identify:

1. The dollar amount of inventory for each year in end-of-year prices.
2. The end-of-year price index for each year's inventory.
3. The base-year price index.

Using the Spreadsheet:

>S   Load the spreadsheet from the file disk in drive B by typing "/L" followed by "B:LIFO,A".

>L   Load the spreadsheet from the file disk by pressing the [Alt] key and simultaneously typing the letter "C" from the menu.

When the spreadsheet has finished loading, the screen display should appear similar to that shown in Exhibit 8-1.

Exhibit 8-1

	A	B	C	D	E	F
1|	DOLLAR-VALUE LIFO					
2|	Schedule of Changes in Inventory Layers (Base-Year Prices)					
3		---	---	---	---	---	---
4|					Price	Inventory
5|		Inventory			Index	in Base-Year
6|		End-of-Year	End-of-Year	Base-Year	(Percent)	Prices
7	Year-end	Prices	Price Index	Price Index	(C/D)	(B/E)
8		---	---	---	---	---	---
9	Base = 0	$0	0	0	.00%	$0
10	1	0	0	0	.00%	0
11	2	0	0	0	.00%	0
12	3	0	0	0	.00%	0
13	4	0	0	0	.00%	0
14	5	0	0	0	.00%	0
15	6	0	0	0	.00%	0
16	7	0	0	0	.00%	0
17	8	0	0	0	.00%	0
18	9	0	0	0	.00%	0
19	10	0	0	0	.00%	0
20						

Example problem: Use the following data for The Citadel Group Companies to try the spreadsheet:

Year	End-of-Year Price Index	Inventory in End-of-Year Prices
0	100	$ 50,000
1	110	60,500
2	115	80,500
3	118	88,500
4	120	78,000
5	125	100,000
6	130	156,000
7	135	135,000
8	140	126,000
9	150	112,000
10	160	192,000

Entering the problem data: You must now enter the required input information in columns B, C, and D.

>SL   **Move the cursor to cell B9 and enter $50,000 as the dollar amount of the base-year inventory.**

This amount should be entered without commas or dollar signs, which will be added automatically.

With certain computers, you may notice that it takes a few seconds before you will be able to continue inputting data. This is caused by the fact that the entire spreadsheet (which is fairly large) must recalculate before you may continue. To speed things up, you can stop the spreadsheet from recalculating each time you input data by using manual recalculation instead of automatic.

>S   **Type "/GM" to turn off the automatic recalculation. When you want the spreadsheet to recalculate, you should type an exclamation point (!).**

(After you have finished inputting the initial data, you may want to turn the automatic recalculation back on. You can do this by typing "/GA".)

>L   **Type "/WGRM" to turn off the automatic recalculation. When you want the spreadsheet to recalculate, you should press the special function key [F9].**

(After you have finished inputting the initial data, you may want to turn the automatic recalculation back on. You can do this by typing "/WGRA".)

>SL   **Moving on to cells B10 through B19, enter the dollar amount of each succeeding year's inventory in end-of-year dollars.**

>SL   **Beginning in cell C9, and continuing through C19, enter the end-of-year price index corresponding to each year's inventory.**

>S   **Type an exclamation point (!) to force a recalculation of the spreadsheet.**
>L   **Press the special function key [F9] to force a recalculation of the spreadsheet.**

Note that the spreadsheet assumes that the Year 0 index is the same as the base-year index. If this is not the case:

>SL   **Enter the base-year price index in cell D9.**

Make sure that you force a recalculation of the spreadsheet after your last input is made!

>S   **Type an exclamation point (!) to recalculate.**
>L   **Press the special function key [F9] to recalculate.**

If you have changed your base-year index, you should see the base-year price index automatically repeated through the remaining input cells in column D.

You should also see that the spreadsheet has calculated a price index for each year (in column E), which is then used to compute each year's inventory in terms of base-year prices (column F).

If your microcomputer has graphics capability, you can view the inventory in terms of base-year prices as a stacked-bar graph.

>SL   **Press the special function key [F10].**

You should see a graph which illustrates the ups and downs of the inventory layers year-by-year. (Only the first six periods are shown in Lotus 1-2-3.)

>SL   **Return to the spreadsheet by pressing any key.**

You can also make a change in any of the inputs and view the revised inventory layers graphically.

>SL   **Change the inventory in end-of-year prices for year 4 (in cell B13) to $120,000.**

>SL   **Make sure that you have either forced a recalculation or returned the spreadsheet to automatic recalculation before continuing!**

>SL   **Press the special function key [F10].**

You should see the newly revised graph!

>SL   **Return to the spreadsheet by pressing any key.**

>SL   **Scroll across the screen to the right.**

You can see that the spreadsheet has also calculated the increase or decrease from the prior year's inventory in base-year prices (column G), and, in columns H through R, has calculated the changes in inventory layers for each year in base-year prices.

>S   **Use the [=] key to move the cursor to cell A21 so that you can view the inventory at end-of-year prices in columns A through F, rows 21 through 40.**

>L   **Use the special function key [F5] to move the cursor to cell A21 so that you can view the inventory at end-of-year prices in columns A through F, rows 21 through 40.**

>SL   **As you scroll to the right, you will see each year's inventory layers and the total inventory value for that year.**

Printing: If your computer is connected to a printer, you may want to print the results. Since this spreadsheet is wider than most printers, you will need to print the spreadsheet in sections. Make sure that your printer is turned on and that it is on-line!

>S   **Type "/GB" to remove the spreadsheet borders (row and column headings).**

The inputs and Schedule of Changes in Inventory Layers must be printed in three sections as follows:

>S   **Type "/ODA1:F19,P"**
>S   **Press any key to continue.**
>S   **Type "/ODG1:L19,P"**
>S   **Press any key to continue.**
>S   **Type "/ODM1:R19,P"**
>S   **Press any key to continue.**

The Computation of Inventory at End-of-Year Prices must be printed in four sections as follows:

>S   **Type "/ODA21:F40,P"**
>S   **Press any key to continue.**

>S   Type "/ODG21:L40,P"
>S   Press any key to continue.
>S   Type "/ODM21:R40,P"
>S   Press any key to continue.
>S   Type "/ODS21:X40,P"
>S   Press any key to continue.

>S   Type "/GB" to replace the spreadsheet borders if you wish to continue.

>L   Press the [Alt] key and "P" simultaneously. (Alt + P)

You should now be ready to manipulate the spreadsheet to see what effects changes in the input variables will have on the ending inventory. For example, you might increase or decrease the level of ending inventory for the most current year. This will help you to determine what would happen to the existing inventory layers if you sell more product (lower inventory) or sell less product (higher inventory). Alternatively, you might change the end-of-year price index and see what effects different rates of inflation or deflation may have on the ending inventory.

If you wish to quit at this time:

>S   Type "/QY" to quit using SuperCalc3.

>L   Type "/QY" to quit using Lotus 1-2-3. (Type "EY" if needed to exit from the Lotus access system menu.)

      After the screen clears and the red in-use light has gone off, you may remove your disks and turn off the computer.

Problems:

1.   The Mohave Oil Company uses the Dollar-Value Lifo method to account for its ending inventory of oil. This method has worked very well for Mohave since its oil has always been relatively uniform in grade.   Thus, Mohave simply determines the cost of its ending inventory of oil in end-of-year prices and applies the Dollar-Value Lifo method to this cost to determine the final balance of ending inventory. The end-of-year inventory balances and relevant price indexes follow:

Year	End-of-Year Price Index	Inventory in End-of-Year Prices
1977	100	$5,600,000
1978	110	5,500,000
1979	112	6,720,000
1980	117	8,190,000
1981	121	7,744,000
1982	128	8,320,000
1983	125	8,125,000
1984	131	8,777,000
1985	137	9,590,000
1986	141	9,306,000
1987	139	9,591,000

A. Compute the balance of the inventory account for each year.

1977 $_____

1978 $_____

1979 $_____

1980 $_____

1981 $_____

1982 $_____

1983 $_____

1984 $_____

1985 $_____

1986 $_____

1987 $_____

2.   Refer to the data from Problem 1. Mohave is contemplating a sale at year-end which would reduce the cost of the ending inventory in 1987 year-end prices from $9,591,000 to $4,865,000. This reduction in inventory would be replaced shortly after year-end. Harry Truxton, the general manager of Mohave, has come to you for advice. He is concerned about showing excessive profits because the company might have to pay a windfall profits tax.

A. Compute the ending inventory balance for 1987 if the sale is made at year-end.

1987 $_____

B. Explain what the effect of this sale would be on the inventory layers which have arisen in prior years.

C. Explain how making the sale before or after year-end can affect the amount of profit to be recognized on the sale. As a part of your answer, calculate any difference in profit that might arise on this transaction because of the timing of the sale. Assume that the replacement of inventory would occur early in 1988 when the price index was still 139.

CHAPTER 9 - RETAIL INVENTORY METHOD

Objective: This spreadsheet will enable you to determine the dollar amount of ending inventory under three different cost assumptions:

1. The conventional retail inventory method (lower of cost or market).
2. The Lifo retail method (stable prices).
3. The Dollar-Value Lifo retail method (fluctuating prices).

The spreadsheet enables you to efficiently evaluate the effects of changes in the retail prices of goods (for example, markups and markdowns), as well as changes in the cost of goods available for sale. It also allows you to compare and contrast the inventory balance under each of the three different cost assumptions for a single period.

Chapter 9

Compatible Textbook Problems: E9-14, E9-15, E9-16, E9-17, E9-18, P9-11, P9-12, P9-13, P9-14, P9-15, P9-16.

Spreadsheet Name: RETAIL

Print Range:
Inputs...A1:F16
Conventional retail inventory method..H1:M30
Lifo retail method..O1:T39
Dollar-Value Lifo retail method V1:Z35

Required Input Information: Before beginning, you should identify:

1. The dollar cost and retail value of the:
   a. Beginning inventory.
   b. Purchases.
   c. Purchase returns and allowances.
2. The dollar cost of freight-in and purchase discounts.
3. The retail value of any:
   a. Markups.
   b. Markup cancellations.
   c. Markdowns.
   d. Markdown cancellations.
   e. Sales.
4. The base year price index and the current year-end price index (if you wish to analyze fluctuating prices).

Using the Spreadsheet:

\>S   Load the spreadsheet from the file disk in drive B by typing "/L" followed by "B:RETAIL,A".

\>L   Load the spreadsheet from the file disk by pressing the [Alt] key and simultaneously typing the letter "D" from the menu.

When the spreadsheet has finished loading, the screen display should appear similar to that shown in Exhibit 9-1.

Example problem: Hinsdale Retailers, Inc. buys and resells merchandise to customers. They currently use the conventional retail inventory method for financial reporting, but are interested in evaluating the effects which the Lifo retail inventory method might have. They are especially interested in Lifo because of recent inflation (the price level went from 180 to 200 in the current year). Hinsdale's management furnishes you with the following data and asks you to prepare an analysis of the effects on ending inventory of using the different variations of the retail method:

	Cost	Retail
Sales		$360,000
Beginning inventory	$ 82,000	123,000
Purchases	260,000	360,000
Freight-in	20,000	
Purchase Returns & Allowances	25,000	40,000
Purchase Discounts	15,000	
Markups		42,000
Markup cancellations		25,000
Markdowns		51,000
Markdown cancellations		20,000

Entering the problem data: You must now enter the required input information in columns E and F.

>SL   **Move the cursor to cell E4 and enter $82,000 as the cost of the beginning inventory.**

All amounts should be entered without commas or dollar signs, which will be added automatically. In addition, all amounts should be entered as *positive* numbers. The template is designed to know which numbers (such as markdowns) will be deducted!

>SL   **In cells E5 through E8 enter the dollar cost of purchases, freight-in, purchase returns and allowances, and purchase discounts, respectively.**
>SL   **In cells F4, F5, and F7, enter the retail values of the beginning inventory, purchases, and purchase returns and allowances, respectively.**

Note that there are no retail values corresponding to freight-in and purchase discounts.

>SL   **In cells F9 through F13, enter the retail values of the markups, markup cancellations, markdowns, markdown cancellations, and sales.**
>SL   **Finally, in cells F15 and F16, enter the base year index of 180 (assumed to be the beginning of the year index) and the year-end price index of 200, respectively, since they are different from the displayed values of 100.**

>SL   **By scrolling across the screen to the right and then scrolling down, you can see that the spreadsheet has calculated the conventional retail inventory at lower of cost or market in columns H through M ($48,300 in cell M29), the**

Lifo retail inventory under stable prices in columns O through T ($46,000 in cell T38), and the Dollar-Value Lifo retail inventory in columns V through Z ($41,400 in cell Z29).

<u>Printing:</u> If your computer is connected to a printer, you may want to print the results; however, since the spreadsheet is wider than most printers, you should print the spreadsheet in sections. Make sure that your printer is turned on and that it is on-line!

>S   Type "/GB" to remove the spreadsheet borders (row and column headings).
>S   Type "/ODA1:F16,P" to print the input section.
>S   Press any key to continue.
>S   Type "/ODH1:M30,P" to print the conventional retail inventory method results.
>S   Press any key to continue.
>S   Type "/ODO1:T39,P" to print the Lifo retail inventory method results.
>S   Press any key to continue.
>S   Type "/ODV1:Z35,P" to print the Dollar-Value Lifo retail inventory method results.
>S   Press any key to continue.
>S   Type "/GB" to replace the spreadsheet borders if you wish to continue.

>L   Press the [Alt] key and "P" simultaneously. (Alt + P)

You may now manipulate the spreadsheet to see what effects changes in the input variables will have on the ending inventory. For example, you might increase or decrease the level of sales reported or projected. Or, you might change the year-end price index for a different rate of inflation.

If you wish to quit at this time:

>S   Type "/QY" to quit using SuperCalc3.

>L   Type "/QY" to quit using Lotus 1-2-3. (Type "EY" if needed to exit from the Lotus access system menu.)

After the screen clears and the red in-use light has gone off, you may remove your disks and turn off the computer.

Exhibit 9-1

	A	B	C	D	E	F	G
1	RETAIL INVENTORY METHOD*						*
2					Cost	Retail	*
3					----------------	------------------	*
4	Beginning inventory				$0	$0	*
5	Purchases				0	0	*
6	Freight-in				0	N/A	*
7	Purchase returns & allowances				0	0	*
8	Purchase discounts				0	N/A	*
9	Markups					0	*
10	Markup cancellations					0	*
11	Markdowns					0	*
12	Markdown cancellations					0	*
13	Sales					0	*
14							*
15	Base year price index					100	*
16	Year-end price index					100	*
17							*
18	* See columns H - M for the conventional retail inventory						*
19	method, columns O - T for the Lifo retail method (stable						*
20	prices), and V - Z for the Dollar-Value Lifo retail method						*

Problems:

1.   Coconino Companies, Ltd., has budgeted the following amounts for inventory related accounts in 1986:

	Cost	Retail
Beginning inventory	$ 85,000	$ 98,000
Purchases	265,000	340,000
Purchase returns and allowances	25,000	32,000
Purchase discounts	15,000	
Freight-in	30,000	

All of the beginning inventory was purchased when the price index was 100. Management is anticipating that the price index will be 120 at year-end. In addition, the Company expects the following markups and markdowns in 1986:

	Amount	Cancellations
Markups	$ 58,000	$ 24,000
Markdowns	76,000	34,000

Sales are currently forecasted to be $266,000 in 1986.

A. Compute the projected ending inventory under:

_____ The conventional retail inventory method.

_____ The Lifo retail inventory method.

_____ The Dollar-Value Lifo retail inventory method.

If management's intent is to maximize net income in 1986, which method would you recommend be used?

B. Assuming that management anticipates prices falling instead of rising (year-end price index = 90), what method would you recommend be used to maximize net income?

C. Assume that prices will remain constant (year-end price index = 100). Management believes that sales can be increased to $300,000 by creating greater sales incentives. Compare the conventional retail inventory method to the Lifo retail inventory method. Explain why the results are the same/different.

2.   Smith and Sayles, Inc. is considering changing their method of accounting for inventories. They currently use the conventional retail inventory method. The following data was prepared for the current year:

	Cost	Retail
Sales		$440,000
Beginning inventory	$105,000	126,000
Purchases	400,000	490,000
Purchase returns and allowances	75,000	100,000
Purchase discounts	20,000	
Freight-in	30,000	

The Company had the following markups and markdowns:

	Amount	Cancellations
Markups	$30,000	$17,000
Markdowns	80,000	33,000

All of the beginning inventory was purchased when the price index was 135. The year-end price index was 150.

A. Compute the ending inventory under:

_____ The conventional retail inventory method.

_____ The Lifo retail inventory method.

_____ The Dollar-Value Lifo retail inventory method.

B. Assume that the previous data reflects all transactions for the year except the following:

Management has negotiated a purchase of inventory which will be shipped on December 26th (year-end is December 31) and is expected to be received in early January. This inventory has a cost of $120,000 and will retail at $175,000. Freight-in will cost $3,000. If the inventory is shipped FOB shipping point, it should be included in Smith and Sayles' December 31 inventory. If it is shipped FOB destination, then it will not be included in the December 31 inventory since it will not arrive until January.

Compute the projected ending inventory assuming the inventory is shipped FOB shipping point under:

_____ The conventional retail inventory method.

_____ The Lifo retail inventory method.

_____ The Dollar-Value Lifo retail inventory method.

C.   Compute the inventory balance in early January after the purchase arrives and assuming the inventory is shipped FOB destination under each method. (The template will not compute these amounts for you.)

_____ The conventional retail inventory method.

_____ The Lifo retail inventory method.

_____ The Dollar-Value Lifo retail inventory method.

D.   If management wishes to maximize their Cost of Goods Sold (minimize inventory), what shipping method would you recommend under each of the three retail inventory methods?

CHAPTER 10 - EXCHANGE OF USED ASSETS

Objective: This spreadsheet will enable you to determine the basis of an asset acquired through an exchange, the gain or loss to be recognized on the exchange, and, if only a portion of the total gain is to be recognized, the amount of any gain not recognized. These calculations are performed under three different assumptions:

1. The tax method is applied to the exchange.
2. The assets exchanged are dissimilar.
3. The assets exchanged are similar.

The spreadsheet provides a fast and efficient means of evaluating the effects that changes in the fair market values of the assets exchanged, as well as the cash paid or received, have on the basis of the asset and the gain or loss to be recognized in income.

Compatible Textbook Problems: E10-9, E10-10, E10-14, P10-7, P10-8, P10-9, P10-10.

Spreadsheet Name: EXCHANGE

Print Range: A1:G40

Required Input Information: Before beginning, you should identify:

1. The costs of the existing asset for each party to the exchange.
2. Any accumulated depreciation on the respective assets.
3. The fair market values of the assets to be exchanged.
4. Any cash (or other boot) to be paid (received).

Using the Spreadsheet:

>S   Load the spreadsheet from the file disk in drive B by typing "/L" followed by "B:EXCHANGE,A".

>L   Load the spreadsheet from the file disk by pressing the [Alt] key and simultaneously typing the letter "E" from the menu.

When the spreadsheet has finished loading, the screen display should appear similar to that shown in Exhibit 10-1.

Example problem: The Sedgwick Corporation has a combine for cutting wheat which it wishes to exchange with Finney Farms, Inc. for a tractor. The combine cost $50,000 when it was new six years ago. Depreciation expense of $30,000 has been taken to date even though the combine is estimated to be worth $25,000. The tractor had a cost of $35,000, and has been depreciated $10,000 even though it is estimated to be worth only $15,000. Finney Farms, Inc. will also pay Sedgwick Corporation

$10,000 in cash.   Determine the amounts at which to record each asset after the exchange and the amount of any gain or loss to be recognized on the exchange by each company.

Entering the problem data: You must now enter the required input information in rows 3 through 7 of columns E and F.

>SL   In cells E3 through E5, enter $50,000 as the cost of the asset to Sedgwick Corporation (Company A), $30,000 as the related accumulated depreciation balance, and $25,000 as the fair market value of the asset, respectively.

These amounts should be entered without commas or dollar signs, which will be added automatically.

>SL   In the corresponding cells in column F, enter $35,000 for the cost of the asset, $10,000 for the accumulated depreciation, and $15,000 as the fair market value for Finney Farms, Inc. (Company B).

>SL   Next, in cell F6, enter the $10,000 of cash to be paid by Finney Farms, Inc.

Note that the corresponding cash to be received by Sedgwick Corporation is automatically entered in cell E7.   In some cases, you may need to enter this amount.

In cells E10 and F10, the spreadsheet automatically computes the book value of each asset, which is then deducted from the corresponding market values to arrive at the implied gain or loss on the exchange for each company's asset in cells E12 and F12.

>SL   By using the cursor to scroll down the spreadsheet, you can see that the basis of each company's new asset and the gain or loss to be recognized on the exchange has been calculated under each of the three different assumptions. In addition, when the assets exchanged are similar, and a gain is implied, any gain not recognized on the exchange is also calculated.

The differences between each of the three assumptions (tax, dissimilar, and similar) are described by each calculation.

Printing: If your computer is connected to a printer, you may want to print the results. Make sure that your printer is turned on and that it is on-line!

>S   Type "/GB" to remove the spreadsheet borders (row and column headings).
>S   Type "/ODA1:G40,P".
>S   Press any key to continue.
>S   Type "/GB" to replace the spreadsheet borders if you wish to continue.

>L   Press the [Alt] key and "P" simultaneously.   (Alt + P)

You may now manipulate the spreadsheet to examine the effect of changes in the input variables. Note, however, that the spreadsheet will not work correctly for a new asset since there is no provision in the inputs for the dealer's profit. Note also that for the results to be meaningful, you must maintain the appropriate relationships between the fair market values of the assets exchanged and any cash paid or received by the two companies.

If you wish to quit at this time:

>S   Type "/QY" to quit using SuperCalc3.

>L   Type "/QY" to quit using Lotus 1-2-3. (Type "EY" if needed to exit from the Lotus access system menu.)

After the screen clears and the red in-use light has gone off, you may remove your disks and turn off the computer.

Exhibit 10-1

	A	B	C	D	E	F	G
1		EXCHANGE OF ASSETS			Company A	Company B	
2							
3		Cost of existing asset			$0	$0	
4		Accumulated depreciation			0	0	
5		Fair market value of asset			0	0	
6		Cash (or other boot) paid			0	0	
7		Cash (or other boot) received			0	0	
8		===					
9		Asset fair market values (FMV)			$0	$0	
10		Less: Asset net book values (NBV)			0	0	
11							
12		Implied gain or (loss)			$0	$0	
13					==============================		
14					Basis of New	Gain (loss)	Gain not
15		Tax Method		Company	Asset	recognized	recognized
16							
17		Basis of new asset equals		A	$0	None	N/A
18		NBV of existing asset					
19		plus (minus) boot given		B	$0	None	N/A
20		up (received).					

Problems:

1. Nimrod Electrical Supply, Inc. is considering exchanging a used spot welder for a used computer-guided welder owned by the Nunley Corporation. Nimrod's spot welder has an original cost of $12,000 and accumulated depreciation of $3,500. The spot welder has been appraised at $6,000. Nunley's computer-guided welder cost $27,000, is four years old, and has been depreciated on a straight-line basis over six years with no estimated salvage value. Nimrod believes that the computer-guided welder is worth $10,000.

    A. How much cash or other boot will Nimrod have to pay to Nunley to make the exchange?

    $_____

    B. Calculate the basis of each company's asset after the exchange under each of the three assumptions.

	Nimrod	Nunley
Basis under the tax method:	$_____	$_____
Basis if the assets are dissimilar:	$_____	$_____
Basis if the assets are similar:	$_____	$_____

    C. Explain why any gain on the exchange was not fully recognized when the assets were considered to be similar.

    D. Sally Blansett, Nimrod's controller, has just discovered that no depreciation was taken on the spot welder in either of the last two years. This expense should have been $1,750 per year. How does this affect Nimrod's basis in the new asset under each assumption? Does it affect Nunley's basis in their new asset? Why or why not?

    E. Prepare all necessary journal entries under part D for Nimrod Electrical Supply, Inc., assuming that the assets exchanged can be considered similar.

2.   Kent Power & Light, Inc. is negotiating an exchange of a used computer for a used computer graphics plotter owned by Newport & Associates, Inc., an architectual firm. Kent's computer has an original cost of $57,000 and accumulated depreciation of $28,500. The computer was appraised to be worth $12,000. Newport's computer graphics plotter cost $30,000 and is two years old. It has been depreciated using the double-declining balance method over five years. Kent believes that the computer graphics plotter is worth $14,000.

Kent would pay Newport $2,000 in cash as part of the exchange.

A. Calculate the basis of each company's asset after the proposed exchange under each of the three assumptions.

	Kent	Newport
Basis under the tax method:	$_____	$_____
Basis if the assets are dissimilar:	$_____	$_____
Basis if the assets are similar:	$_____	$_____

B. Explain for each company why the basis of the assets after the exchange is the same/different when the assets are considered to be similar or dissimilar in nature.

C. Explain what differences might result if Newport had used straight-line depreciation (no salvage value) instead of double-declining balance.

CHAPTER 11 - DEPRECIATION METHODS

Objective: The depreciation spreadsheet will enable you to calculate from a single set of inputs:

1. Straight-line depreciation.
2. Sum-of-the-years'-digits depreciation.
3. Double-declining balance depreciation.

You will be able to evaluate the effect on depreciation expense of differences in the cost of assets, differences in estimated salvage values, and differences in estimated useful lives for up to 25 years. In addition, the spreadsheet will enable you to evaluate the effect on depreciation expense of placing an asset in service in any month of the year. (Note, however, that if you use a twenty-five year life and place the asset in service in any month other than January, the final year's depreciation expense will not be calculated. This is because the final year's depreciaton expense will be a partial year in the 26th period, which is not calculated by the template.)

Compatible Textbook Problems: E11-1ade, E11-2(1,3,4), E11-3ade, E11-19b, P11-1(1,4,5), P11-2.   *Chapter 11*

Spreadsheet Name: DEPR

Print Range: A1:G40

Required Input Information: Before beginning, you should identify:

1. The dollar cost of the asset.
2. The estimated salvage value at the end of the asset's useful life.
3. The estimated useful life of the asset in years.
4. The month in which the asset is first placed in service.

Using the Spreadsheet:

>S   Load the spreadsheet from the file disk in drive B by typing "/L" followed by "B:DEPR,A".

>L   Load the spreadsheet from the file disk by pressing the [Alt] key and simultaneously typing the letter "F" from the menu.

When the spreadsheet has finished loading, the screen display should appear similar to that shown in Exhibit 11-1.

Example problem: The Ferriday Corporation is considering acquiring a new piece of production equipment which would cost $150,000 installed. The equipment is expected to last for 25 years, at which time it would have a salvage value of $7,000. Clayton Bentley, general manager of Ferriday, has asked you to prepare an analysis of the depreciation expense and corresponding book value of the equipment for each year under the straight-line, sum-of-the-years' digits, and double-declining balance methods of depreciation. He will then choose one of the methods to use.

Entering the problem data: You must now enter the required input information in cells E3, E4, E5, and E6.

>SL   **Move the cursor to cell E3 and enter $150,000 as the dollar cost of the asset.**

This amount should be entered without commas or dollar signs, which will be added automatically.

You may need to wait a few moments while the spreadsheet recalculates before entering the next input.

>SL   **In cell E4, enter the estimated salvage value of $7,000.**
>SL   **Enter the estimated useful life in years (25) in cell E5.**
>SL   **Finally, in cell E6, you would normally enter the month in which the asset is first placed in service (for example, January = 1, February = 2, etc.). Let's assume, however, that this asset will be placed in service on January 1. Thus, no entry is needed in cell E6 since it is already equal to 1.**

(Note that depreciation is calculated by the spreadsheet from the first day of the month in which the asset is placed in service.)

In cells E8-E10, the spreadsheet will automatically calculate the depreciable basis of the asset, the denominator for the sum-of-the-years' digits method, and the double-declining balance rate, respectively.

>SL   **By using the cursor to scroll down the spreadsheet, you can see that the annual depreciation expense and the net book value of the asset at the end of each year has been calculated in rows 12 through 40 using each of the three depreciation methods.**

Note that at the end of the asset's useful life, the book value still remains. This would be true until the asset is no longer in service, at which time it would be removed from the company's records.

If your microcomputer has graphics capability, you can view the depreciation expense as a line graph.

>SL   **Press the special function key [F10].**

You should see a graph which illustrates expense behavior under each of the three depreciation methods.

>SL   **Return to the spreadsheet by pressing any key.**

You can also make a change in any of the inputs and view the revised inventory layers graphically.

>SL   **Change the asset cost (in cell E3) to $500,000.**

>SL   **Press the special function key [F10].**

You should see the newly revised graph!

>SL   **Return to the spreadsheet by pressing any key.**

Printing: If your computer is connected to a printer, you may want to print the results. Make sure that your printer is turned on and that it is on-line!

>S   **Type "/GB" to remove the spreadsheet borders (row and column headings).**
>S   **Type "/ODA1:G40,P".**
>S   **Press any key to continue.**
>S   **Type "/GB" to replace the spreadsheet borders if you wish to continue.**

>L   **Press the [Alt] key and "P" simultaneously. (Alt + P)**

It is now possible for you to view the effects that changes in the input variables will have on the annual depreciation expense. You can rapidly evaluate the effect of each depreciation method on net income under different useful life assumptions. Or, you can evaluate the effects of different estimates of the asset's salvage value. You might also use the spreadsheet to evaluate the effect on net income of several different assets which you might be considering acquiring.

You will soon notice that in many cases the double-declining balance method does not fully depreciate the asset. This effect is caused by combining the rapid decrease in the book value of the asset (which is used to calculate each succeeding period's depreciation expense), with a small estimated salvage value and a short estimated useful life. The depreciation expense over the useful life is simply not enough to reduce the book value to the estimated salvage value. In response to this problem, management will normally change to the straight-line method of depreciation for the latter part of the asset's useful life.

Example problem: The Black Company plans to invest in new equipment which will cost $50,000, have an estimated salvage value of $1,000, and an estimated useful life of five years.

>SL   **Enter these data in the appropriate cells in the template.**

Note that the asset is never fully depreciated to its estimated salvage value under the double-declining balance method. The book value of the asset is $3,888 at the end of the fifth year. In order to fully depreciate the equipment, management should change to the straight-line method in the fourth year. Thus, depreciation in each of the fourth and fifth years would be $4,900 ($10,800 net book value at the end of year three less $1,000 estimated salvage value, divided by two years estimated remaining useful life.

If you wish to quit at this time:

>S   Type "/QY" to quit using SuperCalc3.

>L   Type "/QY" to quit using Lotus 1-2-3. (Type "EY" if needed to exit from the Lotus access system menu.)

After the screen clears and the red in-use light has gone off, you may remove your disks and turn off the computer.

Exhibit 11-1

	A	B	C	D	E	F	G
1	DEPRECIATION METHODS						
2							
3	Cost of the asset ....$				0		
4	Salvage value ....$				0		
5	Useful life of the asset (years)				1		
6	Month placed in service (1-12)				1		
7	==						
8	Depreciable basis ....$				0		
9	Sum-of-the-years denominator equals				1		
10	Double-declining rate equals				2		
11							
12		Straight-Line		Sum-of-the-Years'		Double-Declining	
13	Year	Depr Exp	Book Value	Depr Exp	Book Value	Depr Exp	Book Value
14	--						
15	0	0	0	0	0	0	0
16	1	0	0	0	0	0	0
17	2	0	0	0	0	0	0
18	3	0	0	0	0	0	0
19	4	0	0	0	0	0	0
20	5	0	0	0	0	0	0

Problems:

1.   Jamieson Company is currently preparing its budget for next year. One of the major expenditures being considered is the acquisition of fifty microcomputers which will be distributed throughout the company's facilities. These microcomputers are expected to have a total cost of $250,000. Management estimates that the useful life of the microcomputers will be from five to seven years before technological advances will make the hardware obsolete. Estimated salvage values at the end of the fifth, sixth, and seventh years are $60,000, $40,000, and $0, respectively.

A.   Assuming that management wishes to minimize depreciation expense in the initial years the microcomputers are used, what depreciation method and useful life should be selected? Provide supporting documentation for your answer.

Method:_____

Useful Life:_____

B.   Assume, instead, that management wishes to maximize depreciation expense in the first three years, subject to the condition that at least some depreciation expense must be taken in each year. Which depreciation method and useful life should be selected? Provide support for your answer.

Method:_____

Useful Life:_____

2.   Bluffton Corporation is considering purchasing new milling equipment, which would cost $950,000. The equipment will last for 10 years and have a salvage value of $40,000. Management has decided that they would like to purchase the equipment on December 1st of the current year in order to take advantage of certain tax benefits. They are concerned, however, about the financial statement effects of this decision. Normally, Bluffton takes one-half year's depreciation using the double-declining balance method of depreciation on any asset acquisitions in the year of acquisition (as if the asset were purchased on July 1st). They ask you to prepare an analysis of other alternatives which might reduce the amount of depreciation expense to be taken in the current year.

A. Prepare an analysis of the depreciation expense to be taken in the current year using the straight-line, sum-of-the-years' digits, and double-declining balance methods of depreciation if the usual policy of taking one-half year's depreciation in the year of acquisition is followed.

Straight-line depreciation expense: _____

Sum-of-the-years' digits depreciation expense: _____

Double-declining balance depreciation expense: _____

B. Prepare an analysis of the depreciation expense to be taken in the current year using the straight-line, sum-of-the-years' digits, and double-declining balance methods of depreciation if the depreciation expense is determined based on the date of acquisition (December 1) instead of the usual policy.

Straight-line depreciation expense: _____

Sum-of-the-years' digits depreciation expense: _____

Double-declining balance depreciation expense: _____

C. Calculate the net difference for each of the three depreciation methods based on the half-year convention versus the date of acquisition. What would you recommend to management?

                                                    <u>Net difference</u>

Straight-line depreciation expense: _____

Sum-of-the-years' digits depreciation expense: _____

Double-declining balance depreciation expense: _____

CHAPTER 12 - BONDS PAYABLE

Objective: The bonds payable spreadsheet will enable you to determine the present value of a bond issue and, correspondingly, whether or not the bond will sell at a premium or a discount. The spreadsheet can be used to rapidly evaluate the effects of differences between the rates of interest which a bond pays and the interest demanded by investors. The spreadsheet also prepares an amortization schedule of up to twenty periods using the effective interest method. Data from this schedule may be used to prepare journal entries.

Chapter 14

Compatible Textbook Problems: E14-9, P14-2, P14-4, P14-6.

Spreadsheet Name: BONDS

Print Range: A1:F40

Required Input Information: Before beginning, you should identify:

1. The dollar amount of bond principal.
2. The stated interest rate *per period*.
3. The effective interest rate *per period*.
4. The number of *interest periods*.

Using the Spreadsheet:

>S   Load the spreadsheet from the file disk in drive B by typing "/L" followed by "B:BONDS,A".

>L   Load the spreadsheet from the file disk by pressing the [Alt] key and simultaneously typing the letter "G" from the menu.

When the spreadsheet has finished loading, the screen display should appear similar to that shown in Exhibit 12-1.

Example problem: On January 1, Wabash, Inc. issued $200,000 of 12%, 10-year bonds which pay interest June 30 and December 31 each year. Similar bonds were paying 14% at the date the bonds were sold. Determine the selling price of the bonds and prepare an amortization schedule for each period's interest expense.

Entering the problem data: You must now enter the required input information in cells F3, F4, F5, and F6.

>SL Move the cursor to cell F3 and enter $200,000 as the dollar amount of bond principal.

This amount should be entered without commas or dollar signs, which will be added automatically.

>SL   In cell F4, enter the stated interest rate of 6% (the rate of interest actually paid in cash).

>SL   In cell F5, enter the effective interest rate of 7% (the market rate of interest demanded by investors).

Each of these interest rates must be input as a decimal (for example, 12% equals .12) and must be the rate *per period* (for example, 12% compounded semiannually is 6% per semiannual interest period).

>SL   In cell F6, enter 20 as the number of interest periods.

Note that a 10-year bond paying interest semiannually results in 20 semiannual interest periods. Also note that the spreadsheet has calculated the present values of the bond interest payments (row 8), the bond principal (row 9), and the bond issue as a whole (row 11).

>SL   By using the cursor to scroll down to line 40, you can see that the spreadsheet has provided an effective interest method amortization schedule for up to twenty periods in rows 14 through 40.

While the spreadsheet will accept a larger number of interest periods (>20), the amortization schedule will only display the first twenty interest periods.

Printing: If your computer is connected to a printer, you may want to print the results. Make sure that your printer is turned on and that it is on-line!

>S   Type "/GB" to remove the spreadsheet borders (row and column headings).
>S   Type "/ODA1:F40,P".
>S   Press any key to continue.
>S   Type "/GB" to replace the spreadsheet borders if you wish to continue.

>L   Press the [Alt] key and "P" simultaneously. (Alt + P)

You may now manipulate the spreadsheet to examine the effect of changes in the input variables. The spreadsheet may be used to evaluate the effects of market interest rates both above and below the bond's stated rate of interest on the bond's selling price. This information may be used to evaluate the effect of a bond sale on a company's net income. Thus, a predicted change in market interest rates might lead a company to accelerate or defer a bond issue date, or to increase or decrease the principal amount of a bond issuance to effect a change in the amount of interest expense.

If you wish to quit at this time:

>S   Type "/QY" to quit using SuperCalc3.

>L   Type "/QY" to quit using Lotus 1-2-3. (Type "EY" if needed to exit from the Lotus access system menu.)

After the screen clears and the red in-use light has gone off, you may remove your disks and turn off the computer.

Exhibit 12-1

	A	B	C	D	E	F
1	BONDS PAYABLE					
2						
3	Amount of principal..					$0
4	Stated interest rate (per period)...					0
5	Effective interest rate (per period)...					0
6	Number of interest periods (max=20)..					0
7	==					
8	Present value of interest payments equals...............................					$0
9	Present value of principal equals...					0
10						----------------
11	Present value of bonds payable equals......................................					$0
12						===========
13						
14	Schedule of Bond Premium or Discount Amortization					
15	Effective Interest Method					
16						
17		Credit	Interest	(Prem)Disc	Unamort.	Carrying
18	Period	Cash	Expense	Amortiz.	Prem(Disc)	Value
19	---					
20	0	0	0	0	0	0

Problems:

1.   Bilko Manufacturing, Inc. is planning to issue $5,000,000 of 12%, 10-year bonds, which would pay interest annually. Bilko's management has been unable to decide whether to issue the bonds currently, or to use short term financing for the next year and issue the bonds one year from now (they would still be due ten years from the date of issuance). Currently, similar bonds are paying a market rate of interest of 11%. Management is afraid that the value of their 12% bonds will decline since interest rates are predicted to climb to 14% by year end.

A. Calculate the selling price of the bond issue under both interest rate assumptions. Ignoring the short term cost of financing for the next year, and assuming that management wishes to maximize the amount received for Bilko's bonds, when would you recommend that Bilko's bonds be issued?

$_____ Current selling price.

$_____ Selling price one year from now.

Decision:

B. Assume, instead, that management is not concerned with the selling price of the bonds, but is instead concerned with the amount of annual interest expense from long term debt shown on the income statement. Assuming that the bonds will not be sold until year end (when the market rate of interest will be 14%), and that management must decide whether or not to pay interest annually or semiannually, prepare a calculation of the annual interest expense under each alternative for the first three years. What decision would you recommend to management? Why?

| | Interest Expense | |
	Annual Interest	Semiannual Interest
Year 1	_____	_____
Year 2	_____	_____
Year 3	_____	_____

Decision:

2.   The Chambers Company, Inc. issued $10,000,000 of 10%, 10-year bonds two years ago to yield 12%. These bonds pay interest semi-annually. Interest rates have increased dramatically over the last two years and are currently at 18% for similar bonds. Management of Chambers has been considering whether or not to purchase and retire the outstanding bonds, and reissue new debt at the 18% interest rate for the remaining term of the original issue.

A. Calculate the selling price of the original bond issue and prepare an amortization schedule for the first five years.

Period	Credit Cash	Interest Expense	(Prem)Disc Amortiz.	Unamort. Prem(Disc)	Carrying Value
0	___	___	___	___	___
1	___	___	___	___	___
2	___	___	___	___	___
3	___	___	___	___	___
4	___	___	___	___	___
5	___	___	___	___	___

B.   Calculate the purchase price of the original bond issue at the present time.

$_____ Current purchase price.

C.   Calculate the selling price of the proposed bond issue and prepare an amortization schedule for the first three years.

Period	Credit Cash	Interest Expense	(Prem)Disc Amortiz.	Unamort. Prem(Disc)	Carrying Value
0	___	___	___	___	___
1	___	___	___	___	___
2	___	___	___	___	___
3	___	___	___	___	___

D.   Calculate the gain(loss) on the bond retirement and the difference in interest expense for the first three years between the two bond issues.

Gain (loss) on retirement: _____

Difference in interest expense:
_____ First year
_____ Second year
_____ Third year

E.   Would you recommend that the bonds be refinanced? Why or why not?

CHAPTER 13 - SERIAL BONDS PAYABLE

Objective: The serial bonds payable spreadsheet will enable you to determine the present value of a serial bond issue and, correspondingly, whether or not the bond will sell at a premium or a discount. The spreadsheet can be used to rapidly evaluate the effects of differences between the rates of interest which a serial bond pays and the interest demanded by investors. The spreadsheet also prepares an amortization schedule of up to twenty periods using the effective interest method. Data from this schedule may be used to prepare journal entries.

Compatible Textbook Problems: P14-16e, P14-17.

Spreadsheet Name: SERIAL

Print Range: A1:G40

Required Input Information: This spreadsheet requires four inputs:

1. The dollar amount of bond principal.
2. The number of *interest periods*.
3. The stated interest rate *per period*.
4. The effective interest rate *per period*.

Using the Spreadsheet:

\>S   Load the spreadsheet from the file disk in drive B by typing "/L" followed by "B:SERIAL,A".

\>L   Load the spreadsheet from the file disk by pressing the [Alt] key and simultaneously typing the letter "H" from the menu.

When the spreadsheet has finished loading, the screen display should appear similar to that shown in Exhibit 13-1.

Example problem: On January 1, Oak Creek Power & Light, Inc., issued $10,000,000 of 9%, 10-year serial bonds which require interest and principal to be paid annually each December 31. Similar issuances of serial bonds were paying 12% on January 1. Determine the selling price of the bonds and prepare an amortization schedule for each period's interest expense and principal repayment.

Entering the problem data: You must now enter the required input information in cells F3, F4, F5, and F6.

\>SL   Move the cursor to cell F3 and enter $10,000,000 as the dollar amount of bond principal.

This amount should be entered without commas or dollar signs, which will be added automatically.

76

>SL   **In cell F4, enter 10 as the number of interest periods.**

This amount must be the interest periods, not necessarily the number of years. For example, a 10-year bond paying interest semiannually results in 20 semiannual interest periods.

>SL   **In cells F5 and F6, respectively, enter the stated interest rate of 9% (the rate of interest actually paid in cash) and the effective interest rate of 12% (the market rate of interest demanded by investors).**

Each of the interest rates must be input as a decimal (for example, 12% equals .12) and must be *the rate per period* (for example, 12% compounded semiannually is 6% per semiannual interest period).

Note that while the spreadsheet will accept a larger number of interest periods, the amortization schedule will only display the first twenty interest periods.

You can see that the spreadsheet has calculated the present values of the bond interest payments (row 8), the bond principal (row 9) and the bond issue as a whole (row 11). You should have a present value (selling price) for the bond issue of $8,912,556.

>SL   **If you scroll over to columns G through Z, you will see the periodic cash flows for this serial bond (The spreadsheet assumes that prinicipal is to be repaid in equal periodic installments). The cash flows shown in columns G through Z were used to calculate the present values in rows 8, 9, and 11.**

>SL   **Press the [Home] key to return to cell A1. Then, by using the cursor to scroll down to row 40, you can see that the spreadsheet has provided an effective interest method amortization schedule for up to twenty periods in rows 14 through 40.**

Printing: If your computer is connected to a printer, you may want to print the results. Make sure that your printer is turned on and that it is on-line!

>S   **Type "/GB" to remove the spreadsheet borders (row and column headings).**
>S   **Type "/ODA1:G40,P".**
>S   **Press any key to continue.**
>S   **Type "/GB" to replace the spreadsheet borders if you wish to continue.**

>L   **Press the [Alt] key and "P" simultaneously. (Alt + P)**

You may now manipulate the spreadsheet to examine the effect of changes in the input variables. The spreadsheet may be used to evaluate the effects of market interest rates both above and below the bond's stated rate of interest on the bond's selling price. This information may be used to evaluate the effect of a bond sale on a company's net income. Thus, a predicted change in market interest rates might lead a company to accelerate or defer a bond issue date, or to increase or decrease the principal amount of a bond issuance to effect a change in the amount of interest to be expensed.

If you wish to quit at this time:

>S   **Type "/QY" to quit using SuperCalc3.**

>L   **Type "/QY" to quit using Lotus 1-2-3. (Type "EY" if needed to exit from the Lotus access system menu.)**

After the screen clears and the red in-use light has gone off, you may remove your disks and turn off the computer.

Exhibit 13-1

	A	B	C	D	E	F	G
1	SERIAL BONDS PAYABLE						
2							
3	Amount of principal...					$0	
4	Number of interest periods (max=20)................................					0	1
5	Stated interest rate (per period)					0	0
6	Effective interest rate (per period)...................................					0	0
7	==						
8	Present value of interest payments equals........................					$0	
9	Present value of principal equals					0	
10						----------------	
11	Present value of bonds payable equals........................					$0	
12						==========	
13							
14	Schedule of Bond Premium or Discount Amortization						
15	Effective Interest Method						
16							
17		Credit	Interest	(Prem)Disc	Unamort.	Debit Bonds	Carrying
18	Period	Cash	Expense	Amortiz.	Prem(Disc)	Payable	Amount
19	---						
20	0	0	0	0	0	0	0

Problems:

1. The board of directors of Ventura Mining & Manufacturing, Inc. plans to issue $10,000,000 of 10-year serial bonds next January 1. The directors are concerned, however, with the effect that recent fluctuations in bond interest rates may have on the selling price of the bonds. Bob Sutter, treasurer of Ventura, is particularly concerned because of the need to start repayment of the bond principal at the end of the first year. The stated interest rate of the bond issue is 12%, payable each December 31, which was planned when similar bond issues were selling at 11%. Recently, however, the interest rate for similar bond issues has climbed as high as 15%. That rate, which has currently dipped back down to 14%, is projected to go as high as 17% by January 1, the intended date of sale of Ventura's bonds. Bob has argued with the board that because the company is issuing serial bonds, they should accelerate the sale of the bonds to take advantage of the current interest rates, or plan to increase the stated rate of interest, in order to make it easier to repay the principal.

    A. Calculate the selling price of the bonds (i) which Ventura's board of directors had originally expected, (ii) at the current interest rate, and (iii), at the projected interest rate for January 1.

    $_____ Selling price as originally planned

    $_____ Current selling price

    $_____ January 1 selling price

    B. The proceeds from this bond issue are intended to be used in a plant expansion, requiring $6,500,000 of the proceeds, and to increase the company's working capital. The plant expansion will not begin earning a return until it is completed one year after the bond issue is sold. If the sale of the bond issue is accelerated, the plant expansion will also need to be accelerated, which will add $500,000 to the cost of the project. What would you recommend to the board of directors? Show calculations to support your recommendation.

2.   The MacGregor Corporation issued $5,000,000 of 10-year serial bonds on January 1, 1985. These bonds called for interest of 13% and principal payments to be made each December 31st. They were issued to yield an effective interest rate of 11%.

By January 1, 1987, interest rates increased to 16% for similar bonds. Management of MacGregor, concerned about the poor performance projected for 1987, decided to repurchase and retire the outstanding bonds. They plan to issue a new serial bond issue which will pay the current interest rate. The new issue will cover the remaining life of the original issue.

A. Calculate the price management will have to pay for the original serial bonds on January 1, 1987.

$_____ Current purchase price at January 1, 1987

B. Calculate the selling price (amount to be received) for the new serial bonds on January 1, 1987.

$_____ Current selling price at January 1, 1987

C. Explain the effects of this series of transactions on the income statement of MacGregor Corporation in 1987. Include both the effect on the interest expense to be reported and the gain (loss) on refinancing the serial bond issue. Will this decision to refinance the serial bond issue improve the performance of the company?

CHAPTER 14 - EARNINGS PER SHARE--SIMPLE CAPITAL STRUCTURE

Objective: This spreadsheet will enable you to determine the weighted average number of shares outstanding and the simple earnings per share for a company. The weighted average can include up to four stock transactions during the year, and is calculated on a daily basis.

The spreadsheet enables you to evaluate the effects of stock dividends or splits, as well as the effects of other issuances and purchases of shares on the weighted average number of shares outstanding for the year.

Compatible Textbook Problems: E17-15, E17-16, E17-18, E17-21.

Chapter 7

Spreadsheet Name: SIMPLEPS

Print Range: A1:F40

Required Input Information: Before beginning, you should identify:

1. The number of shares outstanding at the beginning of the year.
2. The increase (decrease) in the number of shares resulting from stock transactions during the year.
3. The net income (loss) for the year.
4. The amount of any preferred stock dividends for the year.

Using the Spreadsheet:

>S   Load the spreadsheet from the file disk in drive B by typing "/L" followed by "B:SIMPLEPS,A".

>L   Load the spreadsheet from the file disk by pressing the [Alt] key and simultaneously typing the letter "I" from the menu.

When the spreadsheet has finished loading, the screen display should appear similar to that shown in Exhibit 14-1.

Example problem: The Lime Springs Chemical Corporation is preparing its financial statements for the year ended December 31, 1985. The company has a simple capital structure, with only common stock and preferred stock. The January 1, 1985 balances of these two accounts are shown below:

Preferred Stock, 6%, $100 par value, 10,000 shares issued
  and outstanding $1,000,000
Common Stock, $10 par value, 200,000 shares issued
  and outstanding $2,000,000

On April 1, Lime Springs Chemical Corporation declared a 10% stock dividend on the common stock. On July 1, 15,000 shares were repurchased for the treasury. Later, on November 15, these shares were resold to the public.

The only item affecting the preferred stock was the declaration and payment of its annual dividend. Net income for the year was $300,000.

Entering the problem data: You must now enter the required input information. There are two input areas you need to complete: One for the weighted average computation and a second for the earnings per share calculation.

>SL **Move the cursor to cell F10 and enter 200,000 as the number of common stock shares outstanding at the beginning of the year (January 1, 1985).**

This amount should be entered without a comma, which will be added automatically.

>SL **Next, move the cursor to cell A11.**

>S **Enter April 1, 1985, as the date of the first stock transaction during the year. This date must be entered in date format. This format is "DAT(mm,dd,yy)". You can enter "DAT(4,1,85)" for April 1, 1985.**

Or, rather than retyping the date command, you can edit the command which is currently in cell A11, and is displaying 12/31/1985. Type "/E" and press the [enter] key.   Then using the left cursor movement key, move the flashing cursor on the third status line beneath the 1 in 12 for the month of December. Type "04" to replace 12 for December with 4 for April. Use the right cursor movement key to move the flashing cursor beneath the 3 in 31 for the day of the month. Type "01" to replace 31 for the thirty-first day of the month with 1 for the first day of the month.   The third status line should now read "DAT(04,01,85)". If it does, press the [enter] key. If it does not, use the cursor movement keys to go back and continue editing the formula until it reads correctly. Then press the [enter] key.

After pressing the enter key, 4/1/1985 should be displayed in cell A11!

>L **Enter April 1, 1985, as the date of the first stock transaction during the year. This date must be entered in date format.   This format is "@DATE(yy,mm,dd)". You can enter "@DATE(85,4,1)" for April 1, 1985.**

Or, rather than retyping the date command, you can edit the command which is currently in cell A11, and is displaying 31-Dec-85. Press the special function key [F2]. The second line of the control panel at the top of the screen will display the contents of cell A11 for editing. Using the left cursor movement key, move the flashing cursor beneath the 1 in 12 for the month of December. Type "4" and press the [Del] key twice to replace 12 for December with 4 for April. Use the right cursor movement key to move the flashing cursor beneath the 3 in 31 for the day of the month. Type "1" and press the [Del] key twice to replace 31 for the thirty-first day of the month with 1 for the first day of the month. The second line of the control panel should now read "@DATE(85,4,1)". If it does, press the [enter] key. If it does not, use the cursor movement keys to go back and continue editing the formula until it reads correctly. Then press the [enter] key.

After pressing the enter key, 01-Apr-85 should be displayed in cell A11!

>SL   **Now move the cursor to cell B11 and enter 20,000 as the number of shares issued in the 10% stock dividend.**

Note that the restatement factor in cell C11 is 1.10, indicating that a ten percent stock dividend was issued.

>SL   **Move the cursor back to cell A12 and enter July 1, 1985 using the procedures described earlier for entering a date.**

>SL   **Move to cell E12 and enter 15,000 as the number of shares repurchased as treasury shares.**

>SL   **Move the cursor back to cell A13 and enter November 15, 1985 using the procedures described earlier for entering a date.**

>SL   **Move to cell D13 and enter 15,000 as the number of treasury shares resold to the public.**

>SL   **By scrolling down the screen, you can see that the spreadsheet has calculated the weighted share days for the exact number of days between each stock transaction. Note that the number of shares outstanding from January 1 April 1 has been retroactively restated to account for the stock dividend on April 1.**

The weighted share days were then used to compute the weighted average number of shares outstanding. You should have 214,370 shares as the weighted average if you have made your entries correctly.

You may also see that one (1) day appears in cell E24. This is necessary because of the manner in which days in a year are calculated by the template. When we take the difference in the number of days between January 1 and December 31, we get 364 days--one day short of a full year! We should calculate this number from January 1 of the first year to January 1 of the second year in order to get the correct number of days. In other words, December 31 is omitted when we take the difference between January 1 and December 31. This day is added in cell E24 and thus a one (1) appears in that cell.

>SL   **Move the cursor down to cell F33 and let's complete the calculation of simple earnings per share.**

>SL   **Enter the net income of $300,000.**

>SL   **Move the cursor to cell F34 and enter the preferred stock dividend of $60,000.**

In cell F39, you should see the earnings per common share of $1.12 displayed!

Printing: If your computer is connected to a printer, you may want to print the results. Make sure that your printer is turned on and that it is on-line!

>S   **Type "/GB" to remove the spreadsheet borders (row and column headings).**

>S   **Type "/ODA1:F40,P".**

>S   **Press any key to continue.**

>S   **Type "/GB" to replace the spreadsheet borders if you wish to continue.**

>L   **Press the [Alt] key and "P" simultaneously. (Alt + P)**

You may now manipulate the spreadsheet to see what effects changes in the input variables will have on the earnings per share. For example, instead of reselling the treasury shares on November 15, you might purchase additional shares. Or perhaps double the number of shares through a two-for-one stock split. What effects will these changes have on your earnings per share?

If you wish to quit at this time:

>S   Type "/QY" to quit using SuperCalc3.

>L   Type "/QY" to quit using Lotus 1-2-3. (Type "EY" if needed to exit from the Lotus access system menu.)

After the screen clears and the red in-use light has gone off, you may remove your disks and turn off the computer.

Exhibit 14-1

	A	B	C	D	E	F
1	EARNINGS PER SHARE--SIMPLE CAPITAL STRUCTURE					
2						
3	Computation of Weighted Average Number of Shares					
4	---					
5	Number of Shares Transacted Through:					
6	---					
7	Transaction	Dividends	(Restatement	Other		Outstanding
8	Date	or Splits	Factor)	Issuances	Purchases	Balance
9	--					
10	1/ 1/1985	N/A	N/A	N/A	N/A	0
11	12/31/1985	0	.00	0	0	0
12	12/31/1985	0	.00	0	0	0
13	12/31/1985	0	.00	0	0	0
14	12/31/1985	0	.00	0	0	0
15	---				=============
16			Cumulative			
17	Beginning	Ending	Restatement	Restated	Days	Weighted
18	Date	Date	Factor	Balance	Outstanding	Share Days
19	--					
20	1/ 1/1985	12/31/1985	0.00	0	364	0

Note: Lotus 1-2-3 users will see dates displayed in the format DD-MMM-YY. For example, December 31, 1985 will be displayed as 31-Dec-85.

Problems:

1. Great River Brewing Company, Inc. had the following capital stock accounts at January 1, 1985:

Preferred Stock, 9%, $100 par value, 50,000 shares issued
and outstanding $5,000,000
Common Stock, $20 par value, 400,000 shares issued
and outstanding $8,000,000

During 1985, Great River entered into the following transactions:

March 25--Purchased 20,000 common shares for the treasury at $32 per share.
June 6--Sold 20,000 treasury shares at $45 per share.
September 28--Sold 50,000 newly issued common shares for $52 per share.
December 1--Declared and paid the annual preferred stock dividend.

At December 20th, management is projecting the net income for 1985 to be $2,000,000. They are very concerned, however, about the market price of their common shares, which has been rising steadily and is currently at $54 per share.

Roger Blansett, vice-president of Finance, has suggested that the company issue a two-for-one stock split. He suggests that this should result in cutting the market price per share approximately in half, while not costing the company anything. Jerry Tabor, vice-president of Marketing, argued that the market price would probably fall substantially more than one-half, because the earnings per share would be drastically reduced by the split.

A. Compute the projected earnings per share if no stock split occurs.

$_____ Earnings per common share

B. Assume that the two-for-one stock split occurs on December 20th. Compute the earnings per share.

$_____ Earnings per common share

C. Comment on the likelihood of the market price per share falling by more or less than approximately one-half as a result of the split.

2.   Caldwell Industries, Inc., had the following capital stock accounts at January 1, 1985:

Preferred Stock, 12%, $100 par value, 300,000 shares issued
    and outstanding $30,000,000
Common Stock, $50 par value, 1,000,000 shares issued
    and outstanding $50,000,000

During 1985, Caldwell entered into the following transactions:

February 8--Issued a 10% stock dividend on the common shares. The market price was $62 per share.
April 27--Sold an additional 50,000 common shares at $63 per share.
November 20--Due to a drop in the market price of the common stock, 200,000 common shares were repurchased for the treasury at $43 per share.
December 15--Declared and paid the annual preferred stock dividend.

In early December, management projects the net income for 1985 to be $27,000,000. The market price of the common shares has recovered, and they are considering reselling the treasury shares on the open market. They are concerned, however, that reissuing the shares might cause the earnings per share to decline significantly.

A. Compute the projected earnings per share if the treasury shares are not resold.

$_____ Earnings per common share

B. Assuming that the treasury shares are resold on December 15th for $59 per share, compute the earnings per share.

$_____ Earnings per common share

C. Assuming that the treasury shares are resold on December 31st for $59 per share, compute the earnings per share.

$_____ Earnings per common share

D. Comment on which date, in your opinion, management should resell the treasury shares.

CHAPTER 15 - EARNINGS PER SHARE--COMPLEX CAPITAL STRUCTURE

Objective: This spreadsheet will enable you to determine the primary and fully diluted earnings per share for a company with a complex capital structure. This structure can include up to two options (warrants) and three convertible securities. Because of the large number of inputs, the spreadsheet is interactive and requires that you make certain judgments in order to complete the spreadsheet. It requires that you have already computed the components of simple earnings per share--these amounts will be used as inputs in the calculation of the primary and fully diluted earnings per share.

The spreadsheet enables you to evaluate the effects of potentially dilutive securities on the primary and fully diluted earnings per share.

Compatible Textbook Problems: E17-22, E17-23, E17-24, E17-27, P17-8b, P17-9.   *chapter 17*

Spreadsheet Name: COMPLEPS

Print Range:
Inputs and determination of common stock equivalents............. A1:A37
Per share effect of options (treasury stock method)................... H1:M40
Calculation of per share effect of options and
    convertible securities.. N1:S37
Ranking of per share effects, Computation of primary
    earnings per share, Computation of fully diluted
    earnings per share, Materiality test.............................. U1:Z40

Required Input Information: Before beginning, you should identify:

1. The components of simple earnings per share (net income, preferred stock dividends, and the weighted average number of shares outstanding) It may be possible to use the simple EPS template to find these numbers.
2. The average income tax rate.
3. The number of common shares outstanding at year-end.
4. The interest rate to be used if debt is reduced or investments are made using excess proceeds from the assumed exercise of options.
5. The dates of the beginning and end of the fiscal year.
6. The applicable average Aa corporate bond yields and the effective yields of each convertible security.
7. The number of common shares issuable under options.
8. The exercise price of each option.
9. The average and end-of-year market prices per common share.
10. The dates on which the convertible securities were issued.
11. The par value of each convertible security and the total par value of each convertible security outstanding.
12. The conversion ratio of each convertible security.
13. The interest rate on convertible debt.
14. The dividend on convertible preferred stock.

Using the Spreadsheet:

>S   Load the spreadsheet from the file disk in drive B by typing "/L" followed by "B:COMPLEPS,A".

>L   Load the spreadsheet from the file disk by pressing the [Alt] key and simultaneously typing the letter "J" from the menu.

When the spreadsheet has finished loading, the screen display should appear similar to that shown in Exhibit 15-1.

Example problem: Suffield Corporation is preparing its financial statements for the year ended December 31, 1985. The company has a complex capital structure. Selected information appears below:

Long-term debt:
  8% convertible bonds payable $2,500,000
  10% convertible bonds payable 2,500,000

Stockholders' equity:
  10% cumulative, convertible preferred stock, par value $100,
    25,000 shares outstanding $2,500,000
  Common stock, par value $1, 500,000 shares outstanding 500,000

Other Information:
- Options were granted in July, 1983, to purchase 50,000 common shares at $20 per share. The average market price of common stock was $25 in 1985. At year-end, the market price per common share was $30. No options have been exercised.
- Both the 8% and 10% convertible bonds were issued in 1984 at face value. The 8% issue was sold when the average Aa corporate bond yield was 13%, while the 10% issue was sold when the average Aa corporate bond yield was 14%. Each $1,000 bond is convertible into 40 common shares.
- The 10%, cumulative, convertible preferred stock was issued at the beginning of 1985 at par, when the average Aa corporate bond yield was 16%. Each $100 share is convertible into 4 common shares.
- None of the bonds or preferred stock have been converted during 1985.
- The average income tax rate is 40%.
- There have been no changes in the number of common shares outstanding during the year.
- Net income was $1,750,000 in 1985.

Entering the problem data: You must now enter the required input information. This must be done in several locations throughout the template. Be careful not to enter data in the wrong locations since that may alter the template. If you do enter data in a cell where you should not have, you are best advised to *erase* the template from the screen, *reload* COMPLEPS and *start again!*

>SL   Move the cursor to cell F5 and enter $1,750,000 as the net income for 1985.

All amounts should be entered without commas or dollar signs, which will be added automatically.

100%

>SL   **Move the cursor to cell F6 and enter $250,000 as the amount of preferred stock dividends.**

Note that since the preferred stock is cumulative, it doesn't matter whether or not these dividends have been declared--they are still deducted. However, if the preferred stock was not cumulative, only the amount of declared dividends would be entered here.

You may need to wait a few moments while the spreadsheet recalculates before entering the next input.

>SL   **Move the cursor to cell F9 and enter 500,000 as the weighted average number of common stock shares outstanding during 1985.**

The simple earnings per share should display as $3.00 in cell F11.

Note that the weighted average is also displayed in cell F16. If the number of shares outstanding at year-end is different from the weighted average, then you should enter this number in cell F16 over the weighted average.

>SL   **In cell F14, enter the average income tax rate as ".40". It should display as 40.00%.**

Note that no entry is needed in this problem for the interest rate used to reduce debt or invest in government securities if there are excess proceeds from the assumed exercise of the options. Thus, you need not enter anything in cell F19.

>SL   **In cells E22 and F22, you would normally enter the beginning and ending dates for the fiscal year under consideration. However, since our year begins on January 1, 1985 and ends on December 31, 1985, we need not make any entries here. The procedures for using the date function are described at the end of the chapter for both SuperCalc3 and Lotus 1-2-3 should you wish to change a date.**

Now let's prepare our schedule to determine which securities are common stock equivalents.

>SL   **Use the arrow keys to move the cursor to cell C33 and enter the average Aa corporate bond yield (13%) when the 8% bonds (Security #1) were issued. Enter this as a decimal (.13).**

The spreadsheet will automatically calculate two-thirds of this amount for our common stock equivalent test.

>SL   **Move the cursor to cell C34 and enter the average Aa corporate bond yield (14%) when the 10% bonds (Security #2) were issued.**

>SL   **Move the cursor to cell C35 and enter the average Aa corporate bond yield (16%) when the preferred stock (Security #3) was issued.**

>SL   **Move the cursor to cell E33 and enter the effective yield on the 8% bonds. Since the bonds were issued at their face amount, this yield is 8%. Again, make sure that you enter percentages as decimals (.08).**

>SL   **Move the cursor to cell E34 and enter the effective yield on the 10% bonds. Since these bonds were also issued at their face amount, this yield is 10%.**

>SL   **Finally, move the cursor to cell E35 and enter the effective yield on the preferred stock. The preferred stock was also issued at par, so the effective yield is 10%.**

You should note at this point that the 8% bonds and the preferred stock are common stock equivalents and that the 10% bonds are not common stock equivalents. Note also that no entries were made for the options since options are always common stock equivalents.

Now let's determine the effects of any options on the components of earnings per share.

>S   **Use the [=] key to jump to cell H1 so that you can see columns H through M.**
>L   **Use the special function key [F5] to jump to cell H1 so that you can see columns H through M.**

>SL   **Move the cursor to cell K5 and enter 50,000 as the number of shares which could be issued under option #1.**
>SL   **In cell K6, enter the option exercise price of $20.**

The spreadsheet then calculates the proceeds from the assumed exercise of the options. (Since we only have one option outstanding, skip cells K8 and K9.)

>SL   **Move the cursor down to cell K13 and enter $25, the average market price per share during the year.**
>SL   **Move the cursor to cell K14 and enter $30, the market price at December 31st.**

The spreadsheet calculates the number of shares which can be purchased using the proceeds from the assumed exercise of the options in cells L16 and M16.

These are compared with 20 percent of the outstanding shares as shown in cells L20 (40,000) and M20 (33,333) to ensure that we do not assume the repurchase of too many shares. Since 40,000 and 33,333 are less than 100,000 (20% of the outstanding shares of 500,000), we will assume that these are the numbers of treasury shares which can be purchased (shown in cells L23 and M23) for primary and fully diluted earnings per share.

The number of incremental shares to be issued is shown in cells L25 (10,000) and M25 (16,667). These figures are the difference between the total number of shares to be issued under options (50,000) and the number of shares assumed to be repurchased as treasury shares.

>SL   **If you continue to scroll down to row 40, you will see the computation of the incremental income effect of the options under the treasury stock method.**

Note that since we did not violate the 20% maximum for repurchase of treasury shares, there is no incremental income effect (as shown by the zeroes (0) in cells L39 and M39).

Now let's continue by calculating the remaining incremental per share effects.

>S   **Use the [=] key to jump to cell N1 so that you can see columns N through S.**

>L   Use the special function key [F5] to jump to cell N1 so that you can see columns N through S.

In rows 5, 7, and 9, the per share effects of the options are summarized. The net per share effect of the options, as measured by the ratio of the incremental income effect to the incremental shares is zero for both primary and fully diluted earnings per share. We will use this information again after we compute the per share amounts for the convertible securities.

>SL   Move the cursor to cell Q13.

This cell contains the date January 1, 1985. This date should be the date of the beginning of the year or the date of issuance of the convertible security, whichever is later. It ensures that we include the convertible securities only for that part of the year for which they have been outstanding.

Since the 8% bonds were issued in 1984, the later date is January 1, 1985 and we do not need to change this amount. The same is true for the 10% bonds and the preferred stock and we need not change either cells R13 or S13. Thus, each of our securities has been outstanding throughout the entire year.

>SL   In cells Q15, R15, and S15, enter the total par values of each convertible security. These amounts are $2,500,000 for each security.

>SL   In cells Q16, R16, and S16, enter the par value per security. These amounts are $1,000 for each of the bond issues, and $100 for the preferred stock.

If entered correctly, you should see 2,500 as the number of bonds outstanding for each bond issue and 25,000 as the number of shares of preferred stock outstanding as shown in row 18.

>SL   In cells Q19, R19, and S19, enter the conversion ratios of common shares per convertible security.

These are 40 to one (or 40/1) for the bond issues and 4 to one (or 4/1) for the preferred stock.

>SL   If you scroll down the spreadsheet, you will see the number of shares issuable calculated in row 21, the number of days the security was outstanding in 1985 in row 23 (365 for each of our securities since all three were outstanding the entire year), and the weighted average number of incremental shares in row 25.

>SL   Move the cursor to cell Q27 and enter 8% (.08) as the interest rate on Security #1.

>SL   In cell R27, enter 10% (.10) as the interest rate on Security #2.

>SL   Move the cursor down and over to cell S28 and enter 10% (.10) as the dividend rate on Security #3, the preferred stock.

Note that it is important that you enter these rates in the correct row (27 or 28) since interest is tax-deductible and dividends are not. Thus, the incremental income calculated in row 33 for each of the securities is on an after-tax basis.

>SL   **If you scroll down to row 36, you will see the per share index for each of the three convertible securities.**

Finally, we are ready to compute the primary and fully diluted earnings per share figures.

>S   **Use the [=] key to jump to cell U1 so that you can see columns U through Z.**
>L   **Use the special function key [F5] to jump to cell U1 so that you can see columns U through Z.**

At the top of the screen, you will see a schedule for ranking the per share effects of the options and each security. This schedule shows the incremental income and incremental shares which would result from each item, as well as the per share effect of each item.

Note that Security #2, the 10% bonds, are not listed since they were not a common stock equivalent.

>SL   **Move the cursor to cell W13.**

Choose the item shown in the first schedule with the lowest per share effect. This should be the options, since their effect is zero (0).

>SL   **Since zero (0) is already in cell W13, we do not have to change the amount of income. Move the cursor to cell W14.**
>SL   **Enter 10,000, the incremental shares to be issued assuming exercise of the options.**

The calculation of primary earnings per share displayed in cell W17 should be $2.94 as a result of this entry.

Now, choose the next lowest earnings per share effect in the ranking schedule. This should be Security #1, the 8% bonds.

>SL   **Move to cell X13 and enter $120,000 as the incremental income effect.**
>SL   **Move to cell X14 and enter 100,000 as the incremental shares effect.**

As a result of these entries, the primary earnings per share displayed in cell X17 should be $2.66.

Finally, include Security #3 (the preferred stock) since its per share effect is 2.50 which is still less than the primary earnings per share figure of $2.66.

>SL   **Move to cell Y13 and enter $250,000 as the incremental income effect.**
>SL   **Move to cell Y14 and enter 100,000 as the incremental shares effect.**

As a result of these final entries, the primary earnings per share displayed in cell Y17 will be $2.63.

>SL   **Scroll down the screen until rows 20 through 39 can be seen. Repeat the process you just used for calculating the primary earnings per share to calculate the fully diluted earnings per share calculation.**

In rows 20 through 27, you will see the schedule for ranking the per share effects. Below that, in rows 29 through 36, you can calculate the fully diluted earnings per share.

>SL Move the cursor to cell W32 and enter 16,667 shares to be issued assuming exercise of the options (since the options have the lowest per share effect again).

This should reduce primary earnings per share to $2.90, which is displayed in cell W35.

Now, choose the next lowest earnings per share effect in the ranking schedule. This will again be Security #1, the 8% bonds.

>SL Move to cell X31 and enter $120,000 as the incremental income effect.
>SL Move to cell X32 and enter 100,000 as the incremental shares effect.

As a result of these entries, the fully diluted earnings per share displayed in cell X35 should be $2.63.

Next, choose the lowest remaining earnings per share effect in the ranking schedule. This will again be Security #2, the 10% bonds.

>SL Move to cell Y31 and enter $150,000 as the incremental income effect.
>SL Move to cell Y32 and enter 100,000 as the incremental shares effect.

As a result of these entries, the fully diluted earnings per share displayed in cell Y35 should be $2.47.

Finally, consider Security #3 (the preferred stock). Since the per share effect is 2.50, which is more than the current fully diluted earnings per share shown in cell Y35, **STOP!** Adding in this security would be antidilutive--that is, it would increase the earnings per share.

As a final check, we need to find out if the primary and fully diluted earnings per share meet the 3% materiality test. Move the cursor down so that you can see rows 37 through 40. Cell Z39 contains 97% of the simple earnings per share. If the primary or fully diluted earnings per share amounts are not less than this amount, then they do not have to be reported. However, since primary earnings per share was $2.63, and fully diluted earnings per share was $2.47, both of which are less than $2.91, both primary and fully diluted earnings per share must be reported as calculated.

Printing: If your computer is connected to a printer, you may want to print the results. However, you will need to print the spreadsheet in sections. Make sure that your printer is turned on and that it is on-line!

>S Type "/GB" to remove the spreadsheet borders (row and column headings).
>S Type "/ODA1:F37,P".
>S Press any key to continue.
>S Type "/ODH1:M40,P".
>S Press any key to continue.
>S Type "/ODN1:S37,P".
>S Press any key to continue.

>S   Type "/ODU1:Z40,P".
>S   Press any key to continue.
>S   Type "/GB" to replace the spreadsheet borders if you wish to continue.

>L   Press the [Alt] key and "P" simultaneously. (Alt + P)

You may now manipulate the spreadsheet to see what effects changes in the input variables will have on the earnings per share. For example, instead of assuming that the preferred stock was issued on January 1, 1985, you might assume that it was issued on July 1, 1985. Note that if you make such a change, you may need to rework the *entire* computation of primary and fully diluted earnings per share.

If you wish to quit at this time:

>S   Type "/QY" to quit using SuperCalc3.

>L   Type "/QY" to quit using Lotus 1-2-3. (Type "EY" if needed to exit from the Lotus access system menu.)

After the screen clears and the red in-use light has gone off, you may remove your disks and turn off the computer.

Exhibit 15-1

	A	B	C	D	E	F
1	EARNINGS PER SHARE--COMPLEX CAPITAL STRUCTURE					
2						
3		Computation of Earnings per Share--Simple Capital Structure				
4	--				
5	Net income					$0
6	Less: preferred dividends					0
7						-------------------
8	Net income applicable to common shareholders					$0
9	Weighted average number of common shares outstanding					0
10						-------------------
11	Earnings per common share					$.00
12						==============
13	Other inputs:					
14	Average income tax rate					.00%
15						==============
16	Number of outstanding shares at year-end...................					0
17						==============
18	Interest rate (to reduce debt or invest in government					
19	securities if excess proceeds from options are available)					.00%
20						==============

Instructions for changing dates:

Let's input a fiscal year beginning on July 1, 1985 and ending on June 30, 1986. These dates must be entered in cells E22 and F22 in date format.

>SL   Move the cursor to cell E22.

>S   Date format in SuperCalc3 is "DAT(mm,dd,yy)". You can enter July 1, 1985 as "DAT(7,1,85)".

Or, rather than retyping the date command, you can edit the command which is currently in cell E22, and is displaying 1/1/1985. Type "/E" and press the [enter] key. Then using the left cursor movement key, move the flashing cursor on the third status line beneath the first 1 which indicates the month of January. Type "7" to replace 1 for January with 7 for July. The third status line should now read "DAT(07,01,85)". If it does, press the [enter] key. If it does not, use the cursor movement keys to go back and continue editing the formula until it reads correctly. Then press the [enter] key.

After pressing the enter key, 7/1/1985 should be displayed in cell E22! Repeat this process in cell F22 to enter June 30, 1986.

>L   Date format in Lotus 1-2-3 is "@DATE(yy,mm,dd)". You can enter "@DATE(85,7,1)" for July 1, 1985.

Or, rather than retyping the date command, you can edit the command which is currently in cell E22, and is displaying 01-Jan-85. Press the special function key [F2]. The second line of the control panel at the top of the screen will display the contents of cell E22 for editing. Using the left cursor movement key, move the flashing cursor beneath the first 1 (middle number in the formula) which indicates the month of January. Type "7" and press the [Del] key once to replace 1 for January with 7 for July. The second line of the control panel should now read "@DATE(85,7,1)". If it does, press the [enter] key. If it does not, use the cursor movement keys to go back and continue editing the formula until it reads correctly. Then press the [enter] key.

After pressing the enter key, 01-Jul-85 should be displayed in cell E22! Repeat this process in cell F22 to enter June 30, 1986.

Problems:

1.   Perry International, Inc. is preparing its financial statements for the year ended December 31, 1985. Selected information from the accounts follows:

Long-term debt:
  10% convertible bonds payable $5,000,000
  14% convertible bonds payable 2,000,000

Stockholders' equity:
  8% cumulative, convertible preferred stock, par value $100,
  50,000 shares outstanding $5,000,000
  6% cumulative, nonconvertible preferred stock, par value
  $50, 20,000 shares outstanding 1,000,000
  Common stock, par value $10, 1,000,000 shares outstanding 10,000,000

Other Information:
- Options were granted in May, 1984, to purchase 300,000 common shares at $15 per share. The average market price of common stock was $18 in 1985. At year-end, the market price per common share was $25. No options have been exercised. All excess proceeds from the assumed exercise of options can be used to reduce an 8% nonconvertible bond issue.
- Both the 10% and 14% convertible bonds were issued in 1984 at face value. The 10% issue was sold when the average Aa corporate bond yield was 16%, while the 14% issue was sold when the average Aa corporate bond yield was 17%. Each $1,000, 10% bond is convertible into 50 common shares. Each $1,000, 14% bond is convertible into 40 common shares.
- The 8%, cumulative, convertible preferred stock was issued on June 29, 1985 at par, when the average Aa corporate bond yield was 15%. Each $100 share is convertible into 6 common shares. The 6% preferred stock was issued on January 1, 1980, when the bank prime interest rate was 10%.
- None of the bonds or preferred stock have been converted during 1985.
- The average income tax rate is 40%.
- There have been no changes in the number of common shares outstanding during the year.
- Net income was $2,200,000 in 1985.

A.   Calculate the required earnings per share disclosures for the year ended December 31, 1985.

$_____ Primary earnings per share
$_____ Fully diluted earnings per share

B.   Assuming that the 8% preferred stock had been issued on January 1, 1985, instead of June 29, 1985, calculate the required earnings per share disclosures for the year ended December 31, 1985.

$_____ Primary earnings per share
$_____ Fully diluted earnings per share

2.   Garland Company Inc. is preparing its financial statements for the year ended December 31, 1985. Selected information from the accounts follows:

Long-term debt:
12% convertible bonds payable $2,000,000
8% convertible bonds payable 3,000,000

Stockholders' equity:
18% cumulative, convertible preferred stock, par value $200,
10,000 shares outstanding $2,000,000
Common stock, par value $25, 200,000 shares outstanding 5,000,000

Other Information:
- Options were granted in 1983 to purchase 30,000 common shares at $30 per share. The average market price of common stock was $35 in 1985. At year-end, the market price per common share was $34. No options have been exercised. Any excess proceeds from the assumed exercise of options can be used to retire debt from an 11% nonconvertible bond issue.
- Both the 12% and 8% convertible bonds were issued in 1983. The 12% bonds were issued at face value but the 8% bonds were issued to yield a 9% effective yield. Both issues were sold when the average Aa corporate bond yield was 15%. Each $1,000, 12% bond is convertible into 25 common shares. Each $1,000, 8% bond is convertible into 40 common shares.
- The 18%, cumulative, convertible preferred stock was issued on January 1, 1985 at $360 per share, when the average Aa corporate bond yield was 16%. Each $200 share is convertible into 8 common shares.
- None of the bonds or preferred stock have been converted during 1985.
- The average income tax rate is 40%.
- There have been no changes in the number of common shares outstanding during the year.
- Net income was $6,000,000 in 1985.

A.   Calculate the required earnings per share disclosures for the year ended December 31, 1985.

$_____ Primary earnings per share
$_____ Fully diluted earnings per share

B.   Assuming that the net income was only $1,000,000 instead of $6,000,000, calculate the required earnings per share disclosures for the year ended December 31, 1985.

$_____ Primary earnings per share
$_____ Fully diluted earnings per share

CHAPTER 16 - MARKETABLE EQUITY SECURITIES

Objective: The marketable equity securities template prepares schedules to calculate for two periods and up to seven securities:

1. The total cost of securities.
2. The realized gains (losses) on sales or portfolio transfers (to the long-term portfolio) of marketable equity securities.
3. The dividend income from short-term marketable equity securities.
4. The lower of cost or market in the aggregate for the short-term marketable equity securities.

These schedules may be used to prepare the necessary journal entries for the short-term marketable equity securities portfolio. The spreadsheet can also help you to evaluate the effects of selling or reclassifying a security from short-term to long-term on the income statement. It also enables you to determine the proper balance to be disclosed on the balance sheet and provides you with the amounts to be used to determine the gross unrealized gains and losses on the short-term portfolio.

Compatible Textbook Problems: E18-1, P18-1, P18-2, P18-3a.

Spreadsheet Name: MES

Print Range: Cost of securities (both periods).. A1:F35
Realized gain or loss (both periods).. H1:L35
Dividend income and Lower of cost or market (both pds.)........N1:T40

Required Input Information: Before beginning, you will need to determine for each period:

1. The securities invested in:
   a. Number of shares.
   b. Cost per share.
   c. Incidental costs (broker's fees, etc.).
2. The securities sold or transferred to the long-term portfolio:
   a. Number of shares.
   b. Selling (market) price per share.
   c. Incidental expenses (broker's fees, etc.)
3. The dividends per share received on each security during the year.
4. The market price per share for each security at year-end.

Using the Spreadsheet:

>S   Load the spreadsheet from the file disk in drive B by typing "/L" followed by "B:MES,A".

>L   Load the spreadsheet from the file disk by pressing the [Alt] key and simultaneously typing the letter "K" from the menu.

When the spreadsheet has finished loading, the screen display should appear similar to that shown in Exhibit 16-1.

Example problem: The Farmington Company, Inc. invested excess cash in marketable equity securities during 1986 and 1987. These investments and related transactions are detailed below:

Beginning Portfolio - 1986	Number of shares	Cost per share	Dividends per share	Market price at year-end
Thunder Mtn. Mining Corp.	1,000	$28.50	$.75	$32.00
Cleveland Power & Light, Inc.	2,000	17.00	.50	16.00
Pinellas Industries, Inc.	5,000	42.00	-0-	35.00

Transactions - 1987

Sold all of the Pinellas Industries stock for $40 per share.
Sold one-half of the Thunder Mtn. Mining Corp. stock for $33.50 per share.
Purchased 3,000 shares of Seminole Products, Inc. for $22.00 per share.
No dividends were received in 1987.
At year-end, the securities had the following market prices:

Thunder Mtn. Mining Corp.	$35.00
Cleveland Power & Light, Inc.	18.00
Seminole Products, Inc.	21.00

To *summarize*, you must now enter the required input information as follows:

Enter a description of the securities' names in column A.
Enter the number of shares purchased in column C.
Enter the costs of acquiring the securities in columns D and E.

Enter the selling price of securities sold in column H.
Enter the number of shares sold in column I.
Enter any incidental selling expenses in column J.

Enter any dividends per share in column N.

Enter the market price per share at year-end in column Q.

Entering the problem data:

Period 1

>SL   **Move the cursor to cell A7, type "Thunder Mtn. Mining Corp." and press the [enter] key.**

>SL   **Move the cursor to cell A8, type "Cleveland Power & Light, Inc." and press the [enter] key.**

Note that your entry is truncated (that is, cut off) by column C. If you wish, you might abbreviate your entry as just "Cleveland Power & Light" so that the entry "fits" in columns A and B.

>SL   Move the cursor to cell A9, type "Pinellas Industries, Inc." and press the [enter] key.

>SL   Now move the cursor to cell C7 and enter 1,000 as the number of shares of Thunder Mtn. Mining Corp. stock.

This amount should be entered without a comma, which will be added automatically.

You may need to wait for a few moments while the spreadsheet recalculates before entering the next input.

>SL   In cells C8 and C9, enter 2,000 and 5,000, respectively for our other two investments.

>SL   Next, in cells D7, D8, and D9, enter $28.50, $17, and $42, respectively, as the cost per share for each company's securities.

These amounts should be entered without dollar signs. Note that the template computes the total cost of each investment and the total cost of all three investments ($272,500) in column F.

>SL   Column E is available for entering any incidental expenses such as broker's fees. Our example doesn't include any, so skip this column.

(Incidental expenses should be entered as the total expense for all of the shares, not as the expense per share.)

Before scrolling to the right, let's "fix" columns A and B as titles so that we can continue to see the names of the investments as we scroll to the right.

>S   Move the cursor to any cell in column B and type "/TV". (To remove fixed titles, type "/TC".)

>L   Move the cursor to any cell in column C and type "/WTV". (To remove fixed titles, type "/WTC".)

>S   Scroll to the right to column H.

>L   Scroll to the right to column G.

Note how columns A and B are still visible, but column C has disappeared!

>SL   Continue scrolling to the right until column L is the right-most column.

(Note that in columns H through L, any realized gain or loss on marketable equity securities is calculated. Since we didn't have any sales or transfers from the short-term to the long-term portfolio of securities, we will scroll past this section.)

>SL   Continue scrolling to the right until columns N and O are displayed.

>SL   In cell N7, enter $.75 as the amount of dividend income per share of Thunder Mtn. Mining Corp. stock.

>SL   In cell N8, enter $.50 as the amount of dividend income per share of Cleveland Power & Light, Inc. stock.

The total dividends ($1,750) are calculated for you in column O based on the total number of shares owned (as given in column C).

>SL   Scroll to the right so that you can see columns Q, R, S, and T.

In these columns, we will calculate the aggregate cost and market of our portfolio, and the balance required in the valuation allowance at year-end.

>SL   Move the cursor to cell Q7 and enter $32 as the year-end market price of a share of the Thunder Mtn. Mining Corp. stock.

>SL   In cells Q8 and Q9, enter $16 and $35, respectively, as the year-end market prices per share of each of the other two investments.

Note that the total market value and cost are calculated in row 15, and the balance required for the allowance account is calculated in cell T17 ($33,500). The gross unrealized gains and losses are also displayed in column C. With this information, you can prepare your year-end journal entries and other disclosures.

Period 2

>SL   Move the cursor back to column C.

Note that if you use the cursor movement keys to try to enter column B, you will not be able to do so.

>S   Type "/TC" to remove the fixed titles and move the cursor to cell A26.

>L   Type "/WTC" to remove the fixed titles and move the cursor to cell A26.

>SL   In cells A26, A27, and A28, enter the descriptions of the three investments outstanding at the end of 1986 (period one).

>SL   In cell A29, enter "Seminole Products, Inc." as a description of the new investment made during the year.

>SL   In cells C26 through C29, enter the number of shares held at the beginning of the year or purchased during the year, as appropriate, for each of the four investments. (There were no sales of securities in 1986.)

>SL   In cells D26 through D29, enter the corresponding cost per share for each of the four investments.

You should see a total cost of $338,500 displayed in cell F34. If not, check your inputs to make sure that they are correct.

Before continuing, let's "fix" columns A and B as titles once again.

>S   Move the cursor to any cell in column B and type "/TV".

>L   Move the cursor to any cell in column C and type "/WTV".

>S   Use the [=] key to jump to cell H21 so that you can see columns H through L.

>L   Use the special function key [F5] to jump to cell H21 so that you can see columns H through L.

>SL   In cell H26, enter the selling price of $33.50 per share for the Thunder Mtn. Mining Corp. shares. In cell I26, enter 500 since one-half of the shares have been sold.

>SL   In cell H28, enter the selling price of $40 per share for the Pinellas Industries, Inc. shares. In cell I28, enter 5,000 since all of the shares have been sold.

Column J is reserved for incidental selling expenses. Since we do not have any, skip this column. (Incidental selling expenses should be input in total for all of the shares sold, not on a per share basis.)

>SL   Continue scrolling to the right until columns K and L are displayed.

Column K is used to compute the net selling price of the investments sold and column L is used to compute the realized gain or loss on marketable equity securities. You should see a realized loss of $7,500 displayed in cell L34.

Since there were no dividends in the second period:

>S   Use the [=] key to jump to cell Q21 so that you can see columns Q through T.
>L   Use the special function key [F5] to jump to cell Q21 so that you can see columns Q through T.

>SL   Enter the appropriate year-end market prices in cells Q26 through Q29.

Note that the total market value and cost are calculated in row 34, and the balance required for the allowance account is calculated in cell T36. Since there is now an aggregate gain on the portfolio, no allowance is needed, ($0), and there will be a recovery of $33,500. The gross unrealized gains and losses are also displayed in column T. With this information, you can prepare your year-end journal entries and other disclosures.

Period 3

If you wish to analyze a third period, you will need to copy the second period's descriptions and information from cells A26 through T32 into the locations for the first period's data in cells A7 through T13. Then you may input the third period information in the locations for the second period.

In effect, you are inputting the second period information into the first period's cells, and the third period information into the second period's cells. The second period becomes period 1 and the third period becomes period 2!

Printing: If your computer is connected to a printer, you may want to print the results. Since the spreadsheet is wider than most printers, you should print the spreadsheet in sections. Make sure that your printer is turned on and that it is on-line!

>S   Type "/GB" to remove the spreadsheet borders (row and column headings).
>S   Type "/ODA1:F35,P" to print the cost of securities for both periods.
>S   Press any key to continue.
>S   Type "/ODH1:L35,P" to print the realized gain or loss for both periods.
>S   Press any key to continue.
>S   Type "/ODN1:T40,P" to print the dividend income and the calculation of lower of cost or market for both periods.
>S   Press any key to continue.

>S   Type "/GB" to replace the spreadsheet borders if you wish to continue.

>L   Press the [Alt] key and "P" simultaneously. (Alt + P)

If you wish to quit at this time:

>S   Type "/QY" to quit using SuperCalc3.

>L   Type "/QY" to quit using Lotus 1-2-3. (Type "EY" if needed to exit from the Lotus access system menu.)

After the screen clears and the red in-use light has gone off, you may remove your disks and turn off the computer.

Exhibit 16-1

	A	B	C	D	E	F
1	MARKETABLE EQUITY SECURITIES					
2				Cost of Marketable Equity Securities		
3	Period 1		---------	---------	---------	---------
4	Short-term Marketable		Number of	Cost per	Incidental	
5	Equity Securities		Shares	Share	Expenses	Total Cost
6	-------					
7			0	.00	0	0
8			0	.00	0	0
9			0	.00	0	0
10			0	.00	0	0
11			0	.00	0	0
12			0	.00	0	0
13			0	.00	0	0
14	-------					
15					Total Cost	$0
16					=============	
17						
18						
19						
20						

Problems:

1.   Early in 1986, the Barbour Corporation projected an excess of cash. Management decided to use this excess cash as it became available to invest in a portfolio of marketable equity securities in the hopes of obtaining short-term profits. During the latter part of 1986, they made the following investments:

Security	Shares	Cost/share	Incidental Expenses
Trinity Corporation common stock	1,000	$16.00	$ 220
Klamath Companies, Inc. common stock	2,000	13.50	500
Shasta Power & Light common stock	6,000	6.00	400
Lassen Technologies, Inc. preferred	4,500	28.00	1,175

By the end of 1986, Barbour had sold the Trinity Corporation common stock for $18.00 per share. Incidental expenses related to the sale were $250. In addition, the Lassen Technologies, Inc. preferred stock was transferred to the portfolio of long-term investments. The market price per share on the date of transfer was $33.50.

The market prices per share of each investment at December 31, 1986 were:

Klamath Companies, Inc. common stock $13.50
Shasta Power & Light common stock 5.50
Lassen Technologies, Inc. preferred 35.00

By the end of 1987, Barbour had made several sales and acquisitions of temporary investments. Acquisitions included:

Security	Shares	Cost/share	Incidental Expenses
Angeles Forest Products, Inc. common	1,500	$12.00	$ 150
Plumas Electric Corporation common	2,000	17.50	400
Mojave Water Co., Inc. common stock	1,000	8.00	100

Sales in 1987 included:

Security	Shares	Selling Price/share	Incidental Expenses
Angeles Forest Products, Inc. common	1,500	$14.00	$ 250
Klamath Companies, Inc. common stock	2,000	12.00	300
Shasta Power & Light common stock	6,000	8.00	500

The market prices per share of each investment at December 31, 1987 were:

Plumas Electric Corporation common $19.00
Mojave Water Co., Inc. common stock 7.50

A. For each year, prepare a schedule calculating the amount of realized gain or loss to be recognized in income of each year.

B. For each year, calculate the balance required in the valuation allowance at year-end for the current marketable equity securities.

C. Prepare the necessary adjusting entry to reflect the change in the valuation allowance at the end of 1987.

D. Explain why the valuation allowance is considered to be necessary when the aggregate market value falls below the aggregate cost of the temporary investments.

2.   Management of the McCulloch Corporation regularly invests excess cash in a current portfolio of marketable equity securities. Because of fluctuating cash requirements, these securities are purchased and sold within a short period of time, almost always within one year.

At January 1, 1986, the company held the following securities as temporary investments:

Security	Shares	Cost per share	Incidental Expenses	Market Per Share
Scleicher Corporation pref. stock	5,000	$65.00	$3,000	$67.00
Childress Companies, Inc. common	4,000	27.50	2,000	21.00
Knox Industries, Inc. common stk.	1,000	33.00	450	27.00

By the end of 1986, management had sold all three investments as follows:

Security	Shares	Price/share	Expenses
Scleicher Corporation preferred stock	5,000	$68.50	$3,200
Childress Companies, Inc. common	4,000	24.50	1,600
Knox Industries, Inc. common stock	1,000	32.00	400

By December 31, 1986 the following investments had been made (with their respective year-end market values):

Security	Shares	Cost per share	Incidental Expenses	Market Per Share
Burleson Company preferred stock	2,500	$78.00	$2,500	$76.00
Houston Aerotech, Inc. common	2,000	54.00	1,350	55.00

By the end of 1987, management had sold these investments:

Security	Shares	Price/share	Expenses
Burleson Company preferred stock	2,500	$75.00	$2,200
Houston Aerotech, Inc. common	2,000	57.50	1,000

By December 31, 1987 the following investments had been made (with their respective year-end market values):

Security	Shares	Cost per share	Incidental Expenses	Market Per Share
Waco Technologies, Inc. common	8,000	$34.00	$2,400	$18.00
Coryell Air, Inc. common stock	4,500	29.50	2,250	31.00

A. Compute the required balance of the valuation allowance at January 1, 1986.

B. For each year, prepare a schedule calculating the amount of realized gain or loss to be recognized in income of each year.

C. For each year, calculate the balance required in the valuation allowance at year-end for the current marketable equity securities.

D. Prepare the necessary adjusting entry to reflect the change in the valuation allowance at the end of 1986 and 1987.

CHAPTER 17 - PERCENTAGE OF COMPLETION METHOD

Objective: The percentage of completion spreadsheet calculates the revenue to be recognized and the gross profit or loss to be recognized in each period of a long-term construction contract of up to three periods. The spreadsheet can be used to help prepare an initial budget for the contract, which may then be revised as the actual data becomes available. This information may be used to prepare any necessary journal entries.

Compatible Textbook Problems: E19-2, E19-4, E19-5, E19-6, P19-2, P19-3, P19-5, P19-6, P19-7.

Spreadsheet Name: PERCENT

Print Range: A1:F36

Required Input Information: This spreadsheet requires that you specify three inputs for each period. Before beginning, you should identify for each period:

1. The contract price.
2. The estimated cost of construction to date.
3. The estimated cost to complete the contract.

Using the Spreadsheet:

>S   Load the spreadsheet from the file disk in drive B by typing "/L" followed by "B:PERCENT,A".

>L   Load the spreadsheet from the file disk by pressing the [Alt] key and simultaneously typing the letter "L" from the menu.

When the spreadsheet has finished loading, the screen display should appear similar to that shown in Exhibit 17-1.

Example problem: Ludlow Construction Company, Inc. has entered into a long term construction project to rebuild a section of highway. The project is expected to take three years to complete and the contract price is $5,000,000. Costs are projected as follows:

	1986	1987	1988
Estimated costs incurred to date:	$1,200,000	$2,400,000	$4,000,000
Estimated costs to complete:	2,800,000	1,600,000	-0-

Entering the problem data: You must now enter the required input information in rows 5, 7, and 8.

>SL   Move the cursor to cell D5 and enter $5,000,000 as the dollar amount of the contract.

This amount should be entered without commas or dollar signs, which will be added automatically.

You should see the dollar amount of the contract automatically entered in cells E5 and F5. This is because the spreadsheet assumes that the contract price will remain constant. If this is not the case, you would enter the revised contract price(s) for the second and/or third periods in cells E5 and F5, respectively.

>SL   Next, in cells D7, E7, and F7, enter the estimated construction cost to date at the end of periods one, two, and three, respectively. Thus, you would enter $1,200,000 in cell D7, $2,400,000 in cell E7, and $4,000,000 in cell F7.

>SL   Finally, in cells D8, E8, and F8, enter the estimated cost to complete the contract as of the end of periods one, two, and three, respectively. Enter $2,800,000 in cell D8 and $1,600,000 in cell E8.

Note that the spreadsheet is limited to three periods. Since the contract is completed in the third period, leave cell F8 as zero (0).

By examining the spreadsheet, you can see at this point that the spreadsheet has calculated the total estimated cost of the contract in row 10 and the total estimated gross profit at the end of each period in row 12. In row 14, the spreadsheet has calculated the percentage of completion through the end of each period.

>SL   By scrolling down the spreadsheet, you will see that the amount of revenue to be recognized in each period has been calculated in rows 16 through 25. The gross profit to be recognized is calculated in rows 26 through 36.

Normally, the gross profit to be recognized can be found in row 35. However, in the event that a loss is projected for the completed contract, the entire loss should be recognized immediately and the gross profit to be recognized must be adjusted. This adjustment is incorporated in the formulas used in rows 30 through 36.

>SL   For example, press the [Home] key, move the cursor to cell D5, and enter $3,900,000. In row 12, you will see that the contract now projects a $100,000 loss.

>SL   If you scroll down to row 35, you will see that the entire projected loss should be recognized in the first period.

Printing: If your computer is connected to a printer, you may want to print the results. Make sure that your printer is turned on and that it is on-line!

>S   Type "/GB" to remove the spreadsheet borders (row and column headings).
>S   Type "/ODA1:F36,P".
>S   Press any key to continue.
>S   Type "/GB" to replace the spreadsheet borders if you wish to continue.

>L   Press the [Alt] key and "P" simultaneously. (Alt + P)

You may now manipulate the spreadsheet to examine the effect of changes in the contract price or estimated costs. The spreadsheet may be used, for example, to evaluate the effects of unanticipated cost overruns or penalties assessed for late completion of the contract. You may even find that a project which was budgeted to be profitable may be unprofitable due to these types of unforeseen costs.

If you wish to quit at this time:

>S   Type "/QY" to quit using SuperCalc3.

>L   Type "/QY" to quit using Lotus 1-2-3. (Type "EY" if needed to exit from the Lotus access system menu.)

After the screen clears and the red in-use light has gone off, you may remove your disks and turn off the computer.

Exhibit 17-1

	A	B	C	D	E	F
1	PERCENTAGE OF COMPLETION METHOD			Period		
2	(Cost-to-cost basis)					
3				1	2	3
4						
5	Contract price			$0	$0	$0
6	Less estimated cost:					
7	Cost to date			0	0	0
8	Estimated costs to complete			0	0	0
9						
10	Estimated total costs			$0	$0	$0
11						
12	Estimated total gross profit			$0	$0	$0
13						
14	Percentage of completion			.00%	.00%	.00%
15						
16	Revenue to be recognized:					
17	Contract price multiplied			$0	$0	$0
18	times percentage complete			.00%	.00%	.00%
19						
20	Cumulative revenue			$0	$0	$0

Problems:

1. Grand Mesa Industries, Inc. received a contract on February 1, 1987 from the city of Cebolla Junction to construct a new bridge across the Lodore river. The contract was awarded in the amount of $12,000,000 and calls for a completion date of June 1, 1989. Since the city's primary revenues are generated through tourism, and the old bridge will have to be closed in fall of 1988 to facilitate completion of the new bridge, the contract calls for a late completion penalty of one-half of one percent of the total contract price for each week's delay beyond June 1, 1989.

    Grand Mesa estimates that the total cost of constructing the bridge will be $11,000,000. The company's accountants and engineers anticipate that cumulative costs of $4,400,000 will have been incurred by December 31, 1987, and cumulative costs of $8,580,000 by December 31, 1988.

    A. Calculate the estimated percentage of completion of the bridge at the end of each period and the amount of revenue and gross profit (loss) to be recognized at the end of each period.

	1987	1988	1989
Percentage of completion:	____	____	____
Revenue to be recognized:	____	____	____
Gross profit (loss):	____	____	____

    B. At December 31, 1987, only $3,300,000 of the total estimated cost of $11,000,000 had been incurred. This was due to an unanticipated shortage of materials, which resulted in several work delays. Calculate the actual percentage of completion achieved, and the revenue and gross profit (loss) to be recognized for 1987.

Percentage of completion:	____
Revenue to be recognized:	____
Gross profit (loss):	____

    C. At December 31, 1988, total costs of $8,120,000 had been incurred. This was slightly behind the estimated costs, and was attributed to continuing problems due to the materials shortage. In addition, it was now estimated that the completed contract would cost $11,600,000 because of escalating costs for materials. The company's engineers also estimated that there would be an eight-week delay in completing the bridge. Calculate the actual percentage of completion achieved, and the revenue and gross profit (loss) to be recognized for 1988.

Percentage of completion:	____
Revenue to be recognized:	____
Gross profit (loss):	____

(continued)

D. In early 1989, the shortage of materials ended, and progress on the bridge moved ahead. The bridge was completed only five weeks late, instead of eight, and cost $11,500,000, slightly less than what had been expected last year. Calculate the actual percentage of completion achieved, and the revenue and gross profit (loss) to be recognized for 1989.

Percentage of completion: _____
Revenue to be recognized: _____
Gross profit (loss):   _____

2. Scholle Corporation has contracted to build a 50-story office tower at a total contract price of $25,000,000. They estimate the following costs in each year of the three-year contract:

	Period 1	Period 2	Period 3
Estimated costs incurred to date:	$4,000,000	$12,000,000	$20,000,000
Estimated costs to complete.	16,000,000	8,000,000	-0-

A. Calculate the estimated percentage of completion of the tower at the end of each period and the amount of revenue and gross profit (loss) to be recognized at the end of each period.

	Period 1	Period 2	Period 3
Percentage of completion:	_____	_____	_____
Revenue to be recognized:	_____	_____	_____
Gross profit (loss):	_____	_____	_____

B. At the end of the first period, costs were exactly as predicted. In the second period, however, significant cost overruns were incurred. The cost to date was estimated to be $13,200,000, and the estimated cost to complete was now $8,800,000. Calculate the revised percentage of completion of the tower at the end of each period and the amount of revenue and gross profit (loss) to be recognized at the end of each period.

	Period 1	Period 2	Period 3
Percentage of completion:	_____	_____	_____
Revenue to be recognized:	_____	_____	_____
Gross profit (loss):	_____	_____	_____

C. Cost overruns continued to plague the construction of the tower in the third year and the building was completed at a cost of $23,500,000. Calculate the final percentage of completion of the tower at the end of each period and the amount of revenue and gross profit (loss) to be recognized at the end of each period.

	Period 1	Period 2	Period 3
Percentage of completion:	_____	_____	_____
Revenue to be recognized:	_____	_____	_____
Gross profit (loss):	_____	_____	_____

CHAPTER 18 - PENSIONS - MINIMUM & MAXIMUM

Objective: The pensions spreadsheet calculates the annual amounts of past service cost to be amortized and funded for up to twenty periods. These amounts are used to prepare a schedule of the amortization and funding of the past service cost. The spreadsheet also calculates the total pension expense for each set of inputs, which can be compared with the minimum and maximum provisions for pension expense. (The minimum and maximum provisions are calculated by the spreadsheet in additional schedules.) These calculations can be used to ensure that the amount of pension expense conforms with generally accepted accounting principles.

WARNING: This template and the related problems utilize accounting principles which were acceptable prior to the issuance of FASB No. 87. Since these principles will no longer be acceptable beginning in 1987, they have been deleted from Kieso and Weygandt, *Intermediate Accounting*, 5th edition.

Spreadsheet Name: PENSION

Print Range: Inputs and schedule of amortization and funding of
                    past service cost A1:G40
                    Total pension expense H15:H40
                    Computation of minimum provision I14:N40
                    Computation of maximum provision O14:S40

Required Input Information: Before beginning, you will need to determine:

1. The amount of past service cost.
2. The interest (earnings) rate per period.
3. The period over which past service cost will be amortized.
4. The period over which past service cost will be funded.
5. The normal cost per period.

Using the Spreadsheet:

>S   Load the spreadsheet from the file disk in drive B by typing "/L" followed by
      "B:PENSION,A".

>L   Load the spreadsheet from the file disk by pressing the [Alt] key and
      simultaneously typing the letter "M" from the menu.

      When the spreadsheet has finished loading, the screen display should appear
      similar to that shown in Exhibit 18-1.

Example problem: The Rabun Corporation initiated a pension plan for its employees on January 1, 1986. At that date, the total past service cost was actuarially estimated to be $600,000. Mike Toccoa, Rabun's actuary, has suggested that 4% is an appropriate interest rate for the plan. He has calculated the normal cost for Rabun Corporation to be $50,000 annually and has recommended that the company both amortize and fund the past service cost over a twenty-year period.

Entering the problem data: You must now enter the required input information in cells E3 through E6, and cells F7 through Y7.

>SL   **Move the cursor to cell E3 and enter $600,000 as the dollar amount of the past service cost.**

This amount should be entered without commas or dollar signs, which will be added automatically.

You may need to wait for a few moments while the spreadsheet recalculates before entering the next input.

>SL   **In cell E4, enter the 4% interest rate earned per period as a decimal (for example, 4% equals .04).**

>SL   **In cells E5 and E6, enter 20 as the number of periods over which the past service cost is to be both amortized, and funded, respectively.**

>SL   **Finally, in cell F7, enter the normal cost of $50,000 for the first period.**

>SL   **By scrolling over to the right, you should see that the dollar amount of the normal cost has been automatically entered in cells G7 through Y7.**

This is because the spreadsheet assumes that the normal cost will remain constant. If this is not the case, enter the normal cost(s) in future periods in the appropriate cells ranging from G7 through Y7.

>SL   **Press the [Home] key to return to cell A1.**

By examining rows 9 through 14, you can see that the spreadsheet has calculated the annual amount of past service cost to be amortized and funded.

Immediately below this calculation, in rows 15 through 40, the spreadsheet has prepared a schedule of amortization and funding of the past service cost.

>SL   **Scroll down the spreadsheet so that you can view this schedule.**

(At this point, several columns in the schedule contain zeroes (0's) since the amortization and funding periods are both equal to 20.)

The pension expense calculated in this schedule (column D) is added to the normal cost for each period (cells F7 through Y7) to arrive at the total pension expense. This total is shown to the right of the amortization and funding schedule in column H.

>SL   **Scroll over to the right so that you can view the total pension expense in column H, rows 14 through 40.**

Remember, however, that the total pension expense to be taken is subject to the limits of the minimum and maximum provisions. The minimum provision for pension expense is calculated in columns I through N, rows 14 through 40, immediately to the right of the total pension expense in column H.

>S   **Use the [=] key to jump to cell I14. Scroll down to row 40 so that you can view the calculation of the minimum pension expense for all 20 periods in columns I through N.**

>L   Use the special function key [F5] to jump to cell I14. Scroll down to row 40 so that you can view the calculation of the minimum pension expense for all 20 periods in columns I through N.

Finally, the maximum provision for pension expense is calculated in columns O through S, rows 14 through 40, immediately to the right of the computation of the minimum provision.

>S   Use the [=] key to jump to cell O14. Scroll down to row 40 so that you can view the calculation of the minimum pension expense for all 20 periods in columns O through S.

>L   Use the special function key [F5] to jump to cell O14. Scroll down to row 40 so that you can view the calculation of the minimum pension expense for all 20 periods in columns O through S.

Again, note that several columns have zeroes (0's) since the amortization and funding periods were both set equal to 20.

>SL   Next, compare the total pension expense (in column H) under the data assumptions you have entered with the minimum (in column N) and maximum (in column S) provisions. You should find that the total pension expense is within the minimum and maximum provisions in every period. Thus, the amounts expensed are acceptable.

>SL   Return to cell A1 by pressing the [Home] key.

If your computer has graphics capability, you can also evaluate the amounts expensed using a line-graph.

>SL   Press the special function key [F10].

You should see a line-graph of the pension expense as it compares with the minimum and maximum provisions. It very clearly falls between these two limits.

>SL   Return to your spreadsheet by pressing any key.

Printing: If your computer is connected to a printer, you may want to print the results. However, you will need to print the spreadsheet in sections because of its width. Make sure that your printer is turned on and that it is on-line!

>S   Type "/GB" to remove the spreadsheet borders (row and column headings).
>S   Type "/ODA1:G40,P" to print the inputs, the calculations of annual amounts of past service cost amortized and funded, and the schedule of amortization and funding of past service cost.
>S   Press any key to continue.
>S   Type "/ODH15:H40,P" to print the total pension expense.
>S   Press any key to continue.
>S   Type "/ODI14:N40,P" to print the computation of the minimum provision for pension expense.
>S   Press any key to continue.
>S   Type "/ODO14:S40,P" to print the computation of the maximum provision for pension expense.
>S   Press any key to continue.

>S   Type "/GB" to replace the spreadsheet borders if you wish to continue.

>L   Press the [Alt] key and "P" simultaneously. (Alt + P)

You may now manipulate the spreadsheet to examine the effect of changes in the inputs, especially the periods over which the past service cost is amortized or funded and the interest rate.

Now, let's try making some changes in the inputs! Instead of using equal periods for both amortization and funding of the past service cost, let's enter an amortization period of fifteen periods--five less than the funding period.

>SL   Move the cursor to cell E5 and enter 15.

Compare the total pension expense (in column H) with the minimum (in column N) and maximum (in column S) provisions.

If your computer has graphics capability, evaluate this change by observing the line-graph.

>SL   Press the special function key [F10].

You should see that the amounts expensed are acceptable in all periods. But note that all three amounts (expense, minimum, and maximum) are equal beginning in the sixteenth year (Can you explain why this is so?).

>SL   Return to your spreadsheet by pressing any key.

Let's try another change! Instead of amortizing the past service cost over fifteen periods, let's accelerate the amortization to five periods.

>SL   Enter 5 in cell E5.

Compare the total pension expense (in column H) with the minimum (in column N) and maximum (in column S) provisions.

Remember, if your computer has graphics capability, evaluate this change by observing the line-graph.

You should find that the total pension expense exceeds the maximum for the first five periods. Thus, the total pension expense is not acceptable and Rabun corporation will be limited to the maximum provision.

This limit will affect the amount of deferred pension liability and, correspondingly, the amount of interest to be calculated in future periods in the schedule of amortization and funding of past service cost, and in the computation of the maximum provision.

To evaluate this effect, let's change the amount of pension expense calculated in the schedule of amortization and funding of past service cost. Since Rabun is limited to the maximum provision, let's start by replacing the calculated pension expense with the maximum.

>SL   **Move your cursor to cell S21.**

You will find that the maximum provision for pension expense in period 1 is $110,000. Let's subtract the normal cost in period 1 of $50,000 from the maximum to see how much expense can be related to the past service cost. This gives us $60,000 as the amount of expense related to the past service cost for period 1.

>SL   **Move the cursor back to cell D21 (the pension expense debit for past service cost in period 1). The amount in this cell should be $134,776.**

>SL   **Enter the maximum amount instead--$60,000. Note how this changes the amount of deferred liability (in cell F21) from $90,627 to $15,851.**

Now compare the revised total pension expense for period two (in column H) with the minimum (in column N) and maximum (in column S) provisions--use graphics if you can! (Note that the maximum provision for period 2 is now different.) You should find that the total pension expense for period two also exceeds the maximum. Once again, let's change the amount of pension expense calculated in the schedule of amortization and funding of past service cost, only this time for period two.

The amount related to past service cost in period two is $60,634 (maximum of $110,634 displayed in cell S22 minus $50,000 normal cost).

>SL   **Enter $60,634 in cell D22 and then compare the revised total pension expense for period three (in column H) with the minimum (in column N) and maximum (in column S) provisions.**

By continuing this iterative process of revising the pension expense debit in the schedule of amortization and funding of past service cost, you can arrive at the acceptable amount of pension expense in each period. You can also use this process when the total pension expense is less than the minimum. (In fact, if you continue this example, you will find that the total pension expense will be less than the minimum beginning in period 6!)

WARNING: Since we have been entering fixed dollar amounts in column D (the pension expense debit), we have destroyed the commands which were previously in this column. In order to make another change in the input data, you must restore those commands. That is, you must clear the current spreadsheet from the screen (Type "/ZY" in SuperCalc3 and "/WEY" in Lotus 1-2-3) and reload the template PENSION. You can then begin anew.)

Finally, you may find that with certain combinations of inputs (for example, high interest rates (>10%) and/or unfunded past service costs (funding period = zero)), the minimum provision will exceed the maximum. This is caused by the manner in which costs are included in the formula for computing the maximum. It illustrates deficiencies in the conceptual development of the maximum. If the minimum does exceed the maximum, the minimum should be chosen as the basis for determining the acceptable amounts to be expensed.

If you wish to quit at this time:

>S   Type "/QY" to quit using SuperCalc3.

>L   Type "/QY" to quit using Lotus 1-2-3. (Type "EY" if needed to exit from the Lotus access system menu.)

After the screen clears and the red in-use light has gone off, you may remove your disks and turn off the computer.

Exhibit 18-1

	A	B	C	D	E	F	G
1		PENSIONS - MINIMUM & MAXIMUM Period = 0				1	2
2						-------------------	
3		Past service cost (PSC).............................			$0		
4		Interest rate per period (.00)....................			.00%		
5		Amortization period (max=20)...............			0		
6		Funding period (max=20)........................			0		
7		Normal cost per period...				$0	$0
8		**					
9		Calculation of annual amount of PSC:			(1) Amortized	(2) Funded	
10		Past service cost divided by the				$0	$0
11		Present value of an ordinary annuity				0	0
12		equals					
13		Annual amount of past service cost.............................				$0	$0
14						=======================	
15		Schedule of Amortization and Funding of Past Service Cost					
16		Amortization	0 years		Funding	0 years	
17	--			-------------------------------------			
18		Annual	Interest	Pension	Cash	Deferred expense/liab.	
19	Pd.	Amount	Incr (decr)	Expense Dr.	Credit	Dr (Cr)	12/31 Bal.
20	---						

Problems:

1. Tariffville Printers, Inc. plans to initiate a pension plan for its employees beginning January 1 of next year. The company has hired an actuary, Susan Grandby, to compute the amounts of past service cost to be credited to current employees and the amount of normal cost needed each year to maintain the plan. Susan has calculated the past service cost to be $550,000, and the annual normal cost to be $44,000. She believes that six percent is an appropriate interest rate for the earnings of the plan. Ray Litchfield, president of Tariffville Printers, Inc., is upset because Susan recommended that the past service cost be funded over ten years, a period only one-half as long as the 20-year period she recommended for amortizing the cost. Ray does not want to pay that much cash into the plan each year and wants to know if he can do just the opposite; that is, fund the past service cost over a twenty-year period and amortize the past service cost over ten years.

    A.   Prepare a schedule to compare the total pension expense with the minimum and maximum provisions for pension expense for each period under the plan proposed by Susan:

Period	Total Pension Expense	Minimum Provision	Maximum Provision
1			
2			
3			
4			
5			
6			
7			
8			
9			
10			
11			
12			
13			
14			
15			
16			
17			
18			
19			
20			

Is the total pension expense acceptable in all periods?_____

B.   Prepare a schedule to compare the total pension expense with the minimum and maximum provisions for pension expense for each period under the plan proposed by Ray:

Period	Total Pension Expense	Minimum Provision	Maximum Provision
1			
2			
3			
4			
5			
6			
7			
8			
9			
10			
11			
12			
13			
14			
15			
16			
17			
18			
19			
20			

Is the total pension expense acceptable in all periods?_____

C. Does either plan violate the minimum or maximum provisions for pension expense? If so, prepare schedules to show the total pension expense acceptable as compared with the minimum and maximum provisions for pension expense for each period:

<u>Susan's Proposal</u>

Period	Acceptable Expense	Minimum Provision	Maximum Provision
1			
2			
3			
4			
5			
6			
7			
8			
9			
10			
11			
12			
13			
14			
15			
16			
17			
18			
19			
20			

<u>Ray's Proposal</u>

Period	Acceptable Expense	Minimum Provision	Maximum Provision
1			
2			
3			
4			
5			
6			
7			
8			
9			
10			
11			
12			
13			
14			
15			
16			
17			
18			
19			
20			

2.   Essex Foods, Inc. is planning to initiate a pension plan   for   its   employees beginning January 1 of 1986. The company's insurance agency provided an actuary to compute the amounts of past service cost to be credited to current employees, and the amount of normal cost needed each year to maintain the plan. The past service cost was actuarially estimated to be $300,000 and the annual normal cost to be $30,000. Implicit in these calculations is an interest rate of six percent for the earnings of the plan.

Since the amount of past service cost is relatively small, the actuary recommended that it be funded over 10 years and amortized over the same period.

A.   Prepare a schedule to compare the total pension expense with the minimum and maximum provisions for pension expense for each period under the plan proposed by the actuary.

Period	Total Pension Expense	Minimum Provision	Maximum Provision
1			
2			
3			
4			
5			
6			
7			
8			
9			
10			

(continued)

B. Does the plan violate the minimum or maximum provisions for pension expense? If so, prepare a schedule to show the total pension expense acceptable as compared with the minimum and maximum provisions for pension expense for each period:

Period	Acceptable Expense	Minimum Provision	Maximum Provision
1			
2			
3			
4			
5			
6			
7			
8			
9			
10			
11			
12			
13			
14			
15			
16			
17			
18			
19			
20			

When you reach period 10, what happens to the pension expense in relation to the minimum and maximum provisions?

Objective: The pension expense template calculates the annual amounts of net pension cost to be recognized. The template can be used to calculate these amounts for up to twenty periods.

The template includes a schedule of amortization of unrecognized prior service cost. The results from this schedule are included in the schedule of the projected benefits obligation, in the schedule of plan assets (the fair value is assumed to be the same as the market-related asset value), and in the determination of the pension expense. The template will also calculate the accrued/prepaid pension cost and, with the addition of data on the accumulated benefit obligation, will also calculate the minimum liability at the end of each year. The information from these calculations can be used to prepare the necessary journal entries for pension expense and any related assets or liabilities.

Compatible Textbook Problems: E21-3, E21-4, E21-5, E21-6. (The template may also be used to find the amortization of prior service costs in several other exercises and problems.)

Spreadsheet Name: NEWPEN

Print Range: Inputs and schedule of amortization of unrecognized
   prior service cost A1:F40
   Schedule of projected benefits obligation G14:K40
   Schedule of plan assets L14:P40
   Determination of pension expense Q14:U40
   Calculation of the minimum liability V12:Z40

Required Input Information: Before beginning, you will need to determine:

1. The rate(s) to be used in determining interest costs (settlement rate) and the return on pension plan assets.
2. Any prior service cost information:
   a. The number of employees granted retroactive credit to the plan.
   b. The rate of employee departure (through retiring or quitting).
   c. The dollar amount of the prior service cost.
   d. The year in which the prior service cost took effect (through adoption or amendment of a plan).
3. The annual service cost (actuarial present value of benefits).
4. The annual funding of service cost.
5. The annual amount of benefits paid from pension assets each year, if any.
6. The accumulated benefit obligation at the end of each period.

Using the Spreadsheet:

>S   **Load the spreadsheet from the file disk in drive B by typing "/L" followed by "B:NEWPEN,A".**

>L   Load the spreadsheet from the file disk by pressing the [Alt] key and simultaneously typing the letter "N" from the menu.

When the spreadsheet has finished loading, the screen display should appear similar to that shown in Exhibit 19-1.

Example problem: The Rabun Corporation initiated a pension plan for its employees on January 1, 1986. At that date, the total prior service cost was actuarially estimated to be $600,000. Mike Toccoa, Rabun's actuary, has suggested that 12% is an appropriate interest rate for the plan. He has calculated the annual service cost to be funded by Rabun Corporation as $50,000 and has recommended that the company both amortize and fund the prior service cost using the "expected future years of service of participants" method. Rabun currently has 60 active employees, five percent of whom are expected to depart each year through retirement or quitting. Initially, payments from pension fund assets are expected to be $25,000 annually.

Entering the problem data: You must now enter the required input information beginning in cell F5 and cells F8 through F11. You will also need to input data in cells G21 through G40 (annual service cost), cells J21 through J40 (annual benefit payments from plan assets), cells L21 through L40 (annual funding of service cost), and cells X21 through X40 (the accumulated benefit obligation at each year-end).

>SL   Move the cursor to cell F5 and enter 12 percent as the rate to be used in determining interest cost and the return on plan assets.

This amount should be entered as a decimal. For example, 12% should be entered as ".12". The percent sign will be added automatically.

You may need to wait for a few moments while the spreadsheet recalculates before entering the next input.

>SL   In cell F8, enter sixty (60) as the number of employees covered by the retroactive provisions of adopting the pension plan.
>SL   In cell F9, enter 5 percent (.05) as the expected rate of employee departure through retirement and quitting.
>SL   In cell F10, enter $600,000 as the dollar amount of the prior service cost granted retroactively to current employees.

Remember, this amount should be entered without commas or dollar signs.

>SL   Finally, since this prior service cost arises at the date at which the pension plan was initiated, leave the year in cell F11 as one (1).

If the prior service cost arose from a plan amendment at a later date, then you would enter the appropriate number in cell F11. For example, if the plan amendment occurred at the beginning of the fifth year, you would enter "5" in cell F11. Note that there is no provision in the template for more than one event giving rise to prior service cost. Thus, the data entered in cells F8 through F11 represent the only provision for prior service cost. In addition, the template does not contain any provision for gains and losses which are not covered by the rate used in determining interest cost and the return on plan assets.

>SL   At this point, you may scroll down the spreadsheet. As you do, you will see that a schedule of amortization of unrecognized prior service cost has been prepared in columns A through F, rows 13 through 40. This schedule is prepared using the "expected future years of service of participants" method. You should see zero (0) as the unamortized balance of the unrecognized prior service cost in cell F40. If you do not, go back and recheck your inputs to see that they are correct.

The template uses the amount of amortization calculated in this schedule in determining the pension expense and the amount funded each year. If you wish to adopt a different amortization policy or change the amount of prior service cost funded, you will have to enter these amounts manually. These changes will be discussed when we examine the remaining schedules in the template.

>S   Use the [=] key to jump to cell A12 so that row 12 is at the top of your screen.

>L   Use the special function key [F5] to jump to cell A12 so that row 12 is at the top of your screen.

>S   With the cursor in column A, type "/TV" to *lock* column A in place as a vertical title. (Later, if you wish to remove the vertical title, type "/TC". This will clear the title.)

>L   Place the cursor in any cell in column B and type "/WTV" to *freeze* column A (which is the only column to the left of column B) in place as a vertical title. (Later, if you wish to remove the vertical title, type "/WTC". This will clear the title.)

Now when you scroll to the right, you will continue to see column A and you will know what period each row corresponds to.

>S   Scroll to the right until you can see columns G through K (or use the [=] key to jump to cell G12).

>L   Press the [tab] key to move one screen to the right. (You can then use the backtab key [shift] +[tab] to move one screen to the left.)

Columns G through K contain the schedule of projected benefits obligation. As you can see, the schedule is incomplete--it lacks the annual service cost and the benefits paid in each year.

>SL   Move the cursor to cell G21 and enter $50,000, the amount of annual service cost.

The template will automatically enter $50,000 as the service cost for each year as a convenience. If the service costs in each year are different, however, then each year's cost must be entered separately in column G. (If this is the case, you may wish to turn the program's automatic recalculation off by typing "/GM" in SuperCalc3 or "/WGRM" in Lotus 1-2-3. When you finish entering the data, type "/GA" in SuperCalc3 or "/WGRA" in Lotus 1-2-3 to turn the automatic recalculation back on. Make sure that you then press the exclamation point (!) key in SuperCalc3 or the special function key [F9] in Lotus 1-2-3 to force the spreadsheet to recalculate after your data has been entered.)

>SL   **Move the cursor to cell J21 and enter $25,000 as the annual benefit to be paid from the pension plan assets each year.**

Again, the template will automatically enter $25,000 as the amount of benefit payments in each year as a convenience. If these payments vary from year to year, you will need to input each year's payment separately in column J.

This completes the schedule of the projected benefits obligation.

>S   **Now scroll over to the right so that you can see columns L through P (or use the [=] key to jump to cell L12).**
>L   **Press the [tab] key to move one screen to the right.**

Columns L through P contain the schedule of plan assets. At this point, this schedule is also incomplete, since it lacks the amounts of annual service cost which have been funded.

>SL   **Move the cursor to cell L21 and enter $50,000, the amount of service cost that was recommended for funding.**

Once again, the template will automatically enter $50,000 as the amount of service cost funded in each period. If these amounts vary from year to year, then you will need to enter each year's funded amount separately in column L.

If you examine column M, you will see that the amount of prior service cost funded is the same as the amount of prior service cost amortized (calculated in column E). The template assumes that the amount funded each year will be the same as the amount amortized. If you wish to fund amounts which are different than the amounts being amortized each period, then you will have to manually enter the amount of prior service cost funded in each year in column M.

This completes the schedule of plan assets since the benefits to be paid have already been copied by the template into column O from our schedule of projected benefit obligation.

At last we can examine the amount of pension expense!

>S   **Scroll to the right until you can see columns Q through U (or use the [=] key to jump to cell Q12).**
>L   **Press the [tab] key to move one screen to the right.**

Columns Q through U contain a schedule which summarizes the components of pension expense (not including additional gains and losses, which the template is not designed for). In columns Q through T, you will see four components of pension expense: (1) Service cost, (2) Interest on the projected benefit obligation, (3) Return on plan assets, and (4) the amortization of prior service cost. Column U contains the total pension expense for each year.

You should note that the pension expense in column U is the sum of the service cost, the interest on the projected benefit obligation, and the amortization of prior service costs, less the return on plan assets.

In addition, the amount of amortization used in calculating the pension expense is based on the expected future years of service of participants method. If you use a different amortization method, then you will need to manually enter the amortization for each separate year in column T.

>S   **Finally, scroll over to the right so that you can see columns V through Z (or use the [=] key to jump to cell V12).**

>L   **Press the [tab] key to move one more screen to the right.**

Columns V through Z will contain the calculation of the accrued/prepaid pension cost, the amount of accumulated benefit obligation at the end of each year, and the minimum liability to be disclosed.

In column V, the increase or decrease in the accrued/prepaid pension cost is shown. This should show a liability balance of $72,000 (in cell V21) for the first period--the excess of the pension expense over the amount actually funded. In column W, the cumulative balance of the increases and decreases in accrued/prepaid pension cost is computed. Thus, the balance is $72,000 (in cell W21) at the end of the first year, $145,783 (in cell W22) at the end of the second, etc.

Column X contains space for the accumulated benefit obligation. Remember, the calculation of the projected benefit obligation is normally based on expected future salaries whereas the accumulated benefits obligation is oftentimes based on current salary levels (which are likely to be substantially lower than future salaries). Thus, the accumulated benefit obligation will normally always be lower than the projected benefit obligation.

>S   **Scroll back to the schedule of projected benefits obligation in columns G through K (or use the [=] key to jump to cell G12).**

>L   **Press the backtab key three times (simultaneously press the [shift] key and the [tab] key).**

Note that the balance of projected benefits obligation for the first period is $697,000 (cell K21). Most of this amount arises from the prior service cost granted to current employees ($600,000 in cell H21 plus $72,000 interest on the prior service cost in cell I21). Since this amount is based on expected future salaries of employees when they retire, we would expect that the accumulated benefit obligation (based on current salaries) would be considerably less. Let's assume that it is $400,000.

>S   **Scroll back to cell X21 (or use the [=] key to jump to cell V12 and then move to cell X21) and enter $400,000.**

>L   **Press the [tab] key three times. Move the cursor to cell X21 and enter $400,000.**

Once more, the template automatically enters $400,000 in column X for each year's accumulated benefit obligation. If the accumulated benefit obligation varies from year to year (which it probably will), you will need to enter the amount of each year's obligation separately.

Note, however, the final two columns, Y and Z. In column Y, the template computes the unfunded accumulated benefit obligation. This is the difference between the plan assets and the accumulated benefit obligation.

Thus, to the extent that the plan assets are less than the accumulated benefit obligation, a liability must be disclosed.

However, in order to determine the amount needed to adjust the accounts and arrive at the correct net amount of liability, we must take the accrued/prepaid pension cost into account. Thus, in column Z, the unfunded accumulated benefit obligation is compared with the net accrued/prepaid pension cost in order to determine any additional liability to be disclosed.

In period one, we see that the unfunded accumulated benefit obligation is $317,857 (cell Y21). But we already have a net liability of $72,000 (cell W21) shown as the accrued/prepaid pension cost. Thus, these liabilities can be used to offset one another and the additional liability adjustment shown in cell Z21 need only be the difference of $245,857.

In period two, since the minimum liability (unfunded accumulated benefit obligation) has decreased to $228,714 (cell Y22), and the liability balance of the accrued/prepaid pension cost has increased to $145,783 (cell W22), we can recapture some of the additional liability that was established in period one. Thus, we would decrease the additional liability by $162,926 (cell Z22). This leaves the balance of the additional liability at $82,931 ($228,714-145,783).

This process continues into each future period. In period three, the liability balance of the accrued/prepaid pension cost actually exceeds the minimum liability and thus no additional liability is needed. We would then recapture the remaining additional liability of $82,931 (cell Z23) in this period.

Given the assumptions in our problem, the accrued/prepaid pension cost continues to exceed the minimum liability in each future period, and we need not establish any further additional liability!

Printing: If your computer is connected to a printer, you may want to print the results. However, you will need to print the spreadsheet in sections because of its width. Make sure that your printer is turned on and that it is on-line!

>S   Type"/GB" to remove the spreadsheet borders (row and column headings).

>S   Type"/ODA1:F40,P" to print the inputs and schedule of amortization of unrecognized prior service cost.

>S   Press any key to continue.

>S   Type"/ODG14:K40,P" to print the schedule of projected benefits obligation.

>S   Press any key to continue.

>S   Type "/ODL14:P40,P" to print the schedule of plant assets.

>S   Press any key to continue.

>S   Type "/ODQ14:U40,P" to print the determination of pension expense.

>S   Press any key to continue.

>S   Type "/ODV12:Z40,P" to print the calculation of the minimum liability.

>S   Press any key to continue.

>S   Type "/GB" to replace the spreadsheet borders if you wish to continue.

>L   Press the [Alt] key and "P" simultaneously. (Alt + P)

You may now manipulate the spreadsheet to examine the effect of changes in the inputs, especially the period in which prior service cost arises, the funding of service cost, and the accumulated benefit obligation at the end of each year.

If you wish to quit at this time:

>S   Type "/QY" to quit using SuperCalc3.

>L   Type "/QY" to quit using Lotus 1-2-3. (Type "EY" if needed to exit from the Lotus access system menu.)

After the screen clears and the red in-use light has gone off, you may remove your disks and turn off the computer.

Exhibit 19-1

	A	B	C	D	E	F
1	PENSION EXPENSE AND MINIMUM LIABILITY					
2						
3	Current information:					
4	Interest rate on obligation (settlement rate)					.00%
5	Expected return on pension plan assets					.00%
6						
7	Prior service cost information:					
8	Number of employees granted retroactive credit					0
9	Rate of employee departure (retire or quit)					.00%
10	Dollar amount of prior service cost					0
11	Change was made at the beginning of year (1-20) ?					1
12						
13	Amortization of Unrecognized Prior Service Cost					
14	Expected Future Years of Service of Participants Method					
15	--					
16						Balance of
17				Amortization	Periodic	Unrecognized
18	Period	Numerator	Denominator	Rate	Amortization	Prior S.C.
19	--					
20	0					0

Problems:

1.   Tariffville Printers, Inc. plans to initiate a pension plan for its employees beginning January 1 of next year. The company has hired an actuary, Susan Grandby, to compute the amounts of prior service cost to be credited retroactively to current employees and the amount of service cost needed each year to maintain the plan. Susan has calculated the prior service cost to be $6,000,000, and the first year's service cost to be $800,000. The company will fully fund the service cost each year. Payments from plan assets are expected to be $450,000 in the first year. The service costs, service cost funding, and benefit payments are expected to increase by 10 percent each year.

Susan believes that 14 percent is an appropriate interest rate for determining interest cost and the return on the plan assets (assuming that the fair value of assets and the market-related asset value are the same). She recommends that any prior service cost be amortized and funded using the "expected future years of service of participants" method. Tariffville currently has 600 employees who will be covered by the plan. Five percent of those employees are expected to retire or quit each year.

For your assistance, the following table of service cost, service cost funding, benefit payments, and the accumulated benefit obligation has been prepared. Note that the anticipated increase of 10 percent has been incorporated into the table. In addition, the accumulated benefit obligation is estimated as 75% of the total balance of projected benefits obligation at each year-end.

| Service Cost | | | Accumulated Benefit Obligation | |
Benefits/Years of Service	Funded	Benefits Paid	No Prior Service Cost	With Prior Service Cost
800,000	800,000	450,000	262,500	5,392,500
880,000	880,000	495,000	588,000	6,436,200
968,000	968,000	544,500	987,945	7,654,893
1,064,800	1,064,800	598,950	1,475,645	9,075,966
1,171,280	1,171,280	658,845	2,066,561	10,730,927

A. Assuming that the company chooses not to give any retroactive credit to current employees (no prior service cost), prepare schedules for the first five years of the plan to compute (1) the projected benefits obligation, (2) the plan assets, (3) the pension expense, and (4) the amount of any accrued/prepaid pension cost and any provision for minimum liability to be established.

B.   Assuming that the company does wish to grant retroactive credit to current employees when the plan is initiated, prepare schedules for the first five years of the plan to compute (1) the projected benefits obligation, (2) the plan assets, (3) the pension expense, and (4) the amount of any accrued/prepaid pension cost and any provision for minimum liability to be established.

2.   Essex Foods, Inc. is planning to initiate a pension plan for its employees beginning January 1 of 1986. The company's insurance agency provided an actuary to compute the amount of service cost needed each year to maintain the plan. The company does plan to grant any retroactive credit to current employees when the plan is initiated. Using the benefits/years of service method, the service cost in the first year was estimated to be $200,000. It is expected to increase by 10 percent each year of the plan. Implicit in this calculation is a rate of ten percent for the interest cost and the return on plan assets (the fair value of assets and the market-related asset value are assumed to be the same).

For your assistance, the following table of service cost, service cost funding, benefit payments, and the accumulated benefit obligation has been prepared. Note that the anticipated increase of 10 percent has been incorporated into the table. In addition, the accumulated benefit obligation is estimated as 80% of the total balance of projected benefits obligation at each year-end.

| | Service Cost | | | Accumulated Benefit Obligation | |
Benefits/Years of Service	Funded	Benefits Paid	No Prior Service Cost	With Prior Service Cost
200,000	200,000	60,000	112,000	112,000
220,000	220,000	66,000	246,400	246,400
242,000	242,000	72,600	406,560	2,166,560
266,200	266,200	79,860	596,288	2,532,288
292,820	292,820	87,846	819,896	2,949,496

A.   Prepare schedules for the first five years of the plan to compute (1) the projected benefits obligation, (2) the plan assets, (3) the pension expense, and (4) the amount of any accrued/prepaid pension cost and any provision for minimum liability to be established.

B.   At the end of year two, the company realized that the failure to give current employees retroactive benefits at the time the plan was initiated was having a negative impact on productivity. Thus, management decided that the plan would be amended to provide retroactive credit to all current employees effective at the beginning of the third year. This prior service cost was estimated to be $2,000,000. The plan amendment covers 200 current employees, who are expected to retire or quit at the rate of 5 percent per year. The company will amortize and fund the prior service cost using the "expected future years of service of participants" method.

Prepare schedules for the first five years of the plan to compute (1) the projected benefits obligation, (2) the plan assets, (3) the pension expense, and (4) the amount of any accrued/prepaid pension cost and any provision for minimum liability to be established.

CHAPTER 20 - LEASE AMORTIZATION SCHEDULE

Objective: The lease spreadsheet determines the interest rate applicable to the lessee and lessor, and calculates the present value of the mimimum lease payments for the lessee and the implied fair value of the asset for the lessor under a capital lease. The spreadsheet also prepares lease amortization schedules for both the lessee and the lessor for up to twenty periods on an annuity due basis (payments are made at the beginning of each period). These schedules may be used to prepare the necessary journal entries for the lessee and the lessor.

The spreadsheet will enable you to evaluate the effects of changes in the inputs (such as adding a bargain purchase option or guaranteed residual value to the lease, or changing the lease term) on the amounts to be capitalized and expensed by the lessee and the income to be recognized by the lessor.

Compatible Textbook Problems: E22-3, E22-4, E22-5, E22-6, E22-8, E22-9, P22-3, P22-4, P22-5, P22-7, P22-8, P22-12, P22-13, P22-14, P22-16.

Spreadsheet Name: LEASE

Print Range: Inputs and lessee calculations...A1:F40
                     Inputs and lessor calculations H1:M40

Required Input Information: Before beginning, you will need to determine the following:

1. Minimum rental payment (net of any executory costs).
2. Amount of any bargain purchase option or residual value guaranteed by the lessee.
3. Amount of any unguaranteed residual value accruing to the lessor at the end of the lease-term.
4. Number of periods covered by the lease (lease-term).
5. Lessee's incremental borrowing rate.
6. Lessor's implicit rate of return.
7. Whether or not the lessor's implicit rate of return is known by the lessee.

Using the Spreadsheet:

>S   Load the spreadsheet from the file disk in drive B by typing "/L" followed by "B:LEASE,A".

>L   Load the spreadsheet from the file disk by pressing the [Alt] key and simultaneously typing the letter "O" from the menu.

       When the spreadsheet has finished loading, the screen display should appear similar to that shown in Exhibit 20-1.

Example problem: The Clayton Office Supply Co., Inc., leased a new automobile from Bentley Motor Works, Inc. The lease calls for annual payments of $3,000 at the beginning of each year, commencing on the first day of the lease. In addition, at the end of the seven-year lease term, Clayton can purchase the automobile for the nominal amount of $17! Any executory costs (taxes, license, insurance, etc.) on the automobile are the responsibility of Clayton Office Supply Co., Inc., as the lessee. Bentley's implicit rate of return is 13%, which is known to Clayton and is equal to Clayton's incremental borrowing rate. Compute the present value of the minimum lease payments and prepare lease amortization schedules for both lessee and lessor.

Entering the problem data: You must now enter the required input information in cells F2 through F8.

>SL   **Move the cursor to cell F2 and enter $3,000 as the dollar amount of the annual minimum rental payment.**

This amount should be entered without commas or dollar signs, which will be added automatically.

You may need to wait for a few moments while the spreadsheet recalculates before entering the next input.

If the lessor is responsible for paying the executory costs (taxes, insurance, etc.) related to the asset, then these costs must be deducted from the lessee's rental payments to determine the minimum rental payments.

Example: If the rental payments are $3,000 annually and Clayton (lessee) is responsible for paying executory costs of $500 (taxes, license, and insurance) per year, then the minimum lease payment is $3,000. If, however, the lessor must pay the executory costs, then the minimum lease payments are $2,500 ($3,000 less $500 for taxes, license, & insurance). This is because the lessor must pay the executory costs from the amount received from the lessee; thus, the $500 is not considered to be a part of the minimum rental payment for the asset, but is instead an indirect payment of the taxes on the asset.

>SL   **In cell F3, enter $17 as the amount of the bargain purchase option (or guaranteed residual value at the end of the lease term, if it applies).**

If there were no transfer of title, bargain purchase option or guaranteed residual value, you would enter the unguaranteed residual value which will accrue to the lessor at the end of the lease-term in cell F4. Otherwise, this cell should be zero (0). *Note that if there is a transfer of title, or if there is a bargain purchase option or guaranteed residual value in cell F3, then cell F4 must be zero; otherwise, the lessor's amortization schedule will be incorrect!*

>SL   **In cell F5, enter seven (7) as the number of periods in the lease term.**

>SL   **In cell F6, enter Bentley's incremental borrowing rate of 13%.**

This should be input as a decimal (for example, 13% equals .13).

Note that the lessor's implicit rate of return is assumed by the spreadsheet to be the same as the lessee's incremental borrowing rate. If this is not the case, enter the lessor's implicit rate of return in cell F7.

>SL   Finally, in cell F8, indicate whether or not the lessee is aware of the rate of return used by the lessor in calculating the lease rental payments. If the lessee is not aware of the lessor's implicit rate of return, enter a zero in this cell; otherwise, leave the cell in its default setting of one, which indicates that the lessee knows what the lessor's implicit rate of return is.

Once you have entered the data, you will see that the spreadsheet has selected the appropriate interest rate applicable to the lessee in cell F10 and calculated the present value of the minimum lease payments for the lessee in cell F11.

>SL   If you scroll down the spreadsheet, to rows 13 through 40, you will see that the spreadsheet has prepared the lessee's lease amortization schedule on an annuity due basis.

>S   Use the [=] key to jump to cell H13.
>L   Use the special function key [F5] to jump to cell H13.

In columns H through M, you will find that the spreadsheet has prepared the corresponding calculations and schedules for the lessor. By scrolling down to row 40, you can examine the entire schedule.

Printing: If your computer is connected to a printer, you may want to print the results. Since the spreadsheet is wider than most printers, you should print the spreadsheet in sections. Make sure that your printer is turned on and that it is on-line!

>S   Type "/GB" to remove the spreadsheet borders (row and column headings).
>S   Type "/ODA1:F40,P" to print the inputs, the lessee's interest rate, the present value of the minimum lease payments, and the lessee's lease amortization schedule.
>S   Press any key to continue.
>S   Type "/ODH1:M40,P" to print the inputs, the lessor's interest rate, the implied fair value of the lessor's asset, and the lessor's lease amortization schedule.
>S   Press any key to continue.
>S   Type "/GB" to replace the spreadsheet borders if you wish to continue.

>L   Press the [Alt] key and "P" simultaneously. (Alt + P)

You may now manipulate the spreadsheet to examine the effect of changes in the inputs, especially the alternatives related to the residual value of the leased asset at the end of the lease-term, and the lessee's and lessor's interest rates. *Note that if you change the lease term, however, you will need to recalculate the amount of the minimum rental payments!*

If you wish to quit at this time:

>S   **Type "/QY" to quit using SuperCalc3.**

>L   **Type "/QY" to quit using Lotus 1-2-3. (Type "EY" if needed to exit from the Lotus access system menu.)**

After the screen clears and the red in-use light has gone off, you may remove your disks and turn off the computer.

Exhibit 20-1

	A	B	C	D	E	F
1	LEASE AMORTIZATION SCHEDULE					
2	Minimum rental payment (net of executory costs)					$.00
3	Bargain purchase option or guaranteed residual value					$0
4	Unguaranteed residual value accruing to the lessor					$0
5	Lease term (maximum = 20 periods)					0
6	Lessee's incremental borrowing rate					.00%
7	Lessor's implicit rate of return					.00%
8	Lessor's rate known by lessee? (0=No, 1=Yes)					1
9	==					
10	Interest rate applicable to lessee					.00%
11	Present value of minimum lease payments (lessee)					$0
12						
13	Lessee's Lease Amortization Schedule (Annuity due basis)					
14						
15		Annual	Interest	Reduction		
16		Lease	on Unpaid	of Lease	Lease	
17	Period	Payment	Obligation	Obligation	Obligation	
18	--					
19	0				0	
20	0	0	0	0	0	

Problems:

1.   Utica Furniture, Inc. manufactures and wholesales furniture throughout the midwest. George La Salle, vice-president of marketing, recently announced that the company would be expanding sales to other regions of the country in an attempt to become national in scope. Because of the high cost of the additional debt (15% incremental borrowing rate) required to finance expansion of the manufacturing facilities of Utica, George does not want Utica to purchase the tractor-trailer rigs needed to transport furniture to other parts of the country. Instead, he has arranged to lease a fleet of tractor-trailers for an eight-year period.

The lease requires that eight equal annual rental payments of $86,237.75 be made to the Peru Leasing Corporation at the beginning of each year, commencing on January 1, 1987, the first day of the lease term. Peru Leasing based these payments on their implicit 12% rate of return and their cost of $500,000 for the tractor-trailers. George was not aware of this implicit rate of return. The lease also contains a bargain purchase option whereby, at the end of the lease term, Utica will be able to purchase the tractor-trailers for $50,000, one-half of their expected residual value at that date. Utica will be responsible for paying all taxes, insurance, and other executory costs of the tractor-trailers during the lease-term.

A.   Based on this information, calculate the amount of the asset to be capitalized by Utica Furniture, Inc. and the implied fair value of the asset owned by Peru Leasing Corporation on January 1, 1987.

Amount to be capitalized by lessee: _____

Implied fair value of lessor's asset: _____

Are these amounts the same? Explain why or why not.

What type of lease is this for Peru Leasing Corporation? (Assume that the collectibility of payments is reasonably predictable and that there are no important uncertainties surrounding the amount of unreimbursable costs yet to be incurred by the lessor.) Explain.

B. Assuming the same information, except that George La Salle is aware of Peru's implicit rate of return of 12%, calculate the amount of the asset to be capitalized by Utica Furniture, Inc. and the implied fair value of the asset owned by Peru Leasing Corporation on January 1, 1987.

Amount to be capitalized by lessee: _____

Implied fair value of lessor's asset: _____

Are these amounts the same? Explain why or why not.

Prepare an amortization schedule for the lessee.

Period	Annual Lease Payment	Interest on Unpaid Obligation	Reduction of Lease Obligation	Lease Obligation
0				
0				
1				
2				
3				
4				
5				
6				
7				
8				

C. Assume, again, that George La Salle is aware of Peru's implicit rate of return of 12%, but that there is no bargain purchase option and the residual value will accrue to the lessor. What type of lease is this for the lessor? Explain.

D. Assume, instead, that George is not aware of Peru's implicit rate of return, and that there is no bargain purchase option and any residual value will accrue to the lessor. If the useful life of the tractor-trailers is 12 years, what type of lease is this for the lessee? For the lessor? Explain.

2.   Torrance Metal Products, Inc. has arranged with the Cutter Leasing Company, Inc. to lease a new production facility. This building is being specially constructed by Cutter at a cost of $250,000 to meet the requirements of Torrance, and is expected to have a useful life of only ten years, at which time its salvage value will be $20,000.

The lease requires that ten equal annual rental payments of $41,135.19 be made to the Cutter Leasing Company, Inc. at the beginning of each year, commencing on January 1, 1988, the first day of the lease term. Cutter Leasing based these payments on their implicit 14% rate of return, their cost of $250,000, and the expected residual value of $20,000. Torrance, which has worked with Cutter in the past, is aware of this implicit rate of return, which is also equal to their incremental borrowing rate. The lease contains no transfer of title or bargain purchase option, and the unguaranteed residual value will accrue to Cutter Leasing Company, Inc. Torrance will be responsible for paying all taxes, insurance, and other executory costs of the building during the lease-term.

A. Determine what type of lease this would be classified as for (1) the lessor and (2) the lessee. Assume that the collectibility of payments is reasonably predictable and that there are no important uncertainties surrounding the amount of unreimbursable costs yet to be incurred by the lessor. Explain these classifications.

B. Based on the information, calculate the amount of the asset to be capitalized by Torrance Metal Products, Inc. and the implied fair value of the asset owned by Cutter Leasing Company, Inc. on January 1, 1988.

Amount to be capitalized by lessee: _____

Implied fair value of lessor's asset: _____

Are these amounts the same? Explain why or why not.

C. Assume, instead, that Torrance Metal Products, Inc. has an incremental borrowing rate of 16%. What effect will this have on the amount of the asset to be capitalized? Explain.

Would it make a difference if Torrance was not aware of Cutter's implicit rate of return? Explain.

D. Assume, instead, that Torrance Metal Products, Inc. has an incremental borrowing rate of 12%. What effect will this have on the amount of the asset to be capitalized? Explain.

CHAPTER 21 - PURCHASING POWER GAIN OR LOSS

Objective: The purchasing power gain or loss template calculates the gain or loss on net monetary items for a specified time period. It can be used to rapidly calculate the gain or loss using either the average-for-the-year price-level index or the end-of-year price-level index. The effects of potential changes in the monetary items on the amount of the purchasing power gain or loss can be evaluated using the template.

Compatible Textbook Problems: E25-5, E25-8, P25-1a, P25-2a. (The template can also be used to calculate the purchasing power gain or loss required in P25-10 and P25-12.)

Spreadsheet Name: PPGAIN

Print Range: A1:H40

Required Input Information: Before beginning, you will need to determine the following:

1. The types and amounts of the net monetary assets and liabilities at the beginning of the year.
2. The average-for-the-year Consumer Price Index and the end-of-year Consumer Price Index.
3. The changes in net monetary items resulting from transactions during the year.
4. The Consumer Price Index applicable to specific dates on which changes to the net monetary items occurred.

Using the Spreadsheet:

>S   Load the spreadsheet from the file disk in drive B by typing "/L" followed by "B:PPGAIN,A".

>L   Load the spreadsheet from the file disk by pressing the [Alt] key and simultaneously typing the letter "P" from the menu.

When the spreadsheet has finished loading, the screen display should appear similar to that shown in Exhibit 21-1.

Example problem: Sunbury Corporation is in the process of preparing its financial statements for the year ended December 31, 1986. As a part of its financial statements, the purchasing power gain or loss on net monetary items must be disclosed. Management intends to use the average-for-the-year price-level index for the purpose of making this calculation. However, for managerial purposes, they are considering preparing a full set of price-level adjusted financial statements using the end-of-year price-level index. Information about net monetary items, changes in those items, and the relevant price-level indexes follows:

January 1, 1986

Monetary Items:

Cash and receivables	$ 220,000
Other monetary assets	80,000
Current monetary liabilities	(66,000)
Long-term monetary liabilities	(100,000)

Price-level index 120

Changes in monetary items during the year:

Sales	$800,000
Purchases	500,000
Selling and Administrative expense	180,000
Income taxes	40,000
Cash dividends	10,000

Assume that all income related changes in monetary items occurred uniformly throughout the year. The average-for-the-year price-level index was 126. The dividends were declared and paid at year-end when the price-level index was 132.

Required:

Prepare a computation of the purchasing power gain or loss on net monetary items for the year ended December 31, 1986 using both the average-for-the-year price-level index and the end-of-year price-level index.

Entering the problem data: You must now enter the required input information in cells H1 and H2, and in columns D, E, and F.

>SL   **In cell H1, enter 132 as the end-of-year price-level index.**
>SL   **In cell H2, enter 126 as the average-for-the-year price-level index.**

Note that the template automatically enters the average-for-the-year index in column E. This represents the price-level index which we wish to translate our monetary items **TO**.

>SL   **If you scroll down the spreadsheet, you will see that the price-level index has also been entered in several cells in column F.**

The average-for-the-year index has been entered in each of the cells corresponding to income related accounts.

For example, the cells in columns E and F which correspond with sales (row 17) both have 126 entered in them. In cell G17, you will see 1.00 as the restatement ratio. A restatement ratio of one means that sales on a restated basis will be exactly the same as they are before restatement. This is one of the advantages of calculating the purchasing power gain or loss using the average-for-the-year price-level index.

In addition, the end-of-year index has been entered in cell F26, which relates to the dividends. (Dividends are assumed to be declared and paid at the end of the year.)

>SL   **Skip cell H4 for the moment and move the cursor down to cell D9. Enter $220,000 as the amount of cash and receivables.**

This amount should be entered without dollar signs or commas, which will be displayed automatically.

>SL   **Move the cursor to cell D10 and enter the other monetary assets of $80,000.**
>SL   **In cell D11, enter the amount of current liabilities. This amount should be entered as a negative number, so enter "-66,000".**
>SL   **In cell D12, the long-term liabilities should also be entered as a negative number. Enter "-100,000".**

The beginning balance of the net monetary items (which should be $134,000 in cell D14) can be restated to average-for-the-year dollars by entering the beginning-of-the-year price-index in cell F14.

>SL   **In cell F14, enter 120.**

You should get $140,700 as the restated balance.

Let's enter the remaining data.

>SL   **In cell D17, enter $800,000, the amount of sales.**

(If there were other sources of monetary items, such as a sale of plant assets, these items would be entered as other sources in cell D18.)

>SL   **In cells D23 through D26, enter purchases of $500,000, selling and administrative expenses of $180,000, income taxes of $40,000, and dividends of $10,000, respectively.**

Note that if the sales, purchases, selling and administrative expenses, or income taxes did not occur uniformly throughout the year, you would need to change the corresponding index in column F. Similarly, if the dividends were not declared and paid at the end of the year, you would need to change the index in cell F26.

>SL   **Scroll down to row 40.**

You will be able to see that the spreadsheet has calculated the net monetary items at the end of the year on an historical basis ($204,000 in cell D32) and on a restated basis ($211,155 in cell H32).

In rows 34 to 39, the purchasing power gain or loss on net monetary items is calculated. To do this, the net monetary items as restated are compared with either (1) the net monetary items on an historical basis (if using the end-of-year index) or (2) the historical net monetary items restated to average-for--the-year dollars (if using the average-for-the-year index).

In this case, since we are using the average-for-the-year index, the net monetary items at year-end ($204,000 in cell C37) are restated to average-for-the-year dollars ($194,727 in cell H37). This leaves a purchasing power loss on net monetary items of $16,427 ($211,155 in cell H34 minus $194,727 in cell H37).

Now let's try changing to the end-of-year price-level index to calculate the purchasing power gain or loss on net monetary items.

>SL   **Move the cursor to cell H4.**

Cell H4 is used to indicate which price-level index is to be used. If zero (0) is entered in cell H4, then the average-for-the-year price-level index is used to calculate the purchasing power gain or loss on net monetary items.

If one (1) is entered in cell H4, then the end-of-year price-level index will be used to calculate the purchasing power gain or loss on net monetary items.

>SL   **In cell H4, enter "1".**

Note that all of the index numbers in column E have changed to 132, the end-of-year price-level index.

>SL   **Scroll down to row 40.**

You will see that the purchasing power gain or loss on net monetary items has been recalculated simply by changing one number. Note that now the calculation compares the net monetary items as restated ($221,210 in cell H34) with the historical amount of net monetary items at year-end ($204,000 in cell H35). This leaves a purchasing power loss on net monetary items of $17,210.

Printing: If your computer is connected to a printer, you may want to print the results. Make sure that your printer is turned on and that it is on-line!

>S   **Type "/GB" to remove the spreadsheet borders (row and column headings).**
>S   **Type "/ODA1:H40,P" to print the spreadsheet.**
>S   **Press any key to continue.**
>S   **Type "/GB" to replace the spreadsheet borders if you wish to continue.**

>L   **Press the [Alt] key and "P" simultaneously. (Alt + P)**

If you wish to quit at this time:

>S   Type "/QY" to quit using SuperCalc3.

>L   Type "/QY" to quit using Lotus 1-2-3. (Type "EY" if needed to exit from the Lotus access system menu.)

After the screen clears and the red in-use light has gone off, you may remove your disks and turn off the computer.

Exhibit 21-1

	A	B	C	D	E	F	G	H
1	COMPUTATION OF PURCHASING POWER			End-of-year price index				.00
2	GAIN OR LOSS		Average-for-the-year index					.00
3	Statements prepared in end-of-year or average-for-the-year							
4	dollars? (end-of-year=1, average-for-the-year=0)							0
5	--
6					Restatement Ratio			Restated
7	Net monetary items--historical		Historical	To/From=Ratio			Dollars
8	Beginning of year:		---				
9	Cash and receivables		$0				
10	Other monetary assets		0				
11	Current liabilities (monetary)		0				
12	Long-term liabilities (monetary)		0				
13			----------------				
14	Net monetary items--beginning		$0	0	0	.00		$0
15			----------------					----------------
16	Add (sources of monetary items):						
17	Sales		$0	0	0	.00		$0
18	Other sources		0	0	0	.00		0
19			----------------					----------------
20	Total sources		$0					$0

Problems:

1.   Sparland Corporation is preparing disclosures of the effects of changing price-levels for the year ended December 31, 1985. You have selected the following data from the basic financial statements for use in calculating the purchasing power gain or loss on net monetary items:

Cash	$ 200,000
Receivables	350,000
Cash surrender value of life insurance	75,000
Current liabilities	320,000
Long-term liabilities	400,000
Sales	1,400,000
Purchases	750,000
Selling and administrative expenses	320,000
Income taxes	180,000
Cash dividends	80,000

In addition, Sparland spent $300,000 of cash for a new plant on February 10th. Sparland sold their existing plant for $200,000 on November 15th.

Assume that all income-related monetary items were incurred uniformly during the year and that the cash dividends were declared and paid at December 31.

The Consumer Price Index at different times during the year was as follows:

January 1	100
February 10	102
November 15	110
December 31	112
Average-for-the-year	105

A. Based on this information, calculate the amount of the purchasing power gain or loss on net monetary items in average-for-the-year dollars and in end-of-year dollars.

_____ Average-for-the-year dollars (price-level)

_____ End-of-year dollars (price-level)

B. Explain why the company was subject to this gain or loss.

2.   Fairmont Companies, Inc. is preparing its annual disclosures for changing price-levels for the year ended December 31, 1987. Data which may be useful in calculating the purchasing power gain or loss on net monetary items follow:

Cash ....$ 450,000
Receivables 350,000
Other monetary assets 220,000
Current liabilities 350,000
Long-term liabilities 500,000
Sales 2,500,000
Purchases 1,450,000
Selling and administrative expenses 400,000
Income taxes 270,000
Cash dividends 100,000

During 1987, Fairmont issued $500,000 of common stock. This stock was issued shortly after January 1, 1987, when the general price-level index was 190. Assume that all income related monetary items were incurred uniformly during the year and that the cash dividends were declared and paid at December 31.

The Consumer Price Index at different times during the year was as follows:

January 1 190
December 31 200
Average-for-the-year 198

A. Based on this information, calculate the amount of the purchasing power gain or loss on net monetary items in average-for-the-year dollars and in end-of-year dollars.

_____ Average-for-the-year dollars (price-level)

_____ End-of-year dollars (price-level)

B. Joleen Lansing, head of corporate finance, has insisted that it would have been advantageous for the company to have invested excess cash in marketable securities. Not only would the company be able to earn a return on the investment, but because the securities would be non-monetary, the investment would also reduce any purchasing power loss (or increase any gain). Assuming the use of average-for-the-year dollars, how much better off (or worse off) would the company have been had it invested $200,000 of cash on January 1, 1987 in marketable securities? (For simplicity, ignore any dividends or changes in the market value of the investment.)

$_____

PART III

A. TUTORIAL TEMPLATES
SUPERCALC^3

CHAPTER 22 - INCOME STATEMENT

Objective: This partially completed spreadsheet provides an introduction to SuperCalc3. It illustrates how the spreadsheet can be used to help prepare a condensed multiple-step income statement. Formatting columns and individual cells to change the way in which text and numbers are displayed is illustrated. The importance of calculations being performed in a logical order is also demonstrated as well as the need to consider formats (display options) before beginning to create a spreadsheet. The completed income statement allows you to change the inputs and see what effects this has on net income and earnings per share.

The spreadsheet emphasizes the use of the FORMAT command, including user-defined formats. It also demonstrates how to use the HELP screens in constructing a spreadsheet. The GLOBAL command (global means affecting the entire spreadsheet) and WINDOW command (windows allow you to see two different areas of the spreadsheet at the same time instead of just one) are also illustrated.

Part A of the spreadsheet requires the construction of a multiple-step income statement. Part B completes the income statement by preparing the earnings per share disclosures. These two parts may be worked *sequentially* at different times by saving the results of Part A on a disk.

Spreadsheet Name: INCOME

Required Input Information: Before beginning, you should identify from the problem data on the following page:

1. The amount of sales and the relationships of cost of goods sold and selling and administrative expense to sales.
2. Other income or expense attributable to continuing operations.
3. The income tax rate.
4. Any other items affecting the determination of net income including:
   a. Discontinued operations.
   b. Extraordinary items.
   c. The cumulative effect of a change in accounting principle.
5. The average number of common shares outstanding.

Using the Spreadsheet:

If you have not already done so, load SuperCalc3 into your computer following the instructions given in Part I.

Load the partially completed spreadsheet from the file disk in drive B.

>S   Enter "/L" followed by "B:INCOME,A".

When the spreadsheet has finished loading, the screen display should appear similar to that shown in Exhibit 22-1.

151

You must now enter the required input information and complete the template. Partial instructions for completing the template are given below. (You may wish to refer to your textbook for certain formulas and relationships in order to complete the template.)

Problem:

As the controller of the Unknown Company, Inc., you are responsible for the preparation of the annual financial statements. You assign Ms. Susan Kern, your newly hired assistant, to prepare a *projected* income statement for the company for the year ending December 31, 1985. Several days later, Ms. Kern presents you with the following condensed income statement:

Unknown Company, Inc.
Income Statement
For the Year Ended December 31, 1985

Revenues:	
Sales	$10,000,000
Investment (dividend) income	200,000
Income during 1985 from Sutter Company operations	1,400,000
Gain from sale of plant located in town of Plumas, one of three such plants owned by the company	2,300,000
Total revenues	$13,900,000
Expenses:	
Cost of Goods Sold	$ 6,000,000
Loss on sale of Sutter Company, a line of business which, with this sale, the company has discontinued	2,800,000
Interest expense	175,000
Selling and administrative expense	1,500,000
Cumulative effect of change from straight-line method of depreciation to double-declining balance method	425,000
Loss due to expropriation of foreign assets	1,000,000
Loss on sale of investments	200,000
Total Expenses	$12,100,000
Net income before taxes	$ 1,800,000
Income taxes (40 %)	720,000
Net income	$ 1,080,000
Net income per common share	$1.08

(Average number of common common shares outstanding = 1,000,000)

You immediately realize that the income statement is based on the single-step approach and does not disclose all of the required per share amounts. Unfortunately, you forgot to tell Susan that you wanted a multiple step income statement. Instead of having Susan rework the entire income statement on her own, however, you ask her to help you finish a spreadsheet you have been working on which will help prepare a multiple step income statement.

Required:

A.   Prepare a multiple step income statement for the Unknown Company, Inc. for the year ending December 31, 1985.

B.   Prepare the necessary earnings per share disclosures so that your completed statement conforms with generally accepted accounting principles.

Exhibit 22-1

	A	B	C	D	E	F	G	H
1			Unknown Company, Inc.					
2			Income Statement					
3			For the Year Ended December 31, 1985					
4								
5	Sales revenue							
6	Cost of goods sold							
7							--------------	
8	Gross profit							
9	Selling and administrative expense							
10							--------------	
11	Income from operations							
12	Other revenues and gains							
13	Item #1							
14	Item #2							
15						--------------		
16	Other expenses and losses							
17	Item #1							
18	Item #2							
19						--------------------------		
20	Income from continuing operations before income taxes							

Completing the spreadsheet - Part A:

Step 1 - Let's begin by calculating the income from operations.

>S   **Move the cursor to cell G5.**
>S   **Enter the dollar amount of sales, $10,000,000.**

This amount should be entered without dollar signs or commas. If you do enter the dollar signs or commas, the program will assume that you meant to enter text instead of a number in this cell, in which case you will not be able to perform any mathematical operations on the sales amount. The correct entry should appear as 10000000.

>S   **Now move the cursor to cell G6.**
>S   **Enter the cost of goods sold as "G5*.60"**

Since the cost of goods sold is $6,000,000, or 60% of sales ($6,000,000 /$10,000,000), let's enter this relationship instead of a number. That way, if we decide to change the amount of sales, the cost of goods sold will automatically be adjusted to the new sales level. You should see 6000000 displayed in cell G6 and the formula G5*.60 on the first status line.

>S   **Move the cursor to cell G8.**
>S   **Calculate the gross profit by entering "G5-G6" in this cell.**

The gross profit is equal to the sales revenue less the cost of goods sold. You should see 4000000 displayed in cell G8 and the formula G5-G6 on the first status line.

>S   **Move the cursor to cell G9.**
>S   **Enter the selling and administrative expense as "G5*.15"**

The selling and administrative expense should be entered in the same manner as the cost of goods sold. The selling and administrative expense is equal to 15% of sales ($1,500,000/$10,000,000). You should see 1500000 displayed onscreen.

>S   **Finally, move the cursor to cell G11.**
>S   **Enter "G8-G9" to calculate the income from operations.**

The income from operations equals the gross profit less the selling and administrative expense. You should see an income from operations of 2500000 displayed.

>S   **Move the cursor back to cell G5 and enter sales of $500,000.**

Just to make sure your formulas were entered correctly, check to see whether or not you get an income from operations of $125,000. If not, check your formulas by repeating step 1.

>S   **Reenter $10,000,000 of sales revenue in cell G5 if you did get $125,000 in the previous step and let's continue.**

Step 2 - Let's try several techniques to change the appearance of the numbers in our spreadsheet. This is done through formatting--a process which changes the appearance of each cell, but which does not change the contents of the cell. Obviously, large numbers such as 10000000 can be very difficult to read without commas. We might also want to add dollar signs to our numbers as we feel they are needed. For example, 100000 can be formatted to display as $100,000.

We can format a single cell, an individual row or column, a range of consecutive rows or columns, or the entire spreadsheet (referred to as a global format).

First, let's change cell G5 to dollars and cents format. (*If you enter an incorrect keystroke during this process, use the backspace key to eliminate it!*)

>S   **Check to be sure that the cursor is still in cell G5.**
>S   **Press the slash (/) key on the lower right of the keyboard.**

The slash key (don't confuse this with the backslash (\) key) calls up what are referred to as the slash commands. On the second status line, you will see a large part of the alphabet. Each of these letters and other symbols stands for a specific command, several of which you will use in completing this spreadsheet.

>S   **Now press [F1] or [?].**

You should see a brief description of each slash command. If your computer is connected to a printer, you may obtain a hard copy (printout) of these descriptions by pressing the [shift] key and [PrtSc] simultaneously.

>S   **Press any key to return to your spreadsheet.**

>S   **Type "F" to select format.**

The F stands for format. Our selection of this command is shown on the third status line. Immediately above this, the second status line displays your options under Format: These are Global, Column, Row, Entry, or Define.

>S   **Now press [F1] or [?].**

You should see a brief description of each option. If your computer is connected to a printer, you may obtain a hard copy (printout) of these descriptions by pressing the [shift] key and [PrtSc] simultaneously.

>S   **Press any key to return to your spreadsheet.**

>S   **Type "E" to select entry.**

An entry can be either a single cell or a range of cells. On the second status line you are now prompted to enter a range.

>S   **Press the [enter] key to select cell G5 as the range.**

Since the cursor is currently located in cell G5, it will automatically be selected as the range by pressing [enter]. On the second status line the formatting options for your entry (cell G5) are now shown. Each character stands for an option.

>S   **Now press [F1] or [?].**

You should see a brief description of each option. If your computer is connected to a printer, you may obtain a hard copy (printout) of these descriptions by pressing the [shift] key and [PrtSc] simultaneously.

>S   **Press any key to return to your spreadsheet.**

>S   **Type a dollar sign ($) to select dollar and cents notation.**
>S   **Press the [enter] key to complete the formatting for cell G5.**

Unfortunately, the correct dollar amount is not displayed. This is because dollar and cents notation has added a decimal and two zeroes (.00) to the 10000000 already entered in cell G5. Thus, the display format (10000000.00) is now eleven characters long--and cell G5 is only nine characters wide. In addition, the program reserves one space for a minus sign, used to indicate whether a number is positive or negative. Thus, we need a cell which is at least twelve characters wide before our new format can be displayed. The program indicates this problem by displaying a series of greater-than symbols (>>>>>>>>) in cell G5.

Step 3 - In order to make this number display in dollar and cents format, we need to make column G wider. Let's begin by increasing the width of *all* of the columns in the spreadsheet.

>S   **You can leave the cursor in any cell for this operation.**
>S   **Press the slash (/) key to call up the slash commands.**
>S   **Next, type "F" for format, and "G" for global.**

Global means that whatever option you select will affect the *entire* spreadsheet! On the second status line, you will see that the last option for globally defined formats is "column width". By entering a number, you can select the width of the columns in your spreadsheet.

>S   **Type "13" and press the [enter] key.**

Each column will be expanded to 13 characters wide. Our only problem now is that we can only see columns C through G on the screen. Columns A and B are to the left. Since this didn't work so well, let's go back to 9 characters per column and start over.

>S   **Type "/FG" followed by "D" and press the [enter] key.**

This returns you to the default setting of 9 characters per column. You should now see columns C through J.

>S   **Press the [Home] key to return the cursor to cell A1 so that you will be able to see all of your original screen.**

Instead of changing the global format, let's change only columns E, F, and G: the columns in which we will be entering numbers.

>S   **Type "/F" to select format.**
>S   **Type "C" for column.**

You will now be prompted on the second status line for a column range.

>S   **Type "E:G,"--make sure that you don't omit the comma!**

"E:G" indicates the column *range* of E through G. Thus, all cells in columns E, F, and G will be affected. Once you have entered the comma, you should see the format options prompt again.

>S   **Type "13" and press the [enter] key.**

You should now be able to see columns A through G, and 10000000.00 is finally displayed on the screen!

Step 4 - Let's return cell G5 to its original display format so that we can experiment with some additional formatting options.

>S   **Move the cursor back to cell G5.**

Note that only our entry in cell G5 is in dollar and cents notation and that this notation only added two decimal places to our number. It did not add a dollar sign. We can see what display format cell G5 is using by looking at the first status line. This line now shows a dollar sign ($) before the description of the contents of cell G5.

Cell G5 is the only cell displaying the ($) notation because display formats are arranged in a sequence of priority. The format of an individual cell (such as dollars and cents in cell G5) takes priority over any other format. A format for a row is next in priority for the cells in that row. A column format is third in priority (such as 12 characters per column in columns E, F, and G). Finally, the global format will determine the display of all other cells.

Thus, when developing a spreadsheet, you should first determine the type of display which is best for the majority of cells. By entering this display format globally, you can minimize the number of rows, columns, or cells which you need to format on an individual basis. Similarly, once the global format has been set, you should next determine any different formats by row or column, and then finally format individual cells or cell ranges. Using this technique can save you a lot of time when formatting!

We could continue to format all of the other cells which will contain numbers in dollars and cents format, but we can see that this format didn't really accomplish what we wanted to do--we would like commas in all of our numbers, and dollar signs on those numbers where we believe dollar signs are appropriate.

>S   **Type "/FE" and press the [enter] key to select cell G5 as the range.**
>S   **Type "D" for default and press the [enter] key.**

         This reformats cell G5 to the default display format--that we originally started with! If done correctly, 10000000 should be displayed in cell G5.

Step 5 - Commas (and dollar signs) can be added by applying user-defined formats. These allow you to add many different formatting options, tailored to your needs. Let's define several format options!

>S   **To begin, type "/F" for format, followed by "D" for define.**

         Onscreen, you should see a list of options and choices corresponding to eight user-defined formats. Thus, you may customize up to eight format options in addition to the regular options available. Let's define two options--numbers 1 and 2.

>S   **Type "N" for no in place of the Y currently listed under format option 1 for the dollar sign (floating $) choice.**

         The floating $ choice is defined as no since most of our numbers do not need to display a dollar sign.

>S   Using the cursor movement keys, move the cursor down one row to the embedded commas row.

We would like our numbers to have commas, so leave this choice as yes.

>S   Move the cursor down to the minus in ( ) row.
>S   Type "Y" in place of the N currently listed under format option 1.

The minus in ( ) allows you to display negative numbers inside parentheses instead of using a minus (-) sign. Many businesspeople prefer this, so let's change this choice to Y for yes. (That way, if you have a net loss, it will display inside of parentheses.)

>S   Move the cursor down four rows to the decimal places row.

The zero as blank, percentage (%), and scaling factor choices should be left at their current settings.

>S   Type "0" in place of the 2 currently listed under format option 1.

Changing the decimal places choice to zero will eliminate any cents from being displayed since zero characters to the right of the decimal will be shown. But, with our large numbers (for example, $10,000,000), we really don't need to display cents. (If you should choose to display cents, you will need to make columns E through F even wider than 12 characters in order to see them.)

You have now finished specifying option 1!

>S   You should define option 2 in exactly the same manner as option 1 with one exception--leave the floating $ choice as yes.

We'll use option 2 to format the beginning of each column and the final totals. You do not need to change any of the other option numbers (3-8) unless you wish to use those options as well as options 1 and 2!

>S   To return to your spreadsheet, press the special function key [F2]. You should see your spreadsheet reappear.

Step 6 - Let's begin using our new formats by formatting columns E through G with user-defined option 1.

>S   Type "/FC" to select format and column.
>S   Type "E:G," in response to the prompt for the column range--again, don't forget the comma!

After you enter the comma, the format options will appear on the second status line.

>S   Type "U" for user-defined.
>S   Type "1" for option 1.
>S   Press the [enter] key.

The numbers in column G should now be displayed with commas!

Step 7 - Finally, let's format the sales revenue in cell G5 so that a dollar sign is also displayed. You can do this with user-defined option 2.

>S **Check to be sure that the cursor is still in cell G5.**
>S **Type "/FE" and press the [enter] key to select cell G5.**
>S **Type "U" followed by "2" for option 2, and then press the [enter] key.**

You should now see $10,000,000 displayed in cell G5!

If you examine the numbers in column G, you will see that they are no longer right-hand justified in each cell--each number is one space to the left of the right-hand side. For example, look at cell G5. You will see that there is one character space to the right of $10,000,000.

This is because the right-most space is reserved for the right parenthesis, should we need it to display a negative number. Thus, if you plan to use parentheses for negative numbers, you should make your columns one space wider then would otherwise be necessary.

You are probably starting to see the need to plan your cell sizes according to the sizes of the numbers that you may expect to encounter in a problem. Increasing or decreasing the width of a column once you have done a substantial amount of work can be very inconvenient!

Now let's return to our income statement!

Step 8 - Let's enter the amounts of any *other* revenues and gains and calculate the total amount of other revenues and gains.

>S **In cells F13 and F14, enter the amounts of any other revenues or gains. (Refer to the original data.)**
>S **In cell G14, enter "F13+F14" to total the other revenues and gains.**

(These revenues and gains are simply labeled Item #1 and Item #2 on your spreadsheet--don't bother to change these labels for now.)

Step 9 - Let's enter the amounts of any *other* expenses or losses and calculate the total amount of other expenses and losses.

>S **In cells F17 and F18, enter the amounts of any other expenses or losses. (Refer to the original data.)**
>S **In cell G18, enter "F17+F18" to total the other expenses and losses.**

(These expenses and losses are simply labeled Item #1 and Item #2 on your spreadsheet--don't bother to change these labels for now.)

Step 10 - Calculate the income from continuing operations before income taxes by adding the gross profit to the other revenues and gains and subtracting the other expenses and losses.

>S   **In cell G20, enter "G11+G14-G18".**

You should get $4,625,000 if all steps have been completed correctly.

Step 11 - Next, let's prepare to calculate the amount of income taxes and the income from continuing operations. Since income taxes are calculated as a percentage of income, and rates may change, let's input the tax rate in a separate cell. Then, if we wish to change rates later, we can simply change the amount in one cell.

>S   **In cell D21, enter the tax rate.**

Make sure that you enter the tax rate as a decimal (for example, 40% equals .40).

Step 12 - When the tax rate is correctly entered, you should see only .4 displayed--the zero is dropped by the program. This provides us with another opportunity to apply the user-defined formats.

>S   **Type "/FD" to begin another user-defined format.**
>S   **When the format option screen appears, use the cursor keys to move to the column for option 3.**
>S   **Type "N" for all of the Yes or No choices except for the percentage (%) choice. Type "Y" for yes for this choice.**

Since tax rates are usually even percentages, you may want to change the decimal places choice to zero (0). The scaling factor should still be set at zero.

>S   **Return to your spreadsheet by pressing the special function key [F2].**
>S   **Check to make sure that the cursor is still in cell D21.**

>S   **Type "/FE", press the [enter] key to select cell D21, type "U3", and press the [enter] key.**

You should see the tax rate appear as either 40% or 40.00%, depending upon how many decimal places you specified!

Step 13 - Now let's finish calculating the dollar amount of income taxes and the income from continuing operations.

>S   **Move the cursor to cell G21.**
>S   **Enter "G20*D21".**

This will multiply the income from continuing operations before tax by the tax rate to determine the amount of income taxes.

>S   **Move the cursor to cell G23.**
>S   **Enter "G20-G21".**

This calculation subtracts the income taxes from the income from continuing operations before tax to arrive at the after-tax income from continuing operations. You should get $2,775,000 if your entries have been correct.

Step 14 - Next, the effects of any additional components of net income should be calculated. Since you have already calculated the income taxes in determining income from continuing operations, each additional item which affects net income must be disclosed net-of-tax. However, the amount of tax expense related to each of these items should also be shown on the income statement.

These special items include: (a) discontinued operations, (b) extraordinary items, and (c) cumulative effects of changes in accounting principles.

Step 14a - Let's begin with discontinued operations. Any net gain or loss on discontinued operations must be segregated into (i) the income or loss during the year from operating the discontinued operations and (ii) the gain or loss on disposal of the discontinued operations.

>S   **Move the cursor to cell E25.**

>S   **Enter the income (loss) from operations of a discontinued operation. (Refer to the original data.)**

>S   **Move the cursor to cell E26.**

>S   **Enter "E25*D21" to calculate the income tax effect of the income (loss) from operations of the discontinued operations.**

>S   **Move the cursor to cell F26.**

>S   **Enter "E25-E26".**

This calculates the net-of-tax income (loss) from operations of the discontinued operation by subtracting the income tax effect from the gross amount.

>S   **Move the cursor to cell E28.**

>S   **Enter the gain or loss on disposal of the discontinued operation. (Refer to the original information.)**

Remember to enter any losses as negative numbers. For example, a loss of $2,800,000 is entered as -2800000 (on some monitors, negative numbers are shadowed to help distinguish them from positive numbers).

>S   **Move the cursor to cell E29.**

>S   **Enter "E28*D21" to calculate the income tax effect of the gain (loss) on disposal of the discontinued operations.**

>S   **Move the cursor to cell F29.**

>S   **Enter "E28-E29".**

This calculates the net-of-tax gain (loss) on disposal of the discontinued operation by subtracting the income tax effect from the gross amount.

>S   **Move the cursor to cell G29.**

>S   **Enter "F26+F29".**

This calculation totals the net gain or loss on discontinued operations by summing the net-of-tax amounts from operating and disposing of the discontinued operations.

>S   **Move the cursor to cell G31.**
>S   **Enter "G23+G29".**

The net gain or loss on discontinued operations is added to the income from continuing operations to arrive at the income before extraordinary items and cumulative effect of a change in accounting principle. If done correctly, you should have $1,935,000 for the income before extraordinary items and the cumulative effect of a change in accounting principle.

Step 14b - Now let's calculate the effects of any extraordinary items.

>S   **Move the cursor to cell F33.**
>S   **Enter the total gross amount of any extraordinary gains or losses. (Refer to the original information.)**

Remember to enter any losses as negative numbers.

>S   **Move the cursor to cell F34.**
>S   **Enter "F33*D21" to calculate the income tax effect of the extraordinary gains or losses.**
>S   **Move the cursor to cell G34.**
>S   **Enter "F33-F34" to calculate the net-of-tax extraordinary gain or loss.**

Step 14c - Now let's calculate the effects of any cumulative effects of changes in accounting principles.

>S   **Move the cursor to cell F36.**
>S   **Enter the total gross amount of any cumulative effects of changes in accounting principles. (Refer to the original information.)**

Remember to enter any losses as negative numbers.

>S   **Move the cursor to cell F37.**
>S   **Enter "F36*D21" to calculate the income tax effects of the cumulative effects of changes in accounting principles.**
>S   **Move the cursor to cell G37.**
>S   **Enter "F36-F37" to calculate the net-of-tax cumulative effect of changes in accounting principles.**

Step 15 - Finally, compute the net income by summing the income before extraordinary items and cumulative effect of a change in accounting principle with the net gain or loss from extraordinary items and the cumulative effects of changes in accounting principles.

>S   **Move the cursor to cell G39.**
>S   **Enter "G31+G34+G37".**

Your final net income should be $1,080,000, the same amount as was calculated by Ms. Kern. You may wish to reformat this cell to display the dollar sign. (Remember, type "/FE", press the [enter] key, and then type "U2".)

>S   **Press the [Home] key to move the cursor to cell A1.**

Step 16 - At this point, you may wish to **save** your work and complete part B of the problem at a later date. Use the procedures given in Chapter 5 to save your work.

Printing: You might also want to print the spreadsheet if your computer is connected to a printer. If you wish to do this:

>S   **Type "/GB" to remove the spreadsheet borders (row and column headings).**
>S   **Type "/ODA1:G40,P" to print the income statement.**
>S   **Press any key to continue.**
>S   **Type "/GB" to replace the spreadsheet borders if you wish to continue.**

If you wish to quit at this time:

>S   **Type "/QY" to quit using SuperCalc3.**

After the screen clears and the red in-use light has gone off, you may remove your disks and turn off the computer.

Completing the spreadsheet - Part B:

If you saved your earlier work and now wish to retrieve your template, use the procedures in Chapter 5 for retrieving a file.

Step 17 - Let's begin calculating the earnings per share disclosures for our income statement. First, you need to enter the weighted average number of common shares outstanding.

>S   **Use the [=] key to jump to cell I1 (type "=I1" and press the [enter] key) so that you can view columns I through P.**

This will enable you to view the earnings per share section of the template.

>S   **Move the cursor to cell P1 and enter 1,000,000, the weighted average number of shares outstanding.**

Step 18 - Next, let's add the necessary labels for our earnings per share calculations.

>S   **Move the cursor to cell I6 and type: "Income from continuing operations"**

>S   **Press the [enter] key.**

This enters what you have typed as text in cell I6. Text is left-hand justified in each cell, unlike the numbers and formulas you entered earlier, which were right-hand justified in each cell.

Also, the program allows your entry to "spillover" into cells J6, K6, and L6. This "spillover" is allowed by the program unless there is an entry in one of the cells your text spills over into. For example, if we had made an entry in cell L6, then only "Income from continuing oper" would display. The balance of the text would not display because of the overlapping of our entries in cells I6 and L6!

Now let's add the remaining text!

>S   **Enter the following text in the corresponding cells:**

Cell	Text to be entered
I7	**Income (loss) from operations of discontinued operations,**
I8	** net of tax**
I9	**Gain (loss) on disposal of discontinued operation, net of tax**

Note that the program will not allow you to enter spaces when you begin the entry in cell I8. Before you may begin an entry with a space, you must tell the program that you wish to enter text in cell I8. To do this, type a double quotation mark (") before entering the spaces. This tells the program that the spaces are text and you will then be able to enter them as part of your entry.

Step 19 - Now you can calculate the per share amounts.

>S   **Move the cursor to cell P6.**
>S   **Enter "G23/P1".**

This is the income from continuing operations per common share. You should see 2.775 displayed if done correctly. (We'll reformat this cell and the other per share amounts to display dollars and cents in a moment.)

>S   **Move the cursor to cell P8.**

Let's use the cursor as a *pointer* to find the numbers which we want to enter in this cell.

>S   **Press the [Esc] key. This activates the cursor as a pointer.**

On the third status line, cell P8 has appeared since this is where the cursor is currently located.

>S   **Using the cursor movement keys, move one cell to the left (cell O8) Note how the cell reference on the third status line is now cell O8!**
>S   **Continue moving the cursor to cell F26, the cell which contains the amount of income (loss) from operations of the discontinued operations. Note that the cell reference on the third status line is now cell F26!**
>S   **Press the slash key (/) to indicate that you wish to divide cell F26 by another number.**

The cursor will automatically return to cell P8--where we started from! On the third status line, the partially completed command "F26/" is displayed.

>S   Using the cursor movement keys, move the cursor to cell P1, which contains the average number of common shares outstanding. On the third status line, the formula "F26/P1" will be displayed.

>S   Enter this formula in cell P8 by pressing the [enter] key.

This is the income (loss) from operations of the discontinued operations per common share. You should see .84 displayed if done correctly.

If you got confused, you can always start over after pressing the [enter] key (or simply enter "F26/P1" in cell P8).

>S   Move the cursor to cell P9.

>S   Activate the pointer by pressing the [Esc] key and move the cursor to cell F29.

>S   Press the slash (/) key to indicate that you wish to divide.

>S   Move the cursor to cell P1 and press the [enter] key.

This is the gain (loss) from disposal of the discontinued operations per common share. You should see -1.68 displayed if done correctly. (In summary, you should have entered "F29/P1" in cell P9.)

>S   Move the cursor to cell P12.

>S   Activate the pointer and use it to enter "G31/P1".

This is the income (loss) before extraordinary items and the cumulative effect of a change in accounting principle per common share. You should see 1.935 displayed if done correctly.

>S   Move the cursor to cell P13.

>S   Activate the pointer and use it to enter "G34/P1".

This is the income (loss) from extraordinary items per common share. You should see -.6 displayed if done correctly.

>S   Move the cursor to cell P15.

>S   Activate the pointer and use it to enter "G37/P1".

This is the income (loss) from the cumulative effect of a change in accounting principle per common share. You should see -.255 displayed if done correctly.

>S   Move the cursor to cell P17.

>S   Activate the pointer and use it to enter "G39/P1".

This is the final net income (loss) per common share. You should see 1.08 displayed if done correctly.

Step 20 - Let's format the per share amounts to show dollars and cents. Let's begin by preparing two additional user-defined formats.

>S   Type "/FD" to see the options screen.

>S   Define options #4 and #5 exactly like options #1 and #2, respectively, except leaving the decimal places choice as 2.

This will enable you to display the dollar sign using option #5, and to display negative numbers in parentheses instead of with a minus (-) sign for both options. In addition, under both options, two decimal places will be displayed, corresponding with dollars and cents.

>S   **To return to your spreadsheet, press the special function key [F2]. You should see the spreadsheet reappear.**

>S   **Move the cursor to cell P6.**
>S   **Type "/FE" and press the [enter] key to select cell P6 as the range.**
>S   **Type "U" followed by "5" for option 5 and then press the [enter] key.**

You should now see $2.78 displayed in cell P6.

>S   **Move the cursor down to cell P17, type "/FE", press the [enter] key to select cell P17 as the range, type "U5" and press the [enter] key to format this cell in the same manner.**

You should now see $1.08 displayed in cell P17.

>S   **Move the cursor up to cell P8.**
>S   **Type "/FE" to begin formatting.**
>S   **Type "P8:P15," to specify a range of cells to be formatted instead of a single cell--be careful not to omit the comma.**
>S   **Type "U4" to select user-defined option #4 and press the [enter] key to complete the formatting.**

The numbers in the range from cell P8 to cell P15 should now be displayed with two decimals (cents) and with negative numbers in parentheses.

Step 21 - Let's try changing the amount of sales revenue to see what effect it has on net income and the related earnings per common share.

>S   **Move the cursor one column to the right so that you can see column Q (which is blank).**
>S   **Next, move the cursor left to any cell in column P.**
>S   **Type "/W" for window, followed by "V" for vertical.**

You should see a split in the viewing screen with the cursor on the right-hand side of the split. Since we can see the earnings per share amounts on the right, let's move the cursor to the left side of the screen so that we can see the amount of sales revenue at the same time.

>S   **Type a semi-colon (;).**

You should see the cursor jump to the opposite side of the split in the screen.

>S   **Move the cursor left until you can see columns E, F, G, and H.**

You should now be able to view both the earnings per share amounts and the right-hand side of the income statement.

>S   Move the cursor to cell G5, which is the cell containing the amount of sales revenue.

>S   Examine the numbers on the spreadsheet very carefully, especially the earnings per share amounts in column P.

>S   Enter $20,000,000 of sales instead of $10,000,000.

You should see several of the numbers on the income statement change as the program recalculates the amounts, but no changes in the earnings per share amounts. This doesn't seem quite right, however. How could we double the amount of sales without changing the earnings per share? Let's check to see if net income changed.

>S   Move the cursor down to cell G39.

Notice that when you move the cursor to cell G39 that the left side of your viewing screen moves independently of the right side. That is, the two screens are unsynchronized. If you wish, you may synchronize the two screens by typing "/WS".

Indeed, cell G39 displays a net income of $2,580,000--whereas it was $1,080,000 when sales were only $10,000,000. So why didn't the program recalculate the earnings per share?

The reason the earnings per share was not correctly recalculated is that we have a logical error as a result of the manner in which the program recalculates. The program recalculates the spreadsheet by either columns or rows. In this spreadsheet, it is recalculating by rows. Thus, it recalculates all of the cells in row 1 first, then row 2, then row 3, etc.

When we entered $20,000,000 in cell G5, the program began this process. When it reached row 6, it recalculated not only the cost of goods sold in cell G6, but also the income from continuing operations per common share in cell P6. Since the command in cell P6 is G23/P1, the program looks for the numbers in cells G23 and P1. Since row 23 comes after row 6, the new income from continuing operations has not yet been calculated and the program uses the same number as we had before. Thus, the earnings per share amounts, all of which contain such forward references, are incorrect.

There are two ways to avoid this problem.

First, by forcing the spreadsheet to recalculate for each consecutive forward reference, you can arrive at the correct answers. Let's try this first.

>S   Make sure that you can see the earnings per share data in column P and press the exclamation point (!) key to manually force a recalculation.

You should see the earnings per share amounts recalculated to the correct amounts.

Since it may be difficult to tell how many forward references a spreadsheet has (and thus how many recalculations to force), it is best to plan ahead so that there aren't any! In this spreadsheet, we can eliminate this problem by having the program recalculate by columns instead of by rows. Let's do this!

>S   **Type "/G" for global.**

On the second status line, you will see the options available under global.

>S   **Now press [F1] or [?].**

You should see a brief description of each slash command. If your computer is connected to a printer, you may obtain a hard copy (printout) of these options by pressing the [shift] key and [PrtSc] simultaneously.

>S   **Press any key to return to your spreadsheet.**

>S   **Type "C" for column-wise recalculation.**

The program will now recalculate this spreadsheet on a column by column basis instead of a row by row basis. If you save your spreadsheet, this command will also be saved.

>S   **Move the cursor to cell G5 and re-input $10,000,000.**

Check the earnings per share amounts. Did you get the correct amounts as before? For example, does the net income per common share in cell P17 equal $1.08? If not, repeat these last few steps to make sure that you are in column-wise recalculation.

>S   **Type "/WC" to clear the split screen and return to a single screen.**
>S   **Press the [Home] key to move the cursor to cell A1.**

Step 22 - At this point, you may wish to **save** your work. Use the procedures given in Chapter 5 to save your work.

Printing: You might also want to print the spreadsheet if your computer is connected to a printer. You must do this in two sections: (1) the income statement, and (2) the earnings per common share.

>S   **Type "/GB" to remove the spreadsheet borders (row and column headings).**
>S   **Type "/ODA1:G40,P" to print the income statement.**
>S   **Press any key to continue.**
>S   **Type "/ODI1:P18,P" to print the earnings per share amounts.**
>S   **Press any key and type "/GB" to replace the spreadsheet borders if you wish to continue.**

If you wish to quit at this time:

>S   **Type "/QY" to quit using SuperCalc3.**

After the screen clears and the red in-use light has gone off, you may remove your disks and turn off the computer.

CHAPTER 23 - ACCOUNTS RECEIVABLE AGING

Objective: This tutorial introduces you to the use of SuperCalc3 by illustrating a simple spreadsheet which can be used in conjunction with an aging of accounts receivable. The spreadsheet which will result from the tutorial will enable you to determine the balance of the accounts receivable and the allowance for uncollectible accounts at any given date. It will also enable you to determine the effects of changes in the amounts due and the percentages of uncollectible accounts on the balance of the allowance account.

The spreadsheet introduces the REPLICATE, INSERT, BLANK and EDIT commands. It also uses the FORMAT command for text formatting, and demonstrates how to use REPEATING TEXT. The SUM function is used in the spreadsheet for several totals.

Part A of the preparation of the spreadsheet introduces these commands and formulas. Part B, the completion of the spreadsheet, reviews several of these concepts. These two parts may be worked sequentially at different times by saving the results of Part A on a disk.

Required Input Information: Before beginning, you should identify:

1. The balance of each customer's account and an aging of his/her account.
2. The percentage estimated to be uncollectible for each age category.

Problem:

The Lemhi Bearing Company regularly sells to customers on account. Presented below are the account balances for Lemhi's four customers. These balances are broken down into four aging categories along with the percentage of bad debts expected for each age category:

Customer	Less than 30 days	31-60 days	61-120 days	More than 120 days
Chamberlain Mftg.	$190,000	$30,000		
Bargamin Distributors	92,000	42,000	$14,000	
Stibnite Products Co.	214,000	62,000	17,000	
Tendoy Company, Inc.		16,000	28,000	$42,000
Percentage uncollectible	1%	3%	6%	25%

Building a Spreadsheet Template

If you have not already done so, load SuperCalc3 into your computer following the instructions given in Part I. When the blank spreadsheet appears on the screen, you are ready to begin.

Step 1 - Before beginning the spreadsheet, however, let's turn the automatic cursor advance off.

>S   **Type a slash (/).**

The slash key (don't confuse this with the backslash (\) key) accesses what are referred to as the slash commands. On the second status line, you will see a large part of the alphabet. Each of these letters and other symbols stands for a specific command, many of which you will use in constructing this spreadsheet.

>S   **Type "G" for global.**
>S   **Type "N" for next.**

This means that the cursor will no longer automatically advance to the next cell when you press the [enter] key. This is indicated on the first status line by the fact that the character in front of the cell reference has disappeared.

(The automatic cursor can be very useful if you are entering large amounts of data and can be turned back on by typing the same set of keystrokes-- "/GN".)

Part A - Calculating the Accounts Receivable Balance

Step 2 - Let's begin by preparing a schedule which will total the accounts receivable for each age category. First, we need to enter column headings.

>S   **In cell A2, type "Customer".**

Note how this appears on the third status line to let you know what you have typed.

>S   **Press the [enter] key.**

When you press the [enter] key, "Customer" will appear in cell A2. This is also shown on the first status line, which indicates that text has been entered in cell A2.

>S   **Move the cursor to cell D1 and enter "Less than".**
>S   **In cell D2, enter "30 days".**
>S   **In cell E1, enter "31-60".**

Note what happens! The program has subtracted 60 from 31 and arrived at negative 29! The first status line indicates that this is not text, but is instead a formula. An entry composed entirely of numbers and numeric operations is assumed to be a formula, and the operation implied by that formula has been performed. In order to have 31-60 display, instead of -29, you need to tell the program that this entry should be considered as text, not as a formula. To do this, type a double quote mark (") before entering 31-60.

>S   **Reenter 31-60 by typing a double quotation mark (") first and your entry will be interpreted as text.**

Note that 31-60 is left-hand justified in cell E1--we'll adjust that later.

>S   **In columns E, F, and G, enter the remainder of the headings for the four age categories (as given in the problem data) following the process described in step 2.**

Your completed headings should appear as in Exhibit 23-1.

Exhibit 23-1

	A	B	C	D	E	F	G	H
1|				Less than	31-60	61-120	More than	
2|	Customer			30 days	days	days	120 days	
3|								
4|								
5|								
6|								
7|								
8|								
9|								
10|								

Step 3 - Next, let's enter Lemhi's customer names in cells A4 through A7.

>S   **In cell A4, enter "Chamberlain Mftg."**

This entry is too wide for cell A4, which is only 9 characters wide, but it is allowed to "spillover" into cell B4. This spillover is possible as long as an entry doesn't spillover into a cell which already has an entry. For example, if cell B4 already had an entry, then only the first nine letters of Chamberlain Mftg. would display--those that fit in cell A4.

>S   **In cells A5, A6, and A7, enter the remaining customer names.**

Step 4 - Enter the aged balances of accounts receivable. All numbers should be entered without dollar signs and commas or they will be interpreted as text instead of numbers. Thus, $190,000 is entered as 190000. Enter a zero if a company's balance in a category is zero.

>S   **In cells D4 through G7, enter the aged balances.**

Your spreadsheet should appear as in Exhibit 23-2.

Exhibit 23-2

	A	B	C	D	E	F	G	H
1				Less than	31-60	61-120	More than	
2	Customer			30 days	days	days	120 days	
3								
4	Chamberlain Mftg.			190000	30000	0	0	
5	Bargamin Distributors			92000	42000	14000	0	
6	Stibnite Products Co.			214000	62000	17000	0	
7	Tendoy Company, Inc.			0	16000	28000	42000	
8								
9								
10								

Step 5a - Let's total the accounts outstanding for less than 30 days.

>S   In cell A9, enter "Total".
>S   Next, in cell D9, enter "D4+D5+D6+D7".

This totals the accounts which have been outstanding for less than 30 days. You should see the formula on the first status line and the total of $496,000 displayed in cell D9.

Step 5b - Let's total the accounts which have been outstanding for 31 to 60 days. This time, however, let's use the cursor to point to the cells which we would like to total.

>S   Move the cursor to cell E9.
>S   Press the [Esc] key.

This activates the spreadsheet's cursor as a pointer. Notice how the cell where the cursor is presently located (E9) has appeared on the third status line. (If you would like to deactivate the pointer, simply press the [Esc] key a second time.)

>S   Using the arrow keys, move the cursor up to cell E4.

As the cursor moves, the cell reference on the third status line changes. When you reach cell E4, you have pointed to the first cell which you want to total.

>S   Press the plus (+) key.

Note that the cursor immediately returns to its starting cell (E9). You can now point to the second cell you wish to have as a part of the total.

>S   Using the arrow keys, move the cursor to cell E5.
>S   Press the plus (+) key.
>S   Move the cursor to cell E6 and press the plus (+) key a third time.

>S   Finally, move the cursor to cell E7 and, since this is the final cell you wish to total, press the [enter] key.

On the first status line, you will see that cell E9 now contains a formula which is identical to the formula you entered in D9 except that it is in column E instead of column D.

This suggests that perhaps we could recreate, or replicate, this formula in cells F9 and G9 and save a lot of effort. This is exactly what we will do next!

Step 5c - Let's replicate the formula in cell E9 to cell F9.

>S   With the cursor in cell E9, type a slash (/).
>S   Next, type "R" for replicate.

On the second status line, you are prompted to enter the cell range which you would like to replicate *from*.

>S   Press the [Esc] key to activate the pointer.
>S   Press the [enter] key to select cell E9 as the cell range.

Since the cursor is in cell E9, and it contains the formula we wish to replicate, pressing the [enter] key will select cell E9 by default.

You are then prompted to enter the cell range you wish to replicate *to*.

>S   Press the [Esc] key and point to cell F9 (move the cursor to cell F9).
>S   Press the [enter] key to select cell F9 as the cell range.

Since cell F9 is being pointed to, pressing the [enter] key will select it as the cell range. The program automatically replicates the formula and adjusts it to be in column F. If you move the cursor to cell F9, you will see that this cell contains a formula identical to those in cells D9 and E9, except that it has been adjusted to column F.

Step 5d - Repeat this process to total the accounts outstanding for more than 120 days.

>S   Move the cursor to cell F9.
>S   Type "/R" and press the [enter] key.

Note that because the cursor was in the cell we wished to replicate from, it wasn't necessary to activate the pointer. However, to point out the cell range we want to replicate to, you must activate the pointer by pressing the [Esc] key and using the cursor to point out cell G9 (or, since you know that you want to replicate to cell G9, you could type and enter "G9" in response to the prompt instead of pointing to G9).

>S   Type and enter "G9" instead of pointing out G9 as the range we wish to replicate to.

Your spreadsheet should now appear as in Exhibit 23-3.

Exhibit 23-3

	A	B	C	D	E	F	G	H
1				Less than	31-60	61-120	More than	
2	Customer			30 days	days	days	120 days	
3								
4	Chamberlain Mftg.			190000	30000	0	0	
5	Bargamin Distributors			92000	42000	14000	0	
6	Stibnite Products Co.			214000	62000	17000	0	
7	Tendoy Company, Inc.			0	16000	28000	42000	
8								
9	Total			496000	150000	59000	42000	
10								

Step 6a - Now let's add totals in column H for each customer's account.

>S   Move the cursor to cell H2 and enter "Total".
>S   Move the cursor to cell H4.

As you have probably guessed, it can be burdensome to have to point out each and every cell to be totaled. The sum function can be used to speed up this process. What we would like to do is sum the cells from E4 through G4.

>S   Type "SUM(". *(This is the word Sum and a left-hand parenthesis.)*
>S   Press the [Esc] key to activate the pointer, and point to cell D4.
>S   Instead of entering a plus (+), enter a colon (:) at this point.

The colon indicates that cell D4 is the first cell in a continuous range of cells to be summed.

>S   Next, move the pointer over to cell G4 and type the right-hand parenthesis ")".

The formula shown on the third status line should read SUM(D4:G4).

>S   Press the [enter] key and you should get a total of $220,000 in cell H4.

Step 6b - You can now replicate this formula to cells H5, H6, and H7 in order to total the accounts of the other three customers. Rather than doing this one cell at a time, let's replicate the formula to all three cells at once.

>S   With the cursor in cell H4:
>S   Type "/R" and press the [enter] key to indicate that cell H4 is the range to copy from.
>S   Activate the pointer by pressing the [Esc] key and point to cell H5.
>S   Type a colon (:) to indicate that this is the first cell in a range of cells (instead of pressing the [enter] key to select only cell H5).
>S   Point all the way down to cell H9.

Since row 9 also needs to be totaled to arrive at the total accounts receivable, include this in your range. Your range should read H5:H9.

>S   **Press the [enter] key.**

You should see the totals for each row appear. If you move the cursor to any of the cells in the range of cells from H5 through H9, you will see that the formula in each cell has been adjusted to its respective row. Exhibit 23-4 shows how your spreadsheet should now appear.

Exhibit 23-4

	A	B	C	D	E	F	G	H
1				Less than	31-60	61-120	More than	
2	Customer			30 days	days	days	120 days	Total
3								
4	Chamberlain Mftg.			190000	30000	0	0	220000
5	Bargamin Distributors			92000	42000	14000	0	148000
6	Stibnite Products Co.			214000	62000	17000	0	293000
7	Tendoy Company, Inc.			0	16000	28000	42000	86000
8								0
9	Total			496000	150000	59000	42000	747000
10								

One problem remains. Cell H8 has a zero in it. This is because the formula was also replicated to this cell and the spreadsheet is summing the four blank cells in row 8 (cells D8 through G8). You can eliminate this formula by using a slash command.

>S   **Move the cursor to cell H8.**
>S   **Type "/B" for blank and press the [enter] key.**

The formula in cell H8 will be blanked out.

Step 7 - Before continuing with our calculation of the allowance for bad debts, let's clean up the appearance of our first table.

Step 7a - Let's begin cleaning up by adding a heading.

>S   **Press the [Home] key to move the cursor up to cell A1.**

You can add more blank rows at the top of your schedule by using the Insert command.

>S   **Type "/I" for insert, followed by an "R" for row and press the [enter] key.**
>S   **Add a second and a third blank row by the same process so that "Customer" now appears in cell A5.**

>S   **Move the cursor over to a cell that contains a formula (for example, cell H7).**

Note that all of the formulas which you have created in the schedule have automatically been adjusted for the addition of these three rows--you do not have to change the formulas!

>S   **In cell D1, enter "Lemhi Bearing Company".**
>S   **In cell D2, enter "Aging Schedule".**

Since Aging Schedule is not centered with the company's name, let's adjust it.

>S   **With the cursor still in cell D2, type "/E" for edit.**
>S   **Press the [enter] key to edit the current cell, D2.**

You should see Aging Schedule appear on the edit line (the third status line). You can use the left and right arrow keys to move back and forth on the edit line. (Caution: If you move too far left, you will automatically be dumped out of edit mode!)

>S   **Move the flashing cursor on the edit line beneath the A in Aging.**
>S   **Press the [Ins] key.**

This will allow you to insert several blank spaces to the left of the A.

>S   **Press the [space] bar three times to insert three spaces.**
>S   **Press the [enter] key and the edited cell will be entered on the spreadsheet.**

(You can get back out of insert while in edit mode by pressing the [Ins] key a second time. When you are not in insert, you can retype over unwanted characters--or you can use the [Del] key at any time to edit characters out of the cell when you have entered edit mode. Note: Leaving edit mode will also remove you from insert.)

Step 7b - Now let's adjust the column headings. You have probably noticed that text is left-justified and numbers are right-justified in each cell. You can also right-justify text to make it line up better with a column of numbers. This should be done for all of our text in cells D4 through H5.

>S   **Type "/F" for format.**
>S   **Type "E" for entry so that you can define the cell range which you wish to format.**
>S   **Type "D4:H5" and press the [enter] key.**

You are then prompted to select a format.

>S   **Type "TR" for text right and press the [enter] key.**

The column headings should now be right-justified in each cell, resulting in a neater, more organized appearance.

Step 7c - Finally, let's add a dashed line between our headings and our data.

>S   **Move the cursor to Cell A6.**

You could type in 9 dashes (-) in this cell, but it is easier to use the repeating text command.

>S   **Type an apostrophe ('), followed by a dash (-), and press the [enter] key.**

The dash will be repeated throughout each blank cell to the right of the apostrophe. Your spreadsheet should now appear as in Exhibit 23-5.

Exhibit 23-5

	A	B	C	D	E	F	G	H
1				Lemhi Bearing Company				
2				Aging Schedule				
3								
4				Less than	31-60	61-120	More than	
5	Customer			30 days	days	days	120 days	Total
6	----------	---	---	----------	-------	-------	----------	-------
7	Chamberlain Mftg.			190000	30000	0	0	220000
8	Bargamin Distributors			92000	42000	14000	0	148000
9	Stibnite Products Co.			214000	62000	17000	0	293000
10	Tendoy Company, Inc.			0	16000	28000	42000	86000
11								
12	Total			496000	150000	59000	42000	747000
13								

>S   Move the cursor to cell I6, enter an apostrophe (') and press the [enter] key to end the repeating text.
>S   Add a dashed line for your totals in columns D through H (from cell D11 to cell H11) using the same procedures.
>S   Add a double dashed line beneath the final totals (in cells D13 through H13) following the same procedures using an equals sign (=) instead of a dash (-).

Remember to place apostrophes in column I to end each repeating string.

>S   **Press the [Home] key to move the cursor to cell A1.**

Exhibit 23-6 shows what your spreadsheet should now look like.

Exhibit 23-6

	A	B	C	D	E	F	G	H
1			Lemhi Bearing Company					
2			Aging Schedule					
3								
4				Less than	31-60	61-120	More than	
5	Customer			30 days	days	days	120 days	Total
6	---							
7	Chamberlain Mftg.			190000	30000	0	0	220000
8	Bargamin Distributors			92000	42000	14000	0	148000
9	Stibnite Products Co.			214000	62000	17000	0	293000
10	Tendoy Company, Inc.			0	16000	28000	42000	86000
11								
12	Total			496000	150000	59000	42000	747000
13								

Step 8 - At this point, you may wish to **save** your work in case you make an error or wish to complete part B of the problem at a later date. Use the procedures given in Chapter 5 to **save** your work.

Printing: You might also want to print the spreadsheet if your computer is connected to a printer. To do this:

>S   **Type "/GB" to remove the spreadsheet borders (row and column labels).**
>S   **Type "/ODA1:H13,P".**
>S   **Press any key to continue.**
>S   **Type "/GB" to replace the spreadsheet borders if you wish to continue.**

If you wish to quit at this time:

>S   **Type "/QY" to quit using SuperCalc3.**

After the screen clears and the red in-use light has gone off, you may remove your disks and turn off the computer.

Part B - Calculating the Allowance for Uncollectible Accounts

If you saved your spreadsheet earlier and would now like to continue, use the procedures in Chapter 5 to retrieve your file.

Step 9 - Let's begin by entering the appropriate text and formatting for our calculation of the allowance for uncollectible accounts.

	In Cell	Enter text as follows
>S	A17	Age
>S	A19	Under 30 days old
>S	A20	31-60 days old
>S	A21	61-120 days old
>S	A22	Over 120 days
>S	A24	Total
>S	D17	Amount
>S	E15	Percent
>S	E16	Estimated
>S	E17	Uncoll.
>S	F16	Required
>S	F17	Allowance

>S   Type "/FE", "D15:F17,", "TR", and press the [enter] key to adjust your new headings in columns D, E, and F so that they are right-justified in each cell. (Don't forget the comma after specifying "D15:F17".)

>S   Enter dashed lines in rows 18 and 23 from column A through column F.

>S   Enter a double dashed line in cell F25.

Remember, the repeating command begins with an apostrophe (') and should be terminated with an apostrophe (') in a subsequent cell.

>S   Press the [Home] key to move the cursor to cell A1.

Your spreadsheet should now appear as in Exhibit 23-7. (You will need to scroll down to row 24 to see the bottom of the spreadsheet.)

Step 10 - Let's enter the total receivables for each age category in the column for the amount.

>S   Move the cursor to cell D19.

>S   In cell D19, enter the total from cell D12. Either type and enter "D12" in cell D19, or press the [Esc] key to activate the pointer, point to cell D12 and press the [enter] key.

>S   In cells D20, D21, and D22, enter the totals from cells E12, F12, and G12, respectively, using the same procedures.

Step 11 - Enter the percentages estimated to be uncollectible for each age category as given in the problem.

>S   **In cell E19, enter ".01".**
>S   **In cell E20, enter ".03".**
>S   **In cell E21, enter ".06".**
>S   **In cell E22, enter ".25".**

Note that percentages must be entered as decimals (.00).

Exhibit 23-7

	A	B	C	D	E	F	G	H
1				Lemhi Bearing Company				
2				Aging Schedule				
3								
4				Less than	31-60	61-120	More than	
5	Customer			30 days	days	days	120 days	Total
6	---	---	---	---	---	---	---	---
7	Chamberlain Mftg.			190000	30000	0	0	220000
8	Bargamin Distributors			92000	42000	14000	0	148000
9	Stibnite Products Co.			214000	62000	17000	0	293000
10	Tendoy Company, Inc.			0	16000	28000	42000	86000
11								
12	Total			496000	150000	59000	42000	747000
13				==
14								
15					Percent			
16					Estimated	Required		
17	Age			Amount	Uncoll.	Allowance		
18	---	---	---	---	---	---	---	---
19	Under 30 days old							
20	31-60 days old							
21	61-120 days old							
22	Over 120 days							
23	---	---	---	---	---	---	---	---
24	Total							
25						=========		

Step 12 - Calculate the required allowance for uncollectible accounts for each age category by multiplying the amount of receivables in each category by that category's percentage of estimated uncollectible accounts.

>S   **Move the cursor to cell F19.**
>S   **Enter "D19*E19" either by using the pointer or by typing and entering "D19*E19".**

Next, replicate the formula in cell F19 to cells F20 through F22 to compute the remaining uncollectible accounts provisions.

>S   **Make sure that your cursor is in cell F19.**
>S   **Type "/R" and press the [enter] key.**
>S   **Activate the pointer by pressing the [Esc] key and point to cell F20.**
>S   **Enter a colon (:) to indicate that this is the first cell in a range of cells that you wish to replicate to.**
>S   **Point to cell F22.**
>S   **Press the [enter] key.**

You should see the amounts for each row displayed on the screen.

Step 13 - Calculate the total required allowance for uncollectible accounts. That is, sum the amounts calculated for each of the respective age categories by using the sum function.

>S   **In cell F24, enter "SUM(F19:F22)" (or use the pointer to point out the appropriate range).**

The total in cell F24 should be the balance needed in the allowance for uncollectible accounts, which completes your aging schedule. Your schedule should appear as in Exhibit 23-8.

Step 14 - At this point, you may wish to **save** your work. Use the procedures given in Chapter 5 to save your work.

Printing: You might also want to print out the spreadsheet if your computer is connected to a printer. To do this:

>S   **Type "/GB" to remove the spreadsheet borders (row and column labels).**
>S   **Type "/ODA1:H25,P" to print the spreadsheet.**
>S   **Press any key and type "/GB" to replace the spreadsheet borders if you wish to continue.**

You may want to change your input data and see what effects these changes cause on the accounts receivable and allowance for uncollectible accounts balances. For example, change the percentage of estimated uncollectible accounts for 61-120 days old to 10 percent and see what this does to the required allowance for uncollectible accounts. Or, try changing the amount of accounts receivable for Chamberlain Mftg. to include $30,000 of accounts in the over 120 days age category.

If you wish to quit at this time:

>S   **Type "/QY" to quit using SuperCalc3.**

After the screen clears and the red in-use light has gone off, you may remove your disks and turn off the computer.

Exhibit 23-8

	A	B	C	D	E	F	G	H
1				Lemhi Bearing Company				
2				Aging Schedule				
3								
4				Less than	31-60	61-120	More than	
5	Customer			30 days	days	days	120 days	Total
6	--							
7	Chamberlain Mftg.			190000	30000	0	0	220000
8	Bargamin Distributors			92000	42000	14000	0	148000
9	Stibnite Products Co.			214000	62000	17000	0	293000
10	Tendoy Company, Inc.			0	16000	28000	42000	86000
11								
12	Total			496000	150000	59000	42000	747000
13				===				
14								
15					Percent			
16					Estimated	Required		
17	Age			Amount	Uncoll.	Allowance		
18	---							
19	Under 30 days old			496000	.01	4960		
20	31-60 days old			150000	.03	4500		
21	61-120 days old			59000	.06	3540		
22	Over 120 days			42000	.25	10500		
23	---							
24	Total					23500		
25						=========		

CHAPTER 24 - DISCOUNTING NOTES RECEIVABLE

Objective: This partially completed spreadsheet introduces the CALENDAR function and how it might be used in discounting notes receivable. The completed spreadsheet will enable you to determine the due date of the note receivable, and the length of time for which the note is held by both the original holder and by the bank at which the note is discounted. It will also calculate the proceeds from discounting the note receivable and the related interest income or interest expense.

Spreadsheet Name: DISCOUNT

Required Input Information: Before beginning, you should identify:

1. The face value of the note.
2. The number of days to the note's maturity.
3. The stated annual interest rate of the note.
4. The date on which the note is to be issued.
5. The date on which the note is to be discounted.
6. The bank's discount rate.
7. The formula for computing the maturity value of the note.
8. The formula for computing the bank's discount.

Using the Spreadsheet:

If you have not already done so, load SuperCalc3 into your computer following the instructions given in Part I.

Load the partially completed spreadsheet from the file disk in drive B.

>S   Enter "/L" followed by "B:DISCOUNT,A".

When the spreadsheet has finished loading, the screen display should appear similar to that shown in Exhibit 24-1.

You must now enter the required input information and complete the template. Partial instructions for completing the template are given below. (You may wish to refer to your textbook for certain formulas and relationships in order to complete the template.)

Problem:

George Sweeney currently holds a 120-day, 15 percent note receivable written by Frank Koch in the amount of $40,000. The note is dated October 7, 1986. On January 29, 1987, George decides to discount the note at the Como State Bank. On that date, the bank is charging a 16 percent discount rate on notes.

Required:

Determine the due date of the note and the impact of discounting the note on the interest income or expense to be reported.

Exhibit 24-1

```
      |    A    ||    B    ||    C    ||    D    ||    E    ||F ||  G
  1|      DISCOUNTING NOTES RECEIVABLE
  2|
  3| Face value of the note receivable ..........................................
  4| Number of days the note will be outstanding .................
  5| Stated interest rate of the note ............................................
  6| Date of issuance of the note ................................................
  7| Date of discounting the note ...............................................
  8| Bank discount rate ........................................................
  9| ******************************************************************************
 10|
 11| Calculation of the Due Date of the Note Receivable                  Calculat
 12| ------------------------------------------------------------------- ----------
 13| Date of issuance of the note                                        Maturity
 14| Number of days the note will be outstanding                         Less ban
 15|                                             ------------------
 16| Due date of the note                                                Proceeds
 17|                                             ============
 18| Number of Days holding the Note Receivable:
 19|    By original holder:                                              Calculat
 20|                                             ============ ----------
```

Completing the Spreadsheet:

Step 1 - Begin by entering the input information. The template is structured so that all of the required input information will be entered in column E *above* the row of asterisks (***). This will make it easier to use the template when we wish to change the inputs at a later time.

>S   In cell E3, enter $40,000.
>S   In cell E4, enter 120 days.
>S   In cell E5, enter 15% as the interest rate.
>S   In cell E6, enter "DAT(10,7,86)" for October 7, 1986.
>S   In cell E7, enter "DAT(1,29,87)" for January 29, 1987.
>S   In cell E8, enter 16% as the bank discount rate.

Dollar amounts should be entered without dollar signs or commas.

Enter percentages as decimals (for example, 15% equals .15).

When entering the dates of issuing and of discounting the note, use the calendar function. For example, type October 7, 1986 as "DAT(10,7,86)" and press the enter key. Note that if you attempt to enter 10/7/86, you will get the quotient .0166112957! Check to be sure that your dates are correctly entered in date format.

If you have correctly entered your data, then the input area of your screen should appear as in Exhibit 24-2.

Exhibit 24-2

	A	B	C	D	E
1	DISCOUNTING NOTES RECEIVABLE				
2					
3	Face value of the note receivable				40000
4	Number of days the note will be outstanding				120
5	Stated interest rate of the note				.15
6	Date of issuance of the note				10/ 7/1986
7	Date of discounting the note				1/29/1987
8	Bank discount rate				.16
9	**				

Step 2 - Now let's begin our calculations. First, let's determine the due date of the note.

>S   Move the cursor to cell E13.
>S   Enter the date of issuance of the note by either using the cursor to point to cell E6 in the input area, or by entering "E6". (Remember, the cursor can be activated as a pointer by pressing the [Esc] key.)
>S   Move the cursor to cell E14 and enter the number of days the note will be outstanding from cell E4 using the same procedures.
>S   Move the cursor to cell E16 and enter "E13+E14".

This adds the number of days the note will be outstanding to the issuance date. Note how the program provides you with the due date of the note in cell E16!

Step 3 - Next, let's calculate how long the original holder has held the note by subtracting the date of issuance from the date of discount.

>S   In cell E19, enter "E7-E6".

Step 4 - Now let's find out how long the bank will hold the note. This may be calculated by subtracting the date of discounting the note from the due date of the note (which we calculated in cell E16).

>S   **In cell E21, enter "E16-E7".**

At this point, columns A through E of your spreadsheet should appear as in Exhibit 24-3.

Exhibit 24-3

	A	B	C	D	E
1	DISCOUNTING NOTES RECEIVABLE				
2					
3	Face value of the note receivable				40000
4	Number of days the note will be outstanding				120
5	Stated interest rate of the note				.15
6	Date of issuance of the note				10/ 7/1986
7	Date of discounting the note				1/29/1987
8	Bank discount rate				.16
9	***				
10					
11	Calculation of the Due Date of the Note Receivable				
12	---				
13	Date of issuance of the note				10/ 7/1986
14	Number of days the note will be outstanding				120
15					-------------------
16	Due date of the note				2/ 4/1987
17					============
18	Number of Days holding the Note Receivable:				
19	By original holder:				114
20					============
21	By bank:				6
22					============
23					

Step 5 - Calculate the maturity value of the note by summing the face value of the note and the interest to be received at maturity.

>S   **In cell E26, enter the face value of the note by either using the cursor to point to cell E3 in the input area, or by entering "E3".**

>S   **In cell E27, enter the formula for the calculation of the interest on the note to its maturity date.**

Use (reference) the cells in the input area for the amount of principal, the interest rate, and the number of days the note will be outstanding. (For example, your formula might read "E3*E5*E4/360".)

(Note: You may wish to assume either a 360- or 365-day year for all calculations of interest. Alternatively, the length of year to be used could be added as an additional input variable. If you choose to have the length of year as a variable, simply insert a row at line 9 (type "/IR"), enter a description of the variable (for example, Number of days . . .) in cell A9 and enter the number of days you wish to use in cell E9. You may then reference cell E9 in your interest calculations. (*Note that if you insert a row, you will need to adjust the cell references (for cells outside of the input area) in the following instructions by one row.*)

>S   **In cell E29, enter "E26+E27" to sum the principal and interest.**

Step 6 - Calculate the book value of the note by summing the face value of the note and the interest accrued to the date of discount.

>S   **In cell E34, reference the face value of the note from the input area (for example, enter "E3").**
>S   **In cell E35, enter the formula for the calculation of the interest accrued on the note with appropriate references to the cells in the input area and your calculation of the number of days the note has been held.**
>S   **In cell E37, enter the sum of cells E34 and E35 to calculate the book value of the note.**

If you have performed these steps correctly, then the calculations of the maturity value and the book value of the note should appear as in Exhibit 24-4 (assuming a 360-day year).

Exhibit 24-4

	A	B	C	D	E
24	Calculation of the Maturity Value of the Note Receivable				
25	--				
26	Face value of the note				40000
27	Plus interest				2000
28					--------------------
29	Maturity value of the note receivable				42000
30					============
31					
32	Calculation of Book Value of the Note Receivable				
33	--				
34	Face value of the note				40000
35	Interest to date				1900
36					--------------------
37	Book value of the note receivable				41900
38					============

Step 7 - Let's calculate the proceeds from discounting the note by subtracting the bank discount from the maturity value of the note.

>S   Move the cursor over so that columns G through K, rows 11 through 17 are visible.

>S   Move the cursor to cell K13 and enter your previous calculation of the maturity value of the note by referencing the cell where you completed that calculation. (Hint: Activate the pointer and use it to find the cell containing the calculation of the maturity value of the note.)

>S   Then, in cell K14, calculate the bank's discount on the maturity value of the note by entering the discount formula, complete with references to the appropriate input cells.

>S   Move the cursor to cell K16 and enter "K13-K14" to calculate the net proceeds from discounting the note.

Step 8 - Finally, let's calculate the interest income or interest expense by subtracting the book value of the note receivable (calculated previously) from the proceeds from discounting the note receivable (which was just calculated).

>S   In cell K21, enter "K16", the proceeds from discounting the note.

>S   In cell K22, enter "E37", the book value of the note.

>S   In cell K24, enter "K21-K22" to calculate the interest income (expense).

If you have performed these steps correctly, then the calculations of the proceeds from discounting the note and the interest income or expense should appear as in Exhibit 24-5 (assuming a 360-day year). The negative number indicates that interest expense has been incurred!

Exhibit 24-5

	G	H	I	J	K
11|	Calculation of the Proceeds from Discounting the Note				
12|	--				
13|	Maturity value				42000
14|	Less bank discount				112
15|					--------------------
16|	Proceeds from discounting the note				41888
17|					============
18|					
19|	Calculation of Interest Income or Interest Expense				
20|	--				
21|	Proceeds from discounting the note				41888
22|	Less book value of the note receivable				41900
23|					--------------------
24|	Interest Income (Expense)				-12
25|					============

Step 9 - You may wish to "clean up" the appearance of your spreadsheet by changing the formats of certain locations to dollars and cents.

>S   **When you have completed any formatting, press the [Home] key to move the cursor to cell A1.**

Step 10 - At this point, you may wish to **save** your work. Use the procedures given in Chapter 5 to save your work.

You might also want to print the spreadsheet if your computer is connected to a printer. You must do this in two sections:

>S   **Type "/GB" to remove the spreadsheet borders (row and column headings).**
>S   **Type "/ODA1:E40,P" to print the inputs, the calculation of the due date, the calculation of the maturity value, and the calculation of the book value of the note receivable.**
>S   **Press any key to continue.**
>S   **Type "/ODG11:K25,P" to print the calculation of the proceeds and the calculation of interest income or interest expense.**
>S   **Press any key to continue.**
>S   **Type "/GB" to replace the spreadsheet borders if you wish to continue.**

Your spreadsheet should now be ready for you to manipulate the input data and study the effects that changes in the variables, particularly the date of discount, may have on the interest income or expense.

If you wish to quit at this point:

>S   **Type "/QY" to quit using SuperCalc3.**

After the screen clears and the red in-use light has gone off, you may remove your disks and turn off the computer.

CHAPTER 25 - BONDS PAYABLE WITH STRAIGHT-LINE AMORTIZATION

Objective: This partially completed spreadsheet uses the REPLICATE command extensively. It also illustrates how the PRESENT VALUE function might be used in calculating the selling price of a bond issue. The IF function is also introduced. The completed spreadsheet will enable you to determine the selling price (present value) of a bond issue and prepare a schedule of bond premium or discount amortization using the straight-line method. These calculations will provide you with the necessary information to prepare journal entries for each period's transactions.

Part A of the spreadsheet requires the computation of the bond premium or discount and the construction of an amortization schedule for four periods using the straight-line method. Part B asks you to incorporate the inputs needed to calculate the selling price of the bonds, in addition to calculating the bond premium or discount and to expand the amortization schedule to cover up to fifteen periods. These two parts may be worked *sequentially* at different times by saving the results of Part A.

Spreadsheet Name: SLBONDS

Required Input Information: Before beginning, you should identify:

1. The amount of bond principal.
2. The stated interest rate per period.
3. The effective interest rate per period.
4. The number of interest periods.
5. The selling price of the bond issue.

Using the Spreadsheet:

If you have not already done so, load SuperCalc3 into your computer following the instructions given in Part I.

Load the partially completed spreadsheet from the file disk in drive B.

>S   **Enter "/L" followed by "B:SLBONDS,A".**

When the spreadsheet has finished loading, the screen display should appear similar to that shown in Exhibit 25-1.

You must now enter the required input information and complete the template. Partial instructions for completing the template are given below. (You may wish to refer to your textbook for certain formulas and relationships in order to complete the template.)

190

Problem:

The Trinity Corporation issued $100,000 of 10%, 4-year bonds on January 1, 1986. These bonds sold for $93,925 to yield an effective interest of 12%. The company believes that the amount of premium or discount amortization calculated under the straight-line method will not be materially different from the amount which would be calculated using the effective interest method.

Required:

A.   Calculate the amount of any premium or discount on the bond issue and prepare a schedule of bond premium or discount amortization using the straight-line method.

B.   Expand the flexibility of your template to include the necessary inputs to compute the selling price of the bond issue and to cover fifteen time periods.

Exhibit 25-1

	A	B	C	D	E	F
1|	BONDS PAYABLE WITH STRAIGHT-LINE AMORTIZATION					
2							
3|	Amount of bond principal					
4|	Selling price of bond issue					
5|						---------------------
6|	Discount or (Premium) on Bond Issue					
7|						=============
8|	Schedule of Bond Premium or Discount Amortization					
9|	Straight-line Method					
10							
11|		Credit	Disc(Prem)	Interest	Unamort.	Carrying
12|	Period	Cash	Amortiz.	Expense	Disc(Prem)	Value
13|	---					
14							
15							
16							
17							
18							
19							
20							

Completing the Spreadsheet - Part A:

Step 1 - First, let's compute the amount of the premium or discount on the sale of the bond issue.

>S   **Move the cursor to cell F3 and enter $100,000, the amount of bond principal.**

(Remember to enter numbers without dollar signs and commas!)

>S   **In cell F4, enter $93,925, the selling price of the bond issue.**
>S   **Now, in cell F6, enter "F3-F4" to subtract the selling price of the bond issue from the amount of bond principal.**

You should get a discount of $6,075. Note that a discount displays as a positive number while a premium would display as a negative number.

Step 2 - Now we are ready to begin the schedule of bond premium or discount amortization by entering the beginning balances and calculating the first year's interest expense.

Step 2a - Begin by entering the initial account balances at the date of issuance of the bonds.

>S   **In cells A14 through A18, enter each period from 0 to 4, respectively.**

Zero represents the current date, or date of issuance of the bonds. Periods 1-4 represent the end of each year, or the date at which interest is paid.

Since row 14 represents the date of issuance, there is no credit to cash, no amortization and no interest expense.

>S   **In cells B14 through D14, enter zeroes (0). (Or, you may leave these cells blank.)**
>S   **Move the cursor to cell E14 and enter the unamortized balance of the bond discount by referencing cell F6.**

Remember, you can either type and enter "F6" in cell E14, or activate the cursor by pressing the [Esc] key, move the pointer to cell F6 and press the [enter] key.

>S   **Move the cursor to cell F14 and enter the initial carrying value of the bond issue by referencing the selling price of the bond in cell F4. Use the same procedures as in the previous step (or you can subtract the unamortized discount in cell E14 from the amount of bond principal in cell F3).**

Your spreadsheet should now appear similar to Exhibit 25-2.

Step 2b - Now let's calculate the interest expense for the first period.

>S   **In cell B15, enter "F3*.10" to calculate the amount of interest to be paid in cash.**

This amount is equal to the amount of bond principal multiplied times the stated interest rate. Our formula references the amount of bond principal in cell F3 and multiplies this amount by the stated rate of interest of .10. (Make sure that you enter the interest as a decimal and not as a percentage.) You should see 10000 displayed as the credit to cash.

>S   **Next, in cell C15, enter "F6/4" to calculate the straight-line amortization for each period.**

The periodic amortization is equal to the amount of the discount (in cell F6) divided by the life of the bond issue (4 years). You should see 1519 displayed as the amount of amortization.

>S   **Move the cursor to cell D15 and enter (or point) the formula "B15+C15".**

This formula sums the results of cells B15 and C15 to calculate the amount of interest expense for the first period, which is equal to the credit to cash plus the discount amortization. You should get $11,519 as the total interest expense for the first period.

Exhibit 25-2

	A	B	C	D	E	F
1	BONDS PAYABLE WITH STRAIGHT-LINE AMORTIZATION					
2						
3	Amount of bond principal					100000
4	Selling price of bond issue					93925
5						-------------------
6	Discount or (Premium) on Bond Issue					6075
7						=============
8	Schedule of Bond Premium or Discount Amortization					
9	Straight-line Method					
10						
11		Credit	Disc(Prem)	Interest	Unamort.	Carrying
12	Period	Cash	Amortiz.	Expense	Disc(Prem)	Value
13	--------					
14	0	0	0	0	6075	93925
15	1					
16	2					
17	3					
18	4					
19						
20						

Step 2c - Finally, let's calculate the balance of the unamortized discount and the carrying value of the bond issue to complete our calculations for the first period.

>S   **In cell E15, subtract the discount amortization in cell C15 from the unamortized discount in cell E14.**

The unamortized discount is equal to the initial discount less the amortization for the first period. Thus, we subtract the periodic amortization in cell C15 from the unamortized discount in cell E14. You should get $4,556 as the unamortized discount balance.

>S   **In cell F15, subtract the unamortized discount in cell E15 from the amount of bond principal in cell F3.**

The carrying value of the bond issue is equal to the amount of bond principal less the unamortized discount. You should get $95,444 for the carrying value of the bonds at the end of the first year.

Your spreadsheet should appear as in Exhibit 25-3.

Exhibit 25-3

	A	B	C	D	E	F
1|	BONDS PAYABLE WITH STRAIGHT-LINE AMORTIZATION					
2							
3|	Amount of bond principal					100000
4|	Selling price of bond issue					93925
5|						--------------------
6|	Discount or (Premium) on Bond Issue					6075
7|						=============
8|	Schedule of Bond Premium or Discount Amortization					
9|	Straight-line Method					
10							
11|		Credit	Disc(Prem)	Interest	Unamort.	Carrying
12|	Period	Cash	Amortiz.	Expense	Disc(Prem)	Value
13|	---					
14		0	0	0	0	6075	93925
15		1	10000	1519	11519	4556	95444
16		2					
17		3					
18		4					
19							
20							

Step 3 - Let's check our work before moving on.

>S   Move the cursor to each of the following cells and check to see that the formulas are correct. If they are not correct, reenter the correct formula before continuing.

	Cell	Formulas
>S	B15	F3*.10
>S	C15	F6/4
>S	D15	B15+C15
>S	E15	E14-C15
>S	F15	F3-E15

Step 4 - Now that you have established the formulas for calculating the credit to cash, the periodic amortization, the interest expense, the unamortized discount and the carrying value of the bonds for the first period, you can use these formulas as the basis for completing your schedule for periods 2 through 4.

Step 4a - Let's begin by replicating the formula used to calculate the amount of interest to be paid in cash at the end of period 1 to periods 2, 3 and 4.

>S   **Move your cursor to cell B15.**

Note that the first status line shows the formula in this cell to be "F3*.10". We want this exact same formula to be replicated for each period since the cash amount to be paid is the same in each period.

>S   **Type "/R".**
>S   **Press the [enter] key.**

Since you want to replicate the formula *from* cell B15, and your cursor is in that cell, pressing the [enter] key will result in cell B15 automatically being selected as the range to replicate *from*.

>S   **Activate the pointer by pressing the [Esc] key.**
>S   **Move the cursor to cell B16, the first cell in the range you wish to replicate *to*.**
>S   **Type a colon (:) to indicate that cell B16 is the first cell in a range of cells you wish to replicate *to*.**
>S   **Move the cursor to cell B18, the last cell in the range you wish to replicate *to*.**

(The third status line should now read "/Replicate,B15,B16:B18").

>S   **Type a comma (,) followed by "N" for no adjust (the term "no adjust" will be explained shortly).**

You should see 10000 displayed in each of the cells B16 through B18. If you move your cursor to any of these three cells, you should see the formula F3*.10 on the first status line. Your spreadsheet should now appear as in Exhibit 25-4.

Exhibit 25-4

	A	B	C	D	E	F
1		BONDS PAYABLE WITH STRAIGHT-LINE AMORTIZATION				
2						
3	Amount of bond principal					100000
4	Selling price of bond issue					93925
5						-------------------
6	Discount or (Premium) on Bond Issue					6075
7						=============
8		Schedule of Bond Premium or Discount Amortization				
9		Straight-line Method				
10						
11|		Credit	Disc(Prem)	Interest	Unamort.	Carrying
12	Period	Cash	Amortiz.	Expense	Disc(Prem)	Value
13	-------					
14	0	0	0	0	6075	93925
15	1	10000	1519	11519	4556	95444
16	2	10000				
17	3	10000				
18	4	10000				
19						
20						

Step 4b - We could continue to replicate each of the remaining formulas in each column of row 15. This would be tedious, however, if there were a large number of formulas to be replicated. A faster and more efficient method is to replicate several formulas, all at the same time! That is, you can replicate from a range of cells, not just from one cell!

Let's replicate the formulas in cells C15, D15, E15, and F15 to rows 16, 17 and 18 simultaneously.

>S   **Move the cursor to cell C15.**

This is the first cell in the range of cells we wish to replicate *from*.

>S   **Type "/R".**
>S   **Activate the cursor by pressing the [Esc] key.**

You should see C15 automatically display on the third status line.

>S   **Next, type a colon (:) to indicate that cell C15 is the first cell in a range of cells you wish to replicate *from*.**
>S   **Now, move your cursor to cell F15, the final cell in the range of cells you wish to replicate *from* and press the [enter] key.**

If you have done this correctly, the third status line should read "/Replicate,C15:F15," and the second status line should be prompting you for the range you wish to replicate *to*.

If you have made an error and the cursor is still active as a pointer, press the [Esc] key a second time to deactivate the pointer. You can then use the backspace key to eliminate the error and correct your entry.

>S   **Press the [Esc] key to activate the pointer so that you can point out the range you wish to replicate *to*.**

>S   **Move the cursor to cell C16, the first cell you wish to replicate *to*.**

>S   **Type a colon (:) to indicate that this is the first cell in the range of cells you wish to replicate *to*.**

>S   **Then, move the cursor to cell C18 to point out the last cell in the range of cells you wish to replicate *to*.**

>S   **Type a comma (,).**

Note that you did not have to point to cell F18, which would technically be the last cell to which you will be replicating. Since you are replicating *from* a range of cells in four columns (C through F), you need only point out the beginning of the range of rows (16 through 18) you wish to replicate *to*--the spreadsheet will then replicate the formulas from all four columns to each of the succeeding rows!

Now comes the difficult part--determining which cell references in each formula must be adjusted and which ones should not be adjusted.

>S   **Type "A" for ask for adjust.**

On the first status line, you will be prompted to specify whether cell F6 should be adjusted. Note that cell F6 is part of the formula in cell C15, which calculates the discount amortization. This formula is shown on the third status line for your reference.

Since we are using straight-line amortization, we want the formula to always refer to cell F6 (which contains the amount of discount) and divide this amount by 4.

>S   **Type "N" for no adjust to indicate that the reference to cell F6 should always stay the same and should not be adjusted.**

Next, you will be prompted to specify whether cell B15 should be adjusted. This cell is a part of the formula in cell D15, which calculates the total interest expense by adding together the credit to cash and the discount amortization. (The formula in cell D15 is shown on the third status line for your reference.)

Since the total interest expense in period 1 is the sum of cells B15 and C15, and in period 2 would be the sum of cells B16 and C16 (period 3 would be B17 and C17, etc.), we can see that the formula in D15 is relative to, or dependent upon, each succeeding row.

>S   **Type "Y" for yes adjust to have the reference to B15 adjusted to each succeeding row.**

You will then be prompted to specify whether to adjust cell C15 in the same formula.

>S   **For the same reasons as just discussed, type "Y" for yes adjust to have the reference to cell C15 adjusted to each succeeding row.**

Now you will be prompted to specify whether cell E14 should be adjusted. This cell is a part of the formula in cell E15, which calculates the balance of the unamortized discount by subtracting the current period's amortization of discount from the prior period's unamortized discount balance. (This formula is also shown on the third status line for your reference.)

Since the unamortized balance in period 1 is the difference of cells E14 and C15, and in period 2 would be the difference of cells E15 and C16 (period 3 would be E16 and C17, etc.), we can see that the formula in E15 is relative to each succeeding row.

>S   **Type "Y" for yes adjust to have the reference to E14 adjusted to each succeeding row.**

You will then be prompted to specify whether to adjust cell C15 in the same formula.

>S   **For the same reasons as just discussed, type "Y" for yes adjust to have the reference to cell C15 adjusted to each succeeding row.**

You are then prompted to specify whether cell F3 should be adjusted. This cell is a part of the formula in cell F15, which calculates the carrying value of the bond issue by subtracting the unamortized balance of the discount from the amount of principal of the bond issue. (The formula being replicated is again shown on the third status line for your reference.)

Since the carrying value of the bond issue in period 1 is the difference between cells F3 and E15, and in period 2 would be the difference between cells F3 and E16 (period 3 would be F3 and E17, etc.), we can see that the cell reference to F3 is not relative to each row.

>S   **Type "N" for no adjust to have the reference to F3 remain unadjusted in each succeeding row.**

You will then be prompted to specify whether to adjust cell E15 in the same formula. This cell reference, as shown above, is relative to each succeeding row.

>S   **Type "Y" for yes adjust to have the reference to cell E15 adjusted to each succeeding row.**

In summary, your responses to the prompts for adjustment should be:

Cell	Response
F6	N
B15	Y
C15	Y
E14	Y
C15	Y
F3	N
E15	Y

Your spreadsheet for Part A should now be completed and appear as in Exhibit 25-5!

Step 5 - You may wish to "clean up" the appearance of your spreadsheet by changing the formats of certain cells to dollars and cents. Refer to the earlier chapters for instructions on formatting cells.

>S   **After completing your formatting, press the [Home] key to move the cursor to cell A1.**

Step 6 - At this point, you may wish to **save** your work. Use the procedures given in Chapter 5 to save your work.

Printing: You might also want to print the spreadsheet if your computer is connected to a printer.

>S   **Type "/GB" to remove the spreadsheet borders (row and column headings).**
>S   **Type "/ODA1:F18,P" to print the spreadsheet.**
>S   **Press any key to continue.**
>S   **Type "/GB" to replace the spreadsheet borders if you wish to continue.**

If you wish to quit at this time:

>S   **Type "/QY" to quit using SuperCalc3.**

After the screen clears and the red in-use light has gone off, you may remove your disks and turn off the computer.

Exhibit 25-5

	A	B	C	D	E	F
1	BONDS PAYABLE WITH STRAIGHT-LINE AMORTIZATION					
2						
3	Amount of bond principal					100000
4	Selling price of bond issue					93925
5						--------------------
6	Discount or (Premium) on Bond Issue					6075
7						=============
8	Schedule of Bond Premium or Discount Amortization					
9	Straight-line Method					
10						
11		Credit	Disc(Prem)	Interest	Unamort.	Carrying
12	Period	Cash	Amortiz.	Expense	Disc(Prem)	Value
13	--					
14	0	0	0	0	6075	93925
15	1	10000	1519	11519	4556	95444
16	2	10000	1519	11519	3038	96963
17	3	10000	1519	11519	1519	98481
18	4	10000	1519	11519	0	100000
19						
20						

Completing the Spreadsheet - Part B:

If you saved your spreadsheet earlier and would now like to continue, use the procedures in Chapter 5 to retrieve your file.

You will rapidly discover that the only inputs which we can presently change in our spreadsheet are the amount of bond principal and the selling price of the bonds. This is not a very efficient application of the capabilities of the spreadsheet. What we would prefer to have is a spreadsheet which is capable of handling not only different amounts of bond principal and selling prices, but different interest rates and different time periods as well. In fact, it would be nice if the spreadsheet also calculated the selling price of the bond issue for us! So let's modify our spreadsheet to do just that!

Step 7 - Begin by inserting ten rows between the spreadsheet heading and the amount of bond prinicipal to give us room for the additional inputs and calculations.

>S   **Place the cursor in the second row.**
>S   **Type "/I" for insert, followed by "R" for row.**
>S   **When you are prompted to enter a row range, type "2:11" and press the [enter] key.**

Ten blank rows will be inserted, beginning in row 2. Note that your original calculations are still present, but that they have been "pushed" ten rows farther down the spreadsheet.

Step 8 - Enter the following labels in the corresponding cells:

	Cell	Label
>S	A3	**Amount of principal**
>S	A4	**Stated interest rate**
>S	A5	**Effective interest rate**
>S	A6	**Number of interest periods**
>S	A7	
>S	A8	**Present value of interest payments equals**
>S	A9	**Present value of principal equals**
>S	A10	
>S	A11	**Selling price of bonds payable equals**

Step 9 - Enter the following values for the amount of principal, stated interest rate, effective interest rate, and number of interest periods in the corresponding cells.

	Cell	Amount
>S	F3	$100,000
>S	F4	.10
>S	F5	.12
>S	F6	4

These four values represent the inputs for our revised spreadsheet.

When you attempt to enter the interest rates as decimals (which is correct), you will see zeroes (0) on the screen. This is because the spreadsheet is rounding to the nearest whole number. In order to display the decimals, you will need to format cells F4 and F5.

>S   **Move the cursor to cell F4 and type "/F" for format, followed by "E" for entry.**

>S   **Press the [Esc] key to activate the pointer and point out the two cells you wish to reformat (F4 and F5) and press the [enter] key.**

>S   **In response to the prompt to define the format, type either "G" for general, which will display all significant digits, or a dollar sign "$", which will always display two digits to the right of the decimal.**

>S   **Press the [enter] key and you should see the decimals displayed.**

Step 10 - Now let's calculate the selling price of the bonds payable. The selling price is equal to the present value of the bonds, which is comprised of two components--the present value of the interest payments and the present value of the bond principal. Let's calculate these two values in cells F8 and F9.

Step 10a - Let's calculate the present value of the interest payments first:

>S   **In cell F8, enter "PV(" to begin using the present value function.** *(This is PV followed by a left-hand parenthesis.)*

The present value function calculates the present value of an ordinary annuity, such as a series of equal interest payments. The function requires that we specify the amount of each periodic payment, the interest rate, and the number of periods. This data is available through our inputs.

Since our inputs do not include the amount of the interest payments, we will have to calculate this value.

>S   **Press the [Esc] key to activate the pointer and point to cell F3, which contains the amount of principal.**

>S   **Type an asterisk (*) to indicate multiplication and then point to cell F4, which contains the stated interest rate.**

>S   **Press a comma (,) to continue.**

Your function, as shown on the third status line, should now read "PV(F3*F4,".

>S   **Next, point to cell F5, which contains the effective interest rate.**

>S   **Press a comma (,) to continue.**

The function, as shown on the third status line, should now read "PV(F3*F4,F5,".

>S   **Finally, point to cell F6, which contains the number of interest periods. Type the right-hand parenthesis ")" and press the [enter] key.**

Your function should read "PV(F3*F4,F5,F6)" and you should see 30373 as the present value of the interest payments displayed in cell F8.

Step 10b - Now let's find the present value of the bond principal. Unfortunately, there is no function in the program which can be used to directly calculate the present value of a single payment, such as the repayment of principal. There are several alternative approaches to this calculation, one of which is to resort to the mathematical formula for this calculation. This formula is:

$$\frac{\text{Principal}}{(1 + \text{the interest rate})^n}$$

where n = the number of time periods.

>S   **Move the cursor to cell F9, type "F3/(1+F5)**F6" and press the [enter] key.**

Remember, cell F3 is the amount of principal, cell F5 is the effective interest rate, and cell F6 is the number of time periods. The double asterisk means that the quantity inside the parentheses will be raised to the power indicated by cell F6. You should see 63552 displayed in cell F9.

Step 10c - In order to finish calculating the selling price of the bonds, we need to sum the present values of the interest and the principal.

>S   **Move the cursor to cell F11 and sum cells F8 and F9.**

You should get the same selling price as was given earlier in the problem ($93,925).

>S   **Move the cursor to cell F10 and place a dashed line beneath the two present values which are being summed. Remember, the repeating text command begins by typing a single quote mark (').**

>S   **Move the cursor to cell F12 and place a double dashed line beneath the total selling price.**

>S   **Press the [Home] key to move the cursor to cell A1.**

Your spreadsheet should now appear as in Exhibit 25-6.

Step 11 - Let's make one final change before modifying the amortization schedule. In rows 13 through 17, we have a calculation of the bond discount or premium. Let's change the amounts used in that calculation to reference our inputs and calculation of the present value.

>S   **In cell F13, replace the dollar amount with a reference to cell F3, the cell which contains the amount of principal.**

>S   **In cell F14, replace the dollar amount with a reference to cell F11, the calculation of the selling price of the bonds.**

Now our calculation of the discount or premium will automatically incorporate any changes we make in the input data.

>S   **For example, change the stated rate of interest in cell F4 to .09. The selling price of the bonds should now be $90,888 and the amount of discount should be $9,112.**

>S   **Return to the original data (stated interest = .10) and let's continue.**

Exhibit 25-6

	A	B	C	D	E	F
1	BONDS PAYABLE WITH STRAIGHT-LINE AMORTIZATION					
2						
3	Amount of principal					100000
4	Stated interest rate					.10
5	Effective interest rate					.12
6	Number of interest periods					4
7						
8	Present value of interest payments equals					30373
9	Present value of principal equals					63552
10						--------------------
11	Selling price of bonds payable equals					93925
12						==============
13	Amount of bond principal					100000
14	Selling price of bond issue					93925
15						--------------------
16	Discount or (Premium) on Bond Issue					6075
17						==============
18	Schedule of Bond Premium or Discount Amortization					
19	Straight-line Method					
20						

Step 12 - Now we need to see what effects changing our inputs will have on our amortization schedule. Scroll down so that the entire amortization schedule is displayed.

Step 12a - Obviously, four periods is not very many, so let's increase the number of periods to fifteen. We could start this in column A by continuing to enter values for periods 5, 6, 7, . . . 15. There is a faster way to do this, however. Let's enter a formula and replicate it.

>S   Move the cursor to cell A25 (period 1).
>S   Enter "A24+1" in this cell.

Note that while we now have a formula in cell A25, the display is still the number 1.

>S   With the cursor in cell A25, type "/R" and press the [enter] key to indicate that we would like to replicate from this cell.
>S   Then, point out the range of cells we would like to replicate to (A26 through A39) and press the [enter] key to allow for automatic adjustment of the formula .

You should see the numbers 2 through 15 added to the display in column A.

Step 12b - Next, let's replicate our formula for the cash interest to be paid from cell B25. However, first we need to change this formula to reflect our inputs. It should be F3*F4 (the amount of principal times the stated rate of interest).

>S   In cell B25, enter "F3*F4" to calculate the cash credit.
>S   With the cursor in cell B25, type "/R" and press the [enter] key.
>S   Type "B26:B39" as the range of cells to replicate to.
>S   Type a comma (,) followed by "N" for no adjust.

Remember that this formula has a fixed reference to cells F3 and F4. Thus, instead of pressing the [enter] key after you have pointed out the range to replicate to, you should have typed a comma followed by "N" for no adjust.

You should see 10000 displayed in cells B25 through B39. This is, unfortunately, incorrect given our inputs. Remember that our bond issue has a life of only four periods. Thus, the interest should be $10,000 in each of periods one through four, but thereafter it should be zero. To correct this problem, we can use the IF function. This function will allow us to check whether or not we have exceeded the life of the bonds, after which the interest to be paid is zero. Thus, if the period is greater than that given in cell F6 (4 periods in our problem), then the amount in column B should be zero.

>S   In cell B25, enter "IF(A25>F6,0,F3*F4)".

This is interpreted as "if the period as given in cell A25 is greater than the number of interest periods given in cell F6, then set the interest to be paid at zero; otherwise set the interest to be paid equal to the amount of principal (cell F3) times the stated interest rate (cell F4)."

>S   With the cursor in cell B25, type "/R" and press the [enter] key.
>S   Type "B26:B39" as the range of cells to replicate to.
>S   Type a comma (,) followed by "A" for ask for adjust.

Note that cell A25 should be relative to each successive row; that is, we want to compare A25 with F6, A26 with F6, A27 with F6, etc. Make sure that you enter "Y" to adjust cell A25. The remaining variables are all input variables and are fixed and should not be adjusted regardless of the row. If done correctly, your schedule should now appear as in Exhibit 25-7.

Step 12c - We have a similar problem with the formula to calculate the amortization for each period. Updating our formula for the new inputs gives us F16/F6 instead of F16/4. However, if we replicate this formula, the schedule will compute amortization in every period, even after the bond principal has been repaid.

>S   In cell C25, enter "IF(A25>F6,0,F16/F6)" to calculate the periodic amortization.
>S   With the cursor in cell C25, type "/R" and press the [enter] key.
>S   Type "C26:C39" as the range of cells to replicate to.
>S   Type a comma (,) followed by "A" for ask for adjust.

Note again, that A25 is relative to each successive row but that F6 and F16 are fixed relative to each row and should not be adjusted.

Exhibit 25-7

	A	B	C	D	E	F
18|	Schedule of Bond Premium or Discount Amortization					
19|		Straight-line Method				
20|						
21|		Credit	Disc(Prem)	Interest	Unamort.	Carrying
22|	Period	Cash	Amortiz.	Expense	Disc(Prem)	Value
23|	--------	-------	---------	--------	----------	--------
24|	0	0	0	0	6075	93925
25|	1	10000	1519	11519	4556	95444
26|	2	10000	1519	11519	3037	96963
27|	3	10000	1519	11519	1519	98481
28|	4	10000	1519	11519	0	100000
29|	5	0				
30|	6	0				
31|	7	0				
32|	8	0				
33|	9	0				
34|	10	0				
35|	11	0				
36|	12	0				
37|	13	0				
38|	14	0				
39|	15	0				

Step 12d - The remaining three columns calculating interest expense, the unamortized discount balance and the carrying value of the bond issue require no adjustment before replicating. Let's replicate all three columns at one time.

>S   Place the cursor in cell D25 and enter "/R".

>S   Activate the cursor by pressing the [Esc] key, point out the range from cell D25 through cell F25, and type a comma (,).

>S   Next, activate the cursor and point out the range you wish to replicate to--cell D26 through cell D39.

>S   Type a comma (,) and "A" for ask for adjust.

>S   Enter the appropriate responses to indicate whether to adjust or not adjust each cell reference. (All of the cell references should be adjusted except for the reference to cell F13 in the formula contained in cell F25.)

The carrying value of the bonds will increase to $100,000 in the fourth period. Unfortunately, this value continues into the fifth, sixth, and all future periods. Again, you may use an IF function to eliminate this problem.

>S   **In cell F25, enter "IF(A25>F6,0,F13-E25)".**
>S   **Replicate this command to cells F26 through F39.**

Note that the references to cells A25 and E25 are relative and should be adjusted, while the references to cells F6 and F13 are fixed and should not be adjusted.

Your amortization schedule is now completed and should appear as shown in Exhibit 25-8.

Exhibit 25-8

	A	B	C	D	E	F
18|	Schedule of Bond Premium or Discount Amortization					
19|		Straight-line Method				
20							
21|		Credit	Disc(Prem)	Interest	Unamort.	Carrying
22|	Period	Cash	Amortiz.	Expense	Disc(Prem)	Value
23| ----						
24		0	0	0	0	6075	93925
25		1	10000	1519	11519	4556	95444
26		2	10000	1519	11519	3037	96963
27		3	10000	1519	11519	1519	98481
28		4	10000	1519	11519	0	100000
29		5	0	0	0	0	0
30		6	0	0	0	0	0
31		7	0	0	0	0	0
32		8	0	0	0	0	0
33		9	0	0	0	0	0
34		10	0	0	0	0	0
35		11	0	0	0	0	0
36		12	0	0	0	0	0
37		13	0	0	0	0	0
38		14	0	0	0	0	0
39		15	0	0	0	0	0

Step 13 - You may wish to "clean up" the appearance of your spreadsheet by changing the formats of certain cells to dollars and cents, etc. Refer to the earlier chapters for instructions on formatting cells.

>S   **When you have completed any formatting, press the [Home] key to move the cursor to cell A1.**

__Step 14__ - At this point, you may wish to **save** your work. Use the procedures given in Chapter 5 to save your work.

__Printing:__ You might also want to print the spreadsheet if your computer is connected to a printer.

>S   **Type "/GB" to remove the spreadsheet borders (row and column headings).**
>S   **Type "/ODA1:F39,P" to print the spreadsheet.**
>S   **Press any key and type "/GB" to replace the spreadsheet borders if you wish to continue.**

Your spreadsheet should now be ready for you to manipulate the input data and study the effects that changes in the variables may have on the selling price of the bond issue and the amount of interest to be paid and expensed in each period.

If you wish to quit at this time:

>S   **Type "/QY" to quit using SuperCalc3.**

After the screen clears and the red in-use light has gone off, you may remove your disks and turn off the computer.

CHAPTER 26 - DIVIDEND DISTRIBUTION SCHEDULE

Objective: This partially completed spreadsheet illustrates the use of several logic functions. It demonstrates how the IF function and the MINIMUM function might be used in calculating the dividends to be received by each class of stock, preferred and common, when the total amount to be distributed has been set. The completed spreadsheet may also be used to determine the overall percentage dividend received by each class of stock.

Spreadsheet Name: DIVVY

Required Input Information: Before beginning, you should identify:

1. The dollar amount of preferred stock and common stock.
2. The preferred stock dividend rate as a percentage (.00).
3. The limit of preferred stock participation (.00).
4. Whether or not the preferred stock is cumulative.
5. How many years the preferred stock dividend is in arrears.
6. The total dividends to be distributed to the preferred and common stock.

Using the Spreadsheet:

If you have not already done so, load SuperCalc3 into your computer following the instructions given in Part I.

Load the partially completed spreadsheet from the file disk in drive B.

>S   Enter "/L" followed by "B:DIVVY,A".

When the spreadsheet has finished loading, the screen display should appear similar to that shown in Exhibit 26-1.

You must now enter the required input information and complete the template. Partial instructions for completing the template are given below. (You may wish to refer to your textbook for certain formulas and relationships in order to complete the template.)

Problem:

Seminole Distributors, Inc. has the following stock outstanding:

9% Preferred Stock, $100 par value, noncumulative and
   participating to 15%, 4,000 shares authorized,
   2,000 shares issued and outstanding $200,000

Common Stock, $10 par value, 100,000 shares authorized,
   80,000 shares issued and outstanding $800,000

The company wishes to issue the remaining preferred stock next year and will pay $100,000 in cash dividends this year to the preferred and common stockholders. The dividend on the preferred stock is one year in arrears.

Required:

A.   Prepare a schedule to compute the total dividends to be received by each class of stock from the current year's distribution.

B.   Assuming that the company issues the additional preferred stock next year, what amount of dividends will it have to pay if management wishes to maintain the same percentage dividend to the common stockholders as was paid this year?

C.   What difference would it make in each year's distributions if the preferred stock were cumulative?

Exhibit 26-1

	A	B	C	D	E	F
1|	DIVIDEND DISTRIBUTION SCHEDULE					
2|				Preferred	Common	Total
3|				Stock	Stock	Dollars
4|				---------	---------	---------
5|	Par value of stock			200000	800000	
6|				===========================		
7|	Preferred stock dividend (.00)			.09		
8|	Limit of P.S. participation (.00)			.15		
9|	P.S. cumulative? (1=Yes, 0=No)			0		
10|	Number of years in arrears			1		
11|	Amount of dividends to be distributed					100000
12|						============
13							
14|				Amount distributed to:		
15|				---		
16|				Preferred	Common	Yet to be
17|				Stock	Stock	Distributed
18|				---		
19|	Total amount to be distributed			N/A	N/A	100000
20|	P.S. dividends in arrears					

Completing the Spreadsheet - Part A:

Step 1 - After loading the spreadsheet, you will see that the data given in the problem has already been entered. The first step in completing the spreadsheet is to calculate the total par value of the preferred and common stock. This total will be needed later in the distribution schedule.

>S   **Move the cursor to cell F5 and add the corresponding amounts in cells D5 and E5. Either enter "D5+E5" or activate the pointer by pressing the [Esc] key and using the pointer to help enter the formula.**

Step 2 - Now let's begin working on the amounts to be distributed to each class of stock. Let's calculate the amount to be paid to preferred stock for dividends in arrears.

>S   **Move the cursor to cell D20.**

We need to consider two conditions before we enter a formula in this cell.

First, we must find a way to evaluate whether or not the preferred stock is cumulative. If it is noncumulative, then any dividends in arrears are irrelevant and the cell should display a zero. Alternatively, if the preferred stock is cumulative, then the cell should display the dividends to be paid. We can accomplish this using the IF function.

Second, if the stock is cumulative, we still need to determine whether or not the full amount in arrears will be paid. For example, even if the stock is cumulative and there are dividends in arrears, nothing will be paid if no dividends have been declared. We can evaluate this using the MIN function.

The IF and the MIN functions will be "nested" together as one large formula as described below.

Let's examine the IF function in more detail. What we would like is a function which will enable us to select the correct amount from the following two statements:

(A) If the preferred stock is noncumulative, display zero.
(B) If the preferred stock is cumulative, display the amount of dividends in arrears.

If we use a *zero* in cell D9 to indicate that the stock is noncumulative, and a *one* in cell D9 to indicate that the stock is cumulative, then we can accomplish this by using the following function:

      IF(D9=0,0,D5*D7*D10)

This function can be interpreted as follows: If the value in cell D9 equals zero (which indicates that the stock is noncumulative), then display zero; otherwise display the value D5 times D7 times D10 (amount of par value times the dividend rate times the number of years in arrears). Thus, if the value in cell D9 is anything else but zero, the function assumes that the stock is cumulative and calculates and displays the amount of dividends in arrears.

However, as mentioned, we have one further problem. If no dividends have been declared, or if an amount less than the total dividends in arrears has been declared, then the total arrearage cannot be paid. Thus, we need to compare the amount of dividends in arrears with the amount to be paid and choose the lesser of the two values.

For example, if dividends in arrears are $10,000, but no dividends have been declared (cell F11=0), choose zero as the amount to be paid. Alternatively, if dividends in arrears are $10,000, and dividends of $20,000 have been declared, choose $10,000 as the amount to be paid.

This can be done by comparing the results of our IF function with the amount of dividends yet to be distributed (shown in cell F19) and choosing the minimum value. This is shown in the "nested" formula below:

>S   **In cell D20, enter "MIN(F19,IF(D9=0,0,D5*D7*D10))".**

Cell D20 should display a zero. In order to ensure that your formula works, let's temporarily change some of the input data.

>S   **Move the cursor to cell D9 and change the zero (0) to one (1) to indicate that the stock is now cumulative.**

You should now get $18,000 in cell D20--one year's dividend arrearage!

>S   **Move the cursor to cell F11 and enter $10,000 instead of $100,000.**

You should now get $10,000 in cell D20--despite the fact that the dividend arrearage is $18,000, only $10,000 can be paid since that is all that has been declared!

>S   **Reenter the original data ($100,000 of dividends in cell F11 and zero (0) in cell D9) and let's continue.**

Step 3 - Next, let's determine the amount of dividends yet to be distributed after any dividends in arrears on preferred stock are paid.

>S   **Move to cell E20. Since the common stock is not cumulative, enter "N/A" for Not Applicable.**
>S   **Format cell E20 to right-hand justify the text in the cell. (Remember, type "/FE", press the [enter] key to select cell E20, type "TR" for text right and press the [enter] key.)**
>S   **Then in cell F20, subtract the amount of dividends in arrears from the previous amount yet to be distributed (enter, or use the pointer to enter, the formula "F19-D20").**

You should see 100000 displayed since the preferred stock is noncumulative and we are subtracting zero from 100000.

>S   **To check your formula, move to cell D9, enter one (1), and see what happens. You should see 82000 displayed in cell F20.**
>S   **If your answer is correct, reenter a zero (0) in cell D9 and let's continue.**

Step 4 - Now let's calculate the current year's preferred stock dividend. This is not simply the par value of the preferred stock times the dividend rate. Remember again that we must also check to see that there is an adequate amount of dividends yet to be distributed to pay the current year dividend. You can use the MIN function again to do this.

>S   **Move the cursor to cell D21 and enter "MIN(F20,D5*D7)".**

       You should get $18,000 in cell D21.

>S   **To check your formula, move the cursor to cell F11, enter $10,000, and see what happens. You should get $10,000 in cell D21. If correct, reenter $100,000 and continue.**

Step 5 - Let's calculate the amount of dividends yet to be distributed.

>S   **Since the common stock is still not entitled to any dividends, enter "N/A" in cell E21 and format it for text right to right-hand justify this entry (or, instead, replicate the entry from cell E20 to E21).**
>S   **Then, in cell F21, subtract the amount of current dividends (cell D21) from the previous amount yet to be distributed (cell F20).**

       You should see 82000 displayed.

       The distribution schedule of your spreadsheet (in rows 14 through 30) should now appear similar to that shown in Exhibit 26-2.

Exhibit 26-2

	A	B	C	D	E	F
14				Amount distributed to:		
15				----------------------------------		------------------
16				Preferred	Common	Yet to be
17				Stock	Stock	Distributed
18				----------------------------------		------------------
19	Total amount to be distributed			N/A	N/A	100000
20	P.S. dividends in arrears			0	N/A	100000
21	Current P.S. dividends			18000	N/A	82000
22	C.S. dividend to match current P.S...					
23	Participating dividend					
24	Remainder to common stock					
25				----------------------------------		============
26	Total distributed					
27				=======================		
28						
29	Percentage dividend (current year)					
30				=======================		

Step 6 - Now we can calculate the first part of the dividend on the common stock. The common stock is entitled to receive a dividend equivalent to the current preferred stock dividend before any additional participation of the preferred stock needs to be considered.

>S   Move the cursor to cell D22 and enter "N/A" since the preferred stock already has been allocated its current dividend. Format this cell text right.

>S   Move the cursor to cell E22 and enter "MIN(F21,E5*D7)".

You should see 72000. The MIN function is used once again to ensure that the distribution does not exceed the cash yet to be distributed, which is shown in cell F21. The formula E5*D7 calculates a dividend for the common stock which matches the preferred stock dividend on a percentage basis.

Step 7 - Calculate the amount of dividends yet to be distributed.

>S   Move the cursor to cell F22.

>S   Enter a formula to calculate the dividends yet to be distributed.

You should get $10,000 as the amount yet to be distributed.

Step 8 - Now comes the hard part--determining how much of the dividends yet to be distributed that each class of stock should receive under the participation feature! Remember that (in this problem) each class of stock will participate equally (on a percentage of par basis) up to 15%, after which the common stock will be entitled to any remaining dividends.

>S   Move the cursor to cell D23.

>S   In cell D23, enter "IF(F22>=(D8-D7)*F5,(D8-D7)*D5,F22*D5/F5)".

You should get $2,000 in cell D23.

This formula means "if the amount yet to be distributed (cell F22) is greater than or equal to 6% (15% in cell D8 - 9% in cell D7) of the total par value (cell F5), then allocate 6% of the preferred par value (cell D5) to the preferred stock, otherwise allocate the amount yet to be distributed (cell F22) in the proportion of the preferred par value to the total par value (cell D5/cell F5).

A problem arises with this formula, however. What happens if the preferred stock is nonparticipating? That is, if the participation limit is zero (0) percent?

>S   Move the cursor to cell D8 and enter a zero (0).

What result is displayed in cell D23? You should get a negative $18,000, hardly the correct result!

This is because the difference between the preferred stock dividend (cell D7, which is now 9%) and the participation limit (cell D8, which is currently .00) is a negative number (.00 minus .09 = -.09). This is a nonsensical result and can be eliminated by nesting our first IF function inside a second IF function.

To do this, let's edit our entry in cell D23.

>S   **With the cursor in cell D23, type "/E" for edit and press the [enter] key to select the current cell (D23) for editing.**

The formula will now be shown on the third status line for editing. The edit cursor should be flashing at the end of the formula.

>S   **Add a second right-hand parenthesis to the end of the equation by simply typing ")".**

>S   **Now, using the left arrow key, carefully move the flashing cursor to the left until it is located beneath the I in IF.**

(If you move the cursor too far to the left, you will be unceremoniously dumped from edit mode. If this happens, begin editing again as described above. If you accidentally press the [enter] key, your entry will be interpreted as text because of the extra right-hand parenthesis. Because of this, you will need to delete the double quote mark (") at the beginning of the formula (which indicates text rather than a formula) when you reenter the edit function. Move the cursor to this character and press the [Del] key once. Then resume editing.)

>S   **Next, press the [Ins] key once in order to insert additional characters in the formula rather than typing over the existing formula.**

>S   **Enter "IF(D8-D7<=0,0,".**

The formula shown on the third status line should now read:

IF(D8-D7<=0,0,IF(F22>=(D8-D7)*F5,(D8-D7)*D5,F22*D5/F5))

If you make errors in editing, you can press the [Del] key to eliminate any unwanted characters. When you are satisfied that your equation is correct:

>S   **Press the [enter] key and the edited formula will be entered in cell D23.**

If cell D8 still contains zero (0), you should see zero (0) display in cell D23.

>S   **If your display is incorrect, either reenter edit and make the necessary corrections, or enter the entire formula over again in cell D23.**

>S   **When correct, move the cursor back to cell D8 and enter 15% to continue.**

<u>Step 9</u> - We can use this same equation for the common stock calculation in cell E23. Rather than retyping this lengthy formula, use the replicate function.

Before beginning to replicate, however, examine the formula in cell D23 to see which cells are fixed with respect to each column and which are relative to each column.   You should find that all of the cells referenced are fixed (no change) except for cell D5, which should be adjusted to cell E5 during the replication.

>S   With the cursor in cell D23, type "/R" and press the [enter] key to select cell D23 as the only cell in the range you wish to replicate from.

>S   Activate the pointer by pressing the [Esc] key, point to cell E23 and type a comma (,).

>S   Respond to the prompt on the second status line by typing "A" for ask for adjust.

You will then be prompted to specify whether or not to adjust each cell reference in the formula.

>S   Respond to all of the prompts by typing "N" except for when the cell reference is cell D5. (cell D5 will appear twice--respond each time by typing "Y".)

If done correctly, you should get $2,000 in cell D23 and $8,000 in cell E23.   If incorrect, you could either try replicating again, or editing the formula in cell E23, or you could type the entire formula, as adjusted for column E, in cell E23.

Step 10 - Calculate the amount of dividends yet to be distributed. This time we need to deduct both a preferred stock amount (cell D23) and a common stock amount (cell E23) from the previous amount yet to be distributed (in cell F22).

>S   Move the cursor to cell F23 and enter the appropriate formula to calculate the dividends yet to be distributed.

You should get zero (0) as the display in cell F23 after entering the formula.

The distribution schedule of your spreadsheet (in rows 14 through 30) should now appear as shown in Exhibit 26-3.

Step 11 - The final distribution is for the remainder yet to be distributed.   The common stock is entitled to all of this distribution.

>S   In cell D24, enter "N/A".

>S   In cell E24, enter "F23" since the remainder to be distributed to the common stock should be equal to the amount yet to be distributed.

>S   In cell F24, subtract the distribution of the remainder (cell E24) from the amount yet to be distributed (cell F23).

(This final total in cell F24 should always be zero!)

Exhibit 26-3

	A	B	C	D	E	F
				Amount distributed to:		
14						
15						
16				Preferred	Common	Yet to be
17				Stock	Stock	Distributed
18						
19	Total amount to be distributed			N/A	N/A	100000
20	P.S. dividends in arrears			0	N/A	100000
21	Current P.S. dividends			18000	N/A	82000
22	C.S. dividend to match current P.S...			N/A	72000	10000
23	Participating dividend			2000	8000	0
24	Remainder to common stock					
25						
26	Total distributed					
27						
28						
29	Percentage dividend (current year)					
30						

Step 12 - Let's calculate the total amount of dividends to be received by each class of stock.

>S   In cell D26, total the preferred stock dividends in cells D20 through D24 by entering "SUM(D20:D24)". You may wish to use the pointer to do this.

>S   In cell E26, enter the corresponding formula to total the common stock dividends. You may wish to replicate the formula from cell D26 for this calculation.

Don't worry about adding in the N/A's--the spreadsheet will interpret these cells as zeroes (0) and your total will still be correct! You should get $20,000 for the preferred stock and $80,000 for the common stock.

Step 12 - Finally, let's calculate the percentage dividend received by each class of stock for the current year.

>S   In cell D29, enter "(D26-D20)/D5" to compute the percentage dividend received by the preferred stock.

This formula deducts any dividends in arrears from the total dividend in order to get the current year's dividend and divides this amount by the par value of the preferred stock. You should get .1 or 10%.

>S   In cell E29, enter "E26/E5" to compute the percentage dividend received by the common stock. This formula should also result in .1 or 10%.

The completed distribution schedule of your spreadsheet should now appear similar to Exhibit 26-4.

Exhibit 26-4

	A	B	C	D	E	F
1|	DIVIDEND DISTRIBUTION SCHEDULE					
2|				Preferred	Common	Total
3|				Stock	Stock	Dollars
4					---
5|	Par value of stock			200000	800000	1000000
6					==
7|	Preferred stock dividend (.00)			.09		
8|	Limit of P.S. participation (.00)			.15		
9|	P.S. cumulative? (1=Yes, 0=No)			0		
10|	Number of years in arrears			1		
11|	Amount of dividends to be distributed					100000
12|						============
13							
14|				Amount distributed to:		
15|				---		
16|				Preferred	Common	Yet to be
17|				Stock	Stock	Distributed
18|				---		
19|	Total amount to be distributed			N/A	N/A	100000
20|	P.S. dividends in arrears			0	N/A	100000
21|	Current P.S. dividends			18000	N/A	82000
22|	C.S. dividend to match current P.S....			N/A	72000	10000
23|	Participating dividend			2000	8000	0
24|	Remainder to common stock			N/A	0	0
25					--	============
26|	Total distributed			20000	80000	
27					======================================
28							
29|	Percentage dividend (current year)			.1	.1	
30					======================================

Step 13 - You may wish to "clean up" the appearance of your spreadsheet by changing the formats of certain locations to dollars and cents, etc.

>S   When you have completed any formatting, press the [Home] key to move the cursor to cell A1.

Step 14 - At this point, you may wish to **save** your work. Use the procedures given in Chapter 5 to save your work.

Printing: You might also want to print the spreadsheet if your computer is connected to a printer.

>S   Type "/GB" to remove the spreadsheet borders (row and column headings).
>S   Type "/ODA1:F30,P" to print the dividend distribution schedule.
>S   Press any key to continue.
>S   Type "/GB" to replace the spreadsheet borders if you wish to continue.

Completing the Problem - Parts B and C:

Your spreadsheet should now be ready for you to manipulate the input data and study the effects that changes in the variables may have on the amount of dividends distributed to each class of stock.

To find out how large a dividend must be distributed in the following year in order to maintain the same percentage return to the common stock, change the par value of the preferred stock outstanding to $400,000 and then change the amount of dividends to be distributed on an iterative basis. As you increase the amount of dividends to be distributed, examine the percentage return to the common stockholders. When it is equal to 10%, you have found the amount of dividends to be distributed.

If you wish to quit at this time:

>S   Type "/QY" to quit using SuperCalc3.

   After the screen clears and the red in-use light has gone off, you may remove your disks and turn off the computer.

CHAPTER 27 - INSTALLMENT ACCOUNTS RECEIVABLE

Objective: This partially completed spreadsheet introduces the LOOKUP function and the DATA MANAGEMENT command and illustrates how they might be used in calculating the gross profit to be recognized from installment accounts receivable collections. It also reviews the REPLICATE command. The completed spreadsheet will enable you to determine the amount of gross profit to be recognized from cash collections during any given time period from installment sales made over a four year period.

Part A requires the construction of a spreadsheet which will calculate the amount of gross profit to be recognized on installment accounts receivable collected during a period. Part B uses the collections entered in the spreadsheet as a data base to calculate the collections from each year. These two parts may be worked sequentially at different times by saving the results of Part A on a disk.

Spreadsheet Name: INSTALL

Required Input Information: Before beginning, you should identify:

1. The amount of installment sales for each year.
2. The cost of sales for each year.
3. The collections on installment accounts receivable during the period.

Using the Spreadsheet:

If you have not already done so, load SuperCalc3 into your computer following the instructions given in Part I.

Load the partially completed spreadsheet from the file disk in drive B.

>S   **Enter "/L" followed by "B:INSTALL,A".**

When the spreadsheet has finished loading, the screen display should appear similar to that shown in Exhibit 27-1.

You must now enter the required input information and complete the template. Partial instructions for completing the template are given below. (You may wish to refer to your textbook for certain formulas and relationships in order to complete the template.)

Problem:

Potlatch Appliances, Inc. specializes in making sales of new and used appliances to retailers who are considered too risky to obtain credit through other wholesalers. Since the collectibility of receivables is not reasonably assured, Potlatch uses the installment sales method for recognizing profits; that is, no profit is recognized until cash collections are made. Potlatch experienced installment sales and cost of sales over the period from 1985-88 as follows:

	1985	1986	1987	1988
Sales (on installment)	$1,000,000	$2,000,000	$1,800,000	$2,400,000
Cost of sales	760,000	1,600,000	1,350,000	1,680,000

During the month of December, 1988, Potlatch made collections from each year's sales as follows:

Date	Year of Sale	Amount Collected
December 2	1987	$10,000
" 5	1988	15000
" 6	1986	5,000
" 7	1988	6,000
" 7	1987	9,500
" 9	1985	4,200
" 12	1988	7,600
" 13	1988	19,000
" 13	1987	6,300
" 14	1986	7,700
" 15	1987	2,000
" 16	1985	1,300
" 19	1988	4,400
" 19	1987	1,600
" 20	1987	2,200
" 21	1986	1,800
" 22	1988	3,900
" 27	1988	2,700
" 28	1985	800
" 30	1986	1,500

Required:

A. Determine the amount of gross profit which Potlatch should recognize as income in December, 1988. (Ignore any related interest.)

B. Calculate the total gross profit to be recognized in December, 1988, from sales in each of the four individual years, 1985-88. (Ignore any related interest.)

Completing the spreadsheet - Part A:

Step 1 - The installment sales and the cost of those sales (as given in the problem) are already entered for you in the cell range C5:F6. Let's begin by calculating the gross profit for 1985 by subtracting the cost of sales from the installment sales given in column C.

>S   In cell C8, enter "C5-C6".

Exhibit 27-1

	A	B	C	D	E	F
1	INSTALLMENT ACCOUNTS RECEIVABLE					
2						
3			1985	1986	1987	1988
4			----------	----------	----------	----------
5	Sales (on installment)		1000000	2000000	1800000	2400000
6	Cost of sales		760000	1600000	1350000	1680000
7			----------	----------	----------	----------
8	Gross profit					
9			==========	==========	==========	==========
10	Lookup Table:					
11	----------					
12	Year...........................		1985	1986	1987	1988
13	Gross Profit Percent.......					
14	----------					
15	Sales of	Amount	Gross Profit	Gross Profit	Sales of	Amount
16	Year	Collected	Percent	Realized	Year	Collected
17	----------					
18						
19						
20						

This formula can be replicated to calculate the gross profit for 1986-88.

>S   **Make sure that your cursor in cell C8 and type "/R".**
>S   **Since you want to replicate the formula from cell C8, press the [enter] key.**
>S   **Indicate the range you wish to replicate to by typing "D8:F8". (Or point these locations out; remember, press the [Esc] key to activate the pointer.)**
>S   **Press the [enter] key and the formula will automatically be adjusted to calculate the gross profit for the years 1986-88.**

Step 2 - Rows 10 through 14 contain a lookup table. The positioning of rows 12 and 13 of this table is extremely important. These rows will enable you to look up the rate of gross profit corresponding to each year. Thus, the year and the rate of gross profit must be adjacent to each other. (Lookup tables may be set up vertically in adjacent columns as well as horizontally in rows.)

Let's calculate the gross profit percent for 1985 by dividing the gross profit by the installment sales.

>S   **In cell C13, enter or point out the formula "C8/C5".**

Replicate this calculation for 1986-88 to complete the lookup table.

>S   **Make sure that the cursor is still in cell C13, type "/R" and press the [enter] key to select cell C13 as the range you wish to replicate from.**

>S   Indicate the range you wish to replicate to by typing "D13:F13". (Or point these locations out.)

>S   Press the [enter] key and the formula will automatically be adjusted to calculate the gross profit percentages for the years 1986-88.

You should now have four years and four gross profit percentages as shown in Exhibit 27-2.

Exhibit 27-2

	A	B	C	D	E	F
1|	INSTALLMENT ACCOUNTS RECEIVABLE					
2							
3				1985	1986	1987	1988
4|			-------	-------	-------	-------
5|	Sales (on installment)		1000000	2000000	1800000	2400000
6|	Cost of sales		760000	1600000	1350000	1680000
7|			-------	-------	-------	-------
8|	Gross profit		240000	400000	450000	720000
9|			=======	=======	=======	=======
10|	Lookup Table:					
11|	-------					
12|	Year..........................		1985	1986	1987	1988
13|	Gross Profit Percent.......		.24	.2	.25	.3
14|	-------					
15|	Sales of	Amount	Gross Profit	Gross Profit	Sales of	Amount
16|	Year	Collected	Percent	Realized	Year	Collected
17|	-------					
18							
19							
20							

Step 3 - Next, let's enter the cash collections which were made during the year.

>S   In cells A18-A37, enter the years in which the installment sales were made. (You may wish to turn the automatic cursor advance to ease the process of entering these numbers--type "/GN". Later, if you wish to turn the automatic cursor advance off again, type "/GN" a second time.)

>S   In cells B18-B37, enter the dollar amounts of each collection.

Step 4 - When you have finished entering the data in columns A and B, you should be ready to apply the lookup function.

>S   In cell C18, enter "LU(A18,C12:F12)".

This function instructs the program to search the range of cells from C12 to F12 for the value specified in cell A18. Thus, the program searches for 1987 (in cell A18) in the range from 1985-88 (cells C12:F12). When it finds 1987, it returns the value immediately beneath (or adjacent) to 1987. That value is the gross profit percent for 1987 (which is .25) and is displayed in cell C18.

You can use this function for each of the remaining collections. Let's replicate the lookup function to cells C19-C37.

>S   **Check to be sure that the cursor is still in cell C18 and type "/R".**
>S   **Since you want to replicate the formula from this location, press the [enter] key.**
>S   **Indicate the range you wish to replicate to by entering or pointing out "C19:C37".**
>S   **Instead of pressing the [enter] key, however, type a comma (,).**

You are then prompted for another response on the third status line.

>S   **Type "A" for ask for adjust.**

This response allows you to have some cell references adjusted and others fixed or unadjusted. The reference to cell A18 should be adjusted since you want the lookup function to examine the contents of cell A18, then cell A19, then cell A20, etc.

>S   **Type "Y" to respond.**

Cell C12, however, should remain fixed. That is, you always want the lookup function to refer back to the same range of years which are in cells C12 through F12.

>S   **Type "N" to respond to the prompt for cell C12.**
>S   **You should also type "N" when prompted for cell F12.**

If successful, you should see the gross profit percentages which correspond with the year of sale for each collection displayed in column C. If unsuccessful, try step 4 again.

Step 5 - By multiplying the amount collected (column B) by the gross profit percentage (column C), you can calculate the gross profit to be realized on this collection in column D.

>S   **In cell D18, enter "B18*C18".**

You should see 2500 displayed in cell D18. Replicate this formula to cells D19-D37.

>S   **With the cursor in cell D18, type "/R" and press the [enter] key to select cell D18 as the range you wish to replicate from.**
>S   **Indicate the range you wish to replicate to by typing "D19:D37". (Or point these locations out.)**
>S   **Press the [enter] key and the formula will automatically be adjusted to calculate the gross profit amounts for each of the collections.**

Step 6 - Now let's total the amount collected and the gross profit to be recognized in the month of December.

>S   **In cell B39, enter "SUM(B18:B37)" to total the amount collected.**
>S   **Try replicating this formula to cell D39. (If you are unsuccessful, you can always move the cursor to cell D39 and enter "SUM(D18:D37)".)**

When the collections and related calculations section of the spreadsheet is completed, it should appear as in Exhibit 27-3.

Exhibit 27-3

	A	B	C	D
14				
15	Sales of	Amount	Gross Profit	Gross Profit
16	Year	Collected	Percent	Realized
17				
18	1987	10000	.25	2500
19	1988	15000	.3	4500
20	1986	5000	.2	1000
21	1988	6000	.3	1800
22	1987	9500	.25	2375
23	1985	4200	.24	1008
24	1988	7600	.3	2280
25	1988	19000	.3	5700
26	1987	6300	.25	1575
27	1986	7700	.2	1540
28	1987	2000	.25	500
29	1985	1300	.24	312
30	1988	4400	.3	1320
31	1987	1600	.25	400
32	1987	2200	.25	550
33	1986	1800	.2	360
34	1988	3900	.3	1170
35	1988	2700	.3	810
36	1985	800	.24	192
37	1986	1500	.2	300
38				
39		112500		30192
40				

Step 7 - You may wish to "clean-up" the appearance of your spreadsheet by changing the formats of certain locations to dollars and cents, etc.

>S   **When you have completed any formatting, press the [Home] key to move the cursor to cell A1.**

Step 8 - At this point, you may wish to **save** your work. Use the procedures given in Chapter 5 to save your work.

Your spreadsheet can now be used to manipulate the input data and study the effects that changes in the variables, particularly those affecting the gross profit percent, may have on the gross profit to be realized.

You might also want to print the spreadsheet if your computer is connected to a printer.

>S   **Type "/GB" to remove the spreadsheet borders (row and column headings).**
>S   **Type "/ODA1:F40,P" to print the entire spreadsheet.**
>S   **Press any key to continue.**
>S   **Type "/GB" to replace the spreadsheet borders if you wish to continue.**

If you wish to quit at this time:

>S   **Type "/QY" to quit using SuperCalc3.**

After the screen clears and the red in-use light has gone off, you may remove your disks and turn off the computer.

Completing Part B - Data Management

Before starting this task, make sure that you have saved your template with the data you have entered from the problem. This is to insure that you will be able to start over if you happen to make an error. Use the procedures given in Chapter 5 to save your work.

What is a Database?

Simply stated, a database is an organized collection of data. This organization is based on *records* and *fields*. A record represents all of the information which is collected about a certain item. In contrast, a field represents a single piece of information within a record.

In our problem, each individual collection of an installment account receivable represents a record. It is comprised of four fields: (1) the year in which the receivable was created, (2) the amount of the receivable collection, (3) the gross profit percentage related to the collection, and (4) the gross profit to be realized from the collection. Thus, our primary data base consists of 20 records (collections) and a total of 160 fields (20 records times 4 fields per record). Our database must also contain descriptions of the fields and/or records. For example, we will include the headings for each column as a part of the database.

Our database is logically organized into rows and columns. Each row contains a separate record and each column contains all of the information about a single field. Because of this logical organization, you can have SuperCalc3 search through the database for those records which meet certain criteria--criteria which you establish!

For example, you can find the collections which relate to each of the four years by manipulating the database. Before you can do this, however, you will need to define three ranges:

1.   *The input range.* The input range represents the data base from which you can select or extract data. This includes the field names (or variables, such as year, amount, etc.) which you have created and the data records.

2.   *The output range.* This represents the area (cell range) where you would like to display the information which is extracted from your data base.

3.   *The criterion range.* This range specifies what field (variable) should be searched and what value of the field should be searched for.

In defining these ranges, your cursor can be located in any cell. Note that you will not be able to move the cursor when you are defining ranges.

Step 9 - First, let's define the input range. Appropriate field names are listed in row 16 (cells A16-D16). Those names (Year, Collected, Percent, and Realized) can represent our fields. Our data must be located immediately below the field names. Thus, the cell range A17 through D37 contains the numeric records to be searched. (Don't let the dashed line in row 17 confuse you--it won't be any problem since the program will interpret it as zero (0); but it is still part of our records and must be included.) The overall input range, including field names and records is then A16-D37.

>S   **Begin by typing "//D".**

Note that this command requires two slashes be typed, rather than the single slash usually required.

>S   **Respond to the options prompt by typing "I" for input.**

You are then asked for the input range.

>S   **Type "A16:D37" and press the [enter] key.**

Your input range is now defined and you will be returned to the prompt line.

Step 10 - Second, let's define the output range. You don't need to specify field names in the output range, so this range can be one row smaller than the input range. Let's define the output range in the four columns immediately to the right of the input range. Thus, the output range will be in cells E17 through H37. (The template already contains headings for the output range.)

>S   **Start by entering "O" for Output.**

You are then asked to specify the output range.

>S   **Type "E17:H37" and press the [enter] key.**

Your output range is now defined and you will be returned to the prompt line.

Step 11 - Finally, let's define the criterion range.

>S   **Type "R" to exit data management and remain in the spreadsheet.**

This returns you to the spreadsheet and enables you to move your cursor.

>S   **Move the cursor to cell H12.**

This is where we will define the field name to be searched. This field name specification must have the same characters as the field name in our input range--the two field names must be identical. Thus, it is easiest to replicate the field name from the input range to the criterion range.

Since we wish to find the collections from each year, we should specify the Year field, which is located in cell A16.

>S   **Move to cell A16 and replicate its contents to cell H12. (Remember, type "/R", press the [enter] key, type "H12" and press the [enter] key.)**
>S   **Then, move the cursor to cell H13, where we will define what year we are seeking.**
>S   **Type "A17=1985" and press the [enter] key.**

You should see a zero (0) displayed in cell H13. A17 in the formula specifies the first cell where a record in the Year field may be located. Thus, this is the first record SuperCalc3 will look at when it begins to search the database. 1985 specifies the value of the record which should be sought.

Next, you must define these two cells as the criterion range.

>S   **Type "//D" to reenter data management and then type "C" for Criterion.**
>S   **Type "H12:H13" and press the [enter] key.**

The criterion range is now defined and you will be returned to the prompt line. Incidentally, you can also use formulas in the criterion range as well as values.

Step 12 - At this point, you may wish to resave your spreadsheet so that the input, output and criterion ranges will also be saved.

>S   **Type "R" to remain in the spreadsheet.**
>S   **Press the [Home] key to move the cursor to cell A1 and then save your spreadsheet following the procedures in Chapter 5.**
>S   **When you are done saving the spreadsheet, scroll over so that columns E through H appear on the screen.**
>S   **Reenter data management by typing "//D".**

Step 13 - You are now ready to seek the collections from the installment sales of 1985.

>S   **Type "E" for extract.**

The three records representing collections from 1985 should appear in cells E18 through H20.

>S   **Type "R" for remain.**
>S   **Move the cursor to cell F39 and total the amount collected.**

(Hint: You might replicate the formula from cell D39 to do this.) You should have $6,300 of revenue from 1985 sales.

>S   **Move the cursor to cell H39 and total the gross profit realized.**

You should get $1,512 as the gross profit realized this month from 1985 sales.

>S   **If your computer is connected to a printer, you may wish to print the information for 1985.**

>S   **Type "/GB" to remove the spreadsheet borders (row and column headings).**
>S   **Type "/ODE14:H40,P"**
>S   **Press any key to continue.**
>S   **Type "/GB" to replace the spreadsheet borders if you wish to continue.**

Step 14 - Next let's find the collections from 1986.

>S   **Move the cursor to cell H13 and change the formula to "A17=1986".**
>S   **Reenter data management by typing "//D" and then type "E" for extract.**

The four records from 1986 should now appear in the output range.

>S   **Type "R" to exit data management and move the cursor down to check the total collections and gross profit from 1986 sales.**

If you examine cells F39 and H39, you will note that the totals are the same as for 1985! This is because the spreadsheet has not yet recalculated. It has merely extracted a different set of records.

>S   **Type an exclamation point (!).**

This forces a recalculation of the spreadsheet. Note what happens to the totals. They should now be correct for 1986. (You should have $16,000 of revenues and $3,200 as the gross profit to be realized.)

Other considerations:

You can extract the data from 1987 and 1988 in a similar manner. Remember you will need to force a recalculation each time to get the correct totals.

You could also use the Select option to individually select records to be extracted to the output range, or the Find option to simply search the database without extracting any records.

You could also specify many other search criteria. You could search for the Amount instead of the Year. You may also search for values which are greater than or less than a certain limit.

For example, change the field in cell H12 to the field specified in B16. Then change the formula in H13 to B17>8000. When you reenter data management you will now be able to search for all collections greater than $8,000.

Try experimenting with alternatives of your own!

If you wish to quit at this time:

>S   Type "/QY" to quit using SuperCalc3.

After the screen clears and the red in-use light has gone off, you may remove your disks and turn off the computer.

PART III

B. TUTORIAL TEMPLATES
LOTUS 1-2-3

CHAPTER 28 - INCOME STATEMENT

Objective: This partially completed spreadsheet provides an introduction to Lotus 1-2-3. It illustrates how the spreadsheet can be used to help prepare a condensed multiple-step income statement. Formatting columns and individual cells to change the way in which text and numbers are displayed is illustrated. The importance of considering formats (display options) before beginning to create a spreadsheet is illustrated. The completed income statement allows you to change the inputs and see what effects this has on net income and earnings per share.

The spreadsheet emphasizes the use of the FORMAT command. It also demonstrates how to use the HELP screens in constructing a spreadsheet. The GLOBAL command (global means affecting the entire spreadsheet) and WINDOW command (windows allow you to see two different areas of the spreadsheet at the same time instead of just one) are also illustrated.

Part A of the spreadsheet requires the construction of a multiple-step income statement. Part B completes the income statement by preparing the earnings per share disclosures. These two parts may be worked *sequentially* at different times by saving the results of Part A on a disk.

Spreadsheet Name: INCOME

Required Input Information: Before beginning, you should identify from the problem data on the following page:

1. The amount of sales and the relationships of cost of goods sold and selling and administrative expense to sales.
2. Other income or expense attributable to continuing operations.
3. The income tax rate.
4. Any other items affecting the determination of net income including:
   a. Discontinued operations.
   b. Extraordinary items.
   c. The cumulative effect of a change in accounting principle.
5. The average number of common shares outstanding.

Using the Spreadsheet:

If you have not already done so, load Lotus 1-2-3 into your computer following the instructions given in Part I.

Load the partially completed spreadsheet from the file disk:

>L   **Press the [Alt] key and simultaneously type the letter "Q" from the menu.**

When the spreadsheet has finished loading, the screen display should appear similar to that shown in Exhibit 28-1.

You must now enter the required input information and complete the template. Partial instructions for completing the template arc given below. (You may wish to refer to your textbook for certain formulas and relationships in order to complete the template.)

Problem:

As the controller of the Unknown Company, Inc., you are responsible for the preparation of the annual financial statements. You assign Ms. Susan Kern, your newly hired assistant, to prepare a *projected* income statement for the company for the year ending December 31, 1985. Several days later, Ms. Kern presents you with the following condensed income statement:

Unknown Company, Inc.
Income Statement
For the Year Ended December 31, 1985

Revenues:	
Sales	$10,000,000
Investment (dividend) income	200,000
Income during 1985 from Sutter Company operations	1,400,000
Gain from sale of plant located in town of Plumas, one of three such plants owned by the company	2,300,000
Total revenues	$13,900,000
Expenses:	
Cost of Goods Sold	$ 6,000,000
Loss on sale of Sutter Company, a line of business which, with this sale, the company has discontinued	2,800,000
Interest expense	175,000
Selling and administrative expense	1,500,000
Cumulative effect of change from straight-line method of depreciation to double-declining balance method	425,000
Loss due to expropriation of foreign assets	1,000,000
Loss on sale of investments	200,000
Total Expenses	$12,100,000
Net income before taxes	$ 1,800,000
Income taxes (40 %)	720,000
Net income	$ 1,080,000
Net income per common share	$1.08

(Average number of common common shares outstanding = 1,000,000)

You immediately realize that the income statement is based on the single-step approach and does not disclose all of the required per share amounts. Unfortunately, you forgot to tell Susan that you wanted a multiple step income statement. Instead of having Susan rework the entire income statement on her own, however, you ask her to help you finish a spreadsheet you have been working on which will help prepare a multiple step income statement.

Required:

A.   Prepare a multiple step income statement for the Unknown Company, Inc. for the year ending December 31, 1985.

B.   Prepare the necessary earnings per share disclosures so that your completed statement conforms with generally accepted accounting principles.

Exhibit 28-1

	A	B	C	D	E	F	G	H
1			Unknown Company, Inc.					
2			Income Statement					
3			For the Year Ended December 31, 1985					
4								
5	Sales revenue							
6	Cost of goods sold							
7							--------------	
8	Gross profit							
9	Selling and administrative expense							
10							--------------	
11	Income from operations							
12	Other revenues and gains							
13	Item #1							
14	Item #2							
15						--------------		
16	Other expenses and losses							
17	Item #1							
18	Item #2							
19							--------------------------	
20	Income from continuing operations before income taxes							

Completing the spreadsheet - Part A:

Step 1 - Let's begin by calculating the income from operations.

>L   **Move the cursor to cell G5.**
>L   **Enter the dollar amount of sales, $10,000,000.**

This amount should be entered without commas. If you do enter the commas, the program will not allow you to enter this amount in cell G5. If you enter the dollar sign (but no commas), the program will accept your entry, but the dollar sign will not display. The correct entry should appear as 10000000.

>L   **Now move the cursor to cell G6.**
>L   **Enter the cost of goods sold as "+G5*.60"**

Since the cost of goods sold is $6,000,000, or 60% of sales ($6,000,000 /$10,000,000), let's enter this relationship instead of a number. That way, if we decide to change the amount of sales, the cost of goods sold will automatically be adjusted to the new sales level. You should see 6000000 displayed in cell G6 and the formula +G5*.60 on the first line of the control panel at the top of the screen.

Make sure that you type the plus (+) symbol before cell G5. Otherwise, the program will assume that you meant to enter a label (word) instead of a formula. If you made this error, reenter the formula in the same cell using the correct format.

>L   **Move the cursor to cell G8.**
>L   **Calculate the gross profit by entering "+G5-G6" in this cell.**

The gross profit is equal to the sales revenue less the cost of goods sold. You should see 4000000 displayed in cell G8 and the formula +G5-G6 on the first line of the control panel.

>L   **Move the cursor to cell G9.**
>L   **Enter the selling and administrative expense as "+G5*.15"**

The selling and administrative expense should be entered in the same manner as the cost of goods sold. The selling and administrative expense is equal to 15% of sales ($1,500,000/$10,000,000). You should see 1500000 displayed onscreen.

>L   **Finally, move the cursor to cell G11.**
>L   **Enter "+G8-G9" to calculate the income from operations.**

The income from operations equals the gross profit less the selling and administrative expense. You should see an income from operations of 2500000 displayed.

>L   **Move the cursor back to cell G5 and enter sales of $500,000.**

Just to make sure your formulas were entered correctly, check cell G11 to see whether or not you get an income from operations of $125,000. If not, check your formulas by repeating step 1.

>L   **If you did get $125,000 in the previous step, move to cell G5, reenter $10,000,000 of sales revenue, and let's continue.**

Step 2 - Let's try several techniques to change the appearance of the numbers in our spreadsheet. This is done through formatting--a process which changes the appearance of each cell, but which does not change the contents of the cell. Obviously, large numbers such as 10000000 can be very difficult to read without commas. We might also want to add dollar signs to our numbers as we feel they are needed. For example, 100000 can be formatted to display as $100,000.

We can format a single cell, a range of cells within a row or column, a range of cells in a block, or the entire spreadsheet (referred to as a global format).

First, let's change cell G5 to dollars and cents format. (*If you enter an incorrect keystroke during this process, use the [Esc] key to eliminate it!*)

>L   **Check to be sure that the cursor is still in cell G5.**

>L   **Press the slash (/) key on the lower right of the keyboard.**

The slash key (don't confuse this with the backslash (\) key) calls up what are referred to as the slash commands. On the second and third lines of the control panel, you will see a number of words. Each of these words stands for a specific command, several of which you will use in completing this spreadsheet.

>L   **Now press [F1].**

You should see a brief description of how to begin using these commands. If your computer is connected to a printer, you may obtain a hard copy (printout) of this description by pressing the [shift] key and [PrtSc] simultaneously.

>L   **Press the [Esc] key to return to your spreadsheet.**

>L   **Type "R" to select Range. (You can also select a command by using the left and right cursor movement keys to move the cursor to the command and then pressing the [enter] key. For example, instead of typing "R", you could press the right cursor movement key to move the cursor to Range and then press the [enter] key.)**

The R stands for Range. Our command options under Range are now shown on the second line of the control panel. These are Format, Label-Prefix, Erase, Name, Justify, Protect, Unprotect, or Input. The cursor is highlighting our first choice under the Range command--Format.

>L   **Now press [F1].**

You should see a brief description of the Range commands. If your computer is connected to a printer, you may obtain a hard copy (printout) of these descriptions by pressing the [shift] key and [PrtSc] simultaneously.

>L   **Press the [Esc] key to return to your spreadsheet.**

>L   **Type "F" to select Format (or press the [enter] key since the cursor is highlighting the Format command.**

We want to select the Currency option to display the amount of sales with a dollar sign and commas.

>L   **Type "C" or move the cursor to Currency and press the [enter] key.**

The program will now prompt you for the number of decimal places you wish to have displayed. Since we have a large dollar amount, let's choose zero (0).

>L   **Type zero (0) and press the [enter] key.**

You will then be prompted to specify the range to format. A range can be either a single cell (suggested by the prompt which shows G5 . . G5) or a range of cells. Let's format cell G5 only.

>L   **Press the [enter] key to select cell G5 as the range and complete the formatting for cell G5.**

Since the cursor is currently located in cell G5, it will automatically be selected as the range by pressing [enter].

Unfortunately, the correct dollar amount is not displayed. This is because dollar and cents notation has added a dollar sign and commas to the 10000000 already entered in cell G5. Thus, the display format ($10,000,000) is now eleven characters long--and cell G5 is only nine characters wide. In addition, the program reserves one space for indicating a negative number. Thus, we need a cell which is at least twelve characters wide before our new format can be displayed. The program indicates this problem by displaying a series of asterisks (**********) in cell G5.

Step 3 - In order to make this number display in dollar and cents format, we need to make column G wider. Let's begin by increasing the width of *all* of the columns in the spreadsheet.

>L   **You can leave the cursor in any cell for this operation.**
>L   **Press the slash (/) key to call up the slash commands.**
>L   **Next, type "W" for Worksheet and "G" for global.**

Global means that whatever option you select will affect the *entire* spreadsheet! On the second line of the control panel, you will see that the third option for the global command is Column-width. This option will allow you to select the width of the columns in your spreadsheet.

>L   **Type "C" for Column-width followed by "12" and press the [enter] key.**

Each column will be expanded to 12 characters wide. Our problem now is that we can only see six columns (columns B through G if your cursor was still in cell G5) on the screen. Since this didn't work so well, let's go back to 9 characters per column and start over.

>L   **Type "/WGC" followed by "9" and press the [enter] key.**
>L   **Press the [Home] key to return the cursor to cell A1 so that you will be able to see all of your original screen.**

Step 4 - Instead of changing the global format, let's change only columns E, F, and G: the columns in which we will be entering numbers.

>L   **Move the cursor to a cell in column G.**
>L   **Type "/W" to select Worksheet.**
>L   **Now type "C" to select Column-Width instead of Global.**
>L   **Type "S" for set or press the [enter] key.**
>L   **Now type "12" and press the [enter] key.**

You should now be able to see columns A through G, and $10,000,000 is finally displayed on the screen!

>L   **Repeat the process above in columns E and F so that each of those columns is also formatted for 12 characters.**

Step 5 - If your cursor is in cell G5, examine the first line of the control panel. You will see that now the display format for this cell is also shown. The (C0) stands for Currency with zero (0) characters after the decimal point. Thus, you can evaluate the display format of any cell by examining the first line of the control panel.

Cell G5 is the only cell displaying the Currency notation because display formats are arranged in a sequence of priority. The format of an individual cell (such as Currency in cell G5) takes priority over any other format. A format for a range of cells is next in priority for the cells in that range. Finally, the global format will determine the display of all other cells.

Thus, when developing a spreadsheet, you should first determine the type of display which is best for the majority of cells. By entering this display format globally, you can minimize the number of rows, columns, or cells which you need to format on an individual basis. Similarly, once the global format has been set, you should next determine any different formats for large ranges, and then finally format individual cells or small cell ranges. Using this technique can save you a lot of time when formatting!

We could continue to format all of the other cells which will contain numbers in dollars and cents format, but we can see that this format will add dollar signs to all of our numbers, which we don't need. We would, however, like commas in all of our numbers, and dollar signs on those numbers where we believe dollar signs are appropriate.

Step 6 - Let's begin by using a global format to add commas to our numbers and to display dollars only (without cents).

>L   **Type "/WGF" to select Worksheet, Global, and Format.**
>L   **Type a comma (,) to add commas to all of our numbers.**
>L   **Type zero (0) in response to the prompt for the number of decimal places and press the [enter] key.**

The rest of our numbers should now display with commas! Later, we will add formats to other cells or cell ranges as needed.

Step 7 - If you examine the numbers in column G, you will see that they are not fully right-hand justified in each cell--each number is one space to the left of the right-hand side. For example, look at cell G11. You will see that there is one character space to the right of 2,500,000.

This is because the right-most space is reserved for the right parenthesis, should we need it to display a negative number. Thus, if you anticipate negative numbers (such as a net loss), you should make your columns at least one space wider than what would otherwise be the maximum width needed.

You are probably starting to see the need to plan your cell sizes according to the sizes of the numbers that you may expect to encounter in a problem. Increasing or decreasing the width of a column once you have done a substantial amount of work can be very inconvenient!

Now let's return to our income statement!

Step 8 - Let's enter the amounts of any *other* revenues and gains and calculate the total amount of other revenues and gains.

>L   **In cells F13 and F14, enter the amounts of any other revenues or gains. (Refer back to the original information.)**

>L   **In cell G14, enter "+F13+F14" to total the other revenues and gains.**

(These revenues and gains are simply labeled Item #1 and Item #2 on your spreadsheet--don't bother to change these labels for now.)

Step 9 - Let's enter the amounts of any *other* expenses or losses and calculate the total amount of other expenses and losses.

>L   **In cells F17 and F18, enter the amounts of any other expenses or losses. (Refer back to the original information.)**

>L   **In cell G18, enter "+F17+F18" to total the other expenses and losses.**

(These expenses and losses are simply labeled Item #1 and Item #2 on your spreadsheet--don't bother to change these labels for now.)

Step 10 - Calculate the income from continuing operations before income taxes by adding the gross profit to the other revenues and gains and subtracting the other expenses and losses.

>L   **In cell G20, enter "+G11+G14-G18".**

You should get $4,625,000 if all steps have been completed correctly.

Step 11 - Next, let's prepare to calculate the amount of income taxes and the income from continuing operations. Since income taxes are calculated as a percentage of income, and rates may change, let's input the tax rate in a separate cell. Then, if we wish to change rates later, we can simply change the amount in one cell.

>L   **In cell D21, enter the tax rate .**

Make sure that you enter the tax rate as a decimal (for example, 40% equals .40).

Step 12 - When the tax rate is correctly entered, you should see 0 displayed. This is because our global format was for zero decimal places to display. Thus, we need to format cell D21 differently. This provides us with another opportunity to try a special format.

>L   **Check to make sure that the cursor is still in cell D21.**

>L   **Type "/RF" to select Range and Format.**

>L   **When the format options appear, type "P" to select Percent (or use the cursor movement keys to select Percent and then press the [enter] key.**

>L   **The program will then prompt you to enter the number of decimal places. Select the standard setting of "2" by pressing the [enter] key.**

>L   **In response to the prompt for a range to format, simply press the [enter] key since we wish to format only cell D21.**

     You should see the tax rate appear as 40.00%!

Step 13 - Now let's finish calculating the dollar amount of income taxes and the income from continuing operations.

>L   **Move the cursor to cell G21.**

>L   **Enter "+G20*D21".**

     This will multiply the income from continuing operations before tax by the tax rate to determine the amount of income taxes.

>L   **Move the cursor to cell G23.**

>L   **Enter "+G20-G21".**

     This calculation subtracts the income taxes from the income from continuing operations before tax to arrive at the after-tax income from continuing operations. You should get $2,775,000 if your entries have been correct.

Step 14 - Next, the effects of any additional components of net income should be calculated. Since you have already calculated the income taxes in determining income from continuing operations, each additional item which affects net income must be disclosed net-of-tax. However, the amount of tax expense related to each of these items should also be shown on the income statement.

These special items include: (a) discontinued operations, (b) extraordinary items, and (c) cumulative effects of changes in accounting principles.

Step 14a - Let's begin with discontinued operations. Any net gain or loss on discontinued operations must be segregated into (i) the income or loss during the year from operating the discontinued operations and (ii) the gain or loss on disposal of the discontinued operations.

>L   **Move the cursor to cell E25.**

>L   **Enter the income (loss) from operations of a discontinued operation. (Refer to the original information.)**

>L   Move the cursor to cell E26.
>L   Enter "+E25*D21" to calculate the income tax effect of the income (loss) from operations of the discontinued operations.
>L   Move the cursor to cell F26.
>L   Enter "+E25-E26".

This calculates the net-of-tax income (loss) from operations of the discontinued operation by subtracting the income tax effect from the gross amount.

>L   Move the cursor to cell E28.
>L   Enter the gain (loss) on disposal of the discontinued operation.

Remember to enter any losses as negative numbers. For example, a loss of $2,800,000 is entered as -2800000 (on some monitors, negative numbers are shadowed to help distinguish them from positive numbers).

>L   Move the cursor to cell E29.
>L   Enter "+E28*D21" to calculate the income tax effect of the gain (loss) on disposal of the discontinued operations.
>L   Move the cursor to cell F29.
>L   Enter "+E28-E29".

This calculates the net-of-tax gain (loss) on disposal of the discontinued operation by subtracting the income tax effect from the gross amount.

>L   Move the cursor to cell G29.
>L   Enter "+F26+F29".

This calculation totals the net gain or loss on discontinued operations by summing the net-of-tax amounts from operating and disposing of the discontinued operations.

>L   Move the cursor to cell G31.
>L   Enter "+G23+G29".

The net gain or loss on discontinued operations is added to the income from continuing operations to arrive at the income before extraordinary items and cumulative effect of a change in accounting principle. If done correctly, you should have $1,935,000 for the income before extraordinary items and the cumulative effect of a change in accounting principle.

Step 14b - Now let's calculate the effects of any extraordinary items.

>L   Move the cursor to cell F33.
>L   Enter the total gross amount of any extraordinary gains or losses. (Refer to the original information.)

Remember to enter any losses as negative numbers.

>L   Move the cursor to cell F34.
>L   Enter "+F33*D21" to calculate the income tax effect of the extraordinary
       gains or losses.
>L   Move the cursor to cell G34.
>L   Enter "+F33-F34" to calculate the net-of-tax extraordinary gain or loss.

Step 14c - Now let's calculate the effects of any cumulative effects of changes in
accounting principles.

>L   Move the cursor to cell F36.
>L   Enter the total gross amount of any cumulative effects of changes in
       accounting principles. (Refer to the original information.)

       Remember to enter any losses as negative numbers.

>L   Move the cursor to cell F37.
>L   Enter "+F36*D21" to calculate the income tax effects of the cumulative effects
       of changes in accounting principles.
>L   Move the cursor to cell G37.
>L   Enter "+F36-F37" to calculate the net-of-tax cumulative effect of changes in
       accounting principles.

Step 15 - Finally, compute the net income by summing the income before
extraordinary items and cumulative effect of a change in accounting principle with
the net gain or loss from extraordinary items and the cumulative effects of changes
in accounting principles.

>L   Move the cursor to cell G39.
>L   Enter "+G31+G34+G37".

       Your final net income should be $1,080,000, the same amount as was
       calculated by Ms. Kern. You may wish to reformat this cell to display the
       dollar sign. (Remember, type "/RFC", followed by a zero(0), and press the
       [enter] key twice.

>L   Press the [Home] key to move the cursor to cell A1.

Step 16 - At this point, you may wish to **save** your work and complete part B of the
problem at a later date. Use the procedures given in Chapter 5 to save your work.

Printing: You might also want to print the spreadsheet if your computer is
connected to a printer. If you wish to do this:

>L   Type "/PPRA1.G40" and press the [enter] key to specify the print range.
>L   Make sure that your printer's paper is aligned and then type "A" for Align.
>L   Type "G" for Go to print the spreadsheet.
>L   Type "Q" to Quit the print function after the income statement is printed.

If you wish to quit at this time:

>L   **Type "/QY" to quit using Lotus 1-2-3. (Type "EY" if needed to exit the Lotus access system menu.)**

After the screen clears and the red in-use light has gone off, you may remove your disks and turn off the computer.

Completing the spreadsheet - Part B:

If you saved your earlier work and now wish to retrieve your template, use the procedures in Chapter 5 for retrieving a file.

Step 17 - Let's begin calculating the earnings per share disclosures for our income statement. First, you need to enter the weighted average number of common shares outstanding.

>L   **Use the special function key [F5] to jump to cell I1 so that you can view columns I through P.**

This will enable you to view the earnings per share section of the template.

>L   **Move the cursor to cell P1 and enter 1,000,000, the weighted average number of shares outstanding.**

Step 18 - Next, let's add the necessary labels for our earnings per share calculations.

>L   **Move the cursor to cell I6 and type: "Income from continuing operations"**

>L   **Press the [enter] key.**

This enters what you have typed as text in cell I6. Text is left-hand justified in each cell, unlike the numbers and formulas you entered earlier, which were right-hand justified in each cell.

Also, the program allows your entry to "spillover" into cells J6, K6, and L6. This "spillover" is allowed by the program unless there is an entry in one of the cells your text spills over into. For example, if we had made an entry in cell L6, then only "Income from continuing oper" would display. The balance of the text would not display because of the overlapping of our entries in cells I6 and L6!

Now let's add the remaining text!

>L   **Enter the following text in the corresponding cells:**

Cell	Text to be entered
I7	Income (loss) from operations of discontinued operations,
I8	net of tax
I9	Gain (loss) on disposal of discontinued operation, net of tax

Step 19 - Now you can calculate the per share amounts.

>L   **Move the cursor to cell P6.**
>L   **Enter "+G23/P1".**

This is the income from continuing operations per common share. You should see "3" displayed if done correctly. (We'll reformat this cell and the other per share amounts to display dollars and cents in a moment.)

>L   **Move the cursor to cell P8.**

Let's use the cursor as a *pointer* to find the numbers which we want to enter in this cell.

>L   **Press the plus [+] key. This activates the cursor as a pointer.**

On the second line of the control panel, the plus appears.

>L   **Using the cursor movement keys, move one cell to the left (cell O8). Note how the cell reference on the second line of the control panel is now cell O8!**
>L   **Continue moving the cursor to cell F26, the cell which contains the amount of income (loss) from operations of the discontinued operations. Note that the cell reference on the second line of the control panel is now cell F26!**
>L   **Press the slash key (/) to indicate that you wish to divide cell F26 by another number.**

The cursor will automatically return to cell P8--where we started from! On the second line of the control panel, the partially completed command "+F26/" is displayed.

>L   **Using the cursor movement keys, move the cursor to cell P1, which contains the average number of common shares outstanding. On the second line of the control panel, the formula "+F26/P1" will be displayed.**
>L   **Enter this formula in cell P8 by pressing the [enter] key.**

This is the income (loss) from operations of the discontinued operations per common share. You should see "1" displayed if done correctly.

If you got confused, you can always start over after pressing the [enter] key (or simply enter "+F26/P1" in cell P8).

>L   **Move the cursor to cell P9.**
>L   **Activate the pointer by pressing the plus [+] key and move the cursor to cell F29.**
>L   **Press the slash (/) key to indicate that you wish to divide.**
>L   **Move the cursor to cell P1 and press the [enter] key.**

This is the gain (loss) from disposal of the discontinued operations per common share. You should see "(2)" displayed if done correctly. (In summary, you should have entered "+F29/P1" in cell P9.)

>L   **Move the cursor to cell P12.**
>L   **Activate the pointer and use it to enter "+G31/P1".**

This is the income (loss) before extraordinary items and the cumulative effect of a change in accounting principle per common share. You should see "2" displayed if done correctly.

>L   **Move the cursor to cell P13.**
>L   **Activate the pointer and use it to enter "+G34/P1".**

This is the income (loss) from extraordinary items per common share. You should see "(1)" displayed if done correctly.

>L   **Move the cursor to cell P15.**
>L   **Activate the pointer and use it to enter "+G37/P1".**

This is the income (loss) from the cumulative effect of a change in accounting principle per common share. You should see (0) displayed if done correctly.

>L   **Move the cursor to cell P17.**
>L   **Activate the pointer and use it to enter "+G39/P1".**

This is the final net income (loss) per common share. You should see "1" displayed if done correctly.

Step 20 - Let's format the per share amounts to show dollars and cents.

>L   **Move the cursor to cell P6.**
>L   **Type "/RFC" and press the [enter] key twice.**

You should now see $2.78 displayed in cell P6.

>L   **Move the cursor down to cell P17, type "/RFC" and press the [enter] key twice.**

You should now see $1.08 displayed in cell P17.

>L   **Move the cursor up to cell P8.**
>L   **Type "/RF" followed by a comma (,) and press the [enter] key *once* to begin formatting.**
>L   **Move the cursor down to cell P15 to indicate that you would like to format the range from cell P8 through cell P15 instead of a single cell.**
>L   **Press the [enter] key to complete the formatting.**

The numbers in the range from cell P8 to cell P15 should now be displayed with two decimals (cents) and with negative numbers in parentheses.

Step 21 - Let's try changing the amount of sales revenue to see what effect it has on net income and the related earnings per common share.

>L   **Next, move the cursor left to any cell in column N.**

>L   **Type "/WW" for Worksheet and Window, followed by "V" for Vertical.**

You should see a split in the viewing screen with the cursor on the left-hand side of the split. Since we can see the earnings per share amounts on the right, let's move the cursor to the left so that we can see the amount of sales revenue at the same time. (You can switch sides of the split by pressing the special function key [F6].

>L   **Move the cursor left until you can see columns E, F, G, and H.**

You should now be able to view both the earnings per share amounts and the right-hand side of the income statement (the numbers should be visible).

>L   **Move the cursor to cell G5, which is the cell containing the amount of sales revenue.**

>L   **Examine the numbers on the spreadsheet very carefully, especially the earnings per share amounts.**

>L   **Enter $20,000,000 of sales instead of $10,000,000.**

You should see several of the numbers on the income statement change as the program recalculates the amounts. The earnings per share amounts have also changed!

>L   **Move the cursor down to cell G39 to check the amount of net income..**

Notice that when you move the cursor to cell G39 that the right side of your viewing screen moves along with the left side. That is, the two screens are synchronized. (In some applications, you may wish to unsynchronize the two screens. This can be done by typing "/WWU" (try it sometime--the windows can be synchronized again by typing "/WWS".)

Cell G39 displays a net income of $2,580,000--whereas it was $1,080,000 when sales were only $10,000,000.

>L   **Type "/WWC" to clear the split screen and return to a single screen.**

>L   **Press the [Home] key to move the cursor to cell A1.**

Step 22 - At this point, you may wish to **save** your work. Use the procedures given in Chapter 5 to save your work.

Printing: You might also want to print the spreadsheet if your computer is connected to a printer. You must do this in two sections: (1) the income statement, and (2) the earnings per common share.

>L   Type "/PPRA1.G40" and press the [enter] key to specify the print range for the income statement.

>L   Make sure that your printer's paper is aligned and then type "A" for Align.

>L   Type "G" for Go to print the income statement.

>L   Type "R" for Range, "I1.P18" and press the [enter] key to specify the print range for the earnings per share data.

>L   Make sure that your printer's paper is aligned and then type "A" for Align.

>L   Type "G" for Go to print the earnings per share data.

>L   Type "Q" to Quit the print function.

If you wish to quit at this time:

>L   Type "/QY" to quit using Lotus 1-2-3. (Type "EY" if needed to exit the Lotus access system menu.)

After the screen clears and the red in-use light has gone off, you may remove your disks and turn off the computer.

CHAPTER 29 - ACCOUNTS RECEIVABLE AGING

Objective: This tutorial introduces you to the use of Lotus 1-2-3 by illustrating a simple spreadsheet which can be used in conjunction with an aging of accounts receivable. The spreadsheet which will result from the tutorial will enable you to determine the balance of the accounts receivable and the allowance for uncollectible accounts at any given date. It will also enable you to determine the effects of changes in the amounts due and the percentages of uncollectible accounts on the balance of the allowance account.

The spreadsheet introduces the COPY, INSERT, ERASE and EDIT commands. It also uses the FORMAT command for text formatting, and demonstrates how to use REPEATING TEXT. The @SUM function is used in the spreadsheet for several totals.

Part A of the preparation of the spreadsheet introduces these commands and formulas. Part B, the completion of the spreadsheet, reviews several of these concepts. These two parts may be worked *sequentially* at different times by saving the results of Part A on a disk.

Required Input Information: Before beginning, you should identify:

1. The balance of each customer's account and an aging of his/her account.
2. The percentage estimated to be uncollectible for each age category.

Problem:

The Lemhi Bearing Company regularly sells to customers on account. Presented below are the account balances for Lemhi's four customers. These balances are broken down into four aging categories along with the percentage of bad debts expected for each age category:

Customer	Less than 30 days	31-60 days	61-120 days	More than 120 days
Chamberlain Mftg.	$190,000	$30,000		
Bargamin Distributors	92,000	42,000	$14,000	
Stibnite Products Co.	214,000	62,000	17,000	
Tendoy Company, Inc.		16,000	28,000	$42,000
Percentage uncollectible	1%	3%	6%	25%

Building a Spreadsheet Template

If you have not already done so, load Lotus 1-2-3 into your computer following the instructions given in Part I. When the blank spreadsheet appears on the screen, you are ready to begin.

Part A - Calculating the Accounts Receivable Balance

Step 1 - Let's begin by preparing a schedule which will total the accounts receivable for each age category. First, we need to enter column headings.

>L   **In cell A2, type "Customer".**

Note how this appears on the second line of the control panel as you type to let you know what you have typed. In addition, in the upper right-hand corner of the screen the word "LABEL" appears to indicate that you are entering text, or a label.

>L   **Press the [enter] key.**

When you press the [enter] key, Customer will appear in cell A2. This is then shown on the first line of the control panel. The single quotation mark before Customer means that a label has been entered in cell A2.

>L   **Move the cursor to cell D1 and enter "Less than".**
>L   **In cell D2, type "30 days".**

The program assumes that since you typed the number "30" as the first characters to be entered that you wanted to enter a number. This is indicated in the upper right-hand corner by the word "VALUE."

>L   **Press the [enter] key.**

The program will not allow you to enter "30 days" in cell D2. When the program discovers the word "days" in the same entry, it doesn't know how to interpret this combination of numbers and letters and refuses to let you enter them in the same cell together.

In order to enter "30 days", you must tell the program that you wish this entry to be interpreted as a label instead of a value. You can do this by typing a single quotation mark (') before typing "30 days."

>L   **Press the [Esc] key to start your entry in cell D2 over.**
>L   **Type a single quotation mark ('). (It's on the same key with the double quotation mark.)**
>L   **Now enter "30 days" in cell D2.**

You should now see "30 days" displayed in cell D2.

>L   **In cell E1, enter "31-60".**

Note what happens! The program has subtracted 60 from 31 and arrived at negative 29! The first line of the control panel indicates (by the absence of a single quotation mark before the numbers) that this is not a label, but is instead a formula. An entry composed entirely of numbers and numeric operations is assumed to be a formula, and the operation implied by that formula has been performed. In order to have 31-60 display, instead of -29, you must also tell the program that this entry should be considered as a label, not as a formula. To do this, type a single quote mark (') before entering 31-60.

>L **Reenter 31-60 by typing a single quotation mark (') first and your entry will be interpreted as a label.**

Note that 31-60 is left-hand justified in cell E1--we'll adjust that later.

>L **In columns E, F, and G, enter the remainder of the headings for the four age categories (as given in the problem data) following the process described in step 1.**

Your completed headings should appear as in Exhibit 29-1.

Exhibit 29-1

	A	B	C	D	E	F	G	H
1				Less than	31-60	61-120	More than	
2	Customer			30 days	days	days	120 days	
3								
4								
5								
6								
7								
8								
9								
10								

Step 2 - Next, let's enter Lemhi's customer names in cells A4 through A7.

>L **In cell A4, enter "Chamberlain Mftg."**

This entry is too wide for cell A4, which is only 9 characters wide, but it is allowed to "spill over" into cell B4. This spillover is possible as long as an entry doesn't spill over into a cell which already has an entry. For example, if cell B4 already had an entry, then only the first nine letters of Chamberlain Mftg. would display--those that fit in cell A4.

>L **In cells A5, A6, and A7, enter the remaining customer names.**

Step 3 - Enter the aged balances of accounts receivable. All numbers should be entered without dollar signs and commas. If you enter commas, the program will assume that you wish to enter labels instead of numbers. If you enter the dollar signs, the dollar signs will not display, so there is no reason to enter them. Thus, $190,000 is entered as 190000. Enter a zero if a company's balance in a category is zero.

>L   **In cells D4 through G7, enter the aged balances.**

If you have not already noticed, you can make an entry without pressing the [enter] key. Simply type what you wish to enter in a cell and then, using the cursor movement (arrow) keys, move to another cell. This can greatly speed up data entry!

Your spreadsheet should appear as in Exhibit 29-2.

Step 4a - Let's total the accounts outstanding for less than 30 days.

>L   **In cell A9, enter "Total".**
>L   **Next, in cell D9, enter "+D4+D5+D6+D7".**

This totals the accounts which have been outstanding for less than 30 days. You should see the formula on the first line of the control panel and the total of $496,000 displayed in cell D9.

Exhibit 29-2

	A	B	C	D	E	F	G	H
1				Less than	31-60	61-120	More than	
2	Customer			30 days	days	days	120 days	
3								
4	Chamberlain Mftg.			190000	30000	0	0	
5	Bargamin Distributors			92000	42000	14000	0	
6	Stibnite Products Co.			214000	62000	17000	0	
7	Tendoy Company, Inc.			0	16000	28000	42000	
8								
9								
10								

Step 4b - Let's total the accounts which have been outstanding for 31 to 60 days. This time, however, let's use the cursor to point to the cells which we would like to total.

>L   **Move the cursor to cell E9.**
>L   **Press the plus [+] key.**

This activates the spreadsheet's cursor as a pointer. (If you would like to deactivate the pointer, simply press the [Esc] key.)

>L   **Using the arrow keys, move the cursor up to cell E4.**

As the cursor moves, the cell reference on the second line of the control panel changes. When you reach cell E4, you have pointed to the first cell which you want to total.

>L   **Press the plus (+) key.**

Note that the cursor immediately returns to its starting cell (E9). You can now point to the second cell you wish to have as a part of the total.

>L   **Using the arrow keys, move the cursor to cell E5.**
>L   **Press the plus (+) key.**
>L   **Move the cursor to cell E6 and press the plus (+) key a third time.**
>L   **Finally, move the cursor to cell E7 and, since this is the final cell you wish to total, press the [enter] key.**
       On the first line of the control panel, you will see that cell E9 now contains a formula which is identical to the formula you entered in D9 except that it is in column E instead of column D.

This suggests that perhaps we could copy this formula in cells F9 and G9 and save a lot of effort. This is exactly what we will do next!

Step 4c - Let's copy the formula in cell E9 to cell F9.

>L   **With the cursor in cell E9, type a slash (/).**
>L   **Next, type "C" for Copy.**

On the second status line, you are prompted to enter the cell range which you would like to replicate *from*.

>L   **Press the [enter] key to select cell E9 as the entire cell range which we wish to copy from.**

Since the cursor is in cell E9, and it contains the formula we wish to copy, pressing the [enter] key will select cell E9 by default.

You are then prompted to enter the cell range you wish to copy *to*.

>L   **Using the arrow keys, move the cursor to point to cell F9.**
>L   **Press the [enter] key to select cell F9 as the cell range.**

Since cell F9 is being pointed to, pressing the [enter] key will select it as the cell range. The program automatically copies the formula and adjusts it to be in column F. If you move the cursor to cell F9, you will see that this cell contains a formula identical to those in cells D9 and E9, except that it has been adjusted to column F.

Step 4d - Repeat this process to total the accounts outstanding for more than 120 days.

>L   **Move the cursor to cell F9.**
>L   **Type "/C" and press the [enter] key.**
>L   **Point to cell G9 and press the [enter] key.**

Your spreadsheet should now appear as in Exhibit 29-3.

Exhibit 29-3

	A	B	C	D	E	F	G	H
1|				Less than	31-60	61-120	More than	
2|	Customer			30 days	days	days	120 days	
3|								
4|	Chamberlain Mftg.			190000	30000	0	0	
5|	Bargamin Distributors			92000	42000	14000	0	
6|	Stibnite Products Co.			214000	62000	17000	0	
7|	Tendoy Company, Inc.			0	16000	28000	42000	
8|								
9|	Total			496000	150000	59000	42000	
10|								

Step 5a - Now let's add totals in column H for each customer's account.

>L   Move the cursor to cell H2 and enter "Total".
>L   Move the cursor to cell H4.

As you have probably guessed, it can be burdensome to have to point out each and every cell to be totaled. The @SUM function can be used to speed up this process. What we would like to do is sum the cells from E4 through G4.

>L   Type "@SUM(". *(This is the term @SUM and a left-hand parenthesis.)* The @ symbol is on the same key as the "2" in the upper left-hand corner of the keyboard. Make sure that you hold down the [shift] key while pressing the @ key.
>L   Use the arrow keys to point to cell D4.
>L   Instead of entering a plus (+), enter a period (.) at this point.

The period indicates that cell D4 is the first cell in a continuous range of cells to be summed.

>L   Next, move the pointer over to cell G4 and type the right-hand parenthesis ")".

Notice how the range of cells being summed is highlighted so that it is easy to see what is included in your sum function. The formula shown on the second line of the control panel should read @SUM(D4.G4).

>L   Press the [enter] key and you should get a total of $220,000 in cell H4.

Step 5b - You can now copy this formula to cells H5, H6, and H7 in order to total the accounts of the other three customers. Rather than doing this one cell at a time, let's copy the formula to all three cells at once.

>L   With the cursor in cell H4:
>L   Type "/C" and press the [enter] key to indicate that cell H4 is the range to copy from.
>L   Use the arrow keys to point to cell H5.
>L   Type a period (.) to indicate that this is the first cell in a range of cells (instead of pressing the [enter] key to select only cell H5).
>L   Point all the way down to cell H9.

Note that the cells from H5 to H9 will be highlighted. Since row 9 also needs to be totaled to arrive at the total accounts receivable, include this in your range. Your range (on the right-hand side of the second line of the control panel) should read H5. .H9.

>L   Press the [enter] key.

You should see the totals for each row appear. If you move the cursor to any of the cells in the range of cells from H5 through H9, you will see that the formula in each cell has been adjusted to its respective row. Exhibit 29-4 shows how your spreadsheet should now appear.

Exhibit 29-4

	A	B	C	D	E	F	G	H
1				Less than	31-60	61-120	More than	
2	Customer			30 days	days	days	120 days	Total
3								
4	Chamberlain Mftg.			190000	30000	0	0	220000
5	Bargamin Distributors			92000	42000	14000	0	148000
6	Stibnite Products Co.			214000	62000	17000	0	293000
7	Tendoy Company, Inc.			0	16000	28000	42000	86000
8								0
9	Total			496000	150000	59000	42000	747000
10								

One problem remains. Cell H8 has a zero in it. This is because the formula was also replicated to this cell and the spreadsheet is summing the four blank cells in row 8 (cells D8 through G8). You can eliminate this formula by using a slash command.

>L   Move the cursor to cell H8.
>L   Type "/RE" for Range and Erase and press the [enter] key to select cell H8 as the range to be erased.

The formula in cell H8 will be erased.

Step 6 - Before continuing with our calculation of the allowance for bad debts, let's clean up the appearance of our first table.

Step 6a - Let's begin cleaning up by adding a heading.

>L   Press the [Home] key to move the cursor up to cell A1.

You can add more blank rows at the top of your schedule by using the Insert command.

>L   Type "/WI" for Worksheet and Insert, followed by an "R" for Row and press the [enter] key.

>L   Add a second and a third blank row by the same process so that "Customer" now appears in cell A5.

>L   Move the cursor over to a cell that contains a formula (for example, cell H7).

Note that all of the formulas which you have created in the schedule have automatically been adjusted for the addition of these three rows--you do not have to change the formulas!

>L   In cell D1, enter "Lemhi Bearing Company".

>L   In cell D2, enter "Aging Schedule".

Since Aging Schedule is not centered with the company's name, let's adjust it.

>L   With the cursor still in cell D2, press the special function key [F2] to enter edit.

You should see Aging Schedule appear on the second line of the control panel for editing. You can use the left and right arrow keys to move back and forth on the edit line.

>L   Move the flashing cursor on the edit line beneath the A in Aging.

>L   Press the [space] bar three times to insert three spaces.

>L   Press the [enter] key and the edited cell will be entered on the spreadsheet.

(You can edit out unwanted characters from the second line of the control panel by pressing the [Del] key.)

Step 6b - Now let's adjust the column headings. You have probably noticed that text is left-justified and numbers are right-justified in each cell. You can also right-justify text (or center it) to make it line up better with a column of numbers. This should be done for all of our text in cells D4 through H5.

>L   Move the cursor to cell D4.

>L   Type "/R" for Range.

>L   Type "L" for Label-Prefix, and "R" for Right.

>L   Use the arrow keys to highlight the range of cells from D4. .H5 as the range to be formatted and press the [enter] key.

The column headings should now be right-justified in each cell, resulting in a neater, more organized appearance.

Step 6c - Finally, let's add a dashed line between our headings and our data.

>L   **Move the cursor to Cell A6.**

You could type in 9 dashes (-) in this cell, but it is easier to use the repeating text command.

>L   **Type a backslash (\), followed by a dash (-), and press the [enter] key. (The backslash is at the lower left-hand corner of the keyboard.)**

The dash will be repeated throughout cell A6. Now let's copy this to cells B6 through H6.

>L   **Type "/C" for Copy and press the [enter] key.**
>L   **Use the cursor movement key to move to cell B6. Type a period (.) to indicate that this is the beginning of the range you wish to copy to. Move the cursor to cell H6. (Your range to copy to should now read B6. .H6.) Press the [enter] key.**

The dashed line should be repeated from column A to column H. Your spreadsheet should now appear as in Exhibit 29-5.

Exhibit 29-5

	A	B	C	D	E	F	G	H
1				Lemhi Bearing Company				
2				Aging Schedule				
3								
4				Less than	31-60	61-120	More than	
5	Customer			30 days	days	days	120 days	Total
6	----------	--	--	-----------	-------	--------	-----------	---------
7	Chamberlain Mftg.			190000	30000	0	0	220000
8	Bargamin Distributors			92000	42000	14000	0	148000
9	Stibnite Products Co.			214000	62000	17000	0	293000
10	Tendoy Company, Inc.			0	16000	28000	42000	86000
11								
12	Total			496000	150000	59000	42000	747000
13								

>L   **Add a dashed line for your totals in columns D through H (from cell D11 to cell H11) using the same procedures.**
>L   **Add a double dashed line beneath the final totals (in cells D13 through H13) following the same procedures using an equals sign (=) instead of a dash (-).**

Exhibit 29-6 shows what your spreadsheet should now look like.

Exhibit 29-6

	A	B	C	D	E	F	G	H
1			Lemhi Bearing Company					
2			Aging Schedule					
3								
4				Less than	31-60	61-120	More than	
5	Customer			30 days	days	days	120 days	Total
6	--
7	Chamberlain Mftg.			190000	30000	0	0	220000
8	Bargamin Distributors			92000	42000	14000	0	148000
9	Stibnite Products Co.			214000	62000	17000	0	293000
10	Tendoy Company, Inc.			0	16000	28000	42000	86000
11				---
12	Total			496000	150000	59000	42000	747000
13				===

>L   Press the [Home] key to move the cursor to cell A1.

Step 7 - At this point, you may wish to **save** your work in case you make an error or wish to complete part B of the problem at a later date. Use the procedures given in Chapter 5 to **save** your work.

Printing: You might also want to print the spreadsheet if your computer is connected to a printer. To do this:

>L   Type "/PPRA1.H13" and press the [enter] key to specify the print range for the aging schedule.
>L   Make sure that your printer's paper is aligned and then type "A" for Align.
>L   Type "G" for Go to print the aging schedule.
>L   Type "Q" to Quit the print function.

If you wish to quit at this time:

>L   Type "/QY" to quit using Lotus 1-2-3. (Type "EY" if needed to exit the Lotus access system menu.)

After the screen clears and the red in-use light has gone off, you may remove your disks and turn off the computer.

Part B - Calculating the Allowance for Uncollectible Accounts

If you saved your spreadsheet earlier and would now like to continue, use the procedures in Chapter 5 to retrieve your file.

Step 8 - Let's begin by entering the appropriate text and formatting for our calculation of the allowance for uncollectible accounts. Remember to use the single quote mark to create labels for text that begins with a number.

	In Cell	Enter text as follows
>L	A17	Age
>L	A19	Under 30 days old
>L	A20	31-60 days old
>L	A21	61-120 days old
>L	A22	Over 120 days
>L	A24	Total
>L	D17	Amount
>L	E15	Percent
>L	E16	Estimated
>L	E17	Uncoll.
>L	F16	Required
>L	F17	Allowance

>L   Move the cursor to cell D15 and type "/RL", followed by "R" for Right. Use the arrow keys to highlight the range of cells "D15. .F17". Press the [enter] key to adjust your new headings in columns D, E, and F so that they are right-justified in each cell.

>L   Enter dashed lines in rows 18 and 23 from column A through column F.
>L   Enter a double dashed line in cell F25.

Remember, the repeating command begins with a backslash (\) and may be copied using the "/C" command.

Your spreadsheet should now appear as in Exhibit 29-7.

Step 9 - Let's enter the total receivables for each age category in the column for the amount.

>L   Move the cursor to cell D19.
>L   In cell D19, enter the total from cell D12. Either type and enter "+D12" in cell D19, or press the plus [+] key to activate the pointer, point to cell D12 and press the [enter] key.
>L   In cells D20, D21, and D22, enter the totals from cells E12, F12, and G12, respectively, using the same procedures.

Step 10 - Enter the percentages estimated to be uncollectible for each age category as given in the problem.

>L   In cell E19, enter ".01".
>L   In cell E20, enter ".03".
>L   In cell E21, enter ".06".
>L   In cell E22, enter ".25".

Note that percentages must be entered as decimals (.00).

Exhibit 29-7

	A	B	C	D	E	F	G	H
1				Lemhi Bearing Company				
2				Aging Schedule				
3								
4				Less than	31-60	61-120	More than	
5	Customer			30 days	days	days	120 days	Total
6	----	----	----	----	----	----	----	----
7	Chamberlain Mftg.			190000	30000	0	0	220000
8	Bargamin Distributors			92000	42000	14000	0	148000
9	Stibnite Products Co.			214000	62000	17000	0	293000
10	Tendoy Company, Inc.			0	16000	28000	42000	86000
11								
12	Total			496000	150000	59000	42000	747000
13				===				
14								
15					Percent			
16					Estimated	Required		
17	Age			Amount	Uncoll.	Allowance		
18	----	----	----	----	----	----	----	----
19	Under 30 days old							
20	31-60 days old							
21	61-120 days old							
22	Over 120 days							
23	----	----	----	----	----	----	----	----
24	Total							
25						========		

Step 11 - Calculate the required allowance for uncollectible accounts for each age category by multiplying the amount of receivables in each category by that category's percentage of estimated uncollectible accounts.

>L   Move the cursor to cell F19.
>L   Enter "+D19*E19" either by using the pointer or by typing and entering "+D19*E19".

Next, copy the formula in cell F19 to cells F20 through F22 to compute the remaining uncollectible accounts provisions.

>L   **Make sure that your cursor is in cell F19.**
>L   **Type "/C" and press the [enter] key.**
>L   **Use the arrow keys to move the pointer to cell F20.**
>L   **Enter a period (.) to indicate that this is the first cell in a range of cells that you wish to replicate to.**
>L   **Point to cell F22. (You should see cells F20, F21, and F22 highlighted.)**
>L   **Press the [enter] key.**

You should see the amounts for each row displayed on the screen.

Step 12 - Calculate the total required allowance for uncollectible accounts. That is, sum the amounts calculated for each of the respective age categories by using the sum function.

>L   **In cell F24, enter "@SUM(F19.F22)" using the pointer to specify the appropriate range. Don't forget to enter the right-hand parenthesis before you press the [enter] key.**

The total in cell F24 should be the balance needed in the allowance for uncollectible accounts, which completes your aging schedule. Your schedule should appear as in Exhibit 29-8.

Step 13 - At this point, you may wish to **save** your work. Use the procedures given in Chapter 5 to save your work.

Printing: You might also want to print the spreadsheet if your computer is connected to a printer. To do this:

>L   **Type "/PPRA1.H25" and press the [enter] key to specify the print range for the aging schedule.**
>L   **Make sure that your printer's paper is aligned and then type "A" for Align.**
>L   **Type "G" for Go to print the aging schedule.**
>L   **Type "Q" to Quit the print function.**

You may want to change your input data and see what effects these changes cause on the accounts receivable and allowance for uncollectible accounts balances. For example, change the percentage of estimated uncollectible accounts for more than 120 days old to 10 percent and see what this does to the required allowance for uncollectible accounts (the balance needed in the allowance account drops to $17,200). Or, try changing the amount of accounts receivable for Chamberlain Mftg. (in cell G7) to include $30,000 of accounts in the over 120 days age category (increases the allowance account to $31,000 assuming that 25% of accounts over 120 days old will be uncollectible).

If you wish to quit at this time:

>L   Type "/QY" to quit using Lotus 1-2-3. (Type "EY" if needed to exit the Lotus access system menu.)

After the screen clears and the red in-use light has gone off, you may remove your disks and turn off the computer.

Exhibit 29-8

	A	B	C	D	E	F	G	H
1				Lemhi Bearing Company				
2				Aging Schedule				
3								
4				Less than	31-60	61-120	More than	
5	Customer			30 days	days	days	120 days	Total
6	---	---	---	---	---	---	---	---
7	Chamberlain Mftg.			190000	30000	0	0	220000
8	Bargamin Distributors			92000	42000	14000	0	148000
9	Stibnite Products Co.			214000	62000	17000	0	293000
10	Tendoy Company, Inc.			0	16000	28000	42000	86000
11								
12	Total			496000	150000	59000	42000	747000
13								
14								
15					Percent			
16					Estimated	Required		
17	Age			Amount	Uncoll.	Allowance		
18	---	---	---	---	---	---		
19	Under 30 days old			496000	0.01	4960		
20	31-60 days old			150000	0.03	4500		
21	61-120 days old			59000	0.06	3540		
22	Over 120 days			42000	0.25	10500		
23								
24	Total					23500		
25								

CHAPTER 30 - DISCOUNTING NOTES RECEIVABLE

Objective: This partially completed spreadsheet introduces the DATE function and how it might be used in discounting notes receivable. The completed spreadsheet will enable you to determine the due date of the note receivable, and the length of time for which the note is held by both the original holder and by the bank at which the note is discounted. It will also calculate the proceeds from discounting the note receivable and the related interest income or interest expense.

Spreadsheet Name: DISCOUNT

Required Input Information: Before beginning, you should identify:

1. The face value of the note.
2. The number of days to the note's maturity.
3. The stated annual interest rate of the note.
4. The date on which the note is to be issued.
5. The date on which the note is to be discounted.
6. The bank's discount rate.
7. The formula for computing the maturity value of the note.
8. The formula for computing the bank's discount.

Using the Spreadsheet:

If you have not already done so, load Lotus 1-2-3 into your computer following the instructions given in Part I.

Load the partially completed spreadsheet from the file disk in drive B.

>L   **Load the spreadsheet from the file disk by pressing the [Alt] key and simultaneously typing the letter "R" from the menu.**

When the spreadsheet has finished loading, the screen display should appear similar to that shown in Exhibit 30-1.

You must now enter the required input information and complete the template. Partial instructions for completing the template are given below. (You may wish to refer to your textbook for certain formulas and relationships in order to complete the template.)

Problem:

George Sweeney currently holds a 120-day, 15% note receivable written by Frank Koch in the amount of $40,000. The note is dated October 7, 1986. On January 29, 1987, George decides to discount the note at the Como State Bank. On that date, the bank is charging a 16% discount rate on notes.

Required:

Determine the due date of the note, and the impact of discounting the note on the interest income or expense to be reported.

Exhibit 30-1

	A	B	C	D	E
1	DISCOUNTING NOTES RECEIVABLE				
2					
3	Face value of the note receivable				
4	Number of days the note will be outstanding				
5	Stated interest rate of the note				
6	Date of issuance of the note				
7	Date of discounting the note				
8	Bank discount rate				
9					
10	**				
11					
12	Calculation of the Due Date of the Note Receivable				
13	--				
14	Date of issuance of the note				
15	Number of days the note will be outstanding				
16					-------------------
17	Due date of the note				
18					============
19	Number of Days holding the Note Receivable:				
20	By original holder:				

Completing the Spreadsheet:

Step 1 - Begin by entering the input information. The template is designed so that all of the data will be entered in column E above the row of asterisks (***). This will make it easier to change the inputs at a later time.

>L   **In cell E3, enter $40,000.**

Dollar amounts should be entered without dollar signs or commas.

>L   **In cell E4, enter 120 days.**
>L   **In cell E5, enter 15% as the interest rate.**

Enter percentages as decimals (for example, 15% equals .15).

>L   **In cell E6, enter "@DATE(86,10,7)" for October 7, 1986.**

Note that the number 31,692 displays in cell E6. This is the number which Lotus 1-2-3 assigns to the date October 7, 1986. This number can be used to calculate other dates by adding and subtracting. In a moment we will change the display format so that the date is displayed instead of the number 31,692.

>L   **In cell E7, enter "@DATE(87,1,29)" for January 29, 1987.**

You should see 31,806 displayed in cell E7.

When entering the dates of issuing and of discounting the note, use the calendar function. For example, type October 7, 1986 as "@DATE(86,10,7)" and press the [enter] key. Note that if you attempt to enter 10/7/86, you will get the quotient .0166112957! Check to be sure that your dates are correctly entered in date format.

In order to see the dates displayed, we must change the display format of cells E6 and E7 to date format.

>L   **Move the cursor to cell E6.**
>L   **Type "/R" for range, followed by "F" for format.**

You should see the format options on the second line of the control panel.

>L   **Type "D" for date.**

You are then presented with three different formats for displaying the date. Let's choose the first display (DD-MMM-YY) which shows the day, month, and year.

>L   **Press the [enter] key.**

You will then see a prompt to enter a range on the second line of the control panel.

>L   **Using the "down" cursor movement key, point to cell E7.**

Cells E6 and E7 will be highlighted and the range E6..E7 indicated on the second line of the control panel.

>L   **Press the [enter] key and you should see the dates displayed!**

>L   **Finally, in cell E8, enter 16% as the bank discount rate.**

If you have correctly entered your data, then the input area of your screen should appear as in Exhibit 30-2.

Step 2 - Now let's begin our calculations. First, let's determine the due date of the note.

>L   **Move the cursor to cell E14.**
>L   **Enter the date of issuance of the note by either using the cursor to point to cell E6 in the input area, or by entering "+E6". (Remember, the cursor will be activated as a pointer when you press the [+] key.)**

Note that you will see 31,692 displayed in cell E14.

Exhibit 30-2

	A	B	C	D	E
1		DISCOUNTING NOTES RECEIVABLE			
2					
3	Face value of the note receivable				40000
4	Number of days the note will be outstanding				120
5	Stated interest rate of the note				0.15
6	Date of issuance of the note				07-Oct-86
7	Date of discounting the note				29-Jan-87
8	Bank discount rate				0.16
9					
10	***				

>L   **Reformat cell E14 so that the date will display. (Type "/RFD" and press the [enter] key twice.)**

>L   **Move the cursor to cell E15 and enter the number of days the note will be outstanding by referencing cell E4 (Either point to E4 or enter "+E4").**

>L   **Move the cursor to cell E17 and enter "+E14+E15" (you may wish to point this out rather than typing).**

You should see 31,812 displayed in cell E17. The number of days the note will be outstanding has been added to the date of issue of the note!

>L   **Reformat cell E17 so that the date will display. (Type "/RFD" and press the [enter] key twice.)**

Note how the program provides you with the due date of the note (February 4, 1987) in cell E17!

Step 3 - Next, let's calculate how long the original holder has held the note by subtracting the date of issuance from the date of discount

>L   **In cell E20, enter or point out "+E7-E6".**

Step 4 - Now let's find out how long the bank will hold the note. This may be calculated by subtracting the date of discounting the note from the due date of the note (which we calculated in cell E17).

>L   **In cell E22, enter or point out "+E17-E7".**

At this point, your spreadsheet should appear as in Exhibit 30-3.

Exhibit 30-3

```
|    A    ||    B    ||    C    ||    D    ||    E    |
1|    DISCOUNTING NOTES RECEIVABLE
2|
3| Face value of the note receivable ........................................    40000
4| Number of days the note will be outstanding ..................    120
5| Stated interest rate of the note ........................................    0.15
6| Date of issuance of the note .............................................    07-Oct-86
7| Date of discounting the note ............................................    29-Jan-87
8| Bank discount rate ............................................................    0.16
9|
10| **************************************************
11|
12| Calculation of the Due Date of the Note Receivable
13|-----------------------------------------------------------------------
14| Date of issuance of the note                              07-Oct-86
15| Number of days the note will be outstanding              120
16|                                                        --------------------
17| Due date of the note                                     04-Feb-87
18|                                                        ============
19| Number of Days holding the Note Receivable:
20|      By original holder:                                     114
21|                                                        ============
22|      By bank:                                                   6
23|                                                        ============
```

Step 5 - Calculate the maturity value of the note by summing the face value of the note and the interest to be received at maturity.

>L   **In cell E27, enter the face value of the note by either using the cursor to point to cell E3 in the input area, or by entering "+E3".**

>L   **In cell E28, enter the formula for the calculation of the interest on the note to its maturity date.**

Use (reference) the cells in the input area for the amount of principal, the interest rate, and the number of days the note will be outstanding. (For example, your formula might read "+E3*E5*E4/360".)

(Note: You may wish to assume either a 360- or 365-day year for all calculations of interest. Alternatively, the length of year to be used could be added as an additional input variable. If you choose to have the length of year as a variable, enter a description of the variable (for example, Number of days . . .) in cell A9, and enter the number of days you wish to use in cell E9. You may then reference cell E9 in your interest calculations instead of typing a number.

>L   **In cell E30, enter or point out "+E27+E28" to sum the principal and interest.**

Step 6 - Calculate the book value of the note by summing the face value of the note and the interest accrued to the date of discount.

>L   In cell E35, reference the face value of the note from the input area (for example, enter "+E3").
>L   In cell E36, enter the formula for the calculation of the interest accrued on the note with appropriate references to the cells in the input area and your calculation of the number of days the note has been held (cell E20).
>L   In cell E38, enter the sum of cells E35 and E36 to calculate the book value of the note.

If you have performed these steps correctly, then the calculations of the maturity value and the book value of the note should appear as in Exhibit 30-4 (assuming a 360-day year).

Exhibit 30-4

	A	B	C	D	E
25	Calculation of the Maturity Value of the Note Receivable				
26	--
27	Face value of the note				40000
28	Plus interest				2000
29					-------------------
30	Maturity value of the note receivable				42000
31					============
32					
33	Calculation of Book Value of the Note Receivable				
34	--
35	Face value of the note				40000
36	Interest to date				1900
37					-------------------
38	Book value of the note receivable				41900
39					============

Step 7 - Let's calculate the proceeds from discounting the note by subtracting the bank discount from the maturity value of the note.

>L   Move the cursor to cell E43 and enter your previous calculation of the maturity value of the note by referencing the cell where you completed that calculation. (Hint: Activate the pointer by pressing the [+] key and point to the cell containing the calculation of the maturity value of the note.)
>L   Then, in cell E44, calculate the bank's discount on the maturity value of the note by entering the discount formula, complete with references to the appropriate input cells and earlier calculations.
>L   Move the cursor to cell E46 and enter or point out "+E43-E44" to calculate the net proceeds from discounting the note.

Step 8 - Finally, let's calculate the interest income or interest expense by subtracting the book value of the note receivable (calculated previously) from the proceeds from discounting the note receivable (which was just calculated).

>L   In cell E51, enter "+E46", the proceeds from discounting the note.
>L   In cell E52, enter "+E38", the book value of the note.
>L   In cell E54, enter or point out "+E51-E52" to calculate the interest income (expense).

If you have performed these steps correctly, then the calculations of the proceeds from discounting the note and the interest income or expense should appear as in Exhibit 30-5 (assuming a 360-day year). The negative number indicates that interest expense was incurred.

Exhibit 30-5

	A	B	C	D	E
41	Calculation of the Proceeds from Discounting the Note				
42	---				
43	Maturity value				42000
44	Less bank discount				112
45					-------------------
46	Proceeds from discounting the note				41888
47					============
48					
49	Calculation of Interest Income or Interest Expense				
50	---				
51	Proceeds from discounting the note				41888
52	Less book value of the note receivable				41900
53					-------------------
54	Interest Income (Expense)				-12
55					============

Step 9 - You may wish to "clean up" the appearance of your spreadsheet by changing the display formats of certain locations to dollars and cents, or to add commas to the numbers.

>L   After completing your formatting, press the [Home] key to move the cursor to cell A1.

Step 10 - At this point, you may wish to **save** your work. Use the procedures given in Chapter 5 to save and later to retrieve your work.

Printing: If your computer is connected to a printer, you may want to print the spreadsheet.

>L   Type "/PPRA1.E55" and press the [enter] key to specify the range to print.
>L   Make sure that your printer's paper is aligned and then type "A" for Align.
>L   Type "G" for Go to print your schedules.
>L   Type "Q" to Quit the print function after the schedules are printed.

Your spreadsheet should now be ready for you to manipulate the input data and study the effects that changes in the variables, particularly the date of discount, may have on the interest income or expense.

If you wish to quit at this time:

>L   Type "/QY" to quit using Lotus 1-2-3. (Type "EY" if needed to exit the Lotus access system menu.)

After the screen clears and the red in-use light has gone off, you may remove your disks and turn off the computer.

CHAPTER 31 - BONDS PAYABLE WITH STRAIGHT-LINE AMORTIZATION

Objective: This partially completed spreadsheet uses the COPY command extensively. It also illustrates how the PRESENT VALUE function might be used in calculating the selling price of a bond issue. The IF function is also introduced. The completed spreadsheet will enable you to determine the selling price (present value) of a bond issue and prepare a schedule of bond premium or discount amortization using the straight-line method. These calculations will provide you with the necessary information to prepare journal entries for each period's transactions.

Part A of the spreadsheet requires the computation of the bond premium or discount and the construction of an amortization schedule for four periods using the straight-line method. Part B asks you to incorporate the inputs needed to calculate the selling price of the bonds, in addition to calculating the bond premium or discount and to expand the amortization schedule to cover up to fifteen periods. These two parts may be worked *sequentially* at different times by saving the results of Part A.

Spreadsheet Name: SLBONDS

Required Input Information: Before beginning, you should identify:

1. The amount of bond principal.
2. The stated interest rate per period.
3. The effective interest rate per period.
4. The number of interest periods.
5. The selling price of the bond issue.

Using the Spreadsheet:

If you have not already done so, load Lotus 1-2-3 into your computer following the instructions given in Part I.

Load the partially completed spreadsheet from the file disk:

>L   **Press the [Alt] key and simultaneously type the letter "S" from the menu.**

When the spreadsheet has finished loading, the screen display should appear similar to that shown in Exhibit 31-1.

You must now enter the required input information and complete the template. Partial instructions for completing the template are given below. (You may wish to refer to your textbook for certain formulas and relationships in order to complete the template.)

Problem:

The Trinity Corporation issued $100,000 of 10%, 4-year bonds on January 1, 1986. These bonds sold for $93,925 to yield an effective interest of 12%. The company believes that the amount of premium or discount amortization calculated under the straight-line method will not be materially different from the amount which would be calculated using the effective interest method.

Required:

A.   Calculate the amount of any premium or discount on the bond issue and prepare a schedule of bond premium or discount amortization using the straight-line method.

B.   Expand the flexibility of your template to include the necessary inputs to compute the selling price of the bond issue and to cover fifteen time periods.

Exhibit 31-1

	A	B	C	D	E	F
1	BONDS PAYABLE WITH STRAIGHT-LINE AMORTIZATION					
2						
3	Amount of bond principal					
4	Selling price of bond issue					
5						--------------------
6	Discount or (Premium) on Bond Issue					
7						=============
8	Schedule of Bond Premium or Discount Amortization					
9	Straight-line Method					
10						
11		Credit	Disc(Prem)	Interest	Unamort.	Carrying
12	Period	Cash	Amortiz.	Expense	Disc(Prem)	Value
13	---					
14						
15						
16						
17						
18						
19						
20						

Completing the Spreadsheet - Part A:

Step 1 - First, let's compute the amount of the premium or discount on the sale of the bond issue.

>L   **Move the cursor to cell F3 and enter $100,000, the amount of bond principal.**

(Remember to enter numbers without dollar signs and commas!)

>L   **In cell F4, enter $93,925, the selling price of the bond issue.**

>L   **Now, in cell F6, enter "+F3-F4" to subtract the selling price of the bond issue from the amount of bond principal.**

You should get a discount of $6,075. Note that a discount displays as a positive number while a premium would display as a negative number.

Step 2 - Now we are ready to begin the schedule of bond premium or discount amortization by entering the beginning balances and calculating the first year's interest expense.

Step 2a - Begin by entering the initial account balances at the date of issuance of the bonds.

>L   **In cells A14 through A18, enter each period from 0 to 4, respectively.**

Zero represents the current date, or date of issuance of the bonds. Periods 1-4 represent the end of each year, or the date at which interest is paid.

Since row 14 represents the date of issuance, there is no credit to cash, no amortization and no interest expense.

>L   **In cells B14 through D14, enter zeroes (0). (Or, you may leave these cells blank.)**

>L   **Move the cursor to cell E14 and enter the unamortized balance of the bond discount by referencing cell F6.**

Remember, you can either type and enter "+F6" in cell E14, or activate the cursor as a pointer by pressing the plus [+] key, move the pointer to cell F6 and press the [enter] key.

>L   **Move the cursor to cell F14 and enter the initial carrying value of the bond issue by referencing the selling price of the bond in cell F4. Use the same procedures as in the previous step (or you can subtract the unamortized discount in cell E14 from the amount of bond principal in cell F3).**

Your spreadsheet should now appear similar to Exhibit 31-2.

Exhibit 31-2

	A	B	C	D	E	F
1	BONDS PAYABLE WITH STRAIGHT-LINE AMORTIZATION					
2						
3	Amount of bond principal					100000
4	Selling price of bond issue					93925
5						--------------------
6	Discount or (Premium) on Bond Issue					6075
7						=============
8	Schedule of Bond Premium or Discount Amortization					
9	Straight-line Method					
10						
11		Credit	Disc(Prem)	Interest	Unamort.	Carrying
12	Period	Cash	Amortiz.	Expense	Disc(Prem)	Value
13	--					
14	0	0	0	0	6075	93925
15	1					
16	2					
17	3					
18	4					
19						
20						

Step 2b - Now let's calculate the interest expense for the first period.

>L   Move the cursor to cell B15 and press the plus [+] key to activate the pointer.

>L   Use the arrow keys to point to cell F3. Press the special function key [F4].

On the second line of the control panel, you should see "+$F$3". The dollar signs mean that the reference to cell F3 in our formula is *absolute*. We'll explain what *absolute* means in a moment. You should note that you can also type in the dollar signs rather than using the special function key [F4]. However, using the special function key is usually more convenient.

>L   Now type an asterisk (*)to indicate that you wish to multiply the amount of bond principal by another number. The cursor will return to cell B15.

>L   Type the interest rate of ".10" and press the [enter] key..

Your formula on the first line of the control panel should now read "+$F$4*.10". If it does not, repeat the steps above until it is correct. You should see 10000 displayed as the credit to cash.

This amount is equal to the amount of bond principal multiplied times the stated interest rate. Our formula references the amount of bond principal in cell F3 and multiplies this amount by the stated rate of interest of .10. (Make sure that you enter the interest as a decimal and not as a percentage.)

>L   Next, in cell C15, enter "+$F$6/4" to calculate the straight-line amortization for the first period. (Press the plus [+] key, move the pointer to cell F6, press the special function key [F4], type a slash (/) to indicate division followed by "4" and press the [enter] key.

The periodic amortization is equal to the amount of the discount (in cell F6) divided by the life of the bond issue (4 years). You should see 1519 displayed as the amount of amortization.

>L   Move the cursor to cell D15 and type (or point) the formula "+B15+C15" and press the [enter] key. *Don't* use the special function key [F4] for this entry.

This formula sums the results of cells B15 and C15 to calculate the amount of interest expense for the first period, which is equal to the credit to cash plus the discount amortization. You should get $11,519 as the total interest expense for the first period.

Step 2c - Finally, let's calculate the balance of the unamortized discount and the carrying value of the bond issue to complete our calculations for the first period.

>L   In cell E15, subtract the discount amortization in cell C15 from the unamortized discount in cell E14.

The unamortized discount is equal to the initial discount less the amortization for the first period. Thus, we subtract the periodic amortization in cell C15 from the unamortized discount in cell E14. You should get $4,556 as the unamortized discount balance.

>L   In cell F15, enter "+$F$3-E15" to calculate the carrying value of the bonds at the end of the first period. (Press the plus [+] key, move the pointer to cell F3, press the special function key [F4], type a minus (-) to indicate subtraction, type "E15" and press the [enter] key.

The carrying value of the bond issue is equal to the amount of bond principal less the unamortized discount. You should get $95,444 for the carrying value of the bonds at the end of the first year.

Your spreadsheet should appear as in Exhibit 31-3.

Step 3 - Let's check our work before moving on.

>L   Move the cursor to each of the following cells and check to see that the formulas are correct. If they are not correct, reenter the correct formula before continuing.

Exhibit 31-3

	A	B	C	D	E	F
1	BONDS PAYABLE WITH STRAIGHT-LINE AMORTIZATION					
2						
3	Amount of bond principal					100000
4	Selling price of bond issue					93925
5						--------------------
6	Discount or (Premium) on Bond Issue					6075
7						=============
8	Schedule of Bond Premium or Discount Amortization					
9	Straight-line Method					
10						
11		Credit	Disc(Prem)	Interest	Unamort.	Carrying
12	Period	Cash	Amortiz.	Expense	Disc(Prem)	Value
13	----					
14	0	0	0	0	6075	93925
15	1	10000	1519	11519	4556	95444
16	2					
17	3					
18	4					
19						
20						

	Cell	Formulas
>L	B15	+$F$3*.10
>L	C15	+$F$6/4
>L	D15	+B15+C15
>L	E15	+E14-C15
>L	F15	+$F$3-E15

Step 4 - Now that you have established the formulas for calculating the credit to cash, the periodic amortization, the interest expense, the unamortized discount and the carrying value of the bonds for the first period, you can use these formulas as the basis for completing your schedule for periods 2 through 4.

Step 4a - Let's begin by copying the formula used to calculate the amount of interest to be paid in cash at the end of period 1 to periods 2, 3 and 4.

>L   **Move your cursor to cell B15.**

Note that the first line of the control panel shows the formula in this cell to be "+$F$3*0.10". We want this exact *same* formula to be copied for each period since the cash amount to be paid is the same in each period. This is the reason we used the special function key [F4]. *The dollar signs in the formula tell the program that cell F3 is fixed or absolute and should not be adjusted when we copy it.*

If you fail to specify cell F3 as being an absolute reference, the program will automatically adjust this formula to new cells. For example, if we were to copy the formula in cell B15 to cell B16, the program would adjust the formula "+F3*0.10" to read "+F4*0.10"--one row lower! Since we have specified the reference to cell F3 in our formula as absolute, it will not be adjusted!

>L   **Type "/C" for Copy.**
>L   **Press the [enter] key.**

Since you want to copy the formula *from* cell B15, and your cursor is in that cell, pressing the [enter] key will result in cell B15 automatically being selected as the range to copy *from*.

Once you press the [enter] key, you will be prompted for the range you wish to copy *to*.

>L   **Use the arrow keys to move the cursor to cell B16, the first cell in the range you wish to copy *to*.**

Cell B16 should now be displayed on the right-hand side of the second line of the control panel to indicate that this is the beginning of the cell range you wish to copy to.

>L   **Type a period (.) to indicate that cell B16 is the first cell in a range of cells you wish to copy *to*.**
>L   **Move the cursor to cell B18, the last cell in the range you wish to copy *to*.**

The range of cells from B16 to B18 should now be highlighted to indicate that this is the range that you will copy *to*. The second line of the control panel should also tell you that you will be copying *to* the range B16. .B18. (If this is not the case, press the [Esc] key and begin this step over.)

>L   **Press the [enter] key.**

You should see 10000 displayed in each of the cells B16 through B18. If you move your cursor to any of these three cells, you should see the formula +$F$3*0.10 on the first line of the control panel. Your spreadsheet should now appear as in Exhibit 31-4.

Step 4b - We could continue to copy each of the remaining formulas in each column of row 15. This would be tedious, however, if there were a large number of formulas to be copied. A faster and more efficient method is to copy several formulas, all at the same time! That is, you can copy from a range of cells, not just from one cell!

Let's copy the formulas in cells C15, D15, E15, and F15 to rows 16, 17 and 18 simultaneously.

>L   **Move the cursor to cell C15.**

This is the first cell in the range of cells we wish to copy *from*.

Exhibit 31-4

	A	B	C	D	E	F
1	BONDS PAYABLE WITH STRAIGHT-LINE AMORTIZATION					
2						
3	Amount of bond principal					100000
4	Selling price of bond issue					93925
5						--------------------
6	Discount or (Premium) on Bond Issue					6075
7						=============
8	Schedule of Bond Premium or Discount Amortization					
9	Straight-line Method					
10						
11		Credit	Disc(Prem)	Interest	Unamort.	Carrying
12	Period	Cash	Amortiz.	Expense	Disc(Prem)	Value
13	--					
14	0	0	0	0	6075	93925
15	1	10000	1519	11519	4556	95444
16	2	10000				
17	3	10000				
18	4	10000				
19						
20						

>L   Type "/C" for Copy.

You should see "C15. .C15" automatically display on the second line of the control panel.

>L   Next, move your cursor to cell F15, the final cell in the range of cells you wish to copy *from*. If you have done this correctly, the cells from C15 through F15 should be highlighted.

>L   Press the [enter] key.

When you press the [enter] key, the highlight disappears, but the second line of the control panel will show a range to copy *from* of "C15. .F15" and will be prompting you for the range you wish to copy *to*.

If you have made an error, press the [Esc] key. Each time you press the [Esc] key, you can move one step back in the process of copying.

>L   Move the cursor to cell C16, the first cell you wish to copy *to*.

>L   Type a period (.) to indicate that this is the first cell in the range of cells you wish to copy *to*.

>L   Then, move the cursor to cell C18 to point out the last cell in the range of cells you wish to copy *to* (cells C16 through C18 should be highlighted) and press the [enter] key.

Note that you did not have to point to cell F18, which would technically be the last cell to which you will be copying. Since you are copying *from* a range of cells in four columns (C through F), you need only point out the beginning of the range of rows (16 through 18) you wish to copy *to*--the spreadsheet will then copy the formulas from all four columns to each of the succeeding rows!

Note that in cell C15 we specified the reference to cell F6 as absolute. Because of this, it has not been adjusted. Since we are using straight-line amortization, we want the formula to always refer to cell F6 (which contains the amount of discount) and divide this amount by 4.

All of our cell references in columns D and E are *relative*. If you move the cursor to cell E15, the formula should read "+E14-C15". If you move to cell E16, the formula should read "+E15-C16". Because we did *not* specify these cells as *absolute* in the formulas, the program has automatically adjusted each formula to each new row. Thus, each period's amortization of discount is subtracted from the unamortized balance of the discount.

Move the cursor to cell F15. Remember that this cell calculates the carrying value of the bond issue by subtracting the unamortized balance of the discount from the amount of principal of the bond issue. The formula in this cell should read "+$F$3-E15".

Since the carrying value of the bond issue in period 1 is the difference between cells F3 and E15, and in period 2 would be the difference between cells F3 and E16 (period 3 would be F3 and E17, etc.), we can see that the cell reference to F3 is absolute. Thus, we used the special function key [F4] to indicate that the reference to cell F3 was *absolute*. If you move the cursor to cell F16, you will see that the reference to cell F3 has not been adjusted.

The unamortized discount, however, is *relative* since the balance decreases each period. Thus, in cell F15, we subtracted the balance in cell E15. In cell F16, we subtracted the balance in cell E16 and so forth. Since we did not specify cell E15 as absolute, the program has automatically adjusted this cell reference to each new row.

You should now be seeing how important it is to plan out the development of a spreadsheet so that you will be able to specify any absolute references. Using this feature can greatly increase the efficiency with which you can use the Copy command. *Inappropriate use of the absolute cell designation can result in copied formulas being adjusted when they should not be and/or formulas not being adjusted when they should be!*

Your spreadsheet for Part A should now be completed and appear as in Exhibit 31-5!

Step 5 - You may wish to "clean up" the appearance of your spreadsheet by changing the formats of certain cells to dollars and cents. Refer to the earlier chapters for instructions on formatting cells.

>L   **After completing your formatting, press the [Home] key to move the cursor to cell A1.**

Step 6 - At this point, you may wish to **save** your work. Use the procedures given in Chapter 5 to save your work.

Printing: You might also want to print the spreadsheet if your computer is connected to a printer.

>L   **Type "/PPRA1.F18" and press the [enter] key to specify the print range.**
>L   **Make sure that your printer's paper is aligned and then type "A" for Align.**
>L   **Type "G" for Go to print the spreadsheet.**
>L   **Type "Q" to Quit the print function after the schedule is printed.**

If you wish to quit at this time:

>L   **Type "/QY" to quit using Lotus 1-2-3. (Type "EY" if needed to exit the Lotus access system menu.)**

After the screen clears and the red in-use light has gone off, you may remove your disks and turn off the computer.

Exhibit 31-5

	A	B	C	D	E	F
1	BONDS PAYABLE WITH STRAIGHT-LINE AMORTIZATION					
2						
3	Amount of bond principal					100000
4	Selling price of bond issue					93925
5						--------------------
6	Discount or (Premium) on Bond Issue					6075
7						=============
8	Schedule of Bond Premium or Discount Amortization					
9	Straight-line Method					
10						
11|		Credit	Disc(Prem)	Interest	Unamort.	Carrying
12	Period	Cash	Amortiz.	Expense	Disc(Prem)	Value
13	--					
14	0	0	0	0	6075	93925
15	1	10000	1519	11519	4556	95444
16	2	10000	1519	11519	3038	96963
17	3	10000	1519	11519	1519	98481
18	4	10000	1519	11519	0	100000
19						
20						

Completing the Spreadsheet - Part B:

If you saved your spreadsheet earlier and would now like to continue, use the procedures in Chapter 5 to retrieve your file.

You will rapidly discover that the only inputs which we can presently change in our spreadsheet are the amount of bond principal and the selling price of the bonds. This is not a very efficient application of the capabilities of the spreadsheet. What we would prefer to have is a spreadsheet which is capable of handling not only different amounts of bond principal and selling prices, but different interest rates and different time periods as well. In fact, it would be nice if the spreadsheet also calculated the selling price of the bond issue for us! So let's modify our spreadsheet to do just that!

Step 7 - Begin by inserting ten rows between the spreadsheet heading and the amount of bond prinicipal to give us room for the additional inputs and calculations.

>L   Place the cursor in the second row.
>L   Type "/WI" for Worksheet and Insert, followed by "R" for row.
>L   When you are prompted to enter a row range, use the arrow keys to highlight the range "A2. .A11" and press the [enter] key.

Ten blank rows will be inserted, beginning in row 2. Note that your original calculations are still present, but that they have been "pushed" ten rows farther down the spreadsheet.

Step 8 - Enter the following labels in the corresponding cells:

	Cell	Label
>L	A3	Amount of principal
>L	A4	Stated interest rate
>L	A5	Effective interest rate
>L	A6	Number of interest periods
>L	A7	
>L	A8	Present value of interest payments equals
>L	A9	Present value of principal equals
>L	A10	
>L	A11	Selling price of bonds payable equals

Step 9 - Enter the following values for the amount of principal, stated interest rate, effective interest rate, and number of interest periods in the corresponding cells.

	Cell	Amount
>L	F3	$100,000
>L	F4	.10
>L	F5	.12
>L	F6	4

These four values represent the inputs for our revised spreadsheet.

When you attempt to enter the interest rates as decimals (which is correct), you will see zeroes (0) on the screen. This is because the spreadsheet is rounding to the nearest whole number. In order to display the decimals, you will need to format cells F4 and F5.

>L   **Move the cursor to cell F4 and type "/RF" for Range and Format.**

>L   **Type "F" for Fixed and press the [enter] key to select the standard or default setting of two decimal places.**

>L   **Use the arrow keys to point out the two cells you wish to reformat (F4 and F5) and press the [enter] key. The interest rates will now be displayed as decimals.**

Step 10 - Now let's calculate the selling price of the bonds payable. The selling price is equal to the present value of the bonds, which is comprised of two components--the present value of the interest payments and the present value of the bond principal. Let's calculate these two values in cells F8 and F9.

Step 10a - Let's calculate the present value of the interest payments first:

>L   **In cell F8, enter "@PV(" to begin using the present value function.** *This is @PV followed by a left-hand parenthesis.* **(The @ symbol is on the key with the "2" at the upper left-hand corner of the keyboard. Remember to press the [shift] key to use the @ symbol.)**

The present value function calculates the present value of an ordinary annuity, such as a series of equal interest payments. The function requires that we specify the amount of each periodic payment, the interest rate, and the number of periods. This data is available through our inputs.

Since our inputs do not include the amount of the interest payments, we will have to calculate this value.

>L   **Using the arrow keys, point to cell F3, which contains the amount of principal.**

>L   **Type an asterisk (*) to indicate multiplication and then point to cell F4, which contains the stated interest rate.**

>L   **Press a comma (,) to continue.**

Your function, as shown on the third status line, should now read "@PV(F3*F4,".

>L   **Next, use the arrow keys to point to cell F5, which contains the effective interest rate.**

>L   **Press a comma (,) to continue.**

The function, as shown on the third status line, should now read "@PV(F3*F4,F5,".

>L   **Finally, use the arrow keys to point to cell F6, which contains the number of interest periods. Type the right-hand parenthesis ")" and press the [enter] key.**

Your function should read "@PV(F3*F4,F5,F6)" and you should get $30,373 as the present value of the interest payments in cell F8.

Step 10b - Now let's find the present value of the bond principal. Unfortunately, there is no function in the program which can be used to directly calculate the present value of a single payment, such as the repayment of principal. There are several alternative approaches to this calculation, one of which is to resort to the mathematical formula for this calculation. This formula is:

$$\frac{\text{Principal}}{(1 + \text{the interest rate})^n}$$

where n = the number of time periods.

>L   **Move the cursor to cell F9, type "+F3/(1+F5)^F6" and press the [enter] key.**

Remember, cell F3 is the amount of principal, cell F5 is the effective interest rate, and cell F6 is the number of time periods. The caret (^) means that the quantity inside the parentheses will be raised to the power indicated by cell F6. (The caret is located on the key with the "6" at the top of the keyboard.) You should get $63,552 in cell F9. (You can also use the arrow keys to point to the various cells instead of typing them.)

Step 10c - In order to finish calculating the selling price of the bonds, we need to sum the present values of the interest and the principal.

>L   **Move the cursor to cell F11 and sum cells F8 and F9.**

You should get the same selling price as was given earlier in the problem ($93,925).

>L   **Move the cursor to cell F10 and place a dashed line beneath the two present values which are being summed. Remember, the repeating text command begins by typing a backslash (\\) and then following this with the character to be repeated (a dash).**

>L   **Move the cursor to cell F12 and place a double dashed line (using the equals sign) beneath the total selling price.**

Your spreadsheet should now appear as in Exhibit 31-6.

Step 11 - Let's make one final change before modifying the amortization schedule. In rows 13 through 17, we have a calculation of the bond discount or premium. Let's change the amounts used in that calculation to reference our inputs and calculation of the present value.

>L   **In cell F13, replace the dollar amount with a reference to cell F3, the cell which contains the amount of principal (either type "+F3" or use the arrow keys to point to cell F3).**

>L   **In cell F14, replace the dollar amount with a reference to cell F11, the calculation of the selling price of the bonds.**

Now our calculation of the discount or premium will automatically incorporate any changes we make in the input data.

>L   **For example, change the stated rate of interest in cell F4 to .09. The selling price of the bonds should now be $90,888 and the amount of discount should be $9,112.**

>L   **Return to the original data (stated interest = .10) and let's continue.**

Exhibit 31-6

	A	B	C	D	E	F
1		BONDS PAYABLE WITH STRAIGHT-LINE AMORTIZATION				
2						
3	Amount of principal					100000
4	Stated interest rate					0.10
5	Effective interest rate					0.12
6	Number of interest periods					4
7						
8	Present value of interest payments equals					30373
9	Present value of principal equals					63552
10						----------------
11	Selling price of bonds payable equals					93925
12						============
13	Amount of bond principal					100000
14	Selling price of bond issue					93925
15						----------------
16	Discount or (Premium) on Bond Issue					6075
17						============
18	Schedule of Bond Premium or Discount Amortization					
19	Straight-line Method					
20						

Step 12 - Now we need to see what effects changing our inputs will have on our amortization schedule. Scroll down so that the entire amortization schedule is displayed.

Step 12a - Obviously, four periods is not very many, so let's increase the number of periods to fifteen. We could start this in column A by continuing to enter values for periods 5, 6, 7, . . . 15. There is a faster way to do this, however. Let's enter a formula and copy it.

>L   **Move the cursor to cell A25 (period 1).**
>L   **Enter "+A24+1" in this cell.**

Note that while we now have a formula in cell A25, the display is still the number 1.

>L   **With the cursor in cell A25, type "/C" and press the [enter] key to indicate that we would like to copy from this cell.**

>L   **Then, highlight the range of cells we would like to copy to (A26 through A39) and press the [enter] key to allow for automatic adjustment of the formula .**

You should see the numbers 2 through 15 added to the display in column A.

Step 12b - Next, let's copy our formula for the cash interest to be paid from cell B25. However, first we need to change this formula to reflect our inputs. It should be +F3*F4 (the amount of principal times the stated rate of interest).

>L   **In cell B25, enter "+$F$3*$F$4" to calculate the cash credit.**

Remember to use the pointer and the special function key [F4] to designate the cell references in the formula as absolute. Note that neither the amount of principal nor the stated interest rate will change. Thus, they are absolute.

>L   **With the cursor in cell B25, type "/C" and press the [enter] key to select this cell as the range to copy from.**

>L   **Highlight the range "B26. .B39" as the range of cells to copy to and press the [enter] key.**

Remember that this formula should have absolute references to cells F3 and F4. Thus, if you don't see $10,000 as the amount of cash interest in each period, you should check to make sure that you have designated the cells in the formula correctly.

Ten-thousand dollars in each period is, unfortunately, incorrect given our inputs. Remember that our bond issue has a life of only four periods. Thus, the interest should be $10,000 in each of periods one through four, but thereafter it should be zero. To correct this problem, we can use the @IF function. This function will allow us to check whether or not we have exceeded the life of the bonds, after which the interest to be paid is zero. Thus, if the period is greater than that given in cell F6 (4 periods in our problem), then the amount in column B should be zero.

>L   **In cell B25, enter "@IF(A25>$F$6,0,$F$3*$F$4)".**

(Don't forget the final parenthesis before you press the [enter] key.)

This formula is interpreted as "if the period as given in cell A25 is greater than the number of interest periods given in cell F6, then set the interest to be paid at zero; otherwise set the interest to be paid equal to the amount of principal (cell F3) times the stated interest rate (cell F4)." Note that A25 is a relative variable, whereas F6, F3, and F4 are absolute.

>L   **With the cursor in cell B25, type "/C" and press the [enter] key.**

>L   **Highlight the range "B26. .B39" as the range of cells to copy to and press the [enter] key.**

If done correctly, your schedule should now appear as in Exhibit 31-7.

Exhibit 31-7

	A	B	C	D	E	F
18		Schedule of Bond Premium or Discount Amortization				
19			Straight-line Method			
20						
21		Credit	Disc(Prem)	Interest	Unamort.	Carrying
22	Period	Cash	Amortiz.	Expense	Disc(Prem)	Value
23	-------	-------	-------	-------	-------	-------
24	0	0	0	0	6075	93925
25	1	10000	1519	11519	4556	95444
26	2	10000	1519	11519	3037	96963
27	3	10000	1519	11519	1519	98481
28	4	10000	1519	11519	0	100000
29	5	0				
30	6	0				
31	7	0				
32	8	0				
33	9	0				
34	10	0				
35	11	0				
36	12	0				
37	13	0				
38	14	0				
39	15	0				

Step 12c - We have a similar problem with the formula to calculate the amortization for each period. Updating our formula for the new inputs gives us +$F$16/$F$6 instead of +$F$16/4. However, if we copy this formula, the schedule will compute amortization in every period, even after the bond principal has been repaid.

>L   In cell C25, enter "@IF(A25>$F$6,0,$F$16/$F$6)" to calculate the periodic amortization.

>L   With the cursor in cell C25, type "/C" and press the [enter] key.

>L   Highlight the range "C26. .C39" as the range of cells to copy to and press the [enter] key.

Note again, that A25 is relative to each successive row but that F6 and F16 are absolute in relation to each row and should not be adjusted.

Step 12d - The remaining three columns calculating interest expense, the unamortized discount balance and the carrying value of the bond issue require no adjustment before copying. Let's copy all three columns at one time.

>L   Place the cursor in cell D25 and enter "/C".

>L   Use the arrow keys to highlight the range from cell D25 through cell F25 and press the [enter] key.

>L   Next, highlight the range you wish to copy to--cell D26 through cell D39--and press the [enter] key.

You should see the carrying value of the bonds increase to $100,000 in the fourth period. Unfortunately, this value continues into the fifth, sixth, and all future periods. Again, you may use an @IF function to eliminate this problem.

>L   In cell F25, enter "@IF(A25>$F$6,0,$F$13-E25)".
>L   Copy this command to cells F26 through F39.

Note that the references to cells A25 and E25 are relative and should be adjusted, while the references to cells F6 and F13 are absolute and should not be adjusted.

Your amortization schedule is now completed and should appear as shown in Exhibit 31-8.

Exhibit 31-8

	A	B	C	D	E	F
18|	Schedule of Bond Premium or Discount Amortization					
19|			Straight-line Method			
20							
21|		Credit	Disc(Prem)	Interest	Unamort.	Carrying
22|	Period	Cash	Amortiz.	Expense	Disc(Prem)	Value
23|	---					
24		0	0	0	0	6075	93925
25		1	10000	1519	11519	4556	95444
26		2	10000	1519	11519	3037	96963
27		3	10000	1519	11519	1519	98481
28		4	10000	1519	11519	0	100000
29		5	0	0	0	0	0
30		6	0	0	0	0	0
31		7	0	0	0	0	0
32		8	0	0	0	0	0
33		9	0	0	0	0	0
34		10	0	0	0	0	0
35		11	0	0	0	0	0
36		12	0	0	0	0	0
37		13	0	0	0	0	0
38		14	0	0	0	0	0
39		15	0	0	0	0	0

Step 13 - You may wish to "clean up" the appearance of your spreadsheet by changing the formats of certain cells to dollars and cents, etc. Refer to the earlier chapters for instructions on formatting cells.

>L   **When you have completed any formatting, press the [Home] key to move the cursor to cell A1.**

Step 14 - At this point, you may wish to **save** your work. Use the procedures given in Chapter 5 to save your work.

Printing: You might also want to print the spreadsheet if your computer is connected to a printer.

>L   **Type "/PPRA1.F39" and press the [enter] key to specify the print range.**
>L   **Make sure that your printer's paper is aligned and then type "A" for Align.**
>L   **Type "G" for Go to print the spreadsheet.**
>L   **Type "Q" to Quit the print function after the schedule is printed.**

Your spreadsheet should now be ready for you to manipulate the input data and study the effects that changes in the variables may have on the selling price of the bond issue and the amount of interest to be paid and expensed in each period.

If you wish to quit at this time:

>L   **Type "/QY" to quit using Lotus 1-2-3. (Type "EY" if needed to exit the Lotus access system menu.)**

After the screen clears and the red in-use light has gone off, you may remove your disks and turn off the computer.

CHAPTER 32 - DIVIDEND DISTRIBUTION SCHEDULE

Objective: This partially completed spreadsheet illustrates the use of several logic functions. It demonstrates how the IF function and the MINIMUM function might be used in calculating the dividends to be received by each class of stock, preferred and common, when the total amount to be distributed has been set. The completed spreadsheet may also be used to determine the overall percentage dividend received by each class of stock.

Spreadsheet Name: DIVVY

Required Input Information: Before beginning, you should identify:

1. The dollar amount of preferred stock and common stock.
2. The preferred stock dividend rate as a percentage (.00).
3. The limit of preferred stock participation (.00).
4. Whether or not the preferred stock is cumulative.
5. How many years the preferred stock dividend is in arrears.
6. The total dividends to be distributed to the preferred and common stock.

Using the Spreadsheet:

If you have not already done so, load Lotus 1-2-3 into your computer following the instructions given in Part I.

Load the partially completed spreadsheet from the file disk in drive B.

>L   **Press the [Alt] key and simultaneously type the letter "T" from the menu.**

When the spreadsheet has finished loading, the screen display should appear similar to that shown in Exhibit 32-1.

You must now enter the required input information and complete the template. Partial instructions for completing the template are given below. (You may wish to refer to your textbook for certain formulas and relationships in order to complete the template.)

Problem:

Seminole Distributors, Inc. has the following stock outstanding:

9% Preferred Stock, $100 par value, noncumulative and
participating to 15%, 4,000 shares authorized,
2,000 shares issued and outstanding $200,000

Common Stock, $10 par value, 100,000 shares authorized,
80,000 shares issued and outstanding $800,000

The company wishes to issue the remaining preferred stock next year and will pay $100,000 in cash dividends this year to the preferred and common stockholders. The dividend on the preferred stock is one year in arrears.

Required:

A.   Prepare a schedule to compute the total dividends to be received by each class of stock from the current year's distribution.

B.   Assuming that the company issues the additional preferred stock next year, what amount of dividends will it have to pay if management wishes to maintain the same percentage dividend to the common stockholders as was paid this year?

C.   What difference would it make in each year's distributions if the preferred stock were cumulative?

Exhibit 32-1

	A	B	C	D	E	F
1|	DIVIDEND DISTRIBUTION SCHEDULE					
2|				Preferred	Common	Total
3|				Stock	Stock	Dollars
4							
5	Par value of stock			200000	800000	
6							
7	Preferred stock dividend (.00)			0.09		
8	Limit of P.S. participation (.00)			0.15		
9	P.S. cumulative? (1=Yes, 0=No)			0		
10	Number of years in arrears			1		
11	Amount of dividends to be distributed					100000
12							
13							
14|				Amount distributed to:		
15							
16|				Preferred	Common	Yet to be
17|				Stock	Stock	Distributed
18							
19	Total amount to be distributed			N/A	N/A	100000
20	P.S. dividends in arrears					

Completing the Spreadsheet - Part A:

Step 1 - After loading the spreadsheet, you will see that the data given in the problem has already been entered. The first step in completing the spreadsheet is to calculate the total par value of the preferred and common stock. This total will be needed later in the distribution schedule.

>L   Move the cursor to cell F5 and add the corresponding amounts in cells D5 and E5. Either enter "+D5+E5" or activate the pointer by pressing the plus [+] key and then using the pointer to help enter the formula.

Step 2 - Now let's begin working on the amounts to be distributed to each class of stock. Let's calculate the amount to be paid to preferred stock for dividends in arrears.

>L   Move the cursor to cell D20.

We need to consider two conditions before we enter a formula in this cell.

First, we must find a way to evaluate whether or not the preferred stock is cumulative. If it is noncumulative, then any dividends in arrears are irrelevant and the cell should display a zero. Alternatively, if the preferred stock is cumulative, then the cell should display the dividends to be paid. We can accomplish this using the @IF function.

Second, if the stock is cumulative, we still need to determine whether or not the full amount in arrears will be paid. For example, even if the stock is cumulative and there are dividends in arrears, nothing will be paid if no dividends have been declared. We can evaluate this using the @MIN function.

The @IF and the @MIN functions will be "nested" together as one large formula as described below.

Let's examine the @IF function in more detail. What we would like is a function which will enable us to select the correct amount from the following two statements:

(A) If the preferred stock is noncumulative, display zero.
(B) If the preferred stock is cumulative, display the amount of dividends in arrears.

If we use a *zero* in cell D9 to indicate that the stock is noncumulative, and a *one* in cell D9 to indicate that the stock is cumulative, then we can accomplish this by using the following function:

    @IF(D9=0,0,D5*D7*D10)

This function can be interpreted as follows: If the value in cell D9 equals zero (which indicates that the stock is noncumulative), then display zero; otherwise display the value D5 times D7 times D10 (amount of par value times the dividend rate times the number of years in arrears). Thus, if the value in cell D9 is anything else but zero, the function assumes that the stock is cumulative and calculates and displays the amount of dividends in arrears.

However, as mentioned, we have one further problem. If no dividends have been declared, or if an amount less than the total dividends in arrears has been declared, then the total arrearage cannot be paid. Thus, we need to compare the amount of dividends in arrears with the amount to be paid and choose the lesser of the two values.

For example, if dividends in arrears are $10,000, but no dividends have been declared (cell F11=0), choose zero as the amount to be paid. Alternatively, if dividends in arrears are $10,000, and dividends of $20,000 have been declared, choose $10,000 as the amount to be paid.

This can be done by comparing the results of our @IF function with the amount of dividends yet to be distributed (shown in cell F19) and choosing the minimum value. This is shown in the "nested" formula below:

>L   **In cell D20, enter "@MIN(F19,@IF(D9=0,0,D5*D7*D10))".**

Cell D20 should display a zero. In order to ensure that your formula works, let's temporarily change some of the input data.

>L   **Move the cursor to cell D9 and change the zero (0) to one (1) to indicate that the stock is now cumulative.**

You should now get $18,000 in cell D20--one year's dividend arrearage!

>L   **Move the cursor to cell F11 and enter $10,000 instead of $100,000.**

You should now get $10,000 in cell D20--despite the fact that the dividend arrearage is $18,000, only $10,000 can be paid since that is all that has been declared!

>L   **Reenter the original data ($100,000 of dividends in cell F11 and zero (0) in cell D9) and let's continue.**

Step 3 - Next, let's determine the amount of dividends yet to be distributed after any dividends in arrears on preferred stock are paid.

>L   **Move to cell E20. Since the common stock is not cumulative, type "N/A" for Not Applicable.**
>L   **Format cell E20 to right-hand justify the text in the cell. (Remember, type "/RL" for Range and Label-Prefix followed by "R" for Right and press the [enter] key.)**
>L   **Then in cell F20, subtract the amount of dividends in arrears from the previous amount yet to be distributed (enter, or use the pointer to enter, the formula "+F19-D20").**

You should see 100000 displayed since the preferred stock is noncumulative and we are subtracting zero from 100000.

>L   **To check your formula, move to cell D9, enter one (1), and see what happens. You should see 82000 displayed in cell F20.**
>L   **If your answer is correct, reenter a zero (0) in cell D9 and let's continue.**

Step 4 - Now let's calculate the current year's preferred stock dividend. This is not simply the par value of the preferred stock times the dividend rate. Remember again that we must also check to see that there is an adequate amount of dividends yet to be distributed to pay the current year dividend. You can use the @MIN function again to do this.

>L   **Move the cursor to cell D21 and enter "@MIN(F20,D5*D7)".**

You should get $18,000.

>L   **To check your formula, move to cell F11, enter $10,000, and see what happens. You should get $10,000 in cell D21. If correct, reenter $100,000 in cell F11.**

Step 5 - Let's calculate the amount of dividends yet to be distributed.

>L   **Since the common stock is still not entitled to any dividends, move to cell E21 and enter "N/A". (or copy the entry from cell E20 to E21).**
>L   **Format cell E21 to right-hand justify the text in the cell. This format will automatically be used if you copied from cell E20 to cell E21!**
>L   **Then, in cell F21, subtract the amount of current dividends (cell D21) from the previous amount yet to be distributed (cell F20).**

You should see 82000 displayed.

The distribution schedule of your spreadsheet (in rows 14 through 30) should now appear similar to that shown in Exhibit 32-2.

Exhibit 32-2

	A	B	C	D	E	F
14				Amount distributed to:		
15						
16				Preferred	Common	Yet to be
17				Stock	Stock	Distributed
18						
19	Total amount to be distributed			N/A	N/A	100000
20	P.S. dividends in arrears			0	N/A	100000
21	Current P.S. dividends			18000	N/A	82000
22	C.S. dividend to match current P.S....					
23	Participating dividend					
24	Remainder to common stock					
25						
26	Total distributed					
27						
28						
29	Percentage dividend (current year)					
30						

Step 6 - Now we can calculate the first part of the dividend on the common stock. The common stock is entitled to receive a dividend equivalent to the current preferred stock dividend before any additional participation of the preferred stock needs to be considered.

>L   **Move the cursor to cell D22 and enter "N/A" since the preferred stock already has been allocated its current dividend.**

>L   **Format cell D22 to right-hand justify the text in the cell. This format will automatically be used if you copied from either cell E20 or E21 to cell D22!**

>L   **Move the cursor to cell E22 and enter "@MIN(F21,E5*D7)".**

You should see 72000. The @MIN function is used once again to ensure that the distribution does not exceed the cash yet to be distributed, which is shown in cell F21. The formula E5*D7 calculates a dividend for the common stock which matches the preferred stock dividend on a percentage basis.

Step 7 - Calculate the amount of dividends yet to be distributed.

>L   **Move the cursor to cell F22.**

>L   **Enter a formula to calculate the dividends yet to be distributed.**

You should get 10000 as the amount yet to be distributed.

Step 8 - Now comes the hard part--determining how much of the dividends yet to be distributed that each class of stock should receive under the participation feature! Remember that (in this problem) each class of stock will participate equally (on a percentage of par basis) up to 15%, after which the common stock will be entitled to any remaining dividends.

>L   **Move the cursor to cell D23.**

>L   **In cell D23, enter:**

"@IF($F$22>=($D$8-$D$7)*$F$5,($D$8-$D$7)*D5,$F$22*D5/$F$5)".

Use the arrow keys and the special function key [F4] to designate each of the cell references in this formula as fixed or absolute (indicated by the dollar signs) *except for the reference to cell D5*, which is the par value of the preferred stock. Remember, you can also type in the dollar signs instead of using the special function key.

You should get $2,000 in cell D23.

This formula means "if the amount yet to be distributed (cell F22) is greater than or equal to 6% (15% in cell D8 - 9% in cell D7) of the total par value (cell F5), then allocate 6% of the preferred par value (cell D5) to the preferred stock, otherwise allocate the amount yet to be distributed (cell F22) in the proportion of the preferred par value to the total par value (cell D5/cell F5).

A problem arises with this formula, however. What happens if the preferred stock is nonparticipating? That is, if the participation limit is zero (0) percent?

>L   **Move the cursor to cell D8 and enter a zero (0).**

What result is displayed in cell D23? You should get a negative $18,000, hardly the correct result!

This is because the difference between the preferred stock dividend (cell D7, which is now 9%) and the participation limit (cell D8, which is currently .00) is a negative number (.00 minus .09 = -.09). This is a nonsensical result and can be eliminated by *nesting* our first @IF function inside a second @IF function.

To do this, let's edit our entry in cell D23.

>L   **Move the cursor to cell D23 and press the special function key [F2].**

The formula will now be shown on the second line of the control panel for editing. The edit cursor should be flashing at the end of the formula.

>L   **Add a second right-hand parenthesis to the end of the equation by simply typing ")".**

>L   **Now, using the left arrow key, move the flashing cursor to the left until it is located beneath the @ in @IF.**

(Warning: If you use the backspace key, you will delete characters from your formula. Make sure that you use the left arrow key!)

>L   **Enter "@IF($D$8-$D$7<=0,0,".**

In edit mode, you will have to manually type in the dollar signs to designate cells D8 and D7 as absolute.

The formula shown on the second line of the control panel should now read:

@IF($D$8-$D$7<=0,0,**@IF**($F$22>=($D$8-$D$7)*$F$5,($D$8-$D$7)*D5,$F$22*D5/$F$5))

If you make errors in editing, you can press the [Del] key to eliminate any unwanted characters. When you are satisfied that your equation is correct:

>L   **Press the [enter] key and the edited formula will be entered in cell D23.**

If cell D8 still contains zero (0), you should see zero (0) display in cell D23.

>L   **If your display is incorrect, either reenter edit and make the necessary corrections, or enter the entire formula over again in cell D23.**

>L   **When correct, move the cursor back to cell D8 and enter 15% to continue.**

Step 9 - We can use this same equation for the common stock calculation in cell E23. Rather than retyping this lengthy formula, use the Copy command.

This is why we designated most of the cells as absolute. When we copy, those cells with dollar signs will remain constant. Before beginning to copy, however, reexamine the formula in cell D23 to see which cells are absolute with respect to each column and which are relative to each column. You should find that all of the cells referenced are absolute except for cell D5, which should be adjusted to cell E5 (the par value of the common stock) during the copying.

>L   **With the cursor in cell D23, type "/C" and press the [enter] key to select cell D23 as the only cell in the range you wish to copy *from*.**

>L   **Use the arrow keys to highlight cell E23 as the only cell in the range you wish to copy *to* and press the [enter] key.**

If done correctly, you should det $2,000 in cell D23 and $8,000 in cell E23. If incorrect, you could either try copying a second time, or editing the formula in cell E23 (press the special function key [F2], or you could type the entire formula, as adjusted for column E, in cell E23.

Step 10 - Calculate the amount of dividends yet to be distributed. This time we need to deduct both a preferred stock amount (cell D23) and a common stock amount (cell E23) from the previous amount yet to be distributed (in cell F22).

>L   **Move the cursor to cell F23 and enter the appropriate formula to calculate the dividends yet to be distributed.**

You should get zero (0) as the display in cell F23 after entering the formula.

The distribution schedule of your spreadsheet (rows 14 through 30) should now appear as shown in Exhibit 32-3.

Step 11 - The final distribution is for the remainder yet to be distributed. The common stock is entitled to all of this distribution.

>L   **In cell D24, enter "N/A".**

>L   **Format cell D24 to right-hand justify the text in the cell. This format will automatically be used if you copied from either cell E20, E21, or D22 to cell D24!**

>L   **In cell E24, enter "+F23" since the remainder to be distributed to the common stock should be equal to the amount yet to be distributed.**

>L   **In cell F24, subtract the distribution of the remainder (cell E24) from the amount yet to be distributed (cell F23).**

(This final total in cell F24 should **always** be zero!)

Exhibit 32-3

	A	B	C	D	E	F
				Amount distributed to:		
14						
15				------------------------------------	-------------------	
16				Preferred	Common	Yet to be
17				Stock	Stock	Distributed
18				------------------------------------	-------------------	
19	Total amount to be distributed			N/A	N/A	100000
20	P.S. dividends in arrears			0	N/A	100000
21	Current P.S. dividends			18000	N/A	82000
22	C.S. dividend to match current P.S....			N/A	72000	10000
23	Participating dividend			2000	8000	0
24	Remainder to common stock					
25				------------------------------------	============	
26	Total distributed					
27				=========================		
28						
29	Percentage dividend (current year)					
30				=========================		

Step 12 - Let's calculate the total amount of dividends to be received by each class of stock.

>L   In cell D26, total the preferred stock dividends in cells D20 through D24 by entering "@SUM(D20.D24)". You may wish to use the arrow keys to point to this range. Don't forget to add the right-hand parenthesis before pressing the [enter] key!

>L   In cell E26, enter the corresponding formula to total the common stock dividends. You may wish to copy the formula from cell D26 for this calculation.

Don't worry about adding in the N/A's--the spreadsheet will interpret these cells as zeroes (0) and your total will still be correct! You should get $20,000 for the preferred stock and $80,000 for the common stock.

Step 13 - Finally, let's calculate the percentage dividend received by each class of stock for the current year.

>L   In cell D29, enter "(D26-D20)/D5" to compute the percentage dividend received by the preferred stock.

This formula deducts any dividends in arrears from the total dividend in order to get the current year's dividend and divides this amount by the par value of the preferred stock. You should get .1 or 10%.

>L   In cell E29, enter "+E26/E5" to compute the percentage dividend received by the common stock. This formula should also result in .1 or 10%.

The completed distribution schedule of your spreadsheet should now appear similar to Exhibit 32-4.

Exhibit 32-4

	A	B	C	D	E	F
1	DIVIDEND DISTRIBUTION SCHEDULE					
2				Preferred	Common	Total
3				Stock	Stock	Dollars
4				----------	----------	----------
5	Par value of stock			200000	800000	1000000
6				==========	==========	==========
7	Preferred stock dividend (.00)			0.09		
8	Limit of P.S. participation (.00)			0.15		
9	P.S. cumulative? (1=Yes, 0=No)			0		
10	Number of years in arrears			1		
11	Amount of dividends to be distributed					100000
12						==========
13						
14				Amount distributed to:		
15				----------		----------
16				Preferred	Common	Yet to be
17				Stock	Stock	Distributed
18				----------	----------	----------
19	Total amount to be distributed			N/A	N/A	100000
20	P.S. dividends in arrears			0	N/A	100000
21	Current P.S. dividends			18000	N/A	82000
22	C.S. dividend to match current P.S....			N/A	72000	10000
23	Participating dividend			2000	8000	0
24	Remainder to common stock			N/A	0	0
25				----------	----------	==========
26	Total distributed			20000	80000	
27				==========	==========	
28						
29	Percentage dividend (current year)			0.1	0.1	
30				==========	==========	

Step 14 - You may wish to "clean up" the appearance of your spreadsheet by changing the formats of certain locations to dollars and cents, etc.

>L   **When you have completed any formatting, press the [Home] key to move the cursor to cell A1.**

Step 15 - At this point, you may wish to **save** your work. Use the procedures given in Chapter 5 to save your work.

Printing: You might also want to print the spreadsheet if your computer is connected to a printer.

>L   **Type "/PPRA1.F30" and press the [enter] key to specify the print range for the schedule.**
>L   **Make sure that your printer's paper is aligned and then type "A" for Align.**
>L   **Type "G" for Go to print the dividend distribution schedule.**
>L   **Type "Q" to Quit the print function.**

Completing the Problem - Parts B and C:

Your spreadsheet should now be ready for you to manipulate the input data and study the effects that changes in the variables may have on the amount of dividends distributed to each class of stock.

To find out how large a dividend must be distributed in the following year in order to maintain the same percentage return to the common stock, change the par value of the preferred stock outstanding to $400,000 and then change the amount of dividends to be distributed on an iterative or trial and error basis. As you increase the amount of dividends to be distributed, examine the percentage return to the common stockholders. When it is equal to 10%, you have found the amount of dividends to be distributed.

If you wish to quit at this time:

>L   **Type "/QY" to quit using Lotus 1-2-3. (Type "EY" if needed to exit the Lotus access system menu.)**

After the screen clears and the red in-use light has gone off, you may remove your disks and turn off the computer.

Objective: This partially completed spreadsheet introduces the horizontal LOOKUP function and the DATABASE MANAGEMENT command and illustrates how they might be used in calculating the gross profit to be recognized from installment accounts receivable collections. It also uses the RANGE NAME command and reviews the COPY command. The completed spreadsheet will enable you to determine the amount of gross profit to be recognized from cash collections during any given time period from installment sales made over a four year period.

Part A requires the construction of a spreadsheet which will calculate the amount of gross profit to be recognized on installment accounts receivable collected during a period. Part B uses the collections entered in the spreadsheet as a data base to calculate the collections from each year. These two parts may be worked sequentially at different times by saving the results of Part A on a disk.

Spreadsheet Name: INSTALL

Required Input Information: Before beginning, you should identify:

1. The amount of installment sales for each year.
2. The cost of sales for each year.
3. The collections on installment accounts receivable during the period.

Using the Spreadsheet:

If you have not already done so, load Lotus 1-2-3 into your computer following the instructions given in Part I.

Load the partially completed spreadsheet from the file disk:

>L   **Press the [Alt] key and simultaneously type the letter "U" from the menu.**

When the spreadsheet has finished loading, the screen display should appear similar to that shown in Exhibit 33-1.

You must now enter the required input information and complete the template. Partial instructions for completing the template are given below. (You may wish to refer to your textbook for certain formulas and relationships in order to complete the template.)

Problem:

Potlatch Appliances, Inc. specializes in making sales of new and used appliances to retailers who are considered too risky to obtain credit through other wholesalers. Since the collectibility of receivables is not reasonably assured, Potlatch uses the installment sales method for recognizing profits; that is, no profit is recognized until cash collections are made. Potlatch experienced installment sales and cost of sales over the period from 1985-88 as follows:

	1985	1986	1987	1988
Sales (on installment)	$1,000,000	$2,000,000	$1,800,000	$2,400,000
Cost of sales	760,000	1,600,000	1,350,000	1,680,000

During the month of December, 1988, Potlatch made collections from each year's sales as follows:

Date	Year of Sale	Amount Collected
December 2	1987	$10,000
" 5	1988	15,000
" 6	1986	5,000
" 7	1988	6,000
" 7	1987	9,500
" 9	1985	4,200
" 12	1988	7,600
" 13	1988	19,000
" 13	1987	6,300
" 14	1986	7,700
" 15	1987	2,000
" 16	1985	1,300
" 19	1988	4,400
" 19	1987	1,600
" 20	1987	2,200
" 21	1986	1,800
" 22	1988	3,900
" 27	1988	2,700
" 28	1985	800
" 30	1986	1,500

Required:

A.   Determine the amount of gross profit which Potlatch should recognize as income in December, 1988. (Ignore any related interest.)

B.   Calculate the total gross profit to be recognized in December, 1988, from sales in each of the four individual years, 1985-88. (Ignore any related interest.)

Completing the spreadsheet - Part A:

Step 1 - The installment sales and the cost of those sales (as given in the problem) are already entered for you in the cell range C5:F6. Let's begin by calculating the gross profit for 1985 by subtracting the cost of sales from the installment sales given in column C.

>L   In cell C8, enter "+C5-C6".

Exhibit 33-1

	A	B	C	D	E	F
1	INSTALLMENT ACCOUNTS RECEIVABLE					
2						
3			1985	1986	1987	1988
4			--------	--------	--------	--------
5	Sales (on installment)		1000000	2000000	1800000	2400000
6	Cost of sales		760000	1600000	1350000	1680000
7			--------	--------	--------	--------
8	Gross profit					
9			========	========	========	========
10	Lookup Table:					
11	--------					
12	Year..............................		1985	1986	1987	1988
13	Gross Profit Percent.......					
14			========	========	========	========
15						
16			Sales of	Amount	Gross Profit	Gross Profit
17			Year	Collected	Percent	Realized
18						
19						
20						

This formula can be copied to calculate the gross profit for 1986-88.

>L   **Make sure that the cursor is in cell C8 and type "/C".**
>L   **Since you want to copy the formula from cell C8, press the [enter] key.**
>L   **Indicate the range you wish to copy to by using the arrow keys to highlight "D8. .F8". (Or type this range as "D8.F8".)**
>L   **Press the [enter] key and the formula will automatically be adjusted to calculate the gross profit for the years 1986-88.**

Step 2 - Rows 10 through 14 contain a lookup table. The positioning of rows 12 and 13 of this table is extremely important. These rows will enable you to look up the rate of gross profit corresponding to each year. Thus, the year and the rate of gross profit must be aligned with each other. (Lookup tables may be set up vertically in columns as well as horizontally in rows.)

Let's calculate the gross profit percent for 1985 by dividing the gross profit by the installment sales.

>L   **In cell C13, enter or point out the formula "+C8/C5".**

Copy this calculation for 1986-88 to complete the lookup table.

>L   **Make sure that the cursor is in cell C13, type "/C" and press the [enter] key to select cell C13 as the range you wish to replicate from.**

>L   Use the arrow keys to highlight cells "D13. .F13" as the range that you wish
      to copy to. (Or type the range "D13.F13".)
>L   Press the [enter] key and the formula will automatically be adjusted to
      calculate the gross profit percentages for the years 1986-88.

You should now have four years and four gross profit percentages as shown
in Exhibit 33-2.

Exhibit 33-2

	A	B	C	D	E	F
1	INSTALLMENT ACCOUNTS RECEIVABLE					
2						
3			1985	1986	1987	1988
4			----------	----------	----------	----------
5	Sales (on installment)		1000000	2000000	1800000	2400000
6	Cost of sales		760000	1600000	1350000	1680000
7			----------	----------	----------	----------
8	Gross profit		240000	400000	450000	720000
9			=========	=========	=========	=========
10	Lookup Table:					
11	----------					
12	Year..		1985	1986	1987	1988
13	Gross Profit Percent.......		.24	.2	.25	.3
14			=========	=========	=========	=========
15						
16			Sales of	Amount	Gross Profit	Gross Profit
17			Year	Collected	Percent	Realized
18						
19						
20						

Step 3 - Next, let's enter the cash collections which were made during the year.

>L   In cells C18-C37, enter the years in which the installment sales were made.
>L   In cells D18-D37, enter the dollar amounts of each collection.

Step 4 - When you have finished entering the data in columns C and D, you should
be ready to apply the lookup function.

>L   In cell E18, use the arrow keys and the special function key [F4] to help you
      enter "@HLOOKUP(C18,$C$12.$F$13,1)".

The program searches the *first* row of the range of cells from C12 to F13 for the first value greater than that specified in cell C18. Thus, the program searches for a number greater than 1987 (in cell C18) in the range from 1985-88 (cells C12.F12). When it finds 1988, it selects the previous value--which is 1987--the year we were seeking. Thus, lookup functions must be in ascending order with no duplicates.

The "1" in the function tells it to return the value one row beneath (or offset from) the first row. That value is the gross profit percent for 1987 (which is .25) and is displayed in cell E18.

You can use this function for each of the remaining collections. Let's copy the lookup function to cells E19-E37. Note that since we want the lookup function to always examine the range from C12 to F13, these cell references were specified as absolute in our function.

>L   Check to be sure that the cursor is still in cell E18 and type "/C".
>L   Since you want to copy the formula from this location, press the [enter] key.
>L   Use the arrow keys to highlight the range "E19. .E37" as the range you wish to copy to. (Or type "E19.E37".)
>L   Press the [enter] key.

If successfully done, you should see the gross profit percentages which correspond with the year of sale for each collection displayed in column E. If unsuccessful, try step 4 again.

Step 5 - By multiplying the amount collected (column D) by the gross profit percentage (column E), you can calculate the gross profit to be realized on this collection in column F.

>L   In cell F18, enter "+D18*E18".

You should get $2,500 in cell F18. Copy this formula to cells F19-F37.

>L   With your cursor in cell F18, type "/C" and press the [enter] key to select cell F18 as the range you wish to copy from.
>L   Indicate the range you wish to copy to by using the arrow keys to point to cells "F19. .F37". (Or type the range "F19.F37".)
>L   Press the [enter] key and the formula will automatically be adjusted to calculate the gross profit amounts for each of the collections.

Step 6 - Now let's total the amount collected and the gross profit to be recognized in the month of December.

>L   In cell D39, enter "@SUM(D18.D37)" to total the amount collected.
>L   Try copying this formula to cell F39. (If you are unsuccessful, you can always move the cursor to cell F39 and enter "@SUM(F18:F37)".)

When the collections and related calculations section of the spreadsheet is completed, rows 15 through 40 should appear as in Exhibit 33-3.

Exhibit 33-3

	C	D	E	F
15					
16|	Sales of	Amount	Gross Profit	Gross Profit
17|	Year	Collected	Percent	Realized
18|	1987	10000	.25	2500
19|	1988	15000	.3	4500
20|	1986	5000	.2	1000
21|	1988	6000	.3	1800
22|	1987	9500	.25	2375
23|	1985	4200	.24	1008
24|	1988	7600	.3	2280
25|	1988	19000	.3	5700
26|	1987	6300	.25	1575
27|	1986	7700	.2	1540
28|	1987	2000	.25	500
29|	1985	1300	.24	312
30|	1988	4400	.3	1320
31|	1987	1600	.25	400
32|	1987	2200	.25	550
33|	1986	1800	.2	360
34|	1988	3900	.3	1170
35|	1988	2700	.3	810
36|	1985	800	.24	192
37|	1986	1500	.2	300
38|	---			
39			112500		30192
40|	============			==============

Step 7 - You may wish to "clean up" the appearance of your spreadsheet by changing the formats of certain locations to dollars and cents, etc.

>L   **When you have completed any formatting, press the [Home] key to move the cursor to cell A1.**

Step 8 - At this point, you may wish to **save** your work. Use the procedures given in Chapter 5 to save your work.

Your spreadsheet can now be used to manipulate the input data and study the effects that changes in the variables, particularly those affecting the gross profit percent, may have on the gross profit to be realized.

You might also want to print the spreadsheet if your computer is connected to a printer.

>L   Type "/PPRA1.F40" and press the [enter] key to specify the print range for the collections schedule.

>L   Make sure that your printer's paper is aligned and then type "A" for Align.

>L   Type "G" for Go to print the spreadsheet.

>L   Type "Q" to Quit the print function.

If you wish to quit at this time:

>L   Type "/QY" to quit using Lotus 1-2-3. (Type "EY" if needed to exit the Lotus access system menu.)

After the screen clears and the red in-use light has gone off, you may remove your disks and turn off the computer.

Completing Part B - Database Management

Before starting this task, make sure that you have saved your template with the data you have entered from the problem. This is to insure that you will be able to start over if you happen to make an error. Use the procedures given in Chapter 5 to save your work.

What is a Database?

Simply stated, a database is an organized collection of data. This organization is based on *records* and *fields*. A record represents all of the information which is collected about a certain item. In contrast, a field represents a single piece of information within a record.

In our problem, each individual collection of an installment account receivable represents a record. It is comprised of four fields: (1) the year in which the receivable was created, (2) the amount of the receivable collection, (3) the gross profit percentage related to the collection, and (4) the gross profit to be realized from the collection. Thus, our primary data base consists of 20 records (collections) and a total of 160 fields (20 records times 4 fields per record). Our database must also contain descriptions of the fields and/or records. For example, we will include the headings for each column as a part of the database.

Our database is logically organized into rows and columns. Each row contains a separate record and each column contains all of the information about a single field. Because of this logical organization, you can have Lotus 1-2-3 search through the database for those records which meet certain criteria--criteria which you establish!

For example, you can find the collections which relate to each of the four years by manipulating the database. Before you can do this, however, you will need to define three ranges:

1. *The input range.* The input range represents the data base from which you can select or extract data. This includes the field names (or variables, such as year, amount, etc.) which you have created and the data records.

2. *The output range.* This represents the area (cell range) where you would like to display the information which is extracted from your data base.

3. *The criterion range.* This range specifies what field (variable) should be searched and what value of the field should be searched for.

Range Names:

Lotus 1-2-3 has a special feature which assists in using many of the commands and especially in using databases. This is the Range Name command. This command allows you to associate a name or title with a range. You can then use that name to specify the range instead of having to specify the beginning and ending cells of the range.

For example, you might want to define cells A1 through F40 as the range to be printed. This would have to be specified each time in the print function as the range from "C16. .F17". However, we could *name* the cell range A1. .F40 as "installments" using the Range Name command. Then, instead of always having to type or point out the range of cells A1 through F40, we can simply type "installments" in response to the prompt for a range to print and Lotus 1-2-3 will know that we wish to print cells A1 through F40! Thus, we can use easy to remember words to make commands that require ranges to be specified even easier to use!

The words used as names can be up to *fifteen* characters long. Each name which you use is associated only with the spreadsheet you are using, and those range names are stored with the spreadsheet. Thus, in order to save a range name, you must save the spreadsheet in which the range name has been created.

Step 9 - First, let's name the input range. Appropriate field names for our data are listed in row 17 (cells C17-F17). Those names (Year, Collected, Percent, and Realized) can represent our fields. Our data must be located <u>immediately</u> below the field names. Thus, the cell range C18 through F37 contains the numeric records to be searched. The overall input range, including field names and records is then C17-F37.

>L   **Make sure that the cursor is in cell C17.**
>L   **Begin by typing "/RNC" for Range,Name,Create.**
>L   **Respond to the prompt for a name by typing "INPUTDATA" and then press the [enter] key.**

      (Remember, it doesn't matter whether you type in the names in upper case (capital) or lower case letters--both types will be interpreted in the same manner by the program.)

You are then asked for the range.

>L   **Use the arrow keys to highlight cells "C17. .F37" as the range and press the [enter] key.**

Your input range is now named and you will be returned to the worksheet.

Step 10 - Second, let's name the output range. Let's define the output range in the columns below the input range. Thus, the output range will be in cells C48 through F68. (As you scroll down to this range, you will see that the template already contains headings for the output range.)

>L   **Move the cursor to cell C48.**
>L   **Begin by typing "/RNC" for Range,Name,Create.**
>L   **Respond to the prompt for a name by typing "OUTPUTDATA" and press the [enter] key.**

(You will see the range name "INPUTDATA" automatically appear on the third line of the control panel when you type "/RNC". Since you want a new name to be used (OUTPUTDATA), ignore this prompt and simply type in the new name for the output range.)

You are then asked for the range.

>L   **Use the arrow keys to highlight cells "C48. .F68" as the output range and press the [enter] key.**

Your output range is now defined and you will be returned to the worksheet.

Step 11 - Finally, let's define and name the criterion range. You probably noticed the label "Criterion Range:" when you scrolled down to name the output range. This is where we will specify the criteria used to search and find records in the database. First, we need to define the field names which we would like to be able to search in the first row of the criterion range (row 43). To do this, let's copy the field names to cells C43 through F43. Let's use the Range Names command to facilitate this.

>L   **With the cursor in cell C48 (which is one of the cells containing a field name):**
>L   **Type "/RNC" for Range,Name,Create.**

(You will see the range names "INPUTDATA and "OUTPUTDATA" automatically appear on the third line of the control panel when you type "/RNC". Since you want a new name to be used, ignore this prompt and simply type in the new name for the field name range.)

>L   **Respond to the prompt for a name by typing "FIELDNAMES" and press the [enter] key.**

You are then asked for the range.

>L   **Use the arrow keys to highlight cells "C48. .F48" as the field names range and press the [enter] key.**

The field names range is now defined and you will be returned to the worksheet.

Now let's copy the field names to the criterion range.

>L   **Move the cursor to cell C43.**
>L   **Type "/C" for Copy.**
>L   **In response to the prompt for the range to copy from, press the special function key [F3].**

The range names which we have defined are now displayed on the third line of the control panel. (This feature can be very helpful if you forget what range names you have used. Note: "\M" is the range name of the macro used to return to the Main menu.)

>L   **Make sure that the highlight on the third line is located on FIELDNAMES and press the [enter] key to select this range as the range to copy from.**
>L   **Since the cursor is already in cell C43, the first cell which we wish to copy to, press the [enter] key to complete the copy command.**

The field names should now display in cells C43 through F43.

Now let's name our criterion range.

>L   **Check to make sure that the cursor is still in cell C43.**
>L   **Begin by typing "/RNC" for Range Name Create.**
>L   **Respond to the prompt for a name by typing "CRITERIONRANGE" and press the [enter] key.**

You are then asked for the range.

>L   **Use the arrow keys to highlight cells "C43. .F44" as the criterion range and press the [enter] key.**

The criterion range is now defined and you will be returned to the worksheet.

Next, we need to define the search criteria. Since we wish to find the collections from each year, we should place our search criteria under the Year field, which is located in cell C43.

>L   **Move the cursor to cell C44, where we will define what year we are seeking.**
>L   **Type "1985" and press the [enter] key.**

"1985" specifies the value of the records which should be sought when we begin examining our database.

Step 12 - You are now ready to define the input, output, and criterion ranges needed for manipulating the database.

>L   **Type "/D" for Data, followed by "Q" for Query.**

You will now be asked which options you wish to choose. First, you must specify the ranges needed to define and search the database.

>L   Type "I" for Input, press the special function key [F3], and use the arrow keys to select the range named "INPUTDATA". Press the [enter] key to complete the selection of this range as the input range.

>L   Type "O" for Output, press the special function key [F3], and use the arrow keys to select the range named "OUTPUTDATA". Press the [enter] key to complete the selection of this range as the output range.

>L   Type "C" for Criterion, press the special function key [F3], and use the arrow keys to select the range named "CRITERIONRANGE". Press the [enter] key to complete the selection of this range as the output range.

Step 13 - At this point, you may wish to resave your spreadsheet so that the input, output, field names and criterion ranges will be saved.

>L   Type "Q" to Quit database management.

>L   Press the [Home] key to move the cursor to cell A1 and then save your spreadsheet following the procedures in Chapter 5.

Step 14 - You are now ready to seek the collections from the installment sales of 1985.

>L   Scroll down so that you can see the top of the output range (beginning in row 47).

>L   Type "/D" for Data, "Q" for Query, and "E" for Extract.

The three records representing collections from 1985 should appear in cells C49 through F51.

>L   Type "Q" to Quit database management and return to the worksheet.

>L   Move the cursor to cell D70 and total the amount collected.

(Hint: You might copy the formula from cell D39 to do this.) You should have $6,300 of revenues from 1985.

>L   Move the cursor to cell F70 and total the gross profit realized.

You should get $1,512 of gross profit from 1985 sales to be realized in the current month.

You might also want to print the spreadsheet data for 1985 if your computer is connected to a printer.

>L   Type "/PPRC47.F71" and press the [enter] key to specify the print range.

>L   Make sure that your printer's paper is aligned and then type "A" for Align.

>L   Type "G" for Go to print the spreadsheet.

>L   Type "Q" to Quit the print function.

Step 15 - Next let's find the collections from 1986.

>L   Make sure that the cursor is in cell C44, type "1986" and press the [enter] key.
>L   Reenter database management by typing "/DQE" for Data, Query, and Extract.

The four records from 1986 should now appear in the output range.

>L   Type "Q" to Quit database management and move the cursor down to examine the total collections and gross profit from 1986 sales.

Other considerations:

You can extract the data from 1987 and 1988 in a similar manner to complete the problem assignment. But let's try a couple of other options!

You could also use the Data, Query, Find option to search the database without extracting any records.

>L   Make sure that you have exited from database management.
>L   Make sure that the cursor is in cell C44 and reenter "1985".
>L   Type "/DQF".

The first record in the file from the year 1985 has been located and is highlighted for you!

>L   To see the next record from 1985, press the "down" arrow movement key.
>L   If you wish to see the previous record from 1985, press the "up" arrow key.
>L   Exit from the find option by pressing the [Esc] key.
>L   Type "Q" to Quit database management.

In addition, you can specify many other search criteria. You could search for the Amount instead of the Year. You may also search for values which are greater than or less than a certain limit. For example:

>L   Make sure that the cursor is in cell C44, type "/RE", and press the [enter] key to erase the year.
>L   Move to cell D44, type "+D18>5000" and press the [enter] key.

Note that the formula which you have entered is displayed as "1". This is because cell D18 contains 10000 and our entry (statement) is evaluated by the program as true and assigned a value of "1". If cell D18 had been less than or equal to 5000, then the program would have evaluated the statement as false and displayed a "0".

(When specifying a cell in a search criterion (such as D18), use the first cell with a non-field value in the column to be searched. This will always be the cell in the second row of the input range. Thus, we use D18 since it is the first value as given in the second row of the database.)

>L   Type "/DQE".

All collections of more than $5,000 will be selected.

You can also search using more than one criterion at a time.

>L   **Type "Q" to Quit data management.**
>L   **Move the cursor to cell C44 and enter "1988".**
>L   **Type "/DQE".**

All collections of more than $5,000 *and* from the year 1988 will be selected!

Let's try one final option--sorting the database. Just to be on the safe side, let's do this using our output range and *not* the input range!

>L   **Type "Q" to Quit data management.**
>L   **With the cursor in cell C44, type "/RE", highlight the range C44. .D44, and press the [enter] key to erase the criteria in these cells.**
>L   **Type "/DQE".**

This extracts *all* of the data from the input range and copies it to the ouput range. All of the records are extracted since there are *no* criteria!

>L   **Type "Q" to Quit data management.**
>L   **Type "/D" followed by "S" for Sort.**
>L   **Press the [enter] key (or type "D") to select the Data-Range option.**
>L   **Use the arrow keys to select the range "C49. .F68" and press the [enter] key.**
>L   **Now type "P" to select the primary key on which to sort. Move the cursor to cell C49 (to sort by year) and press the [enter] key.**
>L   **You will then be prompted to specify whether the data should be sorted in ascending or descending order. Press the [enter] key to select the standard setting of ascending order (or type "A" to select Ascending).**
>L   **Type "G" for Go!**

The output range will now be sorted by year! You could also sort by any of the other criteria (amount, percent, or gross profit). Or you can add a secondary key on which to sort. Thus, you could sort by year and, within each year, by amount! Try experimenting with some of your own criteria!

If you wish to quit at this time:

>L   **Type "/QY" to quit using Lotus 1-2-3.**
>L   **Type "EY" to exit the Lotus Access System.**

After the screen clears and the red in-use light has gone off, you may remove your disks and turn off the computer.

CHAPTER 34 - ACCOUNTS PAYABLE

Objective: This tutorial's primary purpose is to provide an introduction to the concepts and uses of MACROS in developing and using spreadsheets. In addition, this tutorial will review and expand the user's knowledge of the DATE, RANGE NAME, and DATABASE MANAGEMENT functions. The MOVE command will also be used. To achieve these objectives we will:

1. Create a macro for setting the width of columns. The macro will incorporate a pause, during which time the user will enter the desired column-width. The column-width macro will then proceed to set the column-width, move to the next column to the right and repeat.

2. Have the user enter accounts payable (the amount and terms of invoices received) into a database. A macro will be created to make the data entry process easier. This macro will also be used to automatically reset the database input range after new invoices are entered to make it easier to manipulate the database.

3. Use the worksheet to calculate the due date and the discount allowed on invoices.

4. Design a macro which will allow the user to enter a "date to pay invoices through" and which will then create a report on the screen which lists all of the invoices due on or before that date. The macro will ask the user to specify items to be used in the criterion range for use in selecting the due date. The report on invoices due will automatically be generated when the macro is invoked. For simplicity, we shall assume that all invoices will be paid on the discount date to take advantage of all possible discounts.

5. Create a print macro to print the report.

6. Create an overall menu structure macro to combine the functions of data entry, query report, and printing into a menu.

7. Refine the data entry macro to incorporate a menu macro. After the user enters a record, this menu macro will ask the user whether or not he/she wishes to enter another record. If the response is yes, the menu macro will call the data entry macro. If the response is no, the macro will return to the overall menu macro.

Saving your work:

Each of the macros can be worked *sequentially.* Should you wish to complete these macros at different times, you will need a formatted disk on which to save your work. Otherwise, when you turn the computer off, all of your work will be lost. You should also save your work each time that you complete an additional step in case you encounter problems in a subsequent step. That way, you can start over on the current step without having to recreate the entire spreadsheet.

Overall Design of the Spreadsheet: Before beginning, we need to consider how the spreadsheet will be structured to accomplish all of our objectives.. We will divide the spreadsheet into five major sections separated by horizontal and vertical lines. This is illustrated in Exhibit 34-1. In columns A through J, we will enter the information about our invoices--the database. In columns L through P, we will have a report selection range for establishing the date to be used in preparing reports, a criterion range for manipulating the database, and a database report range for reporting the output from using the database. In columns R through V, we will enter our macros.

Exhibit 34-1

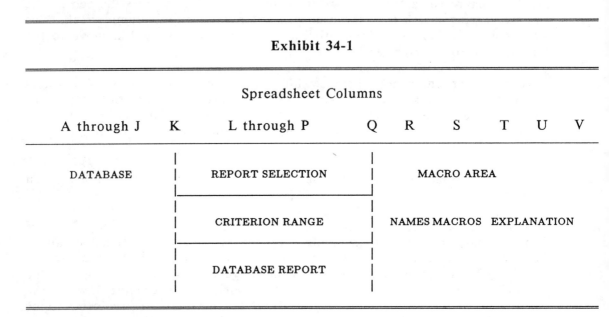

Spreadsheet Columns

A through J	K	L through P	Q	R	S	T	U	V
DATABASE		REPORT SELECTION		MACRO AREA				
		CRITERION RANGE		NAMES MACROS EXPLANATION				
		DATABASE REPORT						

Because of the placement of the macro area immediately to the right of the other ranges, it is extremely important that you *do not insert or delete rows once you have begun.* If you wish to delete, use the Range Erase command to delete a specific range of cells. If you need additional room, use the Move command to move the entries which are in the way to another range in the spreadsheet. If you follow the instructions for this chapter exactly, you should have no need to add or delete rows.

What is a Macro?

A macro is simply a series of keystrokes that is stored by Lotus 1-2-3 which can be recalled and used at any time. This allows you to substitute a single keystroke for a series of multiple steps. Thus, a macro helps you to work more efficiently when you do repetitive operations such as printing or, as in the first example, setting the widths of a large number of columns.

The steps in creating a macro are:

1.   Manually perform the procedure you wish to "record" in a macro. Write down all the keystrokes needed to perform the procedure.
2.   Enter this series of commands as a label in a cell (or range of cells) that is in an out of the way corner of your spreadsheet. (Start each entry with a single quotation mark to indicate that it is a label and not a number or formula.)

3.   Assign the first cell in the macro a range name. The name of the macro must be *one* character from A to Z, preceded by a backslash (\).

4.   To execute or *invoke* the macro, hold down the [Alt] key and type the letter used in the range name of the macro.

It should also be noted that certain keystrokes cannot be entered directly into a macro, but can be entered by using {braces}. For example, pressing the special function keys [F5] and [F2] could be symbolized in a macro by {GOTO} and {EDIT}, respectively. Moving the cursor can be symbolized by specifying {RIGHT}, {LEFT}, {UP}, and {DOWN}, as well as by using the {BS} backspace key. Finally, a critically important keystroke in executing any Lotus command is pressing the [enter] key. This can be symbolized in a macro by typing a tilde (~). *Most errors in entering macros result from forgetting to enter the tilde (~) to symbolize pressing the [enter] key!*

WARNING: Macros are extremely sensitive to missing or extra characters! *Check* and *recheck* your entries before you attempt to use (invoke) a macro!

Using the Spreadsheet:

If you have not already done so, load Lotus 1-2-3 into your computer using the instructions given in Part I. When the blank spreadsheet screen appears on the monitor, you are ready to begin. *Do not use the blank screen available through the main menu!* That "blank" screen contains a macro which will interfere with the macros developed in this chapter! To obtain a completely blank screen from the main menu, type "/WEY" for "/Worksheet,Erase,Yes".

Reminder: It is strongly recommended that you obtain a formatted disk before beginning so that you can save your work should you wish to complete the chapter in stages--you should make it a practice to periodically save your work!

Macro #1 - A Column-Width Setting Macro:

The first step in managing our accounts payable is to create the spreadsheet database for the entry of the invoice information. Before entering the data, we need to enter the column headings and set the width of each column. We can create a macro to save us from having to make the same repetitive keystrokes when we set the column-widths for columns A through K.

Step 1 - Let's manually set the column width of column A to determine the essential keystrokes. Pay close attention to the keystrokes which you use in this process so that you can recreate them in the macro.

>L   For convenience, press the [Caps Lock] key to type all letters in upper case. (Remember, it doesn't matter whether you type upper-case or lower-case letters.)

>L   With the cursor in cell A1, type "/WCS" for Worksheet, Column-Width, Set.

>L   Type in "3" as the desired column width and press the [enter] key.

In our case, we would then move the cursor key to the right since we wish to repeat this procedure in column B. As you see, setting the column width takes us four keystrokes before we type in the desired column size. Then we move to the right and repeat this sequence.

Step 2 - To create a macro to set the column widths for us, we must move to an unused part of our worksheet.

>L   **Move to cell S1.**

>L   **Begin the macro by typing a single quotation mark (') to indicate that you are entering a label.**

>L   **Follow this by typing the slash (/) to indicate that a command is to be executed. (If you failed to type the single quotation mark (') in the previous step, then typing the slash (/) will call up the command menu instead of the slash being entered as the first character in our macro!)**

>L   **Then record the FIRST LETTER of each command you entered when you did the procedure manually. Thus, you should type WCS for Worksheet, Column-Width, Set.**

Your entry should now read <u>'/WCS</u>. *(In order to illustrate the single quote mark clearly, entries using this character will be underlined instead of using double quotation marks.)*

At this point, when we did the procedure manually, we typed in "3" as the desired column width and pressed the [enter] key. Within a macro, we can achieve the same effect by having the macro pause and allow us to enter information. Whenever we want a macro to pause for input, we indicate this by including a question mark in braces {?} to indicate a pause. Then the macro will pause for entry. The macro resumes when we press the [enter] key.

>L   **Type "{?}". (The braces are above and to the left of the [enter] key. Remember to press the [shift] key at the same time that you type the braces.)**

Once we enter the column-width as a number, we need to symbolize pressing the [enter] key. In a macro, pressing the [enter] key is symbolized by the tilde (~).

>L   **Type a tilde "~". (The tilde is on the key to the left of the [enter] key.)**

Your entry should now read <u>'/WCS{?}~</u>.

This macro will only allow us to set one column width at a time. Since we intend to set more than one column width at a time, we will need to add some additional characters. First, we need to tell the program to move to the next column to the right. This can be done by typing "{RIGHT}". Then we need to instruct the program to go to the cell containing our macro and repeat the keystrokes contained in the macro. Lotus will allow us to do this by using a special macro command, "/XG" (read slash XG). The "/XG" command tells Lotus to GOTO a certain cell and start reading the keystrokes found there, thus repeating our macro in the next column.

>L   **Type "{RIGHT}/XG".**

Now we need to tell the program what cell to find the macro in. We can do this by telling the program the name of the macro. Macros are *invoked* using a single letter, so let's refer to our macro as "\W" (read backslash W) to symbolize Width.

>L   **Type "\W~". (The tilde symbolizes the [enter] key.)**

The macro for setting the width of a column and then moving automatically to the column on the right is as follows:

'/WCS{?}~{RIGHT}/XG\W~

>L   **If your entry reads correctly, press the [enter] key to enter the macro in cell S1. Otherwise, go back and edit your entry.**

It is a good idea to document the purpose of our macros so that others can understand them and so that we can remember the purpose of each macro when we return to the spreadsheet at a later date.

>L   **In cell V1, enter "COLUMN WIDTH COMMAND, PAUSE FOR INPUT," and in cell V2 enter "MOVE TO RIGHT AND REPEAT."**

Step 3 -Now we must assign the name "\W" to our macro.

>L   **Move to cell R1 and enter the macro name preceded by the label prefix ('). That is, type a single quotation mark (') followed by "\W "and press the [enter] key. (If you forget to type the label prefix ('), the program will interpret the backslash as the repeating command instead of as a macro range name and "W" will be repeated across cell R1!)**

>L   **Issue the command /Range, Name, Label, Right by typing "/RNLR" and press the [enter] key.**

This command labels the cell to the right of the cursor with the name found in the current cell. Thus, cell R1 contains the name used to denote cell S1.

The macro section of our spreadsheet should now appear as in Exhibit 34-2.

Exhibit 34-2

	R	S	T	U	V	W
\W		/WCS{?}~{RIGHT}/XG\W~			COLUMN WIDTH COMMA	
					MOVE TO RIGHT AND RE	

WARNING: Be sure that you type "/RNLR" and not "/RNR". Typing "/RNR" stands for Range, Name, Reset and will reset all range names. Once we have created more than a few range names, this could be a major inconvenience. To help minimize this danger, we will keep a list of range names beginning in cell AA1 so that if we do accidentally "Reset" the range names, we will be able to reconstruct them from this table. (Lotus 1-2-3 release 2 automatically creates range tables. Users with this version may choose to ignore this step and future steps which ask you to create a range table.)

>L   Move to cell AA1 and enter "NAME". In cell AB1, enter "RANGE".
>L   In cell AA2 enter '\W. In cell AB2, enter "S1".

This documents the existence of our first range and will also help us to recreate the ranges at a later time if necessary.

Using the macro: To use the macro, **move to the leftmost column** for which we wish to change the width (column B since we manually adjusted column A). **Press the [Alt] key and simultaneously press "W"** (the macro name). The macro will pause for you to enter the desired column width. **When you press the [enter] key, it will continue executing** (set the column width, move to the right, and repeat). This is an example of a looping macro.

>L   **Set the width for columns B through K as shown below.**

Column Widths

B	C	D	E	F	G	H	I	J	K
3	3	7	19	9	5	4	10	9	1

To stop (exit) the macro, hold down the [Ctrl] key and press the [Break] key (the break key is on the [Scroll Lock] key in the upper right-hand corner of the keyboard).

Macro #2 - Entering the Accounts Payable Invoice Database:

Step 4 - Set up the following headings in the corresponding cells.

	Cell	Heading
>L	D1	ACCOUNTS PAYABLE INVOICES
>L	A3	INV DATE
>L	A4	MO
>L	B4	DAY
>L	C4	YR
>L	D3	INVOICE
>L	D4	NUMBER
>L	E4	VENDOR
>L	F3	INVOICE
>L	F4	AMOUNT
>L	G3	TERMS
>L	G4	%
>L	H4	DAYS
>L	I4	DATE_DUE
>L	J4	DISCOUNT

Note that the column heading in cell I4 is "Date_Due". Be sure to include the *underline*! Also, include a space before typing "YR" in cell C4 and "NUMBER" in cell D4 (for appearance's sake only).

Let's format our headings to improve their appearance.

>L   **Move to cell A3 and enter "/RLC" for Range, Label-Prefix, Center. Use the arrow keys to highlight the range of cells from A3 through J4 and press the [enter] key to complete the formatting.**

Step 5 - Enter the following data "manually" beginning in cell A5. Note that the "percents" given for column G should be input as whole numbers, not as decimals.

	A	B	C	D	E	F	G	H	I
>L	10	15	86	1332	JKL, INC.	200	2	10	
>L	10	15	86	1234	J & L MFG.	1000.26	2	10	
>L	10	17	86	3258	GLOBAL SUPPLIES	75.06	1	15	

Let's format the cells in column F to display cents.

>L   **Move the cursor to cell F5 and type "/RFF" for Range, Format, Fixed and press the [enter] key to select the default or standard setting of two decimal places. Use the arrow keys to highlight cells F5 through F8 (one more row than data entered) and press the [enter] key to complete the formatting.**

Step 6 - Now we can enter formulas to calculate the date due and the amount of purchase discount. The due date is equal to the date of the invoice plus the number of days allowed for payment as given in the terms section. To use the invoice date in a formula, we will use the date formula @DATE(Year,Month,Day). The purchase discount allowed will be equal to the invoice amount times the discount percentage.

>L   **Move your cursor to cell I5.**
>L   **Enter the formula "@DATE(C5,A5,B5)+H5".**

The serial number assigned to the due date will appear (31710). We need to format cell I5 so that a date is displayed.

>L   **With the cursor still in cell I5, type "/RFD" to issue the command Range, Format, Date. Press the [enter] key to accept the DD-MMM-YY format. Press the [enter] key a second time to complete the formatting and display the date in cell I5.**

The date displayed is the due date--October 25th, which is 10 days after the invoice date!

>L   **Move your cursor to cell J5 so that we can enter the formula to calculate the purchase discount allowed.**
>L   **Start the formula by pressing the plus [+] key. Use the arrow keys to point out the invoice amount in cell F5 and type an asterisk (*) to indicate that you wish to multiply.**
>L   **Use the arrow keys to point out the discount percentage in cell G5 and type "/100" (to divide the percentage by 100) and press the [enter] key.**

The discount of $4 will be displayed in cell J5! Let's format the discount to display cents.

>L   Type "/RFF" for Range, Format, Fixed and press the [enter] key to select the default or standard setting of two decimal places. Press the [enter] key a second time to complete the formatting of cell J5.

Now let's copy the formulas in cells I5 and J5 to rows 6 through 8 so that the date due and the discount will automatically be calculated when we enter invoice amounts. (The formatting will also be copied automatically.)

>L   Move the cursor to cell I5 and type "/C" to begin the copy command.
>L   You will be prompted on the second line of the control panel to specify the range to copy *from*. Use the arrow keys to move one cell to the right so that the range to copy *from* reads I5. .J5, and press the [enter] key.
>L   You are then prompted for the range to copy *to*. Use the arrow keys to move your cursor down one cell to I6 and type a period (.) to indicate that this is the first cell in a range of cells to be copied *to*. Use the arrow keys to move your cursor down to cell I8 (one row past the data we have entered), highlighting the range from I6 to I8.
>L   Press the [enter] key to copy the commands.

When we copy the date due command down the column, however, we get an error message (ERR) in cell I8 for which there is no invoice date. To change the error response to NA (not available), edit your command in I5 (use the special function key [F2] to begin editing) so that it reads:

>L   "@IF(@ISERR(@DATE(C5,A5,B5)),@NA,@DATE(C5,A5,B5)+H5)".

This formula means that if the formula @DATE(C5,A5,B5) returns an "ERR" message (meaning there is no date yet), show the value "NA" (for Not Available); otherwise, show the due date as determined by the formula @DATE(C5,A5,B5)+H5.

>L   Copy this command to cells I6 to I8. The "ERR" message in I8 should be replaced by the "NA" message.

Now let's copy our formulas and formats from row 8 to rows 9 through 16.

>L   Move the cursor to cell A8 and type "/C". Use the arrow keys to highlight the range "A8. . J8" and press the [enter] key.
>L   Use the arrow keys to highlight cells "A9. .A16" as the range to be copied to and press the enter key.

You should see columns I and J extended down through row 16.

Entering Additional Data:

Step 7 - Entering data in a spreadsheet like this one is repetitive in nature. We enter information, then move our cursor to the right. When we finish entering a "record" at the end of a row, we move the cursor down one row and back to the left to start the next "record". This type of spreadsheet data entry is cumbersome, however, because we must enter the month, day, and year in separate columns and because we cannot use the numberpad for data entry and simultaneously use the cursor keys to move around the spreadsheet. We can write a data entry macro, however, to control the movement of our cursor and leave us free to enter numbers using the number pad!

>L   **Move your cursor to cell S3.**

To enter invoice information, we first want to enter the month and then move the cursor to the next cell to the right. Then we want to enter a day and move the cell to the right again. In macro language, this would be denoted as:

{?}	Pause for input.
{RIGHT}	Move to the right.
{?}	Pause for input.
{RIGHT}	Move to the right.

In this model, we will perform this sequence of entering data and moving the cursor to the right eight times to fill in all of the columns.

>L   **In cell S3, enter "{?}{RIGHT}".**
>L   **Move your cursor to cell V3 and type the description "PAUSE FOR INPUT, MOVE CURSOR RIGHT." to document the purpose of the macro sequence.**
>L   **Copy the macro sequence and the related description from cells S3 through V3 to cells S4 through S9.**

After entering information into the eighth column (the number of days allowed for payment), we need to move our cursor down a row and back to column A. In macro language, this would be represented by {?}{DOWN}{END}{LEFT}.

>L   **Move to cell S10 and enter {?}{DOWN}{END}{LEFT}".**
>L   **Move to cell V10 and enter "PAUSE FOR INPUT, MOVE TO NEXT ROW."**

Finally, we want to keep repeating this sequence until we have entered all of our invoices. We can use the special macro command to repeat our macro. If we name our macro "\E" (for data Entry), the command will be "/XG\E~".

>L   **In cell S11, enter '/XG\E~.** *Don't forget to tell the program that this is a label* (type a single quote mark, or label-prefix, to begin the entry). *Also, make sure that you typed the tilde (~) to symbolize pressing the [enter] key.*
>L   **Move to cell V11 and enter "REPEAT MACRO."**

Finally, we need to name our macro.

>L   **Move to cell R3, type '\E, and press the [enter] key to enter the macro name.**
>L   **With the cursor still in cell R3, type "/RNLR" to issue the command Range, Name, Label, Right and press the [enter] key.**

This command labels the item in the cell to the right with the name found in the current cell.

Our completed data entry macro should appear as in Exhibit 34-3.

Exhibit 34-3

	R	S	V	W	X	Y
3	\E	{?}{RIGHT}	PAUSE FOR INPUT, MOVE CURSOR RIGHT.			
4		{?}{RIGHT}	PAUSE FOR INPUT, MOVE CURSOR RIGHT.			
5		{?}{RIGHT}	PAUSE FOR INPUT, MOVE CURSOR RIGHT.			
6		{?}{RIGHT}	PAUSE FOR INPUT, MOVE CURSOR RIGHT.			
7		{?}{RIGHT}	PAUSE FOR INPUT, MOVE CURSOR RIGHT.			
8		{?}{RIGHT}	PAUSE FOR INPUT, MOVE CURSOR RIGHT.			
9		{?}{RIGHT}	PAUSE FOR INPUT, MOVE CURSOR RIGHT.			
10		{?}{DOWN}{END}{LEFT}	PAUSE FOR INPUT, MOVE TO NEXT ROW.			
11		/XG\E~	REPEAT MACRO.			

<u>WARNING:</u> Don't forget to update your list of range names.

>L   In cell AA3 enter '\E. In cell AB3, enter "S3".

This documents the existence of our second range and will assist us if we need to recreate the ranges at a later time.

<u>Using the macro:</u>   To use the macro, **move to the cell where you wish to begin entering data (use the special function key [F5] to jump to cell A8). Press the [Alt] key and simultaneously type "E".** At the top right of the screen, you will see "CMD READY" (for command ready) as the spreadsheet status. This tells you that a macro is currently being executed. If you do not see this status, then something is wrong with your macro. Recheck your macro for errors (especially missing tilde's).

The macro will pause for you to enter the month. **Press the [NumLock] key so that you can enter values using the keypad if you desire, then enter in the month and press the [enter] key.** When you press the [enter] key, the program enters the data, then moves the cursor to the right for the next entry.

>L   **Fill in the following information about the company's payables in rows 8 through 16.**

	A	B	C	D	E	F	G	H	I
>L	10	20	86	45689	NATIONAL TELEPHONE	345.68	0	7	
>L	10	21	86	896	ACME FURNITURE	110	0	7	
>L	10	22	86	5678	UPS	32.5	0	7	
>L	10	21	86	A2310	WEBSTER WHITEWAYS	700.25	1	15	
>L	10	22	86	785555	AMERICAN EXPRESS	550	0	7	
>L	10	22	86	103396	UPS	40.5	0	7	
>L	10	23	86	6784	JACKSON, INC.	6,758	1	15	
>L	10	25	86	8979	SORREL MFG.	575.65	0	7	
>L	10	23	86	7899	GALLEON SHIPPING	123	0	7	

To exit from the macro, hold down the [Ctrl] key and press the [Break] key. (Press the [Num Lock] key a second time in order to use the arrow keys again to move the cursor.)

Database Management:

In order to use the Lotus database management commands to create our reports, we need to define three cell ranges.

1. The *input* range includes all records of our database and the row that contains the column headings (fieldnames).
2. The *criterion* range contains one or more of the column headings used in the input range or database and is used to set criteria for database operations such as search and extract.
3. The *output* range is where items selected through data query operations should be placed.

Step 8 - We will use *named* ranges when we specify the input, criterion, and output ranges in database commands. Let's begin by naming the *input* range.

>L   Move to cell A4. Type "/RNC" to issue the command Range, Name, Create. When prompted to enter the name of the range, type "INPUT" and press the [enter] key. When asked to identify the range, use the arrow keys to highlight cells A4 through J16 and press the [enter] key.

      If we name ranges *within* our database (in other words, name a subset of the database), we will be able to use these names later on. These names can be used to specify ranges in the formulas that we establish in the criterion range.

>L   With your cursor still in cell A4, issue the command "/RNLD" for Range, Name, Label, Down. When asked for the range, use the arrow keys to highlight cells A4 through J4. These cells contain the field names which we will use in manipulating our database.

WARNING: Don't forget to update your list of range names.

>L   In cell AA4 enter "INPUT". In cell AB4, enter "A4.J16".
>L   In cell AA5 enter "FIELDS". In cell AB5, enter "A4.J4".

Step 9 - We will now set up the selection area and specify the *criterion* range for our accounts payable report.

>L   Move the cursor to cell K1. Type a vertical line (|) in this cell (this character is on the backslash key). Copy this character to the cell range K2 through K60.
>L   Move the cursor to cell Q1 and add another vertical line from Q1 through Q60.

      These two lines will offset the input range and the macros from our other ranges.

>L Move the cursor to cell L1. Hold down the [Alt] key and press "W" to call up the column-width setting macro. Set the column-widths for columns L through Q as shown below. Hold down the [Ctrl] key and press [Break] when you wish to stop the execution of the macro.

<u>Column Width</u>

L	M	N	O	P	Q
22	7	11	12	12	1

>L Move the cursor back to cell L1 and enter "FOR ACCOUNTS PAYABLE REPORT, SELECT ALL INVOICES DUE BEFORE:"

>L Move to Cell M2 and enter "MONTH". In cell M3, enter "DATE" and, in cell M4, enter "YEAR".

>L Move to cell N2 and enter "11" for November. In cell N3, enter "1" and, in cell N4, enter "86" for the year 1986.

>L Add a dashed line below these entries by using the repeating label. In cell L5, type "\-" and press the [enter] key. Then, copy the contents of this cell to cells M5 through P5.

>L Move the cursor to cell M2 and use the "/Range, Name, Label, Right" command to name the month, date, and year ranges. Use the arrow keys to highlight cells M2 through M4 when prompted for the range and press the [enter] key.

  Don't forget to update your list of range names. (You may want to use the [tab] key and backtab [shift] key + [tab] key to move back and forth between the range and the range table.)

>L In cell AA6 enter "MONTH". In cell AB6, enter "N2". In cell AA7 enter "DATE". In cell AB7, enter "N3". In cell AA8 enter "YEAR". In cell AB8, enter "N4".

  We will also name the first cell in the selection area as a range so that we will be able to move to this range when we execute our macros later on.

>L Move the cursor to K1, type "/RNC" to issue the command Range, Name, Create. When asked for the range name, type "SELECT" and press the [enter] key twice.

>L In cell AA9 enter "SELECT". In cell AB9, enter "K1".

<u>Step 10</u> - Set up the *criterion* range as given below. Note the use of the named range "DATE_DUE" in the criterion range formula. Also note that the references to cells N4, N2, and N3 (the dates in our selection range) are *absolute* or fixed - their positions never change relative to the records in the database which we will be examining.

>L In cell L6, enter "CRITERION RANGE:"
>L In cell N7, enter "DATE_DUE".
>L In cell N8, enter "+DATE_DUE<=@DATE($N$4,$N$2,$N$3)".

Remember, you can use the special function key [F4] if you use the pointer to specify cells. This will insert the dollar signs to indicate when a cell reference is absolute . For example, when you point to cell N4, press the [F4] key to insert the dollar signs. If you are not using the pointer, you will have to type in each dollar sign.

When you have correctly entered this formula, you should see "1" displayed in cell N8. This is because the spreadsheet is evaluating the first record in the data base to determine if this record has a due date on or before November 1, 1986. Since the first record has a due date before November 1, the formula is evaluated as "true" and assigned the number "1". If the date had been after November 1, the formula would have been evaluated as "false" and assigned a value of "0".

>L   In cell L9, enter "\-" to add a dashed line below these entries. Copy this dashed line to cells M9 through P9.

Let's name the criterion range.

>L   Place the cursor in cell N7 and type "/RNC". Type "CRITERION" and press the [enter] key. Use the arrow keys to highlight cells N7 and N8 as the criterion range and press the [enter] key.

>L   In cell AA10 enter "CRITERION" and in cell AB10, enter "N7.N8" to update our range listing.

Step 11 - Finally, let's set up the accounts payable report section. This is the *output* range of the database and must contain some or all of the column headings used in the input section. The column headings used in the output section (which we will place in row 13) must match *exactly* with the column headings in the input range (which are in row 4), although they do not have to be in the same order. We would like to know the vendor, invoice number, date due, invoice amount and discount available for all invoices due on or before a certain date. To achieve this, set up the output area as follows:

>L   In cell L10, enter "ACCOUNTS PAYABLE DUE ON OR BEFORE:"
>L   In cell O10, enter "@DATE(N4,N2,N3)"
>L   Format cell O10 to display the date. (Type "/RFD" and press the [enter] key twice.)
>L   In both cells M12 and O12, enter "INVOICE".
>L   In cell L13, enter "VENDOR".
>L   In cell M13, enter " NUMBER" (enter a space before NUMBER).
>L   In cell N13, enter "DATE_DUE".
>L   In cell O13, enter"AMOUNT".
>L   In cell P13, enter "DISCOUNT".
>L   Format cells L12 through P13 to center the headings (Hint: type "/RLC" to begin).

>L   With your cursor in cell L13, type "/RNC" to issue the command Range, Name, Create. When prompted for the name of the range type "OUTPUT" and press the [enter] key. When prompted to identify the range, use the arrow keys to highlight cells L13 through P55 and then press the [enter] key.

(We are using rows 13 through 55 to allow enough room so that the report fills one page. If more records match our criterion than will fit in this output range, then an error message will be generated.)

>L   In cell AA11 enter "OUTPUT". In cell AB11, enter "L13.P55".

At this point the selection, criterion, and output areas of your worksheet should appear as in Exhibit 34-4.

Exhibit 34-4

	L	M	N	O	P
1|	FOR ACCOUNTS PAYABLE REPORT, SELECT ALL INVOICES DUE BEFORE:				
2|		MONTH	11		
3|		DATE	1		
4|		YEAR	86		
5|	--				
6|	CRITERION RANGE:				
7|			DATE__DUE		
8				1		
9|	--				
10|	ACCOUNTS PAYABLE DUE ON OR BEFORE:			01-Nov-86	
11						
12|		INVOICE		INVOICE	
13|	VENDOR	NUMBER	DATE__DUE	AMOUNT	DISCOUNT

Step 12 - At this point, we can use the data query extract command to extract a list of all payables due on or before the specified date (11/1/86).

>L   Move your cursor so that you can see the database report area in columns L through P (rows 10 through 29).

>L   Type "/DQ". Type "I" for Input. When asked for the input range, type "INPUT" and press the [enter] key.

>L   Now type "C" for Criterion. When asked for the criterion range, type "CRITERION" and press the [enter] key.

>L   Next, type "O" for Output. When asked for the output range, type "OUTPUT" and press the [enter] key.

>L   Type "E" for Extract to get a list of payables due.

>L   Type "Q" to Quit the data query commands.

Your report area should appear as in Exhibit 34-5.

Exhibit 34-5

	L	M	N	O	P
10	ACCOUNTS PAYABLE DUE ON OR BEFORE:			01-Nov-86	
11					
12		INVOICE		INVOICE	
13	VENDOR	NUMBER	DATE__DUE	AMOUNT	DISCOUNT
14	JKL,INC.	1332	25-Oct-86	200.00	4.00
15	J & L MFG.	1234	25-Oct-86	1000.26	20.01
16	GLOBAL SUPPLIES	3258	01-Nov-86	75.06	0.75
17	NATIONAL TELEPHONE	45689	27-Oct-86	345.68	0.00
18	ACME FURNITURE	896	28-Oct-86	110.00	0.00
19	UPS	5678	29-Oct-86	32.50	0.00
20	AMERICAN EXPRESS	785555	29-Oct-86	550.00	0.00
21	UPS	103396	29-Oct-86	40.50	0.00
22	SORREL MFG.	8979	01-Nov-86	575.65	0.00
23	GALLEON SHIPPING	7899	30-Oct-86	123.00	0.00
24					

Step 13 - We would also like to have totals printed on our report.

>L   Move to cell O56 and enter a dashed line (\-). Copy this dashed line to cell P56.

>L   In cell O58, enter a double-dashed line (\=). Copy this double-dashed line to cells P58 and O60.

>L   In cell L57, type "TOTAL DUE ON OR BEFORE:".

>L   Move to cell N57 and enter "@DATE(N4,N2,N3)". Or, since you have named these cells as ranges, you could enter "@DATE(YEAR,MONTH,DATE)". Format this cell to display the date using the command "/RFD" and pressing the [enter] key twice.

>L   In cell O57, enter the formula "@SUM(O14.O56)". Copy this formula to cell P57.

>L   Move to cell L59 and enter "NET CASH REQUIRED:".

>L   Move to cell O59 and enter "+O57-P57" to calculate the net cash payment required.

>L   Finally, format cells O57 through P59 to display only two decimal places (cents).

Step 14 - Now let's name the range for the report to be printed.

>L   Move to cell L10.

>L   Name the report range by typing "/RNC" for "Range, Name, Create". When prompted for the name of the range type "REPORT" and press the [enter] key. When prompted to show the range to be printed, use the arrow keys to highlight cells L10 through P60 and press the [enter] key.

>L   Update the range table listings by moving to cell AA12 and entering "REPORT". In cell AB12, enter "L10.P60".

Macro #3 - A Print Macro

WARNING: If you do not have access to a printer, you will not be able to use this macro. You should, however, complete this section as the print macro will be referred to later when we develop a menu for operating our accounts payable system.

Consider the keystrokes needed to print:

/PP	Select the command Print to the Printer.
Rreport~	Select the Range to print--the range named REPORT--and press the [enter] key.
AG	Align the printer and Go.
PQ	After printing, advance the Page and Quit

A print macro can save numerous keystrokes each time we print!

Step 14 - Let's create a print macro.

>L   To begin the print macro, move to cell S19.

>L   Enter '**/PP**. In cell V19, enter "SELECT THE COMMAND PRINT TO THE PRINTER."

>L   Move to cell S20 and enter "Rreport~". It is suggested that you type range names in lower-case letters (press the [Caps Lock] key to return to lower case) so that your macro commands will be easier to read.

>L   In cell V20, enter "SELECT THE NAMED RANGE report TO BE PRINTED."

>L   Move to cell S21 and enter "AG".

>L   In cell V21, enter "ALIGN THE PRINTER AND GO."

>L   Move to cell S22 and enter "PQ".

>L   In cell V22, enter "ADVANCE THE PAGE AND QUIT."

>L   Finally move to cell R19 and name the print macro. Enter '\P (for Print macro). Then, with the cursor still in cell R19, type "/RNLR" and press the [enter] key to issue the command Range, Name, Label, Right which completes the naming of the macro.

>L   Move to cell AA13 and enter the range name '\P in our list of range names. In cell AB13, enter "S19".

Your completed print macro should appear similar to Exhibit 34-6.

Exhibit 34-6

	R	S		V	W	X	Y
19	\P	/PP		SELECT THE COMMAND PRINT TO THE PRI
20		Rreport~		SELECT THE NAMED RANGE report TO BE
21		AG		ALIGN THE PAPER AND GO.
22		PQ		ADVANCE THE PAGE AND QUIT.

Using the macro: If your computer is connected to a printer, you can **test the macro by holding down the [Alt] key and pressing "P".** If you are not connected to a printer, you will not be able to test this macro. If you save your work to a disk, you can move to a computer which is connected to a printer and test the print macro.

At this point, we have created a column width setting macro, a data entry macro, a print macro, and used 1-2-3's date and database management functions!

Refining the Data Entry Macro:

There are several reasons for refining our data entry macro. First, as we add more invoices to our database, we will have to redefine the database input range to incorporate these additional records. Second, each time we add a new record, we need to copy the due date and discount amount calculations to the new row. Third, we must check to be sure that the cursor is located in the correct cell to begin data entry before calling the data entry macro.

We can refine our macro by creating a range called BOTTOM which will be a blank bottom row in the input database. This range will contain the calculations for the date due and discount amounts, which we can then copy to a new row for new records. We will also define the input range to include the row BOTTOM. When we wish to enter a new record, we can then move the "bottom" down one row, making room for a new record, and then copy the formulas in the bottom row to the new row.

<u>Step 15</u> - First, let's go back and modify the last row of our input database.

>L   Move to Cell A17 (the first blank row after your database). Type "/RNC" to issue the command Range, Name, Create. When asked for the range name, type "BOTTOM" and press the [enter] key. When asked for the range, use the arrow keys to highlight cells A17 through J17 and press the [enter] key.

>L   In cell AA14, enter "BOTTOM" and in cell AB14 enter "A17.J17" to keep a record of our range.

>L   Move to cell I16 in your database. Type "/C" for Copy. When prompted for the range to copy from, use the arrow keys to highlight cells I16 and J16 and press the [enter] key. When asked for the range to copy to, point out cell I17 and press the [enter] key.

>L   Move to cell F17. Type "/RFF" and press the [enter] key twice to reformat this cell to display two decimal places (cents).

This copies the formulas and formats down to our range BOTTOM.

>L   With the cursor in cell F17, type "/RNC" to issue the command Range, Name, Create. Enter "CALCS" for the range name and point out cells F17 through J17 as the range.

>L   In cell AA15, enter "CALCS" and in cell AB15 enter "F17.J17" to record this range.

Step 16 - Next, let's move the current data entry macro down several rows to give us additional room to refine the macro.

>L   Move to cell S3.

>L   Type "/M" for Move. When prompted for the range to move, use the arrow keys to highlight cells S3 through V11 and press the [enter] key. (Since we're moving the macro commands, we also want to move the descriptions of what each command does.) When prompted for the range to move to, use the arrow keys to point out cell S8 and press the [enter] key.

This will move the existing macro down five rows and allow us to place additional macro commands at the beginning.

Step 17 - Enter the following macro commands and descriptions in the corresponding cells:

>L   In cell S3, enter {GOTO}bottom~. Be sure to enter the tilde (~) to symbolize the [enter] key. In cell V3, enter "GOTO THE RANGE bottom."

>L   Move to cell S4 and enter '/Mbottom~{DOWN}~. In cell V4, enter "MOVE bottom DOWN ONE ROW."

>L   Move to cell S5 and enter {GOTO}calcs~. In cell V5, enter "GOTO THE RANGE calcs."

>L   Move to cell S6 and enter '/Ccalcs~{UP}~. In cell V6, enter "COPY THE RANGE calcs UP ONE ROW."

>L   Move to cell S7 and enter {GOTO}bottom~{UP}. In cell V7, enter "GOTO THE RANGE bottom, THEN UP ONE ROW."

At this point, your data entry macro should appear as in Exhibit 34-7.

Exhibit 34-7

	R	S	V	W	X	Y
3		\E	{GOTO}bottom~	GOTO THE RANGE bottom.		
4			/Mbottom~{DOWN}~	MOVE bottom DOWN ONE ROW		
5			{GOTO}calcs~	GOTO THE RANGE calcs.		
6			/Ccalcs~{UP}~	COPY THE RANGE calcs UP ONE ROW.		
7			{GOTO}bottom~{UP}	GOTO THE RANGE bottom, THEN UP ONE ROW.		
8			{?}{RIGHT}	PAUSE FOR INPUT, MOVE CURSOR RIGHT.		
9			{?}{RIGHT}	PAUSE FOR INPUT, MOVE CURSOR RIGHT.		
10			{?}{RIGHT}	PAUSE FOR INPUT, MOVE CURSOR RIGHT.		
11			{?}{RIGHT}	PAUSE FOR INPUT, MOVE CURSOR RIGHT.		
12			{?}{RIGHT}	PAUSE FOR INPUT, MOVE CURSOR RIGHT.		
13			{?}{RIGHT}	PAUSE FOR INPUT, MOVE CURSOR RIGHT.		
14			{?}{RIGHT}	PAUSE FOR INPUT, MOVE CURSOR RIGHT.		
15			{?}{DOWN}{END}{LEFT}	PAUSE FOR INPUT, MOVE TO NEXT ROW.		
16			/XG\E~	REPEAT MACRO.		

Before completing and using the revised macro, let's consider what may happen. If we were to use this macro without further revision, we would find that when we used the [Ctrl] [Break] key sequence to exit the macro, we would end up with a blank line between our database and the range BOTTOM.

In addition, while this macro can be called regardless of what cell the cursor is in, and while the macro will take you to the correct area for data entry, if we do not invoke (use) the macro from a cell close to the column headings in rows 3 and 4, then we will not be able to see the column headings when we enter data.

To remedy this, we will create a small menu macro which will ask us whether or not we wish to enter an invoice. If the response is "yes", we will move to the input area, set the field names as titles, and call our data entry macro. If the response is "no", we will clear these titles and exit the macro.

Macro #4 - Creating a Menu Macro.

Menu macros are called by using the macro command "/XM" followed by the range name of the menu macro and the tilde (~) to symbolize the [enter] key. This is the only instance in which a macro name can be longer than the backslash plus one letter.

The format of a menu macro is as follows:

NAME	CHOICE 1	CHOICE 2	CHOICE 3
	EXPLANATION 1	EXPLANATION 2	EXPLANATION 3
	MACRO 1	MACRO 2	MACRO 3

The first line contains the name of the macro and the choices that will be displayed when the macro is invoked. It is important that the choices begin with different letters so that they can be selected by typing in their first character in the same manner that we can select commands when we enter the regular Lotus command menu.

Row two contains explanations of the choices in the first row and will appear when the choice in row one is highlighted.

Row three (and subsequent rows) contain the macro to execute when the related choice is selected.

Step 18 - Let's create a menu macro!

>L   To begin the menu macro, let's enter the choices. Move to cell S25 and enter "YES". In cell T25, enter "NO". In cell V25, enter "DATA ENTRY CHOICES."

>L   Move to cell S26 and enter "Enter an Invoice". In cell T26, enter "Quit Invoice Entry". In cell V26, enter "EXPLANATIONS OF CHOICES."

Note that you will not be able to read all of your entry in cell S26 when you enter data in cell T26. However, all of the entry in cell S26 still exists! Cells S26 and T26 simply overlap one another like two sheets of paper! (You can verify this by moving the cursor back to cell S26 and seeing what appears on the first line of the control panel.)

>L   Let's create the macro for our first choice.   Move to cell S27 and enter "{GOTO}input~".

>L   In cell S28, enter "{DOWN}".

>L   In cell S29, enter '/WTH (this sets the field names as titles).

>L   In cell S30, enter '/XG\E~ (to call the data entry macro).

>L   Now let's create the macro for our second choice. Move to cell T27 and enter '/WTC (to clear the titles).

>L   Move to cell T28 and enter '/XQ~. (Use of the "Q" in this command halts the execution of a macro.)

>L   Finally move to cell R25 and name the range of the menu macro. Enter "ENTRY" (for ENTRY menu macro). Then, with the cursor still in cell R25, type "/RNLR" and press the [enter] key to issue the command Range, Name, Label, Right which completes the naming of the menu macro.

>L   Move to cell AA16 and enter the range name "ENTRY" in our list of range names. In cell AB16, enter "S25".

Note that the range name (cell R25), the first choice and its macro (cells S25 through S30), and the second choice and its macro (cells T25 through T28) are in adjacent columns. This is essential to the proper functioning of a menu macro.

Step 19 - Let's return to the data entry macro and finish refining it.

>L   Move to cell S15 and edit the current command "{?}{DOWN}{END}{LEFT}" to "{?}~". (Don't forget to add the tilde "~").

>L   In cell V15, edit the cell to read "PAUSE FOR INPUT."

>L   In cell S16, enter '/XMentry~ to call the entry menu.

>L   In cell V16, enter "CALL MENU MACRO entry."

This completes the data entry macro by having the macro pause for input (YES or NO) from the user and then having the data entry macro call the menu macro ENTRY.

>L   Move to cell R3 and enter "/RNLR" to rename the data entry macro after making the revisions.

You must rename the data entry macro after revising it.

Step 20 - Let's try out our new data entry macro.

>L   Press the [Home] key to move to cell A1 so that you can view the database.

>L   Hold down the [Alt] key and press "E".

The cursor will move to the bottom of the input range and insert an additional data row. it will then pause in row 17 for you to enter additional data.

\>L   **Enter the following data:**

	A	B	C	D	E		F	G	H	I
>L	10	23	86	AZ10506	CDR, INC.		325	0	15	

After the entry of the first complete record, you will be asked whether you wish to enter an invoice or not.

\>L   **Respond by typing "Y" and enter in the following additional invoice:**

	A	B	C	D	E		F	G	H	I
>L	10	23	86	45115	QWIX		50.66	1	10	

\>L   **When you finish entering this invoice, respond by typing "N" and the macro will stop executing.**

Macro #5 - Extracting Payables Due Before a Given Date.

The data query macro will use the dates found in our selection area (cells N2 through N4) to set up the criterion range and select the invoices. These invoices will then be extracted to our output area.

We will make use of the macro command "/XN" which prompts the user with a message (which we will define) to enter a number. After the number is entered, it is copied to a range which is specified as part of the command. We will use the "/XN" command to prompt the user to enter the month, date, and year for the report selection and copy them to the appropriate named ranges. (If a label is entered instead of a number, an error message results. Note: If a label is desired, the "/XL" command can be used to prompt for a label entry.) The format of the command is as follows:

/XNmessage ~location~

One or two spaces should be left after the message and before the tilde which precedes the location to make it easier to differentiate the message from the user's response.

Step 21 - Enter the following macro formulas and descriptions:

	Cell	Macro formula or description
>L	S32	{GOTO}select~
	V32	GOTO SELECTION AREA.
>L	S33	{GOTO}month~
	V33	GOTO THE month RANGE.
>L	S34	'/XNEnter the month ~month~
	V34	PROMPT USER TO ENTER MONTH AND COPY TO month RANGE.
>L	S35	{DOWN}
	V35	MOVE DOWN ONE ROW.
>L	S36	'/XNEnter the day ~date~
	V36	PROMPT USER TO ENTER DATE AND COPY TO date RANGE.
>L	S37	{DOWN}
	V37	MOVE DOWN ONE ROW.

>L   S38   '/XNEnter the year   ~year~
      V38   **PROMPT USER TO ENTER YEAR AND COPY TO year RANGE.**
>L   S39   '/DQIinput~
      V39   **SET DATA INQUIRY RANGE TO input.**
>L   S40   I{UP}~
      V40   **INPUT RANGE FOR DATA QUERY IS input MINUS LAST ROW.**
>L   S41   EQ
      V41   **EXTRACT DATA AND QUIT DATABASE.**

Note: The input range is specified in the macro command in cells S39 and S40. The input range is defined as the range INPUT, then moved up a row so that the range BOTTOM (which contains no data) is not included.

Before we will be able to begin using our macro, however, we will need to revise the range which we previously defined as INPUT to include the data we have added and the range BOTTOM. By including the range BOTTOM as the last row of the range INPUT, we will be able to automatically expand the range INPUT whenever we add more data.

>L   Type "/RNC" followed by "INPUT". Use the cursor to highlight the range from cell A4 through J19 and press the [enter] key.

>L   Move to cell R32 and enter '\Q (note that this is a "Q"). Then type "/RNLR" and press the [enter] key to name the data query macro.

>L   In cell AA17, enter '\Q (note that this is a "Q") and in cell AB17 enter "S32" to update our range table.

Using the macro: Use the data query macro by holding down the [Alt] key and pressing "Q". You should be prompted to enter the month, date, and year for report selection. Enter a date of 10-27-86 (type "10" and press the [enter] key, etc.) to see what happens. After responding to the prompts, the records for invoices due on or before the specified date should be extracted and displayed in the output area. If you are not prompted for an entry when you attempt to invoke the macro, go back and check your macro for errors.

Macro #6 - An Overall Menu Structure

Finally, we can tie our entire worksheet together by writing a menu macro which will offer the options of data entry, extracting a report, printing a report, and quitting macro execution. We will refine each individual macro so that on completion, it returns us to the menu.

Step 22 - Enter the following macro formulas:

	Cell	Macro formula
>L	S44	'/XMmenu~
>L	S46	**DATA_ENTRY**
>L	S47	**Enter Accounts Payable Invoices**
>L	S48	'/XMentry~

	Cell	Macro formula
>L	T46	**EXTRACT_REPORT**
>L	T47	**Select Payables as of a Given Due Date**
>L	T48	**'/XG\Q~**

	Cell	Macro formula
>L	U46	**PRINT_REPORT**
>L	U47	**Print Accounts Payable Report**
>L	U48	**'/XG\P~**

	Cell	Macro formula
>L	V46	**QUIT**
>L	V47	**Quit Macro**
>L	V48	**'/XQ~**

Note that the entries you make will overlap one another and you will not be able to completely read every entry unless you move the cursor to each cell.

Step 23 - Move to cell R44 and name the macro:

>L   **With the cursor in cell R44, enter '\M.**

>L   **In cell R46, enter "MENU".**

>L   **Move back to cell R44 and type "/RNLR". When prompted for a range, use the arrow keys to point out the range R44 through R46 and press the [enter] key to name both menu macro ranges at the same time.**

>L   **In cell AA18, enter '\M and in cell AB18 enter "S44" to update the range list.**

>L   **In cell AA19, enter MENU and in cell AB19 enter "S46" to update the range list.**

Step 24 - We need to refine the print macro, the ENTRY menu macro, and the data query macro so that they return us to the overall menu after being executed.

>L   **Go to cell S23 and enter '/XMmenu~ at the end of the print macro. In cell V23, enter "RETURN TO THE MENU MACRO."**

>L   **Go to cell T28 and enter '/XMmenu~ to the "NO" choice of the ENTRY macro in place of the current command to quit (/XQ).**

>L   **Go to cell S42 and enter '/XMmenu~ to the data query macro. In cell V42, enter "RETURN TO THE MENU MACRO."**

>L   **In cells R19, R25, and R32 rename each of the macros you have modified using the command "/RNLR" and pressing the [enter] key. (Or, you can rename all of the macro ranges at one time. Place the cursor in cell R1 and type "/RNLR". In response to the prompt for a range, use the arrow keys to highlight the range from R1 through R46 and press the [enter] key.)**

Using the macro: Test the menu macro by holding down the [Alt] key and pressing "M" to call up the menu. Test each of the choices by trying them. If one or more fail to work, make sure that you check your entries very carefully to ensure that you have typed all of the essential characters. Again, the most common error is to leave out a tilde (~). Check very carefully for them!

Macro #7 - An Autoloading Macro

We have now written our own "menu driven program". In fact, if we created one additional macro, the menu would be called up automatically when this file is loaded. A macro with the name "\0" (read backslash zero) is automatically executed when the file is loaded.

>L   Go to cell S50 and enter '/XMmenu~ to add this automatic loading feature to your macros. In cell V50, enter "CALL MENU WHEN FILE IS LOADED."

>L   Move to cell R50 and enter '\0 and then type "/RNLR" and press the [enter] key to name the autoloading macro. (Add this range to your range list in columns AA and AB.)

>L   To try this macro, move the cursor to cell A1 and save your spreadsheet. Then, erase the current spreadsheet and retrieve your spreadsheet from the disk file to see if it automatically begins executing.

In addition, any file named AUTO123 will be automatically loaded when 1-2-3 is started. On the file disk you received with this manual, the file with the menu is called AUTO123, which is why the menu is loaded when you first enter Lotus 1-2-3.

There is one final step which should be completed before the template will be practical to use for any length of time. We need to find a way to delete accounts from the data base and then regroup the database after an account has been paid. See if you can find a way to solve this puzzle!

PART IV

PARTIALLY COMPLETED PROBLEMS

P3-11 Taylor Company closes its books only once a year on December 31 but prepares monthly financial statements by estimating month-end inventories and by using worksheets. The company's trial balance on January 31, 1986, is presented below. Selling Expenses and Administrative Expenses are controlling accounts.

Taylor Company
TRIAL BALANCE
January 31, 1986

Cash	8,000	
Accounts Receivable	20,000	
Notes Receivable	5,000	
Allowance for Doubtful Accounts		840
Inventory, Jan. 1, 1986	24,000	
Furniture and Fixtures	28,000	
Accumulated Depreciation of Furniture and Fixtures		7,000
Unexpired Insurance	600	
Supplies on Hand	1,050	
Accounts Payable		6,000
Notes Payable		5,000
Common Stock		20,000
Retained Earnings		31,535
Sales		120,000
Sales Returns and Allowances	1,750	
Purchases	80,000	
Transportation-in	2,000	
Selling Expenses	11,000	
Administrative Expenses	9,000	
Interest Revenue		125
Interest Expense	100	
	---------------	----------------
	190,500	190,500
	==========	==========

Instructions:

Use the template 3P11 to complete the eight-column worksheet.

(a) Prepare adjusting entries for the following transactions and transfer those entries to the appropriate cells in column E and F of the template.
   1. Estimated bad debts, .4% of net sales.
   2. Depreciation of furniture and fixtures, 12% per year.
   3. Insurance expired in January, $80.
   4. Supplies used in January, $80.
   5. Office salaries accrued, $500.
   6. Interest accrued on notes payable, $230.
   7. Interest unearned on notes receivable, $74.
(b) Estimate the January 31 inventory and enter it on the template. The average gross profit earned by the company is 35% of net sales.
(c) Complete the template by adding the appropriate formulas and cell references in those cells which currently contain asterisks (*********).
(d) Print your completed template and/or formulas. Prepare a balance sheet, an income statement, and a statement of retained earnings. Dividends of $5,000 were paid on the common stock during the month.

P4-4 Arshem, Inc., reported income from continuing operations before taxes during 1987 of $820,000. Additional transactions occurring in 1987 but not considered in the $820,000 are as follows:

1. The corporation experienced an uninsured flood loss (extraordinary) in the amount of $60,000 during the year. The tax rate on this item is 46%.
2. At the beginning of 1985, the corporation purchased a machine for $48,000 (salvage value of $6,000) that had a useful life of six years. The bookkeeper uses straight-line depreciation, but failed to deduct the salvage value in computing the depreciation base.
3. Securities sold as a part of its portfolio resulted in a loss of $105,000 (pretax).
4. When its president died, the corporation realized $120,000 from an insurance policy. The cash surrender value of this policy had been carried on the books as an investment in the amount of $56,000 (the gain is nontaxable).
5. The corporation disposed of its recreational division at a loss of $115,000 before taxes. Assume that this transaction meets criteria for discontinued operations.
6. The corporation decided to change its method of inventory pricing from average cost to the FIFO method. The effect of this change on prior years is to increase 1985 income by $50,000 and decrease 1986 income by $10,000 before taxes. The FIFO method has been used for 1987. The tax rate on these items is 40%.

Instructions:
Use the template 4P4 to prepare an income statement for the year 1987 starting with income from continuing operations before taxes. Enter the appropriate numbers in those cells currently containing N's (NNNNNN). Enter formulas or cell references in those cells containing asterisks (********). Compute earnings per share as it should be shown on the face of the income statement. Common shares outstanding for the year are 25,000 shares. (Assume an income tax rate of 40% on all items, unless indicated otherwise.) Print your completed template and/or formulas.

E6-20 Classic Entrees, a manufacturer of low sodium, low cholesterol, TV dinners, would like to increase its market share in the sunbelt. In order to do so, Classic has decided to locate a new factory in the Atlanta area. Classic will either rent or lease a site depending upon which is more advantageous. The site location committee has narrowed down the available sites to the following three buildings.

Building A--Purchase for a cash price of $600,000, useful life 25 years.
Building B--Lease for 25 years with annual lease payments of $79,000 being made at the beginning of the year.
Building C--Purchase for $650,000 cash. This building is larger than needed; however, the excess space can be sublet for 25 years at a net annual rental of $9,000. Rental payments will be received at the end of each year. Classic has no aversion to being a landlord.

Instructions:
Use the template 6E20 to prepare the necessary calculations to complete the investment analysis. Enter the required formulas in the cells currently containing asterisks (********). Print your completed template and/or formulas. In which building would you recommend that Classic locate assuming a 15% cost of funds?

Hint: To calculate the present value factors, use the formulas given in the present value tables in your text. Exponents are indicated in SuperCalc3 by using two asterisks (**) and in Lotus 1-2-3 by using a caret (^).

P7-4 Presented below is information related to Italian Products Company.

Balance per books at October 31, $41,847.85; November receipts, $173,523.91; November disbursements, $166,193.54.
Balance per bank, November 30, $56,274.20.

The following checks were outstanding at November 30:

1224	$1,724.51
1230	2,468.30
1232	3,547.60
1233	482.17

Included with the November bank statement and not recorded by the company were a bank debit ticket for $27.40 covering bank charges for the month, a debit ticket for $465.30 for a customer's check returned and marked NSF, and a credit ticket for $1,200.00 representing bond interest collected by the bank in the name of Italian Products Company. Cash on hand at November 30 recorded and awaiting deposit amounted to $1,833.90.

Instructions:
(a) Use the template 7P4 to prepare a bank reconciliation (to the correct balance) at November 30, 1986, for Italian Products Company from the information above. Enter the appropriate numbers in those cells currently containing N's (NNNNNN) and the appropriate labels beginning in those cells currently containing L's (LLLLLL).   Enter formulas or cell references in those cells containing asterisks (*********). Print your completed template and/or formulas.
(b) Prepare any journal entries required to adjust the cash account at November 30.

E8-12   Mo Lasses Company was formed on December 1, 1985.   The following information is available from Mo Lasses' inventory records for Product Ply:

	Units	Unit Cost
January 1, 1986 (beginning inventory)	700	$8.00
Purchases:		
January 5, 1986	1,200	$9.00
January 25, 1986	1,300	$10.00
February 16, 1986	800	$11.00
March 26, 1986	600	$12.00

A physical inventory on March 31, 1986, shows 1,500 units on hand.

Instructions:
Use the template 8E12 to assist in preparing schedules to compute the ending inventory at March 31, 1986, under each of the following inventory methods:
   (a) FIFO.
   (b) LIFO.
   (c) Weighted average.
Enter the appropriate numbers in those cells currently containing N's (NNNNNN) and the appropriate dates as labels beginning in those cells currently containing D's (DDDDDD).   Enter formulas or cell references in those cells containing asterisks (*********). Print your completed template and/or formulas.

P9-1 Marshmellow Co. follows the practice of valuing its inventory at the lower of cost or market. The following information is available from the company's inventory records as of December 31, 1987.

Item	On Hand Quantity	Unit Cost	Replacement Cost/Unit	Estimated Unit Selling Price	Completion & Disposal Costs/Unit	Normal Unit Profit
A	1,600	$7.50	$8.40	$10.50	$1.50	$1.80
B	1,100	8.20	8.00	9.40	.90	1.20
C	1,000	5.60	5.40	7.20	1.10	.60
D	700	3.80	4.20	6.30	.80	1.50
E	500	6.40	6.30	6.80	.70	1.00

Instructions:
(a) Use the template 9P1 to assist in determining the inventory price that should be used for each item under the lower of cost or market rule. Enter formulas or cell references in those cells containing asterisks (*********). Print your completed template and/or formulas.
(b) Marshmellow applies the lower of cost or market rule directly to each item in the inventory and uses a perpetual inventory system to account for the items above. Give the adjusting entry, if one is necessary, to write down the ending inventory from cost to market.
(c) If Marshmellow applies the lower of cost or market rule to the total of the inventory, what is the proper dollar amount for inventory as of 12/31/87?

P10-12 On March 1, 1986, Gaffknee Corporation acquired a tract of land as a plant site. Gaffknee paid $40,000 cash and gave a $60,000, 3-year, 12% note payable, on which interest is payable annually. Construction was begun immediately on the plant, and it was completed on October 31, 1986. Expenditures for construction were $400,000 monthly for 8 months beginning on March 1. In order to help finance construction, Gaffknee borrowed $3,000,000 on March 1 on a 10%, 2-year note payable. Interest on this note is payable at maturity. Excess funds which are not needed to pay for construction costs were invested in temporary securities at 14%. Other than these two notes, Gaffknee had no outstanding debt during 1986.

Instructions:
(a) Use the template 10P12 to calculate interest revenue, average accumulated expenditures, avoidable interest, total interest cost incurred and interest cost capitalized during 1986. Enter the appropriate numbers in those cells currently containing N's (NNNNNN). Enter formulas or cell references in those cells containing asterisks (********). Print your completed template and/or formulas. In computing avoidable interest, start with the specific borrowing on the land.
(b) Prepare the journal entry needed on the books of Gaffknee at December 31, 1986 to record interest cost incurred and interest cost capitalized.

P11-3 On January 1, 1984, Milton Company, a small machine-tool manufacturer, acquired for $1,350,000 a piece of new industrial equipment. The new equipment was eligible for the investment tax credit and Milton elected to take 80% of the allowed credit and accounted for the amount using the flow-through method. The new equipment had a useful life of 5 years and the salvage value was estimated to be $150,000. Milton estimates that the new equipment can produce 12,000 machine tools in its first year. it estimates that production will decline by 1,000 units per year over the remaining useful life of the equipment. The following depreciation methods may be used:

> Double-declining balance
> Sum-of-the-years' digits
> Straight-line
> Units-of-output

Instructions:
(a) Use the template 11P3 to help determine which depreciation method would maximize net income for financial statement reporting for the three-year period ending December 31, 1986. Enter the appropriate numbers in those cells currently containing N's (NNNNNN). Enter formulas or cell references in those cells containing asterisks (*********). Print your completed template and/or formulas. Prepare a schedule showing the amount of accumulated depreciation at December 31, 1986, under the method selected. Ignore present value, income tax, and deferred income tax considerations.
(b) Which depreciation method would minimize net income for income tax reporting for the three-year period ending December 31, 1986? Prepare a schedule showing the amount of accumulated depreciation at December 31, 1986, under the method selected. Ignore present value considerations.

P12-8 Presented below are financial forecasts related to Harrison Cabinet Company for the next ten years.

Forecasted average earnings (per year)	$60,000
Forecasted market value of net assets, exclusive of goodwill (per year)	260,000

Instructions:
You have been asked to compute goodwill under the following methods. Use the template 12P8 to assist you in your calculations. Enter the appropriate numbers in those cells currently containing N's (NNNNNN). Enter formulas or cell references in those cells containing asterisks (*********). Print your completed template and/or formulas. The normal rate of return on net assets for the industry is 15%.
(a) Goodwill is equal to 5 years' excess earnings.
(b) Goodwill is equal to the present value of 5 years' excess earnings discounted at 12%. Hint: Use the present value formula given in the tables in your text to compute the present value factor in cell E20. Exponents are indicated in SuperCalc3 by using two asterisks (**) and in Lotus 1-2-3 by using a caret (^).
(c) Goodwill is equal to the average excess earnings capitalized at 16%.
(d) Goodwill is equal to average excess earnings capitalized at the normal rate of return for the industry of 15%.

P13-4   This is a payroll sheet for Stamford Printing Company for the month of September, 1986. The company is allowed a 1% unemployment compensation rate by the state; the federal unemployment tax rate is .6% and the maximum for both is $6,000. Assume a 10% federal income tax rate for all employees and a 7% F.I.C.A. tax on employee and employer on a maximum of $39,600 per employee.

Name	Earnings to Aug. 31	September Earnings	Income Tax Withholding	F.I.C.A.	State U.C.	Federal U.C.
D. Kirk	$3,500	$800				
V. Brown	4,900	500				
R. Lauver	6,800	1,000				
D. Mosso	14,700	2,100				
R. Sprouse	39,000	3,400				
A. Wyatt	42,300	3,500				

Instructions:
(a) Use the template 13P4 to complete the payroll record sheet and then make the necessary entry to record the payment of the payroll. Enter formulas or cell references in those cells containing asterisks (*********). Print your completed template and/or formulas.
(b) Make the entry to record the payroll tax expenses of Stamford Printing Company.
(c) Make the entry to pay the payroll liabilities created. Assume that the company pays all payroll liabilities at the end of each month.

P14-4   On January 1, 1986, Seminole Company sold 15% bonds having a maturity value of $200,000 for $221,629.40, which provides the bondholders with a 12% yield. The bonds are dated January 1, 1986, and mature January 1, 1991 with interest payable December 31 of each year. Seminole Company allocates interest and unamortized discount or premium on the effective interest basis.

Instructions:
(a) Prepare the journal entry at the date of the bond issuance.
(b) Prepare the journal entry to record the interest payment and the amortization for 1986. Use the template 14P4 to prepare a partial schedule of interest expense and bond amortization. Enter formulas or cell references in those cells containing asterisks (*********). Print your completed template and/or formulas.
(c) Prepare the journal entry to record the interest payment and the amortization for 1988.

E17-8   Hammerubi Inc. has decided to raise additional capital by issuing $160,000 face value of bonds with a coupon rate of 10%. In discussions with their investment brokers, it was determined that to help the sale of the bonds, detachable stock warrants should be issued at the rate of one warrant for each $100 bond sold. The value of the bonds without the warrants is considered to be $132,000, and the value of the warrants in the market is $24,000. The bonds sold in the market at issuance for $147,000.

Instructions:
(a) Use the template 17E8 to assist with preparing the entry to be made at the time of issuance of the bonds and warrants. Enter numbers in those cells currently containing N's (NNNNNN). Enter formulas or cell references in those cells containing asterisks (*********). Print your completed template and/or formulas.
(b) If the warrants were nondetachable, would the entry be different? Discuss.

E17-13   On December 31, 1985, Leo Tolstoi Book Company issues 200,000 stock appreciation rights to its officers entitling them to receive cash for the difference between the market price of its stock and a preestablished price of $10. The date of exercise is December 31, 1986. The market price fluctuates as follows: 12/31/86--$14; 12/31/87--$8; 12/31/88--$20; 12/31/89--$19. Rights are exercisable only if the officer is employed by the company at the date of exercise.

Instructions:
(a) Use the template 17E13 to prepare a schedule that shows the amount of compensation expense allocable to each year affected by the stock appreciation rights plan. Enter numbers in those cells currently containing N's (NNNNNN). Enter formulas or cell references in those cells containing asterisks (*********). Print your completed template and/or formulas.
(b) Prepare the entry at 12/31/89 to record the compensation expense, if any, in 1989.
(c) Prepare the entry on 12/31/89 assuming that all 200,000 SARs are exercised by all of the eligible officers.

P18-5   On January 1, 1984, Shoestring Company acquires $100,000 of Judy Nolan, Inc., 9% bonds at a price of $92,794. The interest is payable each December 31, and the bonds mature January 1, 1987. The investment will provide Shoestring Company a 12% yield.

Instructions:
(a) Use the template 18P5 to prepare a three-year schedule of interest revenue and bond discount amortization, applying the straight-line method. Enter formulas or cell references in those cells containing asterisks (*********).
(b) Use the template 18P5 to prepare a three-year schedule of interest revenue and bond discount amortization, applying the effective interest method. Enter formulas or cell references in those cells containing asterisks (*********). Print your completed template and/or formulas.
(c) Prepare the journal entry for the interest receipt of December 31, 1986, and the discount amortization under the straight-line method.
(d) Prepare the journal entry for the interest receipt of December 31, 1986, and the discount amortization under the effective interest method.

P20-1 The following facts relate to the Willie Nelson Music Co. for the calendar year 1986.

1. Assets are purchased at the beginning of 1986 at a cost of $140,000. For accounting purposes, straight-line depreciation over an eight-year life is used. For tax purposes, accelerated cost recovery system (ACRS) depreciation over a five-year life is used, under which the company may deduct 15% of the asset cost during 1986.
2. Warranty liability of $8,400 provided for accounting purposes is not deductible for tax purposes until warranty costs are incurred.
3. Accounting income before taxes includes $13,200 related to construction-type contracts still in process that are accounted for on the percentage-of-completion method for accounting purposes and on the completed contract method for tax purposes.
4. Amortization of goodwill of $5,000 is not deductible for tax purposes.
5. Included in pretax accounting income is $4,500 of interest on tax-exempt municipal bonds.
6. Pretax accounting income is $99,800.

Instructions:
Use the template 20P1 to assist in preparing the journal entry to record income taxes payable, income tax expense, and deferred income taxes for the year 1986. Enter the appropriate numbers in those cells currently containing N's (NNNNNN) and the appropriate labels or descriptions beginning in those cells currently containing L's (LLLLLLL). Enter formulas or cell references in those cells containing asterisks (*********). Print your completed template and/or formulas. (WARNING: Be very careful about whether amounts entered or calculated should be added or subtracted in determining taxable income!) Assume that the federal income tax rate is 45%.

E22-4 Trudy Leasing Company leases a new machine that cost $84,000 to Jeremiah Corporation on a three-year noncancelable contract. Jeremiah Corporation agrees to assume all risks of normal ownership including such costs as insurance, taxes, and maintenance. The machine has a three-year useful life and no residual value. the lease was signed on January 1, 1987; Trudy Leasing Company expects to earn an 8% return on its investment. The annual rentals are payable on each December 31.

Instructions:
(a) Discuss the nature of the lease arrangement and the accounting method each party to the lease should apply.
(b) Use template 22E4 to assist in preparing an amortization schedule that would be suitable for both the lessor and lessee and that covers all the years involved. Enter formulas or cell references in those cells containing asterisks (*********). Print your completed template and/or formulas. Use the present value formula given in the tables in your text to compute the present value factor in cell F5. Exponents are indicated in SuperCalc3 by using two asterisks (**) and in Lotus 1-2-3 by using a caret (^).

E23-3 Bach Tool Co. purchased equipment for $348,000 which was estimated to have a useful life of 10 years with a salvage value of $8,000 at the end of that time. Depreciation has been entered for 7 years on a straight-line basis. In 1987, it is determined that the total estimated life should be 15 years with a salvage value of $6,000 at the end of that time.

Instructions:
(a) Complete template 23E3 to assist you in completing parts (b) anc (c). Enter the appropriate numbers in those cells currently containing N's (NNNNNN). Enter formulas or cell references in those cells containing asterisks (*********). Print your completed template and/or formulas. (Hint: Copy (replicate) the formulas in cells B9 through F9 to rows 10 through 22; then, enter the revised useful life and salvage value in cells B15 and C15.)
(b) Prepare the entry (if any) to correct the prior years' depreciation.
(c) Prepare the entry to record depreciation for 1987.

E24-12 Joseph McCormick Co. has recently decided to go public and has hired you as the independent CPA. One statement that the enterprise is anxious to have prepared is a statement of changes in financial position. Financial statements of Joseph McCormick Co., for 1986 and 1987 are provided below:

	12/31/86	12/31/87
Cash	$13,000	$25,000
Accounts receivable	14,000	29,000
Merchandise inventory	35,000	26,000
Property, plant, and equipment	78,000	60,000
Accumulated depreciation	(24,000)	(20,000)
	$116,000	$120,000
Accounts payable	$23,000	$34,000
Federal income taxes payable	30,000	25,000
Bonds payable	33,000	37,000
Common stock	14,000	6,000
Retained earnings	16,000	18,000
	$116,000	$120,000

INCOME STATEMENT
For the Year Ended December 31, 1987

Sales		$220,000
Cost of sales		180,000
Gross profit		40,000
Selling expenses	$18,000	
Administrative expenses	6,000	24,000
Income from operations		16,000
Interest expense		5,000
Income before taxes		11,000
Income taxes		2,000
Net income		9,000

The following additional data were provided:

1. Dividends for the year 1987 were $3,500.
2. During the year equipment was sold for $8,500. This equipment cost $18,000 originally and had a book value of $12,000 at the time of sale. The loss on sale was incorrectly charged to retained earnings.
3. All depreciation expense is in the selling category.

Instructions:
(a) Complete the worksheet in template 24E12 and use this worksheet to prepare a statement of changes in financial position on the cash basis using the indirect approach. All sales and purchases are on account. Enter formulas or cell references in those cells containing asterisks (*********) and labels or descriptions in those cells containing L's (LLLLLLL). Make sure that you reference your entries in the columns provided. Print your completed template and/or formulas.
(b) Use your completed template to prepare a statement of changes in financial position using a working capital basis.

E26-7 Vestpocket Company has been operating for several years, and on December 31, 1987, presented the following balance sheet:

Vestpocket Company
BALANCE SHEET
December 31, 1987

Cash	$40,000	Accounts payable	$75,000
Receivables	75,000	Mortgage payable	130,000
Inventories	80,000	Common stock ($1 par)	150,000
Plant assets (net)	220,000	Retained earnings	60,000
	$415,000		$415,000

The net income for 1987 was $20,000. Projected annual operational expenditures (based on past data) exclusive of depreciation are $50,000. Assume that total assets are the same in 1986 and 1987.

Instructions:
Complete template 26E7 to assist in computing each of the following ratios. Enter the appropriate numbers in those cells currently containing N's (NNNNNN) and labels or descriptions in those cells currently containing L's (LLLLLLL). Enter formulas or cell references in those cells containing asterisks (*********). Print your completed template and/or formulas. For each of the five ratios, indicate the manner in which it is computed and its significance as a tool in the analysis of the financial soundness of the company.
(a) Current ratio.
(b) Acid-test ratio.
(c) Defensive interval measure.
(d) Debt to total assets.
(e) Rate of return on assets.

P26-8 Presented below are comparative balance sheets for the Idaho Company.

Idaho Company
COMPARATIVE BALANCE SHEET
December 31, 1987 and 1986

	December 31	
Assets	1987	1986
Cash	$170,000	$275,000
Accounts receivable (net)	220,000	160,000
Investments	280,000	150,000
Inventories	945,000	980,000
Prepaid Expense	25,000	20,000
Fixed assets	2,700,000	1,900,000
Accumulated depreciation	(1,000,000)	(700,000)
	$3,340,000	$2,785,000

Liabilities and Stockholders' Equity		
Accounts payable	$50,000	$80,000
Accrued expenses	150,000	200,000
Bonds payable	500,000	200,000
Capital stock	2,200,000	1,770,000
Retained earnings	440,000	535,000
	$3,340,000	$2,785,000

Instructions:
(a) Use template 26P8 to assist in parts (b) and (c) below. Enter formulas or cell references in those cells containing asterisks (*********). Print your completed template and/or formulas.
(b) Prepare a comparative balance sheet of Idaho Company showing the percent each item is of the total.
(c) Prepare a comparative balance sheet of Idaho Company showing the dollar change and the percent change for each item.
(d) Of what value is the additional information provided in part (a)?
(e) Of what value is the additional information provided in part (b)?

PART V

COMPREHENSIVE PROBLEMS

Problem 1 - Proof of cash. Presented below is information related to the Danville Companies, Inc.

	Per Bank	Per Books
Cash balance at June 30	$16,702.55	$15,498.28
Receipts during June	78,942.60	77,920.73
Disbursements	85,998.23	74,685.73
Cash balance at July 31	$9,646.92	$18,733.28

A comparision of the June and July bank statements revealed that the following checks were outstanding at the end of each month:

June 30		July 31	
1607	$8,832.50	1679	$28.32
1610	1,323.45	1680	48.50
1612	111.70	1681	129.78
1613	232.67	1682	949.68
1614	15.89	1683	2,777.20
1615	21.05	1684	43.50
1616	88.08	1685	333.99
1617	113.90	1686	826.45
1618	17.56		

In addition, check #1649, written for $1,142.12 had cleared the bank, but through a bookkeeping error had not been recorded in the company's records. A comparison of the deposits made each month as shown on the company's books and in the bank statements showed that the following deposits were in transit at the end of each month:

June 30	July 31
$1,400.00	$7,600.43
2,748.65	1,900.90
5,403.88	642.00

All of the deposits in transit as of June 30 were included on the July bank statement. Other items included on each bank statement and not recorded prior to receipt of the statement included:

	June 30	July 31
Bank Service Charge	$12.50dr	$12.50dr
NSF checks	789.90dr	4,470.00dr
		68.50dr
Interest on account	79.33cr	67.67cr
Note and interest collected by the bank on behalf of the Danville Companies, Inc.		1,545.00cr

The note collected by the bank was a 90-day note, bearing interest at 12%. (Assume a 360-day year.) There was no cash on hand at either month end.

Instructions:
(a) Prepare a proof of cash (four-column bank reconciliation) template to the corrected balance using the data given above for the Danville Companies, Inc. Make your template flexible enough so that it can be used to prepare a proof of cash for each future month's activities. In designing your template you should consider how other types of events (such as bank errors and cash on hand at month-end) would be included in arriving at the corrected balance.
(b) Explain how your template can be used to prepare any necessary journal entries to adjust the cash account at month-end.

Problem 2 - Inventory Methods and Lower of Cost or Market. University Supply, Inc. was formed on August 1, 1986. The company maintains four categories of inventory items as described in the following information from the company's records:

August 1, 1986 (beginning inventory)	Units	Unit Cost
A. Writing implements:		
Pencil sets	10,000	$0.78
Pen sets	12,000	.90
Mechanical pencils	8,000	1.08
B. Paper supplies:		
Tablets	4,000	1.10
Art paper	18,000	1.80
Typing paper	6,000	1.50
Bond paper	9,000	2.40
C. Clothing:		
Sweatpants	1,700	3.20
Sweatshirts	2,000	3.60
Jackets	1,100	5.20
D. Textbooks:		
Management	200	14.30
Economics	600	11.05
Marketing	450	18.85
Finance	300	26.00
Accounting	900	22.75

The company purchases additional inventory before the beginning of each quarter, including the summer term. The quantities and unit costs related to each of these four purchases are detailed below:

Item	Purchase #1	Purchase #2	Purchase #3	Purchase #4
Pencil sets	4,000@.80	6,000@.85	5,000@.90	5,000@.95
Pen sets	8,000@1.05			5,000@1.10
Mech. pencils		2,000@1.05		
Tablets	8,000@1.20	6,000@1.22		10,000@1.30
Art paper			5,000@2.00	
Typing paper	2,000@1.50	2,000@1.50		4,000@1.35
Bond paper		2,000@2.45		
Sweatpants	2,000@3.40		1,500@3.80	2,500@3.90
Sweatshirts		3,500@3.75		2,500@4.00
Jackets		2,000@5.00	1,000@4.80	1,000@4.60
Management texts	400@14.00	300@13.50		400@12.00
Economics texts		300@11.20		400@11.30
Marketing texts		300@18.50		600@17.00
Finance texts	500@24.00		350@20.00	500@21.00
Accounting texts			600@21.00	

The number of units sold, the estimated replacement cost per unit at year-end, and the selling price per unit are given below:

Item	Units Sold	Replacement Cost Per Unit	Sales Price Per Unit
Pencil sets	22,000	$1.00	1.30
Pen sets	15,000	1.10	1.50
Mech. pencils	5,000	1.00	1.80
Tablets	19,000	1.35	2.20
Art paper	8,000	2.00	3.60
Typing paper	5,000	1.30	3.00
Bond paper	5,000	2.50	4.80
Sweatpants	4,200	4.00	8.00
Sweatshirts	4,800	4.00	9.00
Jackets	3,000	4.50	13.00
Management texts	750	10.00	22.00
Economics texts	900	11.50	17.00
Marketing texts	800	16.00	29.00
Finance texts	1,200	21.00	40.00
Accounting texts	600	20.00	35.00

Normal profits (as a percentage of sales price) for each category of goods are: writing implements, 30%; paper supplies, 35%; clothing, 40%; and textbooks, 25%. Costs of disposal for each category of goods are estimated as a percentage of the sales price. These are: writing utensils, 5%; paper supplies, 10%; clothing, 5%; and textbooks, 20%.

Instructions:
1. Prepare a template(s) which can be used to calculate the ending inventory (periodic basis) using the following inventory methods:
    (a) FIFO.
    (b) LIFO.
    (c) Weighted average.

2. University Supply, Inc. plans to follow the practice of valuing its inventory at the lower of cost or market at year-end. Expand the template(s) you prepared under part 1 to incorporate the lower of cost or market convention:
    (a) On an item-by-item basis.
    (b) By category.
    (c) For the entire inventory.

Note: If you are using the educational version of SuperCalc3, you may want to prepare several related templates to complete this problem.

Problem 3 - Troubled Debt Restructuring. The Ogalla Farm Equipment Company, Inc. sells farm equipment on credit. Recent high interest rates coupled with depressed real estate prices have caused many of Ogalla's farming customers to have difficulty making payments on time. Because a large number of Ogalla's customers have been adversely affected by the poor economic conditions, management has adopted a policy of granting concessions to debtors rather than repossessing equipment. These concessions have included: (1) the acceptance of noncash assets, such as interests in crops and real estate, and equity interests (in corporate customers) in payment for all or a part of the amount owed; and (2) renegotiating the amount owed. Renegotiation has included: (a) extending the date for payment, (b) lowering the interest rate, and (c) forgiving all or part of the interest and/or principal owed. To date, Ogalla has not extended any obligations for more than two and one-half years (30 months).

Because of the large number of debt restructurings occurring and their financial consequences to Ogalla, you have been asked to prepare a template which can be used to evaluate the potential income effects of a debt restructuring. You are provided with the following information, which is considered to be a typical debt restructuring situation.

A 3-year note owed by Tom Collins Farms, Inc. is past due and the company is unable to pay. The note, for $450,000 and bearing interest at a 12% rate (interest is payable annually), was issued three years ago by the company in exchange for equipment which it purchased. The company paid the interest on the note in each of the first two years, but this year it has not made any payments. Tom Collins, president of the company, offered Ogalla 40 acres of the company's prime farm land, with a book value of $140,000 and a current fair market value of $100,000 as partial payment of the debt. He has also asked for a two-year extension of the maturity date of the note, a reduction in the future interest rate to 4% (payable annually), forgiveness of the accrued interest, and a reduction in the principal of the note to $300,000 ($450,000 less $150,000 for what Tom believes the land is worth). Management of Ogalla has agreed to accept the land and reduce the principal to $300,000, but not to forgive the accrued interest or lower the interest rate. In addition, they will require monthly payments of interest on the principal amount instead of a lump sum payment of interest at the end of each year (interest is compounded monthly).

Instructions:
Prepare a template which can be used to evaluate the income effects of each alternative on both Ogalla and their customer, Tom Collins Farms, Inc.

The template should calculate the amount of any gain or loss for both the debtor and the creditor on any assets or equity interests transferred as a part of the debt restructuring. In addition, any gain for the debtor or loss for the creditor caused by a modification of terms for debt which is continued should be calculated. Finally, if debt is continued, and no loss should be recognized by the creditor, the template should provide a means of calculating the new effective interest rate and, using that rate, prepare a schedule which shows the cash received by the creditor, the amount of interest income, the reduction in the carrying amount of the debt, and the balance (carrying amount) of debt for each period.

Problem 4 - Stock Appreciation Rights. On January 1, 1983, the Board of Directors of Pendleton Corporation issued 20,000 stock appreciation rights (SAR's) to executives of the company. The plan covered a five-year period and, upon exercise, entitled the executives to receive an amount equal to the appreciation in the market value of the common stock in excess of the pre-established price of $40. At December 31, 1983, the market price of the common stock was only $36. Being unsure of the benefits of the SAR's on management's performance, the board voted not to issue any additional SAR's in 1984.

At the end of 1984, however, the market price of the common stock had increased to $39.50. Encouraged by this increase, the board issued an additional 20,000 SAR's to executives on January 1, 1985. The board established a 3-year period to be covered by this issuance of SAR's. The pre-established price was $38. Because of unforeseen changes in the economy, however, the company's business suffered several setbacks, requiring large write-offs, and the common stock price fell to $32 at year-end.

On January 1, 1986, the board issued 30,000 SAR's, entitling executives to the appreciation on the common stock in excess of a pre-established price of $40 over the next four years. At this point, the board decided to wait and see if the SAR's had a beneficial effect on stock prices before issuing any additional SAR's. At year-end, the market value of the common stock had recovered and increased to $42.

At December 31, 1987, the common stock had a market value of $44. Encouraged by this, several members of the board argued that another, larger SAR plan should be issued on January 1, 1988. They proposed that the SAR's cover a five-year period and have a pre-established price equal to the December 31, 1987 market price of $44. They also argued that the number of SAR's to be issued should be much larger than before, covering a larger group of managers. They proposed that 80,000 SAR's be issued. Several other board members argued that this was excessive and would be too costly if the stock price continued to increase as in the last two years.

The more conservative board members suggested that a projected annual growth rate of 2% in the market value of the common stock would be reasonable. Others argued that a 5% rate was more appropriate, since this was approximately equal to what the company had actually achieved over the last five years. Still others argued that the last two years were more indicative of the potential for growth and that a 10% rate should be used.

Instructions:
Prepare a template which will compute the amount of compensation expense to be recorded in each year from 1983 through 1987. Assume that no SAR's are exercised until the end of the period covered by each plan, and that all SAR's with a pre-established price lower than the market value of the common stock at that date will be exercised.

Include in the template the capability to evaluate the compensation expense which might be expected to be incurred in each of the next five years (1988-92). Your template should be able to incorporate changes in (1) projected annual rates of growth in the common stock prices, (2) the number of SAR's to be issued, (3) the pre-established price of the SAR's, and (4) the number of years covered by the SAR's.

Problem 5 - Weighted Average Shares Computation. Garnet Packaging Plant, Inc. is preparing its earnings per share disclosures for the year ended December 31, 1987. The company had 100,000 shares of $10 par value common stock outstanding at January 1, 1987 and entered into the following transactions during the year:

February 12 - The company issued 20,000 shares of common stock at $40 per share.

March 26 - Because the price of the common stock was dropping, the company repurchased 8,000 shares for the treasury at $30 per share.

April 14 - The company did not pay its usual quarterly dividend at the end of March and the market value of the stock continued to decline. In an effort to bolster the price of the stock, the company purchased an additional 7,000 shares for the treasury at $20 per share.

May 19 - With the stock price beginning to recover, the company resold 4,000 treasury shares at $26 per share.

June 30 - In lieu of the normal quarterly cash dividend, the company issued a 10% stock dividend to stockholders.

July 24 - In response to the additional shares placed on the market from the stock dividend, the market price of the stock declined and the company purchased an additional 8,000 shares at $22 per share.

September 1 - In need of cash, the company sold 9,000 shares of treasury stock at $24 per share.

September 30 - The company issued a second 10% stock dividend in lieu of paying a cash dividend.

November 6 - With improved third quarter results and prospects for an excellent fourth quarter, stock prices rose. The company resold the remaining shares of treasury stock at $38 per share.

At December 31, the company's common stock had risen to a price of $46 per share, and appeared likely to continue increasing. The company was considering issuing additional shares or splitting the stock in order to reduce the per share market value of the stock. By February 15, 1988, prior to the issuance of the financial statements for 1987, the market price had increased to $68 per share and the company decided to issue a two-for-one stock split.

Instructions:

Prepare a template which will compute the weighted average number of common shares outstanding during the year on:

(a) A daily basis.

(b) A monthly basis, (rounded to the nearest month).

(c) A monthly basis, assuming that shares are considered outstanding for the entire month in which they are issued or repurchased.

Problem 6 - Stock Compensation and Earnings Per Share. Watertown Fabrics, Inc. has two nonqualified stock option plans for employees outstanding at December 31, 1987. These plans were intended to compensate employees over the two-year time period covered by each option plan.

Forty-thousand options were granted to employees of the company on January 1, 1986. Each option entitled the employee to acquire 1 share of $10 par value common stock at the end of a two-year period for $20, provided that the employee was still employed by the company at that time. The current market price of the common stock at the date of grant was $23.

An additional 50,000 options were granted to employees on January 1, 1987. These options were identical to the first grant, except that the exercise price of each option was $18 instead of $20. The current market price of the common stock at the date of grant was $22.

The company is considering granting an additional 200,000 stock options on January 1, 1988. These options would have an exercise price of $20 and would otherwise be identical to the options granted previously. The date of measurement for all three stock option plans is the date of grant. The current market price of the common stock at the date of grant is expected to be $25.

Before considering the effects of any of the three option plans, the company's 1987 net income totaled $4,500,000. The weighted average number of common shares outstanding for 1987 (exclusive of options) was calculated to be 460,000 shares. Several members of the board of directors have expressed concern over the granting of such a large number of options. They believe that it will have a serious detrimental effect on the company's earnings per share.

Instructions:
Prepare a template which can be used to calculate the amount of any compensation expense to be recognized from the stock option plans in each year from 1986 through 1989 and the related effect on net income (the average income tax rate is 40% in each year).

Expand your template to include the calculation of the earnings per share for Watertown Fabrics, Inc. for 1987 and 1988. Assume that the net income and the weighted average number of common shares outstanding (exclusive of the effects of the three options) will be the same in each year. All options are exercised on the first day following the end of the two-year period covered by each plan. The average market price of the common stock was $24 during 1987. The year-end market price was $27. In 1988, the average market price of the common stock is projected to be $28, with an end-of-year price of $27. Any excess proceeds from the assumed exercise of the options can be used to reduce $2,000,000 of outstanding debt which carries a 14% interest cost. Any remaining proceeds would be invested in government securities yielding an 8% interest rate.

Use your template to compare the effects on compensation expense and earnings per share if the third set of options are granted or not granted.

Problem 7 - Percentage of Completion. On March 1, 1986, Hudson Falls Construction Corporation received notice that they were the successful bidder on a five-year construction project. The project had a required completion date of August 1, 1990 and carried a penalty of $125,000 per week for each week that it took after this date to complete the project. Hudson Falls estimated the following revenues and costs for each year of the project (000's):

	1986	1987	1988	1989	1990
Revenues	75,000	75,000	75,000	75,000	75,000
Costs incurred	12,000	30,000	40,000	54,000	60,000
Cost to complete	48,000	30,000	20,000	6,000	0

The actual progress year-by-year is given below:

	1986	1987	1988	1989	1990
Revenues	75,000	75,000	75,000	90,000	?
Costs incurred	12,000	30,000	48,000	60,000	80,000
Cost to complete	48,000	30,000	32,000	20,000	0
Progress billings to date	11,250	28,125	36,000	67,500	?
Cash collections	10,000	24,000	32,000	60,000	?

In 1988, a shortage of several critical materials occurred, delaying the project and greatly increasing its cost. Hudson Falls requested a renegotiation of the contract to increase the price to $90,000,000 and to extend the completion date. The price increase was granted, but the client insisted that the date for completion could not be changed. Rather than incur the additional costs to speed completion of the project by the deadline date, Hudson Falls took an additional four months (sixteen weeks) to complete the project. Final billings on and payment for the project was completed by December 31, 1990.

Instructions:
Prepare a template which will calculate the amount of revenues to be recognized each year as well as the amount of gross profit (loss) to be realized in each year. In addition, your template should also calculate the amounts of any inventory/liability and any accounts receivable at the end of each period. Your template should be flexible enough to calculate the project (1) as originally budgeted, (2) as it would have been completed assuming no increase in price was granted, and (3) as it was actually completed.

Problem 8 - Income Tax Loss. The Kingston Corporation, a computer manufacturer, wrote off a major part of its inventory in 1985 because the inventory had become obsolete. Due to the small settlements resulting from the bankruptcies of several of Kingston's major customers, the company also wrote off a significant portion of receivables which had not been previously anticipated. This resulted in a net loss of $4,000,000 in 1985 for tax purposes. Kingston's taxable income in 1982, 1983, and 1984 was $600,000, $700,000, and $500,000, respectively.

Kingston applied an unused investment tax credit carryover of $500,000 to eliminate any taxes payable in 1982 and part of the taxes payable in 1983. The last year in which Kingston could apply this carryover is 1984. Because of previous operating losses and investment tax credits, this $500,000 credit cannot be carried back to any previous years; thus, if they elect to carry back the operating loss, the unused investment tax credit will be lost.

After the write-off in 1985, the company expects to return to a profitable status. They project taxable income to be $600,000 in 1986, and expect that this amount will increase by 10% each year.

Information on relevant income tax rates follows:

	Actual rates-- 1982-1985		Projected rates-- 1986 and later
1st $25,000	15%	1st $50,000	15%
25,000 to 50,000	18%	50,000 to 75,000	25%
50,000 to 75,000	30%	More than 75,000	36%
75,000 to 100,000	40%		
More than 100,000	46%		

In addition, it is expected that taxes payable in 1986 and future years will include an additional 5% tax on any taxable income between $100,000 and $350,000.

Instructions:
Prepare a template to help Kingston Corporation decide whether to carry back the net operating loss to earlier years or to elect to carry forward the entire loss. Your template should compute the amount of taxable income under each alternative, the amount of income tax on that income, and the income taxes actually payable/refundable. In addition, your template should calculate the amount of any estimated future tax benefits from loss carryforward. Finally, your schedule should incorporate any discounting of cash flows needed to arrive at the optimal decision. Assume that 8% is an appropriate discount rate for any cash receipts or payments.

Problem 9 - Financial Statement Analysis.   Presented below are comparative financial statements for the Rawlins Corporation.

Rawlins Corporation
COMPARATIVE BALANCE SHEET
December 31

Assets	1985	1984	1983	1982	1981
Cash	$4,400	$3,600	$3,900	$4,800	$3,600
Marketable Securities	0	14,700	10,100	5,200	9,300
Accounts receivable	20,400	6,800	5,700	5,600	4,800
Inventories	43,000	20,500	18,000	13,600	10,600
Prepaid Expense	2,100	1,500	1,200	1,800	1,000
Land	25,500	18,400	15,500	14,500	15,200
Other fixed assets	72,800	49,800	39,400	34,800	34,100
Accumulated depreciation	(31,600)	(28,000)	(22,300)	(19,200)	(20,000)
Intangibles	8,800	9,300	9,800	9,900	10,400
Other assets	6,000	4,600	5,400	2,200	2,300
Total	$151,400	$101,200	86,700	73,200	71,300

Liabilities and Stockholders' Equity	1985	1984	1983	1982	1981
Accounts payable	$29,400	$14,000	$12,200	$8,500	$6,000
Accrued expenses	14,700	6,300	5,200	4,400	4,400
Other current liabilities	7,800	6,200	2,800	300	1,600
Bonds payable	23,600	15,200	17,200	15,000	18,100
Deferred income tax	12,100	7,400	6,300	5,700	4,500
Capital stock	6,600	3,900	3,800	3,800	3,800
Paid-in Surplus	2,000	1,800	1,700	1,700	1,700
Retained earnings	55,500	46,700	37,800	34,100	31,200
Treasury stock	(300)	(300)	(300)	(300)	0
Total	$151,400	$101,200	86,700	73,200	71,300

Rawlins Corporation
COMPARATIVE INCOME STATEMENT
For the Year Ended December 31

	1985	1984	1983	1982	1981
Sales	$278,500	$211,400	$171,200	$145,200	$133,500
Cost of goods sold	202,400	148,300	127,300	106,200	92,100
Selling & admin. expense	48,500	39,600	31,200	28,400	28,100
Income from operations	27,600	23,500	12,700	10,600	13,300
Interest income	600	300	200	500	700
Interest expense	(1,500)	(900)	(800)	(1,400)	(1,700)
Income before taxes	26,700	22,900	12,100	9,700	12,300
Income taxes	13,100	12,000	6,200	4,900	6,300
Net income	$13,600	$10,900	$5,900	$4,800	$6,000

Instructions:

1. Construct a template which presents the five-year balance sheet and income statement data as horizontal trend analyses.
2. Construct a template which presents the five-year balance sheet and income statement data as common-size (or vertical) analyses.
3. Construct a template which will compute the various ratios which might be useful in evaluating the financial performance and status of the company. Compute each ratio for as many years as possible.
4. If your computer has the ability to do graphics, add this feature to the appropriate parts of each analysis you performed above.

Problem 10 - Interim Financial Reports.   Catskill Companies, Inc. manufactures products which it sells primarily through wholesalers via the company's commercial products division.   In recent years, the company has experimented with selling products directly to consumers through a consumer products division.   Quarterly revenues for each division for the year ended December 31, 1987 are given below:

Division	1st Quarter	2nd Quarter	3rd Quarter	4th Quarter
Commercial	$179,500	$191,400	$197,600	$196,300
Consumer	6,800	8,800	3,900	2,000

Cost of goods sold averages 65% of sales revenue in the commercial products division and 80% of sales revenue in the consumer products division.   However, it was found that the ending inventory in the commercial products division needed to be reduced to reflect the lower of cost or market at the end of the second and fourth quarters. This reduction amounted to $1,180 and $2,700, respectively.   Neither of these declines were believed to be permanent and, in fact, the third quarter inventory value recovered $1,000 from the second quarter decline in value.   Selling and administrative costs average 20% of sales revenues in each division.

In addition to the normal selling and administrative expenses, the company incurred several other important costs.   In the first quarter, $8,000 was spent on advertising for the commercial products division.   These costs are expected to benefit the entire year's sales efforts.   In September, the company shut down manufacturing operations related to the commercial products division for two weeks and undertook major annual repairs costing $18,000.   This cost had been anticipated and included in the budget for 1987.   At December 31, the company also recorded $13,800 of interest expense related to the commercial products division.

In addition to the expenses described above, the consumer products division incurred one other operating expense.   This was an unanticipated writedown of inventories and receivables in the fourth quarter amounting to $2,700.   Because of the marginal profitability of the division in the past, coupled with the loss recorded by the writedown of inventories and receivables, management decided to discontinue the consumer products division.   The shut down of the division in December resulted in an additional loss of $5,200.

Catskill Companies anticipated an income tax rate of 45% on income from the commercial products division.   This rate was used for the first two quarters of 1987. Failure to attain sales goals in the first two quarters resulted in a revision of this estimate to 40% in the third quarter.   This rate was used for the remainder of the year.   The losses in the discontinued consumer products division were used to offset other income, resulting in an income tax effect equal to the company's marginal tax rate of 46%.

Instructions:
Prepare a template which can be used to prepare quarterly income calculations for the Catskill Companies, Inc.   Your template should be able to handle extraordinary items and the cumulative effect of a change in accounting principle as well as discontinued operations.

Appendix A

COMMONLY USED COMMANDS--SUPERCALC3

/Arrange--sorts the spreadsheet.
   Row--arranges columns based on values in one or two rows.
   Column--arranges rows based on values in one or two columns.
      Options under Row and Column include Ascending or Descending order, Yes or
         No for adjustment of cells.

/Blank--erase a cell or a cell range.

/Copy--copy a cell range to another location.
   Options include No adjust, Ask for adjust, Values only.

/Delete--eliminate a row, a column, or a file.

/Edit--edit the contents of a cell.

/Format--controls the appearance or display of cells.
   Global--formats the entire spreadsheet.
      Integer--no decimals are displayed.
      General--displays best fit for the cell (integer, decimal, exponential).
      Exponential--displays in exponential notation.
      $--displays two decimal places (no dollar sign).
      Right--right-hand justifies numbers and formulas.
      Left--left-hand justifies numbers and formulas.
      TR--right-hand justifies text.
      TL--left-hand justifies text.
      User-defined--utilizes a user-defined format (1-8).
      Default--resets display to General, Right, Text-Left, and columns 9 characters
         in width.
      (0-127)--set the width of columns.
   Column--format a column; options as under Format,Global.
   Row--format a row; options as under Format,Global.
   Entry--format a cell or cell range; options as under Format,Global.
   Define--allows access to the user-defined format table.

/Global--affects the entire spreadsheet.
   Formula--displays formulas (contents of cells) on screen.
   Next--turns automatic cursor advance on/off.
   Border--turns column and row headings off.
   Row--recalculates spreadsheet by rows.
   Column--recalculates spreadsheet by columns.
   Manual--recalculates spreadsheet only on command; press the exclamation point (!)
      to recalculate.
   Automatic--recalculates automatically after an entry is made.

/Insert--add a blank column or row to the spreadsheet.

/Load--load a file from disk. Requires specification of the file name.
　　All--load the entire spreadsheet from the disk file.
　　Part--load a cell range from a disk file to the current spreadsheet.
　　Consolidate--combine a cell range from a disk file with the current spreadsheet.

/Move--move an entire column(s) or row(s); with formula adjustment.

/Output--used to print to a disk or printer.
　　Display--print the spreadsheet as displayed (requires specification of a cell range).
　　　Printer--prints to a printer.
　　　Disk--creates a .PRN file on disk.
　　Contents--print the cell contents, one line per cell (requires specification of a cell
　　range). Same options as /Output,Display.

/Protect--restrict access to a cell or cell range.

/Quit--erase the current spreadsheet and exit SuperCalc3. (Specify Yes or No.)

/Replicate--copy a cell or cell range to another location(s). Press [enter] to
　　automatically adjust, press a comma (,) to obtain options.
　　No adjust.
　　Ask for adjust.
　　Values only.

/Save--save the spreadsheet to a disk file (requires specification of a file name).
　　If file already exists, Change name, Backup, Overwrite.
　　All--save the entire spreadsheet with formulas.
　　Values--save only the values as displayed.
　　Part--specify All or Values and a cell range.

/Title--fixes headings (titles) on screen.
　　Horizontal--fixes the current row and all rows above it.
　　Vertical--fixes the current column and all columns to its left.
　　Both--fixes both horizontal and vertical titles.
　　Clear--removes the fixed titles.

/Unprotect--permits access to previously restricted cells.

/Window--splits the screen into two displays. Press the semicolon (;) to move the
　　cursor from one window to another.
　　Horizontal--splits the screen horizontally (by row).
　　Vertical--splits the screen vertically (by column).
　　Clear--returns the display to a single screen.
　　Synchronize--synchronizes windows to scroll together.
　　Unsynchronize--allows windows to scroll independently of each other.

/Zap--erases the current spreadsheet from temporary memory.
　　Yes--proceeds with erasure.
　　No--cancels command and returns to the spreadsheet.

//**Data management**--use database features.
   Input--specify the input range for the database.
   Criterion--specify the criterion range to be used.
   Output--specify where the results of Extract or Select should be output to.
   Find--locate those records matching the criteria.
   Extract--copy those records matching the criteria to the output area.
   Select--copy records matching the criteria upon command (Yes or No).
   Remain--leave database and return to the spreadsheet.

Other special keys:

Help--press the special function key [F1] or [?] to obtain onscreen help.

GoTo--press the equals (=) key, specify a cell, and press the enter key to move to any cell on the spreadsheet.

Repeating text--press the single quotation mark ('), followed by the text to be repeated, and press the [enter] key. The text will be repeated across each empty cell to the right until a nonempty cell is encountered.

Cancel commands, entries--press the special function key [F2] to eliminate commands or entries you do not wish to execute.

Graph--press the special function key [F10] to view a graph.

Appendix B

COMMONLY USED COMMANDS--LOTUS 1-2-3

/Worksheet--commands which affect the spreadsheet as a whole.
  Global--affects the entire spreadsheet.
    Format--controls the appearance or display of numbers.
      Fixed--fixes the number of decimal places (0 to 15).
      Currency--adds dollar signs ($) and commas (,).
      , (comma)--adds commas (,) to numbers.
      General--does not display zeroes after the decimal point.
      Percent--multiplies by 100 and adds a percent symbol (%).
      Date--affects display of dates.
        1 --set the display as Day-Month-Year.
    Label-Prefix--controls the display of words or text.
      Left, Right, or Center are the available options.
    Column-Width--set the column width from 1 to 72 characters.
    Recalculation--controls the order and time of recalculation.
      Natural--recalulates formulas based on whether or not they depend on other
        formulas.
      Automatic--recalculates whenever a change is entered.
      Manual--recalculates only on instruction--press the special function key [F9]
        to recalculate.
    Protection--controls access to cells.
      Enable--turns protection status on.
      Disable--turns protection status off.
  Insert--add a blank column or row to the spreadsheet.
    Column or Row are the two options.
  Delete--remove a column or row from the spreadsheet.
    Column or Row are the two options.
  Column-Width--set the width of a single column.
  Erase--clears the current spreadsheet from temporary memory.
  Titles--fixes headings (titles) on the screen.
    Both--fix both row and column headings to the left and above the cursor.
    Horizontal--fix only the column headings above the cursor.
    Vertical--fix only the row headings to the left of the cursor.
    Clear--removes all titles previously fixed.
  Window--splits the screen into two displays. Press the special function key [F6]
    to move from one window to another.
    Horizontal--splits the screen horizontally (by row).
    Vertical--splits the screen vertically (by column).
    Sync--synchronizes windows to scroll together.
    Unsync--allows windows to scroll independently of each other.
    Clear--returns the display to a single screen.

/Range--affects a range of cells within the spreadsheet.
    Format--controls how numbers in the range are displayed.
        Fixed--fixes the number of decimal places (0 to 15).
        Currency--adds dollar signs ($) and commas (,).
        , (comma)--adds commas (,) to numbers.
        General--does not display zeroes after the decimal point.
        Percent--multiplies by 100 and adds a percent symbol (%).
        Date--affects display of dates.
            1 --set the display as Day-Month-Year.
    Label-Prefix--controls how text in the range is displayed.
        Left, **Right**, or **Center** are the available options.
    Erase--clears the specified range from the spreadsheet. Must also specify **Yes** or **No**.
    Names--provides for the naming of cell ranges.
        Create--establish a named range.
        Delete--eliminate the name of a range.
        Labels--use the label in the current cell to name the next adjacent cell--options are **Right**, **Down**, **Left**, and **Up**.
        Reset--clears all range names.
    Protect--prevents access to the cells in a range.
    Unprotect--allows access to the cells in a range.

/Copy--copy the contents of a cell or range to another location(s).

/Move--move the contents of a cell or range to another location.

/File--manipulate files on a disk.
    Retrieve--load a spreadsheet from a disk file.
    Save--save the current spreadsheet to a disk file.
    Combine--add disk file(s) into the current spreadsheet.
    Xtract--save part of a spreadsheet to a disk file.
    List--list the Lotus 1-2-3 spreadsheet files that are on a disk.

/Print--allows printing of spreadsheets.
    Printer--print to a printer.
        Range--specify the range to be printed.
        Page--advance the paper in the printer to the top of the next page.
        Options--change appearance of page to be printed.
            Other--change the display to be printed.
                As-Displayed--print cells as displayed on the screen.
                Cell-Formulas--print the contents of each cell, one cell per line.
            Quit--leave the options menu and return to the print menu.
        Align--reset the top of the page for printing.
        Go--print!
        Quit--leave printing and return to the spreadsheet.

/Data Commands--use the spreadsheet as a database.
    Sort--sort a range within the spreadsheet.
        Data-Range--specify the range to sort.
        Primary-Key--specify the first column (variable) to sort on.
        Secondary-Key--specify the second column to sort on.
        Reset--delete the sort settings.
        Go--sort!
        Quit--return to /Data Commands menu.
    Query--manipulate the database.
        Input--specify the input range for the database.
        Criterion--specify the criterion range to be used.
        Output--specify where the results of Find or Extract should be output to.
        Find--locate those records matching the criteria.
        Extract--copy those records matching the criteria to the output area.
        Reset--delete the range specifications for the input, criterion, and output
          ranges.
        Quit--leave database and return to the spreadsheet.

/Quit--quit using Lotus 1-2-3 and return to the Access menu or DOS.

Other special keys:

Help--press the special function key [F1] to obtain onscreen help.

Edit--press the special function key [F2] to edit a cell. When done editing, press the [enter] key to return to the spreadsheet.

Absolute--use the special function key [F4] in conjunction with the pointer to specify a cell as absolute when entering a formula.

GoTo--press the special function key [F5], specify a cell, and press the [enter] key to move to any cell on the spreadsheet.

Graph--press the special function key [F10] to view a graph.

Repeating text--press the backslash key (\) followed by the text to be repeated, and press the [enter] key.

Escape--press the [Esc] key to "back" out of any command or entry you have started and do not wish to execute.